Lecture Notes in Computer Science   8405

Commenced Publication in 1973
Founding and Former Series Editors:
Gerhard Goos, Juris Hartmanis, and Jan van Leeuwen

Editorial Board

David Hutchison
  Lancaster University, UK
Takeo Kanade
  Carnegie Mellon University, Pittsburgh, PA, USA
Josef Kittler
  University of Surrey, Guildford, UK
Jon M. Kleinberg
  Cornell University, Ithaca, NY, USA
Alfred Kobsa
  University of California, Irvine, CA, USA
Friedemann Mattern
  ETH Zurich, Switzerland
John C. Mitchell
  Stanford University, CA, USA
Moni Naor
  Weizmann Institute of Science, Rehovot, Israel
Oscar Nierstrasz
  University of Bern, Switzerland
C. Pandu Rangan
  Indian Institute of Technology, Madras, India
Bernhard Steffen
  TU Dortmund University, Germany
Demetri Terzopoulos
  University of California, Los Angeles, CA, USA
Doug Tygar
  University of California, Berkeley, CA, USA
Gerhard Weikum
  Max Planck Institute for Informatics, Saarbruecken, Germany

T0211787

Diana Goehringer
Marco Domenico Santambrogio
João M.P. Cardoso   Koen Bertels (Eds.)

Reconfigurable Computing: Architectures, Tools, and Applications

10th International Symposium, ARC 2014
Vilamoura, Portugal, April 14-16, 2014
Proceedings

 Springer

Volume Editors

Diana Goehringer
Ruhr-Universität Bochum
Universitätsstr. 150, 44801 Bochum, Germany
E-mail: diana.goehringer@rub.de

Marco Domenico Santambrogio
Politecnico di Milano, DEIB
Via Ponzio 34/5, 20133 Milano, Italy
E-mail: marco.santambrogio@polimi.it

João M.P. Cardoso
University of Porto, Faculty of Engineering (FEUP)
Rua Dr. Roberto Frias, s/n, 4200-465 Porto, Portugal
E-mail: jmpc@acm.org

Koen Bertels
Delft University of Technology, Computer Engineering Laboratory
Mekelweg 4, 2628 CD Delft, The Netherlands
E-mail: k.l.m.bertels@tudelft.nl

ISSN 0302-9743   e-ISSN 1611-3349
ISBN 978-3-319-05959-4   e-ISBN 978-3-319-05960-0
DOI 10.1007/978-3-319-05960-0
Springer Cham Heidelberg New York Dordrecht London

Library of Congress Control Number: 2014934369

LNCS Sublibrary: SL 1 – Theoretical Computer Science and General Issues

© Springer International Publishing Switzerland 2014

This work is subject to copyright. All rights are reserved by the Publisher, whether the whole or part of the material is concerned, specifically the rights of translation, reprinting, reuse of illustrations, recitation, broadcasting, reproduction on microfilms or in any other physical way, and transmission or information storage and retrieval, electronic adaptation, computer software, or by similar or dissimilar methodology now known or hereafter developed. Exempted from this legal reservation are brief excerpts in connection with reviews or scholarly analysis or material supplied specifically for the purpose of being entered and executed on a computer system, for exclusive use by the purchaser of the work. Duplication of this publication or parts thereof is permitted only under the provisions of the Copyright Law of the Publisher's location, in ist current version, and permission for use must always be obtained from Springer. Permissions for use may be obtained through RightsLink at the Copyright Clearance Center. Violations are liable to prosecution under the respective Copyright Law.
The use of general descriptive names, registered names, trademarks, service marks, etc. in this publication does not imply, even in the absence of a specific statement, that such names are exempt from the relevant protective laws and regulations and therefore free for general use.
While the advice and information in this book are believed to be true and accurate at the date of publication, neither the authors nor the editors nor the publisher can accept any legal responsibility for any errors or omissions that may be made. The publisher makes no warranty, express or implied, with respect to the material contained herein.

Typesetting: Camera-ready by author, data conversion by Scientific Publishing Services, Chennai, India

Printed on acid-free paper

Springer is part of Springer Science+Business Media (www.springer.com)

Preface

Reconfigurable computing technologies offer the promise of substantial performance gains over traditional architectures via customizing, even at runtime, the topology of the underlying architecture to match the specific needs of a given application. Contemporary configurable architectures allow for the definition of architectures with functional and storage units that match in function, bit-width and control structures the specific needs of a given computation. The flexibility enabled by reconfiguration is also seen as a basic technique for overcoming transient failures in emerging device structures.

The International Symposium on Applied Reconfigurable Computing (ARC, http://www.arc-symposium.org/) aims to bring together researchers and practitioners of reconfigurable computing with an emphasis on practical applications of this promising technology. ARC 2014 is the 10th edition of the symposium and takes place during April 14–16, 2014, in Vilamoura, Algarve, Portugal. The previous editions of ARC took place in Carvoeiro, Algarve, Portugal (ARC 2005), Delft, The Netherlands (ARC 2006), Mangaratiba. Rio de Janeiro, Brazil (ARC 2007), London, UK (ARC 2008), Karlsruhe, Germany (ARC 2009), Bangkok, Thailand (ARC 2010), Belfast, UK (ARC 2011), Hong Kong, People's Republic of China (ARC 2012), and Marina del Rey, California, USA (ARC 2013). ARC 2014 is being organized by the Faculty of Engineering of the University of Porto with the collaboration of the University of Algarve.

Similarly to the first edition of ARC, this year the Portuguese event on Reconfigurable Systems (REC) takes place in Algarve in the day before ARC. We hope that having the two events co-located allows the Portuguese community with interests in reconfigurable hardware to network and discuss ideas with the ARC participants.

We received 57 paper submissions for ARC 2014. The submissions came from 27 countries: USA, UK, Slovakia, Spain, Sweden, The Netherlands, Norway, Pakistan, Poland, Portugal, Qatar, Japan, Republic of Korea, India, Ireland, Australia, Austria, Belgium, Brazil, Canada, People's Republic of China, Cyprus, Denmark, Egypt, Finland, France, and Germany. Each paper was reviewed by at least three members of the Program Committee. Nine papers had three reviews, forty seven had four reviews, and one paper had five reviews. As a result of the reviewing process, we accepted 16 as regular papers (28.07% of acceptance rate) and 18 as short papers (a global acceptance rate of 59.65%). Selected papers will be invited to submit an extended version for consideration for a special issue of the ACM Transactions on Reconfigurable Technology and Systems (TRETS) journal. We would like to acknowledge Steve Wilton and David Thomas for their support.

In addition to the oral and poster presentations of the 34 papers, the symposium program includes invited presentations from prestigious speakers, as well as three special sessions focusing on: EU funded projects related to reconfigurable technology, the FP7 EU-funded ALMA project, and on remote FPGA lab environments.

This year we have the pleasure and honor to host Giovanni De Micheli, from EPFL, Switzerland, as our keynote speaker, and David Thomas, from Imperial College, UK, and Giulio Corradi, from Xilinx Inc., Munich, Germany, as our invited presenters from academia and industry, respectively. We would like to express our gratitude for their presence.

We appreciate the support given by Alfred Hofmann, Vice-President Publishing Computer Science, from Springer International Publishing AG, and Anna Kramer, from Springer Computer Science Editorial.

We also would like to acknowledge, the authors, the ARC 2014 steering and Program Committee members, the external reviewers, and all the colleagues participating in the organization of the symposium. Special thanks go to Gabriel Coutinho for his hard work and dedication as proceedings chair. Gabriel extensively reviewed all the papers regarding the LNCS style and worked with the authors on the required modifications.

We hope you enjoy the symposium, have fruitful and inspiring discussions, have time to network, and have some moments to relax.

Welcome to ARC 2014, the 10th Anniversary of the International Symposium on Applied Reconfigurable Computing, and to Vilamoura in Algarve, Portugal. "Algarve. Europe's most famous secret!"

April 2014
Diana Goehringer
Marco Santambrogio
João M.P. Cardoso
Koen Bertels

Organization

Organizing Committee

General Chairs

João M.P. Cardoso   University of Porto, Portugal
Koen Bertels   Delft University of Technology,
                   The Netherlands

Program Chairs

Diana Goehringer   Ruhr-Universität Bochum, Germany
Marco Santambrogio   Politecnico di Milano, Italy

Finance Chair

João Canas Ferreira   University of Porto, Portugal

Proceedings Chair

José G. Coutinho   Imperial College London, UK

Sponsorship Chair

Horácio Neto   INESC-ID/IST, Lisbon, Portugal

Publicity Chairs

Ray Cheung   City University of Hong Kong, Hong Kong
Eduardo Marques   University of São Paulo, Brazil
Jason H. Anderson   University of Toronto, Canada

Web Chair

João Bispo   University of Porto, Portugal

Local Arrangements

João Lima   University of Algarve, Portugal
Rui Marcelino   University of Algarve, Portugal
José Mariano   University of Algarve, Portugal

Steering Committee

Hideharu Amano	Keio University, Japan
Juergen Becker	Universität Karlsruhe (TH), Germany
Mladen Berekovic	Braunschweig University of Technology, Germany
Koen Bertels	Delft University of Technology, The Netherlands
João M.P. Cardoso	University of Porto, Portugal
Katherine (Compton) Morrow	University of Wisconsin-Madison, USA
George Constantinides	Imperial College of Science, Technology and Medicine, UK
Pedro C. Diniz	USC Information Sciences Institute, USA
Philip H.W. Leong	University of Sydney, Australia
Walid Najjar	University of California Riverside, USA
Roger Woods	The Queen's University of Belfast, UK

In memory of Stamatis Vassiliadis [1951-2007], ARC 2006-2007 Steering Committee member

Program Committee

Andreas Koch	TU Darmstadt, Germany
António Ferrari	University of Aveiro, Portugal
Antonio Miele	Politecnico di Milano, Italy
Carlo Galuzzi	Delft University of Technology, The Netherlands
Chao Wang	University of Science and Technology of China, People's Republic of China
Christian Hochberger	TU Dresden, Germany
Christian Pilato	Politecnico di Milano, Italy
Christos-Savvas Bouganis	Imperial College London, UK
Cyrille Chavet	Université de Bretagne-Sud, France
David Thomas	Imperial College London, UK
Diana Göhringer	Ruhr-Universität Bochum, Germany
Dominic Hillenbrand	Waseda University, Japan
Eduardo Marques	University of São Paulo, Brazil
Erkay Savas	Sabanci University, Turkey
Fearghal Morgan	National University of Ireland Galway, Ireland
Florent de Dinechin	Ecole Normale Superieure de Lyon, France
Frank Hannig	University of Erlangen-Nuremberg, Germany
Gabriel Almeida	Leica Biosystems, Germany
Guy Gogniat	Université de Bretagne-Sud, France
Hayden So	University of Hong Kong, Hong Kong
Horácio Neto	INESC-ID/IST, Portugal

Jason H. Anderson	University of Toronto, Canada
Jim Harkin	University of Ulster, UK
João Bispo	University of Porto, Portugal
João Canas Ferreira	University of Porto, Portugal
João M.P. Cardoso	University of Porto, Portugal
Jongeun Lee	UNIST, Republic of Korea
José C. Alves	University of Porto, Portugal
Jürgen Becker	Karlsruhe Institute of Technology, Germany
Kentaro Sano	Tohoku University, Japan
Kiyoung Choi	Seoul National University, Republic of Korea
Koen Bertels	Delft University of Technology, The Netherlands
Kostas Masselos	University of Peloponnese, Greece
Krzysztof Kepa	Virginia Tech, USA
Kyle Rupnow	Advanced Digital Sciences Center, Singapore
Marco Platzner	University of Paderborn, Germany
Marco Santambrogio	Politecnico di Milano, Italy
Markus Weinhardt	Osnabrück University of Applied Sciences, Germany
Matthias Birk	Karlsruhe Institute of Technology, Germany
Michael Hübner	Ruhr-Universität Bochum, Germany
Mladen Berekovic	Braunschweig University of Technology, Germany
Monica Magalhães Pereira	Universidade Federal do Rio Grande do Norte, Brazil
Neil Bergmann	University of Queensland, Australia
Paul Chow	University of Toronto, Canada
Pedro C. Diniz	USC Information Sciences Institute, USA
Pedro Trancoso	University of Cyprus, Cyprus
Pete Sedcole	Celoxica Ltd., UK
Peter Athanas	Virginia Tech, USA
Peter Zipf	University of Kassel, Germany
Philip Leong	University of Sydney, Australia
Ray Cheung	City University of Hong Kong, Hong Kong
Reiner Hartenstein	University of Kaiserslautern, Germany
René Cumplido	National Institute for Astrophysics, Optics, and Electronics (INAOE), Mexico
Ricardo Jacobi	Universidade de Brasília, Brazil
Robert Esser	Apple Inc., USA
Roman Hermida	Universidad Complutense, Madrid, Spain
Sanjay Rajopadhye	Colorado State University, USA
Seda Ogrenci Memik	Northwestern University, USA

Smail Niar	University of Valenciennes and Hainaut-Cambresis, France
Stephan Wong	Delft University of Technology, The Netherlands
Stephen Brown	Altera Corp., University of Toronto, Canada
Steve Casselman	Altera Corp., USA
Steven Derrien	IRISA, France
Taemin Kim	Intel Corp., USA
Takefumi Miyoshi	The University of Electro-Communications, Japan
Theerayod Wiangtong	MUT, Thailand
Thilo Pionteck	University of Lübeck, Germany
Tim Todman	Imperial College London, UK
Tomonori Izumi	Ritsumeikan University, Japan
Tsutomu Sasao	Meiji University, Japan
Vincenzo Rana	École Polytechnique Fédérale de Lausanne, Switzerland
Waqar Hussain	Tampere University of Technology, Finland
William Marnane	University College Cork, Ireland
Yasushi Inoguchi	Japan Advanced Institute of Science and Technology, Japan
Yoshiki Yamaguchi	Tsukuba University, Japan
Yuchiro Shibata	Nagasaki University, Japan
Yukinori Sato	Japan Advanced Institute of Science and Technology, Japan
Zachary Baker	Los Alamos National Laboratory, USA

Additional Reviewers

Alba Lopes	Universidade Federal do Rio Grande do Norte, Brazil
Alessandro Nacci	Politecnico di Milano, Italy
Andrew Love	Virginia Tech, USA
Anh H. Du Nguyen	Delft University of Technology, The Netherlands
Anthony Brandon	Delft University of Technology, The Netherlands
Alexander Klimm	Karlsruhe Institute of Technology, Germany
Arda Yurdakul	Boğaziçi University, Turkey
Carsten Tradowsky	Karlsruhe Institute of Technology, Germany
Cuong Pham-Quoc	Delft University of Technology, The Netherlands

Eduardo Cuevas-Farfan	INAOE, Mexico
Florian Stock	TU Darmstadt, Germany
Gerald Hempel	TU Dresden, Germany
Hanmin Park	Seoul National University, Republic of Korea
Hamid Mushtaq	Delft University of Technology, The Netherlands
Hiroki Nakahara	Kagoshima University, Japan
Jecel Assumpcao Jr.	University of São Paulo, Brazil
Jose Arnaldo M. De Holanda	University of São Paulo, Brazil
Junxiu Liu	University of Ulster, UK
Kevin Zeng	Virginia Tech, USA
Kyoung Hoon Kim	Seoul National University, Republic of Korea
Luca Cassano	University of Pisa, Italy
Leandro Martinez	University of São Paulo, Brazil
Lukas Jung	TU Darmstadt, Germany
Márcio Brandão	Universidade de Brasília, Brazil
Marcos Da Cruz	Universidade Federal do Rio Grande do Norte, Brazil
Martin Danek	TU Darmstadt, Germany
Matteo Carminati	Politecnico di Milano, Italy
Moritz Schmid	University of Erlangen-Nuremberg, Germany
Oliver Oey	Karlsruhe Institute of Technology, Germany
Paul Kaufmann	University of Paderborn, Germany
Philipp Wehner	Ruhr-Universität Bochum, Germany
Rainer Höckmann	Osnabrück University of Applied Sciences, Germany
Thorsten Wink	TU Darmstadt, Germany
Timo Stripf	Karlsruhe Institute of Technology, Germany
Tomohiro Ueno	Tohoku University, Japan
Vincent Mirian	University of Toronto, Canada
Vlad Mihai Sima	Delft University of Technology, The Netherlands

Table of Contents

Methodologies and Tools I

Architectures I

Short Papers

Applications II

Architectures II

Methodologies and Tools II

Special Session Papers

FPGA-Based Parallel DBSCAN Architecture

Neil Scicluna and Christos-Savvas Bouganis

Imperial College London, EEE Department
London SW7 2AZ, United Kingdom
scicluna.neil@gmail.com, christos-savvas.bouganis@imperial.ac.uk

Abstract. Clustering of a large number of data points is a computational demanding task that often needs the be accelerated in order to be useful in practice. The focus of this work is on the Density-Based Spatial Clustering of Applications with Noise (DBSCAN) algorithm, which is one of the state-of-the-art clustering algorithms, targeting its acceleration using an FPGA device. The paper presents a novel, optimised and scalable architecture that takes advantage of the internal memory structure of modern FPGAs in order to deliver a high performance clustering system. Results show that the developed system can obtain average speed-ups of 32x in real-world tests and 202x in synthetic tests when compared to state-of-the-art software counterparts.

Keywords: Clustering, DBSCAN, FPGA, Parallel Hardware Architectures.

1 Introduction

Clustering is the task of intelligently grouping data points into groups or clusters, where the grouping of the points is based on a particular criterion, such as distance. Clustering has many applications including data mining, statistical data analysis, pattern recognition and image analysis [1–3]. Various clustering algorithms have been developed so far, usually targeting a specific domain of applications by defining suitably the notion of the cluster. With high complexity and long computation times, sometimes even taking hours for large datasets [4], the need to perform clustering as fast as possible is becoming more and more prevalent.

The most widely used clustering algorithms are K-Means [5], Density-Based Spatial Clustering of Applications with Noise (DBSCAN) [1] and Ordering Points To Identify the Clustering Structure (OPTICS) [6]. While K-Means provides a fast solution to the clustering problem, it has been shown to have certain limitations. These include its inability to identify and reject noise in the data and that fact that the achieved clustering of the points is without consideration of the spatial density of the data points [1]. Additionally, the result of the K-Means is heavily dependant on its initialisation and on the number of clusters provided by the user [5]. DBSCAN and OPTICS clustering algorithms address those limitations in exchange for higher complexity.

D. Goehringer et al. (Eds.): ARC 2014, LNCS 8405, pp. 1–12, 2014.
© Springer International Publishing Switzerland 2014

DBSCAN and OPTICS algorithms perform clustering using the spatial density of the data. However, OPTICS does not perform cluster per se but it provides an insight on how to do this, requiring additional processing for the actual clustering to be achieved, making the whole process computationally demanding. DBSCAN on the other hand is faster than OPTICS [1, 6] and serves as a good middle-ground, making it one of the most popular and heavily cited clustering algorithms.

With the increasing requirement of being able to perform clustering on large datasets as fast as possible, running these on generic processors is proving to be inadequate and specialised hardware is often utilised. Even though real-time K-Means implementations have been developed for FPGAs [7], to the best of the authors' knowledge, FPGA implementations of the more complex, density-based methods have not yet been developed. Thus, providing the ability to perform density-based clustering in real-time could open a vast array of possibilities.

In this paper, the an FPGA-based hardware implementation of the DBSCAN algorithm is described. The proposed hardware architecture takes advantage of the dynamic and massively parallel nature of an FPGA device and computes in parallel certain aspects of the algorithm targeting its acceleration. The proposed architecture is highly scalable such that the performance gains are not limited by dataset size, but only by the resources available on the FPGA utilised. Furthermore, this is designed as a fully parametrisable IP core where aspects such as the size and dimensions of the input data, internal precision, pipeline depths and the level of parallelism, can be modified by simply altering the parameters and re-synthesising. Finally, the system is also FPGA target independent, with the only requirement being that the chip used has sufficient amounts of Block Random Access Memory (BRAM). All these aspects make this the most flexible hardware implementation of DBSCAN yet.

2   Background

2.1   DBSCAN Algorithm

The DBSCAN algorithm performs clustering based on the spatial density of the data points. This approach to clustering is intuitive, as the definition of a cluster simply refers to a region where there is a typical density of points which is considerably higher than the outside region of the cluster. Additionally, the density in areas where points can be considered as noise is lower than those of clusters.

The key concept is that in order to form a cluster, there must exist at least *MinPts* data points that are all within the *Eps* radius of each other. The *MinPts* and *Eps* are user specified parameters. Data points which contain at least as many points in their *Eps* neighbourhood as *MinPts*, are considered as core points. If a point contains fewer points than *MinPts* in its neighbourhood, but contains at least one core point, it is considered as a border point. In [1], this point is said to be *directly density-reachable* from a core point but not the other way around. The cluster is then expanded by grouping all the *directly density-reachable* core points and the respective border points. This is referred to as *density reachability* and essentially means that there is a chain of *directly density-reachable* points connecting two particular points. Finally, points which are neither *directly density-reachable*, nor contain at least as many points as *MinPts* in their neighbourhood, are considered as noise.

The algorithm itself works as follows. The first step is to retrieve all the *directly density-reachable* points with respect to *Eps* for each point. If there are less points than *MinPts*, the algorithm moves to the next point, otherwise, the points are assigned to the current cluster (as defined by the cluster identification number). The points obtained in this initial step are referred to as the *immediate neighbourhood points*. The next step is to expand the cluster by pushing all the points retrieved onto a queue. On each iteration, a point is dequeued and all the *density-reachable* points with respect to *Eps* from that point are retrieved. If the number of points is larger or equal to *MinPts*, then these points are added to the cluster and pushed onto the queue. These are referred to as the *extended neighbourhood points*. Subsequently as more *density-reachable* points are found, they are added to the queue to find other points which form part of the cluster. This is repeated until the queue is empty, which signifies that the cluster has been formed completely. The cluster identification number is then incremented and a new point is loaded to start compiling a new cluster. This whole process is repeated until all the points in the dataset have been checked.

DBSCAN also works for multiple dimensions without changes to the core algorithm. This is because the only operation performed on the data is distance measurement, which can be adapted to multiple dimensions. Furthermore, interchanging distance functions such as Euclidean distance and Manhattan distance is also possible. Such change impacts on the shape and radius of points considered in the neighbourhood.

2.2   Related Work

The time complexity of the standard DBSCAN algorithm is $O(n^2)$ (where n is the number of points in the dataset) since a range query, which is done by calculating and checking the distance to all the other points, needs to be performed for each point in the dataset. To improve this, tree data structures such as the R*-Tree [8] used in [1], are adopted to accelerate region queries thereby reducing the time complexity to $O(n * log(n))$. This however adds the requirement of constructing the tree for the dataset, which is also $O(n * log(n))$. Moreover, spatial accesses using an R*-Tree are not always efficient [9].

The Parallel-DBSCAN (P-DBSCAN) algorithm described in [9], adopts a different spatial index called the Priority R-Tree (PR-Tree). Here a form of parallelism is introduced where the database is first separated into several parts and then the computational nodes build their own PR-Tree and carry out the clustering independently. Each node in this system is a desktop PC. Finally, the results are aggregated. An alternative approach to parallelism but on the same platform was taken in MapReduce-DBSCAN (MR-DBSCAN) [4] and Hierarchical-Based DBSCAN (HDBSCAN) [10], where a map-reduce structure is implemented to spread the computation across multiple nodes that can work in parallel using the Hadoop platform. These implementations all aim to solve the problem of very large data clustering. Even though significant performance increases over standard implementations are achieved for datasets with hundreds of thousands of points and more, this is not true for smaller datasets due to the overhead introduced. As a result these methods are suitable only for certain cases and are still dependent on how fast each individual node can perform the clustering.

Thapa et al. [3] propose a Graphics Processing Unit (GPU) implementation of the DBSCAN algorithm that takes advantage of the large amounts of memory and processor cores available on modern GPUs. Two different approaches are explored in attempt to accelerate this algorithm through parallelism. The first involves computing the region query for a particular point, by comparing it to each point in the database in parallel and storing all the results in memory. Alternatively, the second approach involves computing the range queries of all the points in parallel and once again storing the results in memory. While this showed a performance increase of about 2–3x, the advantages are dependent on the size of the dataset.

The fastest implementation so far is the dedicated hardware Very-Large-Scale Integration (VLSI) architecture proposed in [11] and is applied to clustering of image pixel data. In fact this design can only perform 2D clustering and is therefore very application specific. This hardware architecture is designed in such a way that there is a processing element for each pixel and full pixel-parallel processing is achieved. This results in very fast clustering speeds but requires a significant amount of area per pixel and therefore is not feasible for even moderately large datasets, particularly when interconnect requirements are considered. Additionally, it is unclear whether this design is parametrisable in terms of Eps and $MinPts$, maximum sizes of clusters and data precision.

In this work we aim to achieve the performance benefits available through parallelism and hardware implementation, while also maintaining a great level of flexibility. The key contributions are the analysis and development of a novel parallelisation strategy for the DBSCAN algorithm and the design of the first high performance and parametrisable FPGA-based implementation of this clustering algorithm.

3   Concept and Architecture

The major contributor to the time complexity of the algorithm is the range query process that needs to be performed for every point in the dataset. This was also confirmed experimentally through extensive profiling of a custom DBSCAN MATLAB implementation based on [2]. While R*-Trees do indeed improve the time complexity of the algorithm, simulations performed using Elki [12] show that since the tree needs to be reconstructed for each new data sample, this does not provide substantial performance benefits for applications with hard time constraints and in some cases, it is actually detrimental. Furthermore, due to their complexity and highly dynamic nature, R-Trees (which are very similar to

R*-Trees), are shown to be costly in terms of resources to implement efficiently in hardware [13]. Thus the proposed architecture utilises standard indexing instead of a tree based data structure.

For DBSCAN to perform the clustering, two sets of range queries are performed, the first obtains the immediate neighbourhood of the particular point where the second set performs the range queries in order to obtain the extended neighbourhood of points for that cluster. In most cases, this second batch of range queries take the longest portion of execution time. This was corroborated by performing profiling tests in MATLAB with multiple datasets and also varying parameters. These datasets are of varying spatial densities and are obtained from an image processing application and consist of coordinates of local features detected in a variety of images. These results are shown in Table 1.

Table 1. DBSCAN Range query bias analysis

Dataset No.	Size	Eps	MinPts	Imm. Neighb. Range Queries	Ext. Neighb. Range Queries
1	19504	25	10	238	19342
1	19504	25	80	2657	16995
1	19504	55	220	1903	17731
2	2015	25	8	346	1710
3	6472	70	100	193	6310
4	2237	100	90	176	2094
5	2927	80	100	96	2832
6	2003	100	60	2	2003

These extended neighbourhood range queries have no data dependencies and thus can be performed in parallel. Furthermore, the algorithm performs these queries by essentially having a queue of points on which these range queries need to be performed which is constantly appended with new points. Thus, further parallelisation can be extracted. This is achieved by loading all the points in the queue at each iteration and subsequently perform all the range queries for these points concurrently, thereby significantly reducing the computation time.

Figure 1 shows a hardware architecture diagram for the design outlining all the key modules.

The Input Memory element is used to store the data that is going to be clustered, which is not internal to the DBSCAN IP Core in order to allow for maximum flexibility. It is assumed that all the dimensions of the currently addressed data point are available simultaneously. Furthermore, it is assumed that the memory subsystem can provide a data point every clock cycle, which is possible through pipelining or using SRAMs.

The design uses on-chip BRAM resources for all memory elements, however it allows for alternative implementations of the input memory element, as long as the previously mentioned criteria are satisfied. The other two RAM elements in the architecture are the Cluster ID Memory and the Visited Flag Memory which

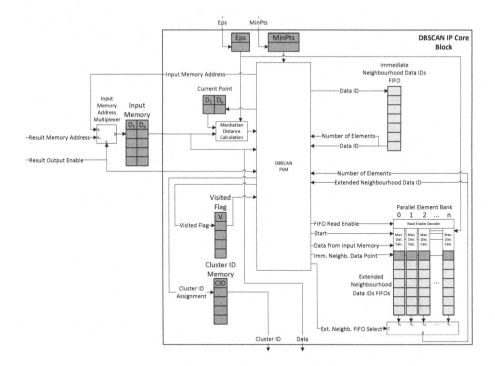

Fig. 1. FPGA DBSCAN Hardware architecture

are internal to the IP Core and are implemented in BRAM. The former stores the cluster identification number for each data point while the latter marks whether a point has been visited.

The immediate neighbourhood range query results are stored in a first in, first out (FIFO) memory element which is implemented using the available BRAM/FIFO resources on the FPGA. This serves as the point queue on which the extended neighbourhood range queries are performed. However, this does not store the actual data points, but just their addresses in main memory.

The main parallelised aspect of the design is the computation of the extended neighbourhood range queries. Towards this, multiple distance measurements are performed simultaneously through the use of the Manhattan Distance Calculation Datapath. This is a dedicated component which is designed to work as a black box, in the sense that, given two data points and the *Eps* parameter value, it provides an output signal signifying whether or not the distance between the two points is smaller than or equal to *Eps*. This element is automatically generated based on the number of dimensions of the input data and it is also pipelined for high clock frequency. Since the data point should only be stored into the queue if that condition is satisfied, this output signal is then used as a write enable for the FIFO which stores the result of the extended neighbourhood range query. The combination of a distance calculation block and a FIFO is referred to as a Parallel Element (PE). As shown in the diagram, multiple PEs can be instantiated depending on the available resources and the target performance. While the results of multiple range queries are obtained simultaneously with these PEs, the cluster identification number and visited flag must be updated serially and therefore, there needs to be a way of selecting between the separate parallel elements. This selection is controlled by the Finite State Machine (FSM) and it is crucial that the read enable signal is high for only one FIFO at a time. Correspondingly, the outputs of the FIFOs also need to be considered individually. This is achieved through the use of a decoder and a multiplexer. If the number of parallel elements is fairly large, the multiplexer would have a very long critical path, resulting in lower clock speeds. To remedy this, the multiplexer is pipelined.

To perform the clustering, the DBSCAN FSM iterates through the points in the data memory and if the data point is not marked as visited in the visited flag memory, a range query is performed by checking the distance of that point to all the other points in the dataset. All the points that are within the Eps neighbourhood are then stored in the immediate neighbourhood data ID FIFO. If the number of elements is greater than or equal to $MinPts$ these points are assigned to the current cluster and the FSM then loads into a register bank as many points as available in the immediate neighbourhood FIFO, or as limited by the number of available PEs. Subsequently it performs this batch of range queries concurrently, with the results stored in each respective FIFO. The element count for each FIFO is then checked against $MinPts$ and if the condition is satisfied, these points are added to the immediate neighbourhood queue to continue expanding the cluster. This whole process is repeated until there are no points left in the queue at which point the next memory element is checked to start forming a new cluster.

4   Experimental Results

The proposed architecture was synthesised for the Xilinx Virtex 7 XC7VX690T-3 FPGA and subsequently, its performance is evaluated using the variety of datasets mentioned in the previous section. Being pixel coordinates, these datasets are therefore two dimensional and each dimension is stored with 16 bit precision. Maximum clock speeds reported by the synthesis tool for this design with 2D input data and 1–710 PEs, range from 350–410 MHz. The simulation results are then compared to a range of software methods run on a desktop computer with an Intel Core i7 2600K 3.4 GHz Sandy Bridge processor and 8GB of DDR3-1066MHz memory. The evaluated design instance targets an image processing application, however, the proposed architecture can be configured to handle multi-dimensional data of any word length without an impact on the latency of the system. Table 2 shows the resource utilisation along with the maximum clock speed and respective power consumption for varying numbers of PEs. The power consumption is estimated using the Xilinx XPower Analyzer tool and includes both the dynamic and static power.

The proposed system was compared against three software implementations. To provide a worst-case comparison, the software time used for each case is the shortest

Table 2. Effects of varying number of PEs (Synthesis Estimates)

No. of PEs	Max Clock Speed (MHz)	LUT Utilisation (%)	BRAM/FIFO Utilisation (%)	Total Power (W)
1	409	0.1	1	0.57
25	413	1	5	0.84
50	393	2	8	1.03
100	395	4	15	1.75
150	391	6	22	2.28
300	378	12	42	3.90
500	372	20	69	6.92
710	353	34	98	8.97

one between three software implementations. The first of these is the MATLAB implementation, while the second and third were measured by ELKI [12], which is a software clustering algorithm performance analysis tool written by the developers of DBSCAN. One of these measurements is with standard indexing, whereas the other was done using R*-Tree indexing. To provide a fair comparison, the R*-Tree timing includes both the time taken for the generation of the tree data structure and the execution of the DBSCAN algorithm accelerated by that data structure. The results for the tests performed, along with the respective chosen parameters are shown in Table 3. The Eps and $MinPts$ parameters in these tests were primarily chosen to provide meaningful results for the targeted image processing application. The obtained results show an average speed-up of 32x. Similarly, Fig. 2 shows how the performance of the fastest software version and the proposed HDL design scale with increasing dataset sizes.

The conducted experiments show that there is a limit as to how much parallelism can be extracted from a dataset and this is dependant on the combination of the spatial density of the data and the parameters used. In spite of this, simulations show that the proposed parallelisation strategy proves significantly beneficial. The choices of the numbers of PEs used in the tests shown in Table 3 were made to ensure that the number of range queries performed in parallel are maximised for each dataset. This is based on a MATLAB model developed to analyse the performance effects of varying numbers of PEs on the system.

Moreover, the results show that for the range of datasets and parameters tested, which provide a wide range of test cases with varying spatial density, most of the performance gains available can be exploited even with a small number of PEs, despite the performance being dataset limited. Figure 3 shows how this applies to two particular test cases. Since the maximum clock speed varies with the number of PEs used in the design, the simulations were performed at the maximum clock speed attainable with the respective number of PEs.

Figure 4(a) shows that the time taken to cluster the dataset increases approximately linearly with the $MinPts$ parameter. This is due to more parallelism potential becoming available in the data as this parameter gets smaller. In this case, when $MinPts = 0$ maximum parallelism is achieved, with the result being a

Table 3. HDL DBSCAN Implementation performance analysis results

Dataset No.	Size	Eps	MinPts	Software Time (s)	Parallel Elements (PEs)	Clock Speed (MHz)	HDL Time (ms)	Speed-Up
1	19504	25	80	7.16	300	377.98	211.88	33.77
1	19504	55	220	11.40	710	353.15	371.51	30.68
2	2015	25	8	0.13	85	405.48	2.77	46.21
3	6472	70	100	1.74	150	391.11	49.56	35.11
4	2237	100	90	0.28	150	391.11	9.76	28.69
5	2927	80	100	0.58	150	391.11	22.34	26.14
6	2003	100	60	0.19	150	391.11	8.64	22.45

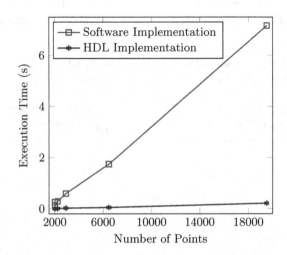

Fig. 2. Graph showing performance scalability with increasing numbers of points

single large cluster, but when $MinPts = 60$ no clusters are formed and therefore, no parallelism can be extracted. Figure 4(b) shows that the relationship is not linear throughout for the Eps parameter. When the Eps parameter is small we encounter the same issue where only a few small clusters are formed and therefore very little performance gain can be obtained through parallelism. As Eps becomes larger, the number of PEs becomes the limiting factor and therefore, more are required to take advantage of the parallelism available in the data. Additionally, as occurs with the standard DBSCAN implementations, with larger Eps the algorithm takes longer to compute.

Furthermore, the proposed system was tested using the datasets that were used in Thapa R. et al. [3], which the authors have kindly provided. It should be noted that unlike the datasets tested previously, these are synthetic datasets and have constant spatial density throughout with the points ordered by cluster. Figure 4 shows the execution times of the various implementations with the parameters set to $Eps = 1.5$ and $MinPts = 4$ as used in [3]. The number of PEs was set to 50 as

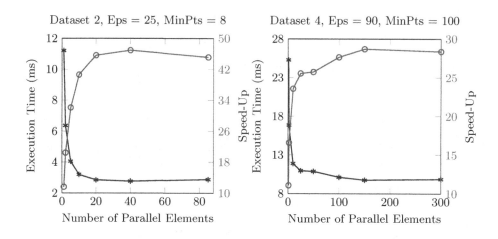

Fig. 3. Execution time (marked by ∗) with varying number of parallel elements and respective speed-up (marked by o)

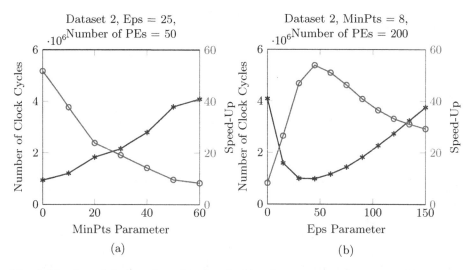

Fig. 4. Number of clock cycles taken (marked by ∗) to compute clustering with varying *MinPts* (a) and *Eps* (b) and respective speed-up (marked by o) over software implementation

this extracts the maximum amount of parallelism available in the data and allows for a clock speed of 393 MHz. The speed-ups achieved in synthetic dataset tests are on average 202x when compared to the software implementations and 143x compared to the GPU implementation.

Table 4. DBSCAN HDL Implementation in comparison to GPU Implementation

Dataset Size	Software Time (s)	Sequential Time (s) [3]	GPU Time (ms) [3]	HDL Time (ms)	Speed-Up over Software	Speed-Up over GPU
5000	0.56	1.33	340	2.6	215.55	130.87
10000	1.69	4.5	1120	8.4	201.14	133.30
15000	3.53	6.82	2490	17.41	202.76	143.02
20000	5.64	9.09	4910	29.62	190.42	165.78

5   Conclusions

The paper presented a novel FPGA-based architecture for the DBSCAN cluster-ing algorithm. The architecture utilises key aspects of the FPGA fabric in order to accelerate the targeted algorithm. When compared to established software meth-ods, the proposed architecture achieves considerable performance increases, which is higher than obtained using the GPU implementation in [3]. Finally, compared to the VLSI implementation in [11], while the performance is not on the same level, the proposed system is significantly more flexible and allows for clustering of consid-erably larger datasets in more dimensions, while still providing high performance.

References

1. Ester, M., Kriegel, H.-P., Sander, J., Xu, X.: A Density-Based Algorithm for Discov-ering Clusters. In: Proc. of 2nd International Conference on Knowledge Discovery and Data Mining, Portland, OR, pp. 226–231 (1996)
2. Daszykowski, M., Walczak, B., Massart, D.L.: Looking for Natural Patterns in Data. Part 1: Density Based Approach. Chemometrics and Intelligent Laboratory Sys-tems 56(2), 83–92 (2001)
3. Thapa, R., Trefftz, C., Wolffe, G.: Memory-Efficient Implementation of a Graphics Processor-Based Cluster Detection Algorithm for Large Spatial Databases. In: Proc. of the IEEE International Conference on Electro/Information Technology (EIT), vol. 1(5), pp. 20–22 (2010)
4. He, Y., Tan, H., Luo, W., Mao, H., Ma, D., Feng, S., Fan, J.: MR-DBSCAN: An Efficient Parallel Density-Based Clustering Algorithm Using MapReduce. In: Proc. of the IEEE 17th International Conference on Parallel and Distributed Systems (ICPADS), vol. 7(9), pp. 473–480 (2011)
5. Hartigan, J.A., Wong, M.A.: A K-Means Clustering Algorithm. Journal of the Royal Statistical Society, Series C 28(1), 100–108 (1979)
6. Ankerst, M., Breunig, M.M., Kriegel, H.-P., Sander, J.: OPTICS: Ordering Points To Identify the Clustering Structure. In: Proc. of the ACM SIGMOD International Conference on Management of Data, vol. 28(2), pp. 49–60 (1999)
7. Maruyama, T.: Real-time K-Means Clustering for Color Images on Reconfigurable Hardware. In: Proc. of 18th International Conference on Pattern Recognition (ICPR), vol. 2(1), pp. 816–819 (2006)

8. Beckmann, N., Kriegel, H.-P., Schneider, R., Seeger, B.: The R*-tree: An Efficient and Robust Access Method for Points and Rectangles. In: Proc. of ACM SIGMOD Int. Conf. on Management of Data, Atlantic City, NJ, pp. 322–331 (1990)

9. Chen, M., Gao, X., Li, H.: Parallel DBSCAN with Priority R-Tree. In: Proc. of the 2nd IEEE International Conference on Information Management and Engineering (ICIME), vol. 16(18), pp. 508–511 (2010)

10. Li, L., Xi, Y.: Research on Clustering Algorithm and Its Parallelization Strategy. In: Proc. of the International Conference on Computational and Information Sciences (ICCIS), vol. 21(23), pp. 325–328 (2011)

11. Shimada, A., Zhu, H., Shibata, T.: A VLSI DBSCAN Processor Composed as an Array of Micro Agents Having Self-Growing Interconnects. In: Proc. of the IEEE International Symposium on Circuits and Systems (ISCAS), vol. 19(23), pp. 2062–2065 (2013)

12. Achtert, E., Kriegel, H.-P., Schubert, E., Zimek, A.: Interactive Data Mining with 3D-Parallel-Coordinate-Trees. In: Proceedings of the ACM SIGMOD International Conference on Management of Data, New York, NY, pp. 1009–1012 (2013)

13. Xiang, X., Tuo, S., Pranav, V., Jaehwan, J.L.: R-tree: A Hardware Implementation. In: Proceedings of the 2008 International Conference on Computer Design (CDES), Las Vegas, NV, pp. 3–9 (2008)

FPGA-Based High Performance AES-GCM Using Efficient Karatsuba Ofman Algorithm

Karim M. Abdellatif, R. Chotin-Avot, and H. Mehrez

LIP6-SoC Laboratory, University of Paris VI, France
{karim.abdellatif,roselyne.chotin-avot,habib.mehrez}@lip6.fr

Abstract. AES-GCM has been utilized in various security applications. It consists of two components: an Advanced Encryption Standard (AES) engine and a Galois Hash (GHASH) core. The performance of the system is determined by the GHASH architecture because of the inherent computation feedback. This paper introduces a modification for the pipelined Karatsuba Ofman Algorithm (KOA)-based GHASH. In particular, the computation feedback is removed by analyzing the complexity of the computation process. The proposed GHASH core is evaluated with three different implementations of AES (BRAMs-based SubBytes, composite field-based SubBytes, and LUT-based SubBytes). The presented AES-GCM architectures are implemented using Xilinx Virtex5 FPGAs. Our comparison to previous work reveals that our architectures are more performance-efficient (Thr. /Slices).

Keywords: AES-GCM, FPGAs, GHASH, Karatsuba Ofman Algorithm (KOA).

1 Introduction

Recently, techniques have been invented to combine encryption and authentication into a single algorithm which is called Authenticated Encryption (AE). Combining these two security services in hardware produces smaller area compared to two separate algorithms.

Galois Counter Mode (GCM) [1] mode is an AE algorithm. It is well-suited for wireless, optical, and magnetic recording systems due to its multi-Gbps authenticated encryption speed, outstanding performance, minimal computational latency as well as high intrinsic degree of pipelining and parallelism. New communication standards like IEEE 802.1ae [2] and NIST 800-38D have considered employing GCM to enhance their performance. The reconfigurability of FPGAs offers major advantages when using them for cryptographic applications. Hence, they are commonly used as an implementation target.

Our Contribution. In this work, we present efficient FPGA-based architectures for AES-GCM by modifying the architecture of the pipelined KOA-based GHASH. Our focus on state of the art of KOA-based GHASHs leads to solve the algorithm complexity resulting from the inherent computation feedback. In

D. Goehringer et al. (Eds.): ARC 2014, LNCS 8405, pp. 13–24, 2014.
© Springer International Publishing Switzerland 2014

addition, three different implementations of AES are evaluated and added to the proposed GHASH in order to increase the flexibility of the presented work.

The major features and the previous work of AES-GCM are described in **Section 2**. After that, our proposed architecture of GHASH is presented (**Section 3**). The overall architecture of AES-GCM is shown in **Section 4**. Implementation details and performance comparison are discussed in **Section 5**. **Section 6** concludes this work.

2   AES-GCM

Recently, Galois Counter Mode (GCM) [1] was considered as a new mode of operation of Advanced Encryption Standard (AES). GCM simultaneously provides confidentiality, integrity and authenticity assurances on the data. It supports not only high speed authenticated encryption but also protection against bit-flipping attacks. It can be implemented in hardware to achieve high speeds with low cost and low latency. Software implementations can achieve excellent performance by using table-driven field operations. GCM was designed to meet the need for an authenticated encryption mode that can efficiently achieve speeds of 10 Gbps and higher in hardware. It contains an AES engine in counter mode and a Galois Hash (GHASH) module as presented in Fig. 1.

As shown in Fig. 1, the GHASH function (authentication part) is composed of chained $GF(2^{128})$ multipliers and bitwise exclusive-OR (XOR) operations. Because of the inherent computation feedback, the performance of the system is usually determined by the $GF(2^{128})$.

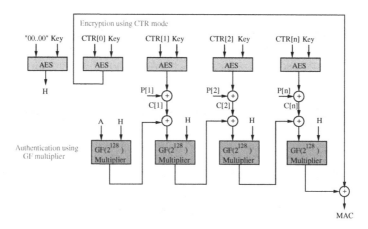

Fig. 1. AES-GCM: Encryption process is performed using counter mode and authentication is done using $GF(2^{128})$, A is an optional 128-bit Additional Authenticated Data which is authenticated but not encrypted

Algorithm 1. GF(2^{128}) multiplier
Input A, H $\in$ GF(2^{128}), F(x) Field Polynomial.
Output X
X=0
for $i = 0$ to 127 do
if $A_i = 1$ then
$X \longleftarrow X \oplus H$
end if
if $H_{127} = 0$ then
$H \longleftarrow rightshift(H)$
else
$H \longleftarrow rightshift(H) \oplus F(x)$
end if
end for
return X

Algorithm 1 describes the GF(2^{128}) multiplier. Serial implementation of **Algorithm 1** performs the multiplication process in 128 clock cycles. Parallel method can be implemented like [3] and it takes only one clock cycle.

In **Algorithm 1**, if **H** is fixed, the multiplier is called a fixed operand GF(2^{128}) multiplier as shown by [4]. This design proposed by [4] can be used efficiently (smaller area) on FPGAs as the circuit is specialized for **H**. We integrated this multiplier proposed by [4] with a key-synthesized AES engine in [5] in order to support slow changing key applications like Virtual Private Networks (VPNs). Also, in [5], we proposed a protocol to secure the FPGA reconfiguration to protect the bitstream because it is a key-based bitstream. The disadvantage of this method is the new reconfiguration which must be downloaded on the FPGA in case of changing the key.

Karatsuba Ofman Algorithm (KOA) is used to reduce the complexity (consumed area) of the GF(2^{128}) multiplier. The single step KOA algorithm splits two m bit inputs A and B into four terms A_h, A_l, B_h, B_l which are m/2 bit terms. The 1-step iteration of KOA shown in Fig.2 can be described as:

$$\begin{cases} D_l &= A_l \times B_l \\ D_{hl} &= (A_h \oplus A_l) \times (B_h \oplus B_l) \\ D_h &= A_h \times B_h \\ D &= D_h X^m \oplus X^{m/2}(D_h \oplus D_{hl} \oplus D_l) \oplus D_l \end{cases} \qquad (1)$$

After the multiplication stage is processed using KOA, the binary field reduction step is used to convert the length of the vector from $2m - 1$ to m as shown in Equation 2.

$$C(x) = D \ mod \ P(x) \qquad (2)$$

where P(x) is the field polynomial used for the multiplication operation.

$$P(x) = x^{128} + x^7 + x^2 + x + 1 \qquad (3)$$

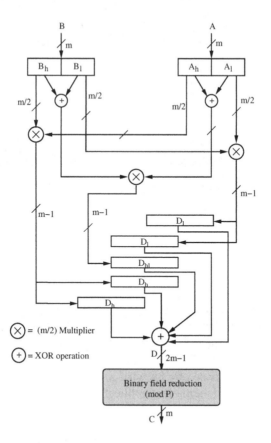

Fig. 2. Polynomial Multiplication using KOA

KOA was used by [6] to reduce the complexity (consumed area) of the $GF(2^{128})$ multiplier as shown in Fig. 3a. From Fig. 3a, the MAC calculation is as follows:

$$MAC = (C_i \oplus Z_{i-1}) \times H \qquad (4)$$

The drawback of the architecture presented in [6] is the the critical delay resulting from the multiplication stage. In order to reduce the data path (critical delay) of the KOA multiplier, pipelining concept was accomplished by [7] as shown in Fig. 3b. Equation 4 was written by [7] as follows:

$$MAC = Q_1 \oplus Q_2 \oplus Q_3 \oplus Q_4, where \qquad (5)$$

$$Q1 = (((C_1 \times H^4 \oplus C_5) \times H^4 \oplus C_9) \times H^4 \oplus ....) \times H^4 \qquad (6)$$

$$Q2 = (((C_2 \times H^4 \oplus C_6) \times H^4 \oplus C_{10}) \times H^4 \oplus ....) \times H^3 \qquad (7)$$

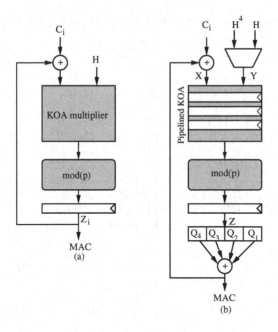

Fig. 3. (a) KOA based GHAH; (b) Pipelined KOA based GHASH

$$Q3 = (((C_3 \times H^4 \oplus C_7) \times H^4 \oplus C_{11}) \times H^4 \oplus ....) \times H^2 \qquad (8)$$

$$Q4 = (((C_4 \times H^4 \oplus C_8) \times H^4 \oplus C_{12}) \times H^4 \oplus ....) \times H \qquad (9)$$

The hardware architecture proposed by [7] (Fig. 3b) is a 4-stage pipelined KOA-based GHASH. An example of data flow control for the GHASH is shown in Table 1, where $C1 .... C_8$ is the input sequence and "-" denotes "don't care". At the beginning, H^4 is passed to port Y. After the input of C_6, H is passed to port Y. The partial GHASH values Q_1, Q_2, Q_3, and Q_4 are ready at the 9th, 15th, 18th, and 12th clock, respectively. As shown from Table 1, the generated MAC resulting from 8 frames of 128-bit is ready after 19 clock cycles. Therefore, the real throughput is calculated as follows:

$$Throughput(Mbps) = F_{max(MHz)} \times 128 \times (\frac{8}{19}) \qquad (10)$$

The last component of Equation 10 is $(\frac{8}{19})$, it is called the reduction factor and the authors of [7] neglected this component in their throughput calculation. Therefore, their presented design of GHASH has not increased the throughput.

Henzen et al. [8] proposed 4-parallel AES-GCM using pipelined KOA. Their design achieved the authentication of 18 frames of 128-bits in 11 clock cycles

Table 1. Data flow control for GHASH calculation by [7]

Clock	C_i	X	Y	Z	Comment
1	C_1	C_1	H^4	0	
2	C_2	C_2	H^4	0	
3	C_3	C_3	H^4	0	
4	C_4	C_4	H^4	0	
5	C_5	$(C_1 \times H^4) \oplus C_5$	H^4	$C_1 \times H^4$	
6	C_6	$(C_2 \times H^4) \oplus C_6$	H	$C_2 \times H^4$	
7	C_7	$(C_3 \times H^4) \oplus C_7$	H	$C_3 \times H^4$	
8	C_8	$(C_4 \times H^4) \oplus C_8$	H	$C_4 \times H^4$	
9	-	-	-	$((C_1 \times H^4) \oplus C_5)H^4$	$z = Q_1$
10	0	$((C_2 \times H^4) \oplus C_6) \times H$	H	$((C_2 \times H^4) \oplus C_6) \times H$	
11	0	$((C_3 \times H^4) \oplus C_7) \times H$	H	$((C_3 \times H^4) \oplus C_7) \times H$	
12	0	-	-	$((C_4 \times H^4) \oplus C_8) \times H$	$z = Q_4$
13	0	-	-	-	
14	0	$((C_2 \times H^4) \oplus C_6) \times H^2$	H	$((C_2 \times H^4) \oplus C_6) \times H^2$	
15	-	-	-	$((C_3 \times H^4) \oplus C_7) \times H^2$	$z = Q_2$
16	-	-	-	-	
17	-	-	-	-	
18	-	-	-	$((C_2 \times H^4) \oplus C_6) \times H^3$	$z = Q_3$
19	-	-	-	-	GHASH

because of the latency resulting from the pipelined KOA. As a result, their throughput is calculated as follows:

$$Throughput(Mbps) = F_{max(MHz)} \times 128 \times \frac{18}{11} \quad (11)$$

The authors of [8] neglected this component ($\frac{18}{11}$) in their throughput calculation and replaced it by 4. Hence, their presented parallel design of GHASH has not increased the throughput by 4 as shown in Equation 11.

3   Efficient KOA-Based GHASH

Four different architectures of FPGAs-based AES-GCM have been presented in the open literature ([5],[7],[6],[8]). It is clear that these contributions do generally have different challenges related to the performance of their architectures. The performance of the architecture presented by [5] is limited because a new reconfiguration is needed in case of changing the key. Also, Zhou et al.[7] claimed the throughput improvement to their previous KOA-based GHASH [6] by using pipelined KOA but we discussed how their method is not efficient for throughput improvement as shown in Equation 10. Also, in [8], the authors claimed that their parallel architecture increased the throughput by 4 because they presented four parallel AES-GCM but we proved that their design is not efficient in terms of increasing the speed as shown in Equation 11.

In this work, in order to improve the performance of AES-GCM, an efficient pipelined KOA-based GHASH is presented. As the targeted platform is FPGA, FPGA-specific properties are considered for performance improvement.

The KOA is selected to reduce the complexity (consumed area) of the classic school multiplication as presented by [7]. Therefore, our presented GHASH uses the KOA for performing the $GF(2^{128})$ multiplication.

As shown in Equation 4, The generation of the MAC is calculated by the multiplication between H and the result of XORing the input C_i and the previous output Z_{i-1}. We propose writing Equation 4 as follows:

$$
\begin{aligned}
MAC &= (C_i \oplus Z_{i-1}) \times H \\
&= (C_i \times H) \oplus (Z_{i-1} \times H) \\
&= (C_i \times H) \oplus [(C_{i-1} \oplus Z_{i-2}) \times H^2] \\
&= (C_i \times H) \oplus (C_{i-1} \times H^2) \oplus [(C_{i-2} \oplus Z_{i-3}) \times H^3] \\
&= (C_i \times H) \oplus (C_{i-1} \times H^2) \oplus (C_{i-2} \times H^3) \\
&\oplus [(C_{i-3} \oplus Z_{i-4}) \times H^4] \\
&= \underbrace{((C_i \times H)} \oplus \underbrace{(C_{i-1} \times H^2)} \oplus \underbrace{(C_{i-2} \times H^3)} \\
&\oplus \underbrace{(C_{i-3} \times H^4)} .... \oplus \underbrace{(C_2 \times H^{i-1})} \oplus \underbrace{(C_1 \times H^i)}
\end{aligned}
\tag{12}
$$

According to Equation 12, the feedback resulting from XORing the input C_i and the previous output Z_{i-1} is removed because the final MAC is calculated from the last two lines of the equation.

Assume that there are 64 frames of 128-bit and the generation of MAC is required. Therefore, Equation 12 will be as follows:

$$
\begin{aligned}
MAC_{64} &= \underbrace{((C_{64} \times H)} \oplus \underbrace{(C_{63} \times H^2)} \oplus \underbrace{(C_{62} \times H^3)} \\
&\oplus \underbrace{(C_{61} \times H^4)} .... \oplus \underbrace{(C_2 \times H^{63})} \oplus \underbrace{(C_1 \times H^{64})}
\end{aligned}
\tag{13}
$$

If the values form H to H^{64} are stored and multiplied to the input C_i as shown in Equation 13, the pipelined architecture can be simply performed. Indeed, the architecture developed for pipelined KOA-based GHASH is in Fig. 4. 4-stage pipelined KOA is used. In terms of the complexity, we used 2-step KOA like [7]. The description of Fig. 4 is presented according to the assumption of calculating the MAC of 64 frames of 128-bit. We divide the process of MAC generation into two steps:

The first step includes storing the H values in the memory. At the beginning, H is passed to X and Y ports. The counter counts up and H^2 will appear on port Z after 4 clock cycles because we use 4-stage pipelined KOA. After, the memory stores H^2 and H^2 is passed to port Y and H to port X in order to generate H^3 and store it in the memory. This process is repeated till filling the memory with the values from H^2 to H^{64}. Filling the memory takes $63 \times 4 = 252$ clock cycles. This is called initialization stage.

After initializing the memory, the second step concerns with MAC generation as presented in Equation 13. The counter starts counting down with the first input. The first input C_1 is passed to port Y and the memory passes H^{64} to

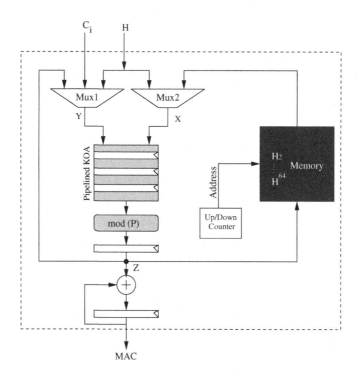

Fig. 4. Proposed pipelined KOA-based GHASH

port X. After one clock cycle, the second input C_2 is passed to port Y and the memory passes H^{63} to port X. This scenario is completed by passing C_{64} to port Y and H to port X.

The MAC is calculated by XORing Z values (Equation 13). In terms of the time taken to generate the MAC, it is 64 clock cycles with 5 additional clock cycles as a latency (4 clock cycles because of the 4-stage pipelined KOA and one cycle because of the last register). Therefore, the throughput of the proposed architecture is as follows:

$$Throughput(Mbps) = F_{max(MHz)} \times 128 \times \frac{64}{69} \qquad (14)$$

The proposed architecture reduces the reduction factor compared to [7] from $\frac{8}{19}$ to $\frac{64}{69}$. Therefore, the developed architecture presents the throughput improvement compared to [7]. In case of changing the key, 252 clock cycles are needed to initialize the memory. Hence, no new reconfiguration is needed in case of changing the key compared to [4].

Because of targeting our architecture on Xilinx Virtex5 FPGAs, we recommend using CLBs for memory implementation because of 6-input Look-Up-Tables (LUT). Otherwise, using BRAMs is another solution.

4   High Throughput AES-GCM

This section describes adding the proposed GHASH to the pipelined AES in order to perform the encryption and the authentication of the input message.

Fig. 5 shows the proposed high throughput architecture for AES-GCM. First, the pipelined AES engine generates H by encrypting "00..00" frame. Second, the proposed GHASH needs 252 clock cycles in order to initialize the memory as we described before. Third, the AES engine changes its mode to be in counter mode for performing encryption and delivering C_i to the proposed GHASH.

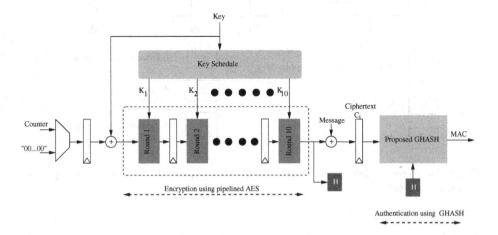

Fig. 5. Proposed AES-GCM architecture

The SubBytes transformation of AES can be implemented either by BRAMs, composite field approach, or direct LUT approach as shown in Fig. 6. Modern FPGAs contain BRAMs. Therefore, implementing SubBytes using BRAMs decreases the consumed slices of the FPGA. The LUT approach is especially interesting on Virtex5 devices because 6-input Look-Up-Tables (LUT) combined with multiplexors allow an efficient implementation of the AES SubBytes stage. Composite field approach uses the multiplicative inverse of $GF(2^8)$ and it is efficient for memoryless platforms.

The proposed architecture of AES-GCM perfectly suits the needs of GCM mode which performs the encryption and the authentication of the input message. As we described before, the encryption and the authentication in GCM are performed using the pipelined AES in counter mode and the proposed GHASH respectively. Therefore, the proposed architecture could also be tuned to handle the decryption and authentication. Indeed, C_i is XORed with the output of the pipelined AES for performing the decryption and also passed to the proposed GHASH for MAC generation.

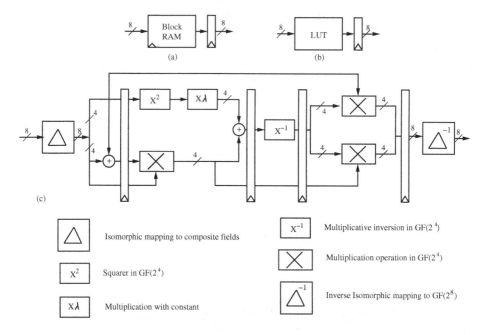

Fig. 6. SubBytes implementation with BlockRAMs (a), with LUTs (b), with composite field approach (c)

5   Hardware Comparison

We coded our proposed scheme in VHDL and targeted to Virtex5 (XC5VLX220). ModelSim 6.5c was used for simulation. Xilinx Synthesize Technology (XST) is used to perform the synthesize and ISE9.2 was adopted to run the Place And Route (PAR).

Table 2 shows the hardware comparison between our results and previous work. Note the filled dots in the "Key" column. The key is synthesized into the architecture when denoted by ∘ which requires a new reconfiguration in case of changing the key. Otherwise, the key schedule is implemented when denoted by ● and no new reconfiguration is needed in case of changing the key.

On Virtex5 platform, our proposed AES-GCM core reaches the throughput of 32.46 Gbps with the area consumption of 3836 slices and 50 BRAMs. In case of using composite field SubBytes, it consumes 7475 slices, however no BRAMs are required. In terms of using LUT SubBytes, the proposed architecture occupies 4770 and reaches the throughput of 36.92 Gbps.

Table 2. Hardware comparison

	FPGA type	Design	key	SubBytes	Slices	BRAMs	Max-Freq MHz	Thr. Gbit/s	Thr./Slice Mbps/Slice
This work	Virtex5	AES-GCM	•	BRAM	3836	50	273.4	32.46	**8.46**
This work	Virtex5	AES-GCM	•	Comp.	7475	0	264.2	31.36	**4.19**
This work	Virtex5	AES-GCM	•	LUT	4770	0	311	36.92	**7.74**
[7]	Virtex5	AES-GCM	•	BRAM	3533	41	314	16.9	4.78
[7]	Virtex5	AES-GCM	•	Comp	6492	0	314	16.9	2.60
[7]	Virtex5	AES-GCM	•	LUT	4628	0	324	17.5	3.77
[8]	Virtex5	AES-GCM	•	BRAM	9561	450	233	48.8	5.1
[8]	Virtex5	AES-GCM	•	Comp	18505	0	233	48.8	2.64
[8]	Virtex5	AES-GCM	•	LUT	14799	0	233	48.8	3.29
[5]	Virtex5	AES-GCM	○	BRAM	2478	40	242	30.9	12.5
[5]	Virtex5	AES-GCM	○	Comp.	5512	0	232	29.7	5.38
[5]	Virtex5	AES-GCM	○	LUT	3211	0	216.3	27.7	8.62

By comparing our results of AES-GCM to [7], the comparison shows that our performance (Thr. /Slice) is better. This improvement results from reducing the reduction factor in the equation of throughput as shown in Equation 10 and Equation 14.

In terms of the 4-parallel AES-GCM by [8], our area consumption (Slices + BRAMs) is smaller compared to them. Also, our performance is better because the throughput presented by [8] is calculated as shown in Equation 11.

Our previous work [5] presented architectures for slow changing key applications like VPNs and the FPGA needs the new reconfiguration when the key changes. Therefore, the proposed architecture in this paper presents better performance compared to [5] because the FPGA does not need a new reconfiguration when the key changes but it needs 252 clock cycles for the memory initialization as described in **Section 3**.

6   Conclusion

In this paper, we presented the performance improvement of AES-GCM (Thr. /Slice). This was achieved by modifying the architecture of the pipelined KOA-based GHASH. With our proposed GHASH, the throughput reduction factor is decreased. Therefore, the throughput of the proposed AES-GCM architectures is increased. In addition, three AES implementations (BRAMs-based SubBytes, composite field-based SubBytes, and LUT-based SubBytes) were evaluated in order to increase the flexibility of the presented work. The throughput of the presented AES-GCM cores ranges from 31.36 to 36.92 using Xilinx Virtex5 FP-GAs. It is shown that the performance of the presented AES-GCM architectures outperforms the previously reported ones.

References

1. McGrew, D.A., Viega, J.: The security and performance of the galois/Counter mode (GCM) of operation. In: Canteaut, A., Viswanathan, K. (eds.) INDOCRYPT 2004. LNCS, vol. 3348, pp. 343–355. Springer, Heidelberg (2004)
2. IEEE Standard for Local and metropolitan area networks–Media Access Control (MAC) Security Amendment 1: Galois Counter Mode–Advanced Encryption Standard– 256 (GCM-AES-256) Cipher Suite. IEEE
3. Satoh, A.: High-Speed Hardware Architectures for Authenticated Encryption Mode GCM. In: IEEE International Symposium on Circuits and Systems (ISCAS), p. 4 (2006)
4. Crenne, J., Cotret, P., Gogniat, G., Tessier, R., Diguet, J.: Efficient Key-Dependent Message Authentication in Reconfigurable Hardware. In: International Conference on Field-Programmable Technology (FPT), pp. 1–6 (2011)
5. Abdellatif, K.M., Chotin-Avot, R., Mehrez, H.: High Speed Authenticated Encryption for Slow Changing Key Applications Using Reconfigurable Devices . In: IEEE Wireless Days (2013)
6. Zhou, G., Michalik, H., Hinsenkamp, L.: Efficient and High-Throughput Implementations of AES-GCM on FPGAs. In: International Conference on Field-Programmable Technology (FPT), pp. 185–192 (2007)
7. Zhou, G., Michalik, H.: Improving Throughput of AES-GCM with Pipelined Karatsuba Multipliers on FPGAs. In: Reconfigurable Computing: Architectures, Tools and Applications, pp. 193–203 (2009)
8. Henzen, L., Fichtner, W.: FPGA Parallel-Pipelined AES-GCM Core for 100G Ethernet Applications. pp. 202–205 (2010)

Efficient Elliptic-Curve Cryptography Using Curve25519 on Reconfigurable Devices

Pascal Sasdrich and Tim Güneysu

Horst Görtz Institute for IT-Security
Ruhr-Universität Bochum, Germany
{pascal.sasdrich,tim.gueneysu}@rub.de

Abstract. Elliptic curve cryptography (ECC) has become the predominant asymmetric cryptosystem found in most devices during the last years. Despite significant progress in efficient implementations, computations over standardized elliptic curves still come with enormous complexity, in particular when implemented on small, embedded devices. In this context, Bernstein proposed the highly efficient ECC instance Curve25519 that was shown to achieve new ECC speed records in software providing a high security level comparable to AES with 128-bit key. These very tempting results from the software domain have led to adoption of Curve25519 by several security-related applications, such as the NaCl cryptographic library or in anonymous routing networks (nTor). In this work we demonstrate that even better efficiency of Curve25519 can be realized on reconfigurable hardware, in particular by employing their Digital Signal Processor blocks (DSP). In a first proposal, we present a DSP-based single-core architecture that provides high-performance despite moderate resource requirements. As a second proposal, we show that an extended architecture with dedicated inverter stage can achieve a performance of more than 32,000 point multiplications per second on a (small) Xilinx Zynq 7020 FPGA. This clearly outperforms speed results of any software-based and most hardware-based implementations known so far, making our design suitable for cheap deployment in many future security applications.

Keywords: FPGA, DSP, ECC, Curve25519, Diffie-Hellman, Xilinx, Zynq.

1 Introduction

With the advent of ubiquitous computing, many applications require an appropriate security level, including complex cryptography. In addition, to avoid bottlenecks due to security requirements, those devices often need to provide a significant amount of cryptographic operations per second regardless the computational constraints of the devices. In particular, modern public key cryptosystems, e.g., RSA, use complex and computation-intensive calculations that are often too slow on embedded hardware. Neal Koblitz and Victor Miller proposed independently in 1985 [11,8] the use of Elliptic Curve Cryptography (ECC) providing similar security compared to RSA but using smaller keys. This benefit

D. Goehringer et al. (Eds.): ARC 2014, LNCS 8405, pp. 25–36, 2014.
© Springer International Publishing Switzerland 2014

allows for greater efficiency when using ECC (160–256 bit) compared to RSA or discrete logarithm schemes over finite fields (1024–4096 bit) while providing an equivalent level of security [9]. In the last years, ECC has become the standard for high-performance asymmetric cryptography, although it still places a high demand on small microprocessors and microcontrollers. Due to this, dedicated cryptographic hardware such as Field-Programmable Gate Arrays (FPGA) are still the preferred choice when high-performance on cryptographic operations is a strict requirement for an embedded application.

Contribution: In this work, we present the first efficient implementation of a special Elliptic Curve Cryptosystem using the Curve25519 [2] on reconfigurable hardware to provide a Diffie-Hellman key agreement suitable for use in high-performance application. It provides inherently timing resistance against simple power attacks (SPA) and a security level comparable to NIST P-256 ECC or AES with 128-bit key. In particular, our design takes advantage of the special-purpose DSP slices of reconfigurable devices in order to increase efficiency and performance. Although ECC using Curve25519 for a Diffie-Hellman key agreement was initially proposed to accelerate primarily its implementation in software, we show that similarly its special characteristics can be exploited in hardware to achieve a compact, space-saving high-performance ECC processor on reconfigurable devices. Our multi-core Curve25519 implementation on a small Xilinx Zynq 7020 FPGA achieves more than 32,000 point multiplications per second with which we can virtually support any high-performance application of asymmetric cryptography.

Outline: The paper is organized as follows: Section 2 provides relevant previous work while Section 3 outlines the Curve25519 function for Diffie-Hellman based key agreement and its special characteristics. Section 4 describes design considerations and decisions, in particular with respect to the arithmetic units. Section 5 describes two different architectures for moderate and high-performance that are evaluated and compared in Section 6. Finally, we conclude our work in Section 7.

2   Previous Work

We briefly summarize previously published results of relevance to this contribution. Since there is a wealth of publication addressing ECC hardware architectures, we refer to the overview in [3] and restrict the discussion of previous works to the most relevant ones. As one of the first works in ECC implementations, Orlando and Paar [13] proposed a design targeting explicitly reconfigurable hardware using Montgomery-based multiplications included with a series of precomputations. This publication was followed by many more, e.g., [7] trying to improve performance on FPGAs by the use of dedicated multipliers or [15] trying to improve the performance in an algorithmic approach. Using integrated Digital Signal Processors (DSP) both for modular multiplication and modular addition was initially proposed in [14] targeting standardized NIST primes P-224 and P-256 using a special reduction scheme.

3   Background

In the following, we will briefly introduce to the mathematical background relevant for this work. We will start with a short review of the Elliptic Curve Cryptosystems (ECC). Please note that only ECC over prime fields $GF(p)$ will be subject of this work.

Let p be a prime with $p > 3$ and $\mathbb{F}_p = GF(p)$ the Galois Field over p. Given the Weierstrass equation of an elliptic curve

$$\mathcal{E} : y^2 = x^3 + ax + b,$$

with $a, b \in GF(p)$ and $4a^3 + 27b^2 \neq 0$, points $\mathcal{P}_i \in \mathcal{E}$, we can compute tuples (x, y) also considered as points on this elliptic curve $\mathcal{E}$. Based on a group of points defined over this curve, ECC arithmetic defines the addition $\mathcal{P}_3 = \mathcal{P}_1 + \mathcal{P}_2$ of two points $\mathcal{P}_1, \mathcal{P}_2$ using the *tangent-and-chord* rule as the primary group operation. This group operation distinguishes the case for $\mathcal{P}_1 = \mathcal{P}_2$ (*point doubling*) and $\mathcal{P}_1 \neq \mathcal{P}_2$ (*point addition*). Furthermore, formulas for these operations vary for affine and projective coordinate representations, i.e., the curve equation for projective coordinates relaxes the one shown above by introducing another variable Z. The use of projective coordinates allows to avoid the costly modular inversion for a point operation at the cost of additional modular multiplications.

Most ECC-based cryptosystems rely on the Elliptic Curve Discrete Logarithm Problem (ECDLP) and thus employ the technique of point multiplication $k \cdot \mathcal{P}$ as cryptographic primitive, i.e., a k times repeated point addition of a base point $\mathcal{P}$. Precisely, the ECDLP is the fundamental cryptographic problem used in protocols and crypto schemes like the Elliptic Curve Diffie-Hellman key exchange [4], the ElGamal encryption scheme [6] and the Elliptic Curve Digital Signature Algorithm (ECDSA) [1]. Note that all these cryptosystems solely employ affine coordinates to guarantee unique solutions, i.e., in case the faster projective coordinates are used for intermediate computations, a final modular inversion needs to be performed to convert projective coordinates back to affine coordinates.

In this work we will focus on the Diffie-Hellman key exchange based on the special elliptic curve Curve25519 which characteristics are given in the following.

3.1   Curve25519 Function

Curve25519 can be considered a function designed to simplify and accelerate the Diffie-Hellmann key agreement over elliptic curves. It defines a point multiplication that provides inherent timing-attack resistance and a conjectured security level comparable to NIST P-256 or AES-128. Using this function, two parties can derive a shared secret with the help of their 32-byte secret key and the public key.

Curve25519 is based on a prime field with a prime close to a power of 2 (Pseudo Mersenne Prime) and defined as follows:

$$E : y^2 = x^3 + 486662x^2 + x \bmod 2^{255} - 19$$

Assume a base point P with $Q = (X_i, Y_i, Z_i)$. Tracking two intermediate points Q, Q' and their difference $Q - Q'$ based on P, Curve25519 defines a combined point doubling and point addition function as a single step of the Montgomery Power ladder [12] with 4 squarings, 5 general multiplications, 1 multiplication by $(A - 2)/4$ and 8 additions or subtractions. An additional benefit of the Curve25519 function is, that only the x-coordinate of each point is required during the computation so that y can be completely omitted in the formulas. Therefore, the point multiplication solely relies on the x and z-coordinate of the two points Q and Q'. Eventually, a combined step is computed by

$$x_2 = (x^2 - z^2)^2 = (x - z)^2(x + z)^2$$
$$z_2 = 4xz(u^2 + Axz + z^2)$$
$$x_3 = 4(xx' - zz')$$
$$z_3 = 4(xz' - zx')x_1$$

3.2   Curve25519 Computations

For the entire scalar multiplication, computing $k \times P$, a total of 255 step function calls (combined point double and addition) are executed followed by a final inversion and a single multiplication calculating $X \times Z^{-1}$.

Figure 1 shows the flow of the algorithm for three points Q, Q' and Q_1 represented in terms of projective coordinates and where Q_1 is $Q - Q'$. Note, that every addition or subtraction is followed by a multiplication and nearly every multiplication is followed by an addition or subtraction. This observation is very helpful for designing an efficient hardware architecture.

In addition, always the same number of operations are performed, independently of the processed data. Therefore, the computation can be done in constant time preventing timing-based attacks.

4   Design Considerations

For most modern standardized elliptic curves, e.g., the NIST P-256, the underlying prime field is based on a Generalized Mersenne Prime which allows a reduction based on few additions and subtractions. For Curve25519 the field is based on a Pseudo Mersenne Prime $2^n - c$ based on a similar but slightly different concept. For the Curve25519 elliptic curve, the reduction can be computed by a multiplication with a small constant, in this case the constant $c = 19$.

However, this prime with a total of 255 bits has some interesting properties since all field elements can be divided into fifteen words of 17 bit width. Processing these chunks is usually inefficient for common processors which operate on 8-, 16-, 32- or 64-bit data words. Recent FPGA devices, however, provide a multitude of dedicated, full-custom DSP slices equipped with an addition, a multiplication and an accumulation stage for integers enhanced with additional register stages to operate at full device speed. Since the multiplication of DSP blocks natively supports signed 25×18-bit wide operands, this is a perfect fit

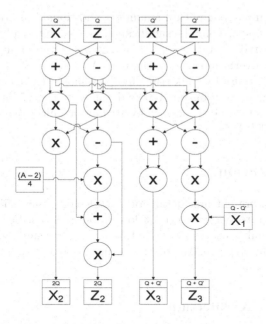

Fig. 1. Double-and-Add formula according to Montgomery's ladder

to our requirement of processing unsigned 17-bit data words. By means of an interleaved multiplication schedule, multiplying two 255-bit field elements can be rearranged over several parallelly operating DSP-blocks so that each DSP block has to compute one 17×17 bit multiplication at a time resulting in one partial product. The full multiplication can then be performed using 15 DSP slices. Additionally, we can use the included accumulation stage per DSP block to add up the intermediate results. Finally, we end up generating an intermediate result in the accumulation stage that is slightly too large but which can be reduced in a subsequent recombination step. The recombination step itself can be implemented by a constant multiplier with $c = 19$, realignment logic to recombine shares of partial products as well as a subtraction stage to correct the result by reducing it modulo P in case it is slightly too large.

Besides the modular multiplication, point doublings and point additions require the computation of modular additions and subtractions. To return a unique result, a final inversion is required to convert the projective coordinates to affine coordinates. The addition respectively subtraction unit can be implemented as cascade of two DSP blocks, one for the main operation and one for the subsequent reduction. For the basic version of an inversion, we plan to use Fermat's Little Theorem. This approach requires solely a modular multiplier which is already provided by the core despite of a small additional state machine. Although inversion based on this approach hardly requires extra hardware, inversion performance will be comparably slow. Another approach would be to implement a dedicated inversion unit based on the Binary Extended Euclidean Algorithm.

This obviously requires a significant amount of additional resources but the computation of the inversion would be significantly faster. Optionally, in a multi-core scenario one dedicated inverter can be shared among several point multiplication cores reducing the overhead costs by resource sharing.

Finally, we plan to use two 36k true dual-port block RAMs (BRAM) to store all intermediate values in a butterfly-wise dataflow. Since 17-bit or 34-bit input and output values need to be processed by arithmetic units, we will specify 34-bit wide ports of the BRAMs.

5   Implementation

In this section, we present first details of a single-core Curve25519 architecture resulting in moderate performance at low resource costs. Second, we extend our design into a multi-core architecture that aims at consuming all available resources of the Xilinx Zynq 7020 device but which is capable to provide maximum throughput.

5.1   Single-Core Architecture

Our single-core Curve25519 implementation is designed to support asymmetric cryptography as a supplementary function and saves most of the FPGA logic for the main application. The cryptographic core is capable to perform a point multiplication in projective coordinates. For use with most cryptographic protocols, the core also needs to implement a final inversion to convert the output in projective coordinates back to affine coordinates. The arithmetic processor therefore supports two basic operation modes: either a combined double-and-add step function or a single modular multiplication. The access to the modular multiplication instruction is required for the final inversion based on Fermat's little theorem, i.e, inversion of a field element $a \in \mathbb{F}_p$ by computing $a^{p-2} \bmod p$. To prevent timing attacks, the arithmetic unit performs the point multiplication running a total 255 double-and-add operations and 266 iterated multiplications for the inversion both in constant time.

In our implementation we follow several of the design suggestions for software implementations as given in the original work on Diffie-Hellman computations over Curve25519 [2]. In particular, each addition or subtraction is always followed by a subsequent multiplication again nearly always succeeded by another addition or subtraction. These facts led to the design presented in Figure 2 using two dual-ported BRAMs in butterfly configuration. More precisely, the first BRAM only receives the results of the addition or subtraction unit and provides the input to the multiplication while the second BRAM stores the multiplication result and feeds the addition unit. This way parallel operation is enabled and pipeline stalls through loading and write-back can be avoided with only little overhead.

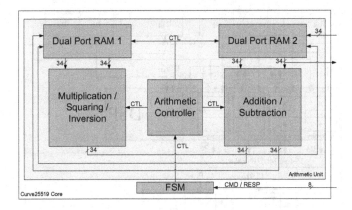

Fig. 2. Overview of the Curve25519 Core

Modular Addition Unit. Centerpiece of the modular addition and subtraction unit computing $c = a \pm b \bmod p$ are two DSP blocks supporting 25x18-bit multiplications and up to 48-bit additions, subtractions or accumulations. The first DSP always performs the main operation (i.e., subtraction or addition $c' = a \pm b$) whereas the second DSP block computes a prediction for a reduced result by $c'' = c' \mp p$. Both, the c' and c'' are stored into the first BRAM and distinguished by a flag obtained from the previous carry/borrow in the prediction operations that indicates in which registers the correct result is stored. In total, modular addition or subtraction takes 10 clock cycles which can be executed in parallel to any multiplication operation. Thus, exploiting the alternating operation flow as mentioned above, the latency for modular addition or subtraction is completely absorbed in the latency for a concurrently running modular multiplication.

Modular Multiplication Unit. The largest component of the arithmetic unit is the multiplication unit and based on 18 DSP blocks – 15 blocks are used to compute partial products, one for a prereduction and two for the final modular reduction. A modular multiplication can be computed in 55 clock cycles of which 34 cycles are required for the actual multiplication and the remaining ones for loading and storing data. Due to the modular design shown in Fig. 3, computation of partials products (stage 1) can be interleaved with the reduction step (stage 2) in pipeline fashion. So a next multiplication operation can be already restarted as soon the first stage (partial products) has completed the previous multiplication Thus, only the first multiplication takes the full 55 clock cycles, each subsequent multiplication is becoming available with a latency of 17 clock cycles only. Since data dependencies need also been taken into account, the combined double-and-add step for Curve25519 finally takes 255 cycles in total.

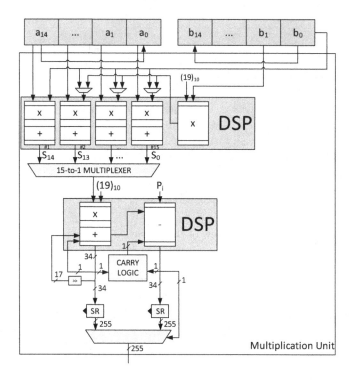

Fig. 3. Architecture of the Modular Multiplication Unit

5.2   Multi-core Architecture

A main caveat with the single-core architecture is the slow inversion. In this work we augment the previously described core design with a dedicated inverter circuit and share it among several cores for an optimal cost-performance trade-off. The number of cores per inverter is upper-bounded by the available resources on the respective device as well as the relation of the cycle count per point multiplication with respect to one final inversion. Since this number directly corresponds to resources available on a given FPGA, we implemented the design generically to allow maximum scalability and flexibility also for other devices. Figure 4 shows the communication interface and the additional controller for distributing incoming packets among the Curve25519 cores. Unlike the hardcore introduced above, all cores of this architecture only support the step function (double-and-add operation) but no modular inversion anymore. The inversion is finally performed by a dedicated inversion unit shared by all cores in a subsequent step.

Dedicated Inversion Unit. In many cases the modular division is the most expensive operation requiring a modular inversion and at least one multiplication. In the single-core approach, we noticed that inversion based on Fermat's

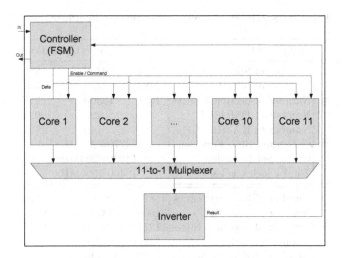

Fig. 4. Overview of the Multi-Core Design

little Theorem is rather ineffective since the inversion requires roughly 20% of the entire time of a Curve25519 computation. Therefore we implemented a modular inverter based on the Binary Extended Euclidean Algorithm as an extension to the existing cores. The inverter uses wide adders/subtracters and uses well-known implementation techniques so that we refrain from giving all details on the implementation. With respect to the multi-core design approach, the inverter receives X and Z as inputs, and computes the final result X/Z in a constant time. Since this inverter is significantly faster compared to a point multiplication, the inverter can serve as subsequent inversion unit for several point multiplication cores (cf. Section 6).

Load Balancing. Due to the concurrent operation of individual cores, we implemented a scheme to distribute incoming data to available cores when they become available. This scheme is basically a round-robin-based loading scheme where the controller unit keeps track of the last active and the next available core. Loading continues until all cores are busy. As soon as one core reports a result, it is handed over to the inversion unit and the core is marked ready again and can be loaded with a next parameter set.

Clock Domain Separation. The point multiplication cores can operate at a clock frequency of 200MHz. However, since the dedicated inversion unit implements 256-bit wide adders and subtracters in logic it only supports a maximum clock frequency of roughly 130MHz. To still operate the implementation at maximum speed, we use different clock domains for the point multiplication cores on the one hand (200 MHz) and the controller and inversion unit on the other hand (100 MHz).

Table 1. Summary of device utilization and performance

	Component	Used	Available	Utilization
Single-Core	Number of Slice Registers	3592	106400	3%
	Number of Slice LUTs	2783	53200	5%
	Number of occupied Slices	1029	13300	7%
	Number of DSP48E1	20	220	9%
	Number of RAMB36E1	2	140	1%
	Cycles per Step Function	64770@200MHz		
	Cycles per Inversion	14630@200MHz		
	Total Clock Cycles	79400@200MHz		
Multi-Core	Number of Slice Registers	43875	106400	41%
	Number of Slice LUTs	34009	53200	63%
	Number of occupied Slices	11277	13300	84%
	Number of DSP48E1	220	220	100%
	Number of RAMB36E1	22	140	15%
	Cycles per Step Function	64770@200MHz		
	Cycles per Inversion	1667@100MHz		
	Total Clock Cycles	34052@100MHz		

6   Results

All results were obtained after place-and-route based on a Xilinx Zynq XC7Z020 using Xilinx ISE 14.5.

6.1   Comparison of the Single- and Multi-Core Architecture

In Table 1 we provide the resource consumption for our single-core and multi-core design, respectively.

The single-core approach only uses a small portion of the (relatively) small Xilinx device, i.e., 7% of the Slices and 9% of the DSP slices. The remaining device components are available for any other function or application that needs to be implemented.

Our single-core architecture has a maximum operation frequency of 200MHz and needs roughly 80,000 clock cycles to perform a Curve25519 operation of which about 20% of the clock cycles are required to compute the final inversion. All in all, the core can perform about 2500 point multiplications per second.

Our multi-core scenario is obviously trimmed for highest performance using a moderately large FPGA. Due to the clock domain separation, the multi-core architecture can compute a point multiplication in about 34,000 cycles at a frequency of 100MHz. In addition, up to 11 operations can be performed in parallel with an initial latency of 1667 clock cycles which is the time that is required for the inversion. This leads to a final throughput of more than 32,000 Curve25519 operations per second.

Table 2. Selected high-performance implementations of public-key cryptosystems

Scheme	Device	Implementation	Logic	Clock	OP/s
Single-Core	XC7Z020	255-bit GF($2^{255} - 19$)	1029 LS/20 DSP	200 MHz	2531
Multi-Core	XC7Z020	255-bit GF($2^{255} - 19$)	11277 LS/220 DSP	100 MHz	21686
ECC [7]	XC4VFX12-12	256-bit GF(p), NIST	1715 LS/32 DSP	490 MHz	2020
ECC [10]	XC2VP125-7	256-bit GF(p), any	15755 LS/256 MUL	39.5 MHz	260
ECC [5]	Intel Core i3	255-bit GF($2^{255} - 19$)	64 bit	2.1 GHz	10810
ECC [5]	AMD FX-4170	255-bit GF($2^{255} - 19$)	64 bit	4.2 GHz	14285
RSA[17]	XC4VFX12-10	1024-bit with DSP	3937 LS/17 DSP	400 MHz	584
RSA[16]	0.5 μm CMOS	1024-bit, unified	28,000 GE	64 MHz	21

6.2   Comparison to Other Work

Despite the fact that this is, to the best of our knowledge, the first implementation of Curve25519 in hardware and that there exist only few implementations in software, we intend to also compare to other relevant work. In Table 2 we list some other implementation results which implement ECC on a comparable security level to Curve25519. Note, however, that due to varying technology of different FPGA generations a fair comparison is actually not accurately possible. In [7] the standardized NIST P-256 curve was implemented using a similar approach on a Xilinx Virtex 4. The authors report that a design to perform point requires more resources at a performance of about 2,000 point multiplications per second. We also like to highlight software results which we obtained e.g. from ECRYPT's eBATS project. According to the reported results, an Intel Core i3 can perform about 10,810 point multiplications per second using the Curve25519 function and an AMD Bulldozer FX-4170, running at 4.2, GHz can compute 14,285 Curve25519 operations per second.

Although comparing software and hardware can be misleading, we still like to emphasize that the moderately large and rather cheap Zynq 7020 FPGA can outperform some recent high-performance processors such as AMD Bulldozer and Intels Core i3. This is slightly surprising since elliptic curve cryptography over prime fields is usually considered a field that is dominated by software implementations with respect to pure performance.

7   Conclusion

In this paper we propose two new architectures for Elliptic Curve Cryptography using the Curve25519 supporting Diffie-Hellman key agreement and other cryptographic primitives. Both architectures provide a security level comparable to AES-128 and process data at constant time. We showed that the design can outperform many recently presented works in hardware and software using only moderate resource requirements.

References

1. ANSI X9.62-2005. American National Standard X9.62: The Elliptic Curve Digital Signature Algorithm (ECDSA). Technical report, Accredited Standards Committee X9 (2005), http://www.x9.org
2. Bernstein, D.J.: Curve25519: New Diffie-Hellman Speed Records. In: Yung, M., Dodis, Y., Kiayias, A., Malkin, T. (eds.) PKC 2006. LNCS, vol. 3958, pp. 207–228. Springer, Heidelberg (2006)
3. de Dormale, G.M., Quisquater, J.-J.: High-speed hardware implementations of elliptic curve cryptography: A survey. J. Syst. Archit. 53(2-3), 72–84 (2007)
4. Diffie, W., Hellman, M.: New directions in cryptography. IEEE Trans. Inf. Theory 22, 644–654 (1976)
5. ECRYPT. eBATS: ECRYPT Benchmarking of Asymmetric Systems. Technical report (March 2007), http://www.ecrypt.eu.org/ebats/
6. ElGamal, T.: A public key cryptosystem and a signature scheme based on discrete logarithms. IEEE Trans. Inf. Theory 31, 469–472 (1985)
7. Güneysu, T., Paar, C.: Ultra High Performance ECC over NIST Primes on Commercial FPGAs. In: Oswald, E., Rohatgi, P. (eds.) CHES 2008. LNCS, vol. 5154, pp. 62–78. Springer, Heidelberg (2008)
8. Koblitz, N.: Elliptic curve cryptosystems. Mathematics of Computation 48, 203–209 (1987)
9. Lenstra, A.K., Verheul, E.R.: Selecting Cryptographic Key Sizes. Journal of Cryptology 14(4), 255–293 (2001)
10. McIvor, C., McLoone, M., McCanny, J.: An FPGA elliptic curve cryptographic accelerator over GF(p). In: Irish Signals and Systems Conference (ISSC), pp. 589–594 (2004)
11. Miller, V.S.: Use of elliptic curves in cryptography. In: Williams, H.C. (ed.) CRYPTO 1985. LNCS, vol. 218, pp. 417–426. Springer, Heidelberg (1986)
12. Montgomery, P.L.: Speeding the Pollard and Elliptic Curve Methods of Factorization. Mathematics of Computation 48(177), 243–264 (1987)
13. Orlando, G., Paar, C.: A scalable $GF(p)$ elliptic curve processor architecture for programmable hardware. In: Koç, Ç.K., Naccache, D., Paar, C. (eds.) CHES 2001. LNCS, vol. 2162, pp. 348–371. Springer, Heidelberg (2001)
14. Örs, S.B., Batina, L., Preneel, B., Vandewalle, J.: Hardware implementation of elliptic curve processor over GF(p). pp. 433–443 (2003)
15. Sakiyama, K., Mentens, N., Batina, L., Preneel, B., Verbauwhede, I.: Reconfigurable Modular Arithmetic Logic Unit for High-Performance Public-Key Cryptosystems. In: Bertels, K., Cardoso, J.M.P., Vassiliadis, S. (eds.) ARC 2006. LNCS, vol. 3985, pp. 347–357. Springer, Heidelberg (2006)
16. Savas, E., Tenca, A.F., Ciftcibasi, M.E., Koc, C.K.: Multiplier architectures for $GF(p)$ and $GF(2^n)$. IEE Proc. Comput. Digit Tech. 151(2), 147–160 (2004)
17. Suzuki, D.: How to Maximize the Potential of FPGA Resources for Modular Exponentiation. In: Paillier, P., Verbauwhede, I. (eds.) CHES 2007. LNCS, vol. 4727, pp. 272–288. Springer, Heidelberg (2007)

Accelerating Heap-Based Priority Queue in Image Coding Application Using Parallel Index-Aware Tree Access

Yuhui Bai[1,2], Syed Zahid Ahmed[2], and Bertrand Granado[2]

[1] Université Cergy Pontoise, ENSEA, UMR CNRS 8051, ETIS, Cergy, France
[2] Sorbonne Universités, UPMC Univ. Paris 06, UMR7606, LIP6,
75005, Paris, France
{yuhui.bai,syed-zahid.ahmed,bertrand.granado}@lip6.fr

Abstract. We present a novel heap-based priority queue structure for hardware implementation which is employed by a wavelet-based image encoder. The architecture exploits efficient use of FPGA's on-chip dual port memories in an adaptive manner. By using 2x clock speed we created 4 memory ports along with intelligent data concatenation of parents and children queue elements, as well as an index-aware system linked to each key in the queue. These innovations yielded in cost effective enhanced memory access. The memory ports are adaptively assigned to different units during different computation phases of operations in a manner to optimally take advantage of memory access required by that phase. We designed this architecture to incorporate in our Adaptive Scanning of Wavelet Data (ASWD) module which reorganizes the wavelet coefficients into locally stationary sequences for a wavelet-based image encoder. We validated the hardware on an Altera's Stratix IV FPGA as an IP accelerator in a Nios II processor based System on Chip. The architectural innovations can also be exploited in other applications that require efficient hardware implementations of priority queue. We show that our architecture at 150MHz can provide 45X speedup compared to an embedded ARM Cortex-A9 processor at 666MHz.

1 Introduction

A wavelet-based image encoder called Öktem coder [1] was developed to efficiently encode the locally stationary image source. In this coder, image samples are transformed by a Discrete Wavelet Transform (DWT) using a Cohen-Daubechies-Feauveau 9/7 wavelet basis, a Scalar Quantization (SQ) is then performed. The quantized coefficients are fed to an Adaptive Scanning of Wavelet Data (ASWD) block which adaptively sorts the coefficients of each subband to maximize the local stationarity of the image, then a Hierarchical ENUmerative Coding (HENUC) is done which models and entropy encodes the locally stationary sequences by independently codify each bit-plane to produce an embedded bit-stream [2]. The Öktem coder is an alternate of the JPEG2000 coder and is demonstrated by our experiments to have higher

D. Goehringer et al. (Eds.): ARC 2014, LNCS 8405, pp. 37–48, 2014.
© Springer International Publishing Switzerland 2014

compression performance than JPEG2000, as the entire subband instead of separate code blocks is processed so that no blocking effect is perceived in the Öktem coder [3,4].

Despite of good image quality provided by the Öktem coder, the algorithmic complexity is high. Haapala *et al.* implemented it on a multi-DSP system called PARNEU using a parallel processor architecture to get the acceleration [4]. The design suffered from high complexity and latency on interprocessor communication due to the distributed memory architecture. We profiled the ASWD (single threaded) on ARM Cortex A9. According to the profiling results, ASWD takes around 65% of the total compression time. Processing single threaded ASWD of a 512×512 grayscale lena image on ARM Cortex A9 at 666MHz takes around 2000 ms. The processing time can only be halved even by using multithreading on dual cores of processor in an ideal case. Since our goal is to integrate Öktem coder on an embedded system to provide real time performance for video compression, this is too slow to reach our requirements, thus, it is mandatory to accelerate the coding. To achieve the high throughput, in the parallel hardware implementation, we leveraged on-chip memory resources of FPGA in efficient and innovative manners using data concatenation and 4 port memory access. We implemented Öktem coder on an Altera Stratix IV FPGA inside a SoC which combines a Nios II processor and several hardwired intellectual properties (IPs). The SoC provides efficient acceleration of computational and memory access intensive tasks, appropriate adaption to an embedded system, as well as possibility to port as an ASIC. The Nios II processor in the SoC manages the control of IPs and provides the flexibility for rapid experiments.

2   Adaptive Scanning of Wavelet Data

The ASWD scheme leverages an efficient exploration of the correlation among inter-band or intra-band wavelet coefficients to increase the compression efficiency. We compared Öktem coder with two state-of-the-art JPEG2000 coders, Lurawave and ACDSee [5]. In our experiments, both the Peak Signal to Noise Ratio (PSNR) measure and the Structural SIMilarity (SSIM) measure [6] of four images were evaluated using a MSU Video Quality Measurement Tool [7]. Compressed image quality was chosen to get approximately same size of output

Table 1. PSNR and SSIM with quantization parameter = 10

Test Image	PSNR (dB)			SSIM		
	Öktem	Lurawave	ACDSee	Öktem	Lurawave	ACDSee
Flower	43.8483	42.1703	43.1402	0.9882	0.9785	0.9825
Sailboat	44.3472	42.8920	44.7435	0.9888	0.9809	0.9866
House	43.9114	42.2677	44.8325	0.9859	0.9785	0.9837
Parrot	44.3102	41.6757	44.9829	0.9810	0.9699	0.9785

file for all codecs. Our test results are depicted in Table 1. We observe that the Öktem coder has higher PSNR than Lurawave. Although the PSNR of Öktem coder is sometimes lower than ACDSee, they are very close to each other. Regarding the SSIM index, as SSIM index has been developed to have a quality reconstruction metric that also takes into account the similarity of the edges between the denoised image and the ideal one, it has become a widely-used image quality assessment metric which is considered to provide a better quality measurement than the PSNR. The Öktem coder shows overall better results than the two JPEG2000 coders in terms of SSIM.

2.1   Heap-Based Priority Queue

A priority queues is one of the fundamental data structures for dynamic ordered sets and is used in a wide variety of applications [8]. In a priority queue, each element is ordered by its associated priority, the basic operations are Insert_key, Extract_max and Increase_key. In practice, the priority queue is implemented with two possible data structure : a *linked list* and a *heap*. A *linked list* sorted by the priority values of the elements is a simple but less efficient way to organize the priority queue. Although a *linked list* can extract the highest priority element in $O(1)$ time, inserting or increasing of the priority of an element takes $O(N)$ time, where N is the number of elements. For large values of N, a *linked list* would be too slow. A second and more efficient way to organize a priority queue is the *heap* data structure. A *heap* is organized as a complete binary tree with all levels completely filled except possibly the lowest level, where each node of the tree corresponds to an element and is associated with an *id* and a *priority* value of that element. In the *heap*, each node has two children, a balanced heap should satisfy the heap-property: each node should have a value greater than its children (max-heap) or less than its children (min-heap). A max-heap or min-heap is built with a Max_Heapify or Min_Heapify operation. A *heap* can extract the max element in $O(1)$ time since this element is stored at the root position due to the heap-property, it can insert or increase the priority of an element in $O(log_2N)$ time so a *heap* is much more efficient than a *linked list*.

2.2   ASWD Using Heap-Based Priority Queue Approach

In Öktem coder, an image is decomposed by the Discrete Wavelet Transform into wavelet coefficients stored in the successive subbands. According to the parent-children link approach developed by Shapiro [9], every coefficient (the parent) at a coarser scale can be related to four coefficients (the children) at the next finer scale of similar orientation, also the children descending from a significant/insignificant parent are more likely to be significant/insignificant. Furthermore, Servetto [10] observed that not only the coefficients descending from a significant parent, but also the morphological neighbors of these coefficients are predicted to be significant. Based on these approaches, in ASWD, the strategies shown in Algorithm 1 are used to exploit the parent-children coefficients correlations and to reorganize them into the locally stationary

---

Algorithm 1. *ASWD using Priority Queue Approach*

1: **for** each coefficient in subband **do**
2:    Calculate EAM for the coefficient;
3: **end for**
4: Build a coefficient heap according to the EAM values with $Max\_Heapify$
5: **while** all the coefficients in subband are not scanned **do**
6:    Pick the coefficient having maximum EAM among the not-yet-scanned coefficients with $Extract\_Max$;
7:    Increase eight morphological neighbor EAMs and update the heap with $Increase\_Key$;
8: **end while**

---

sequences. Firstly, we define a monotonous measure called Expected Activity Measure (EAM) for each coefficient in a subband that relates to an expected energy of the coefficient, where EAM is a function of the coefficients in the parent band and of the previously picked coefficient in the same band. Secondly, we scan the coefficients of the subband into a 1-D array, each time we pick a coefficient whose EAM is the highest among the not-yet-picked coefficients, we update the EAM for its eight morphological neighbor coefficients, i.e., the 3×3 surrounding coefficients within the subband. Finally, we recursively pick and update the coefficients until all the coefficients in the subband have been adaptively scanned. The 1-D array obtained by this adaptive scanning is expected to be a locally stationary sequence due to the fact that the coefficients with similar activity levels are collected together. ASWD is implemented using a priority queue approach, it defines that an EAM is the priority linked with a coefficient thus higher EAM represents higher priority.

The computational complexity of the algorithm is mainly determined by step 4 and 7 in the Algorithm, as the Max_Heapify operation takes $O(N)$ time, while the Extract_Max operation takes $O(8 \cdot N \cdot log_2 N)$ for updating N coefficients in a subband. In ASWD, a coefficient is related to an EAM value stored in a separate EAM memory, each coefficient-EAM relationship is ensured by an index that indicates the location of the coefficient in the subband. This indirect link between an EAM and a coefficient must be known by the encoder during the ASWD. In step 7 of the Algorithm, during each Increase_Key operation, there are up to eight neighbor EAMs which need to be increased, the recursive heap update makes the ASWD into a memory access intensive algorithm.

2.3   ASWD Priority Queue Operations

Max_Heapify (A, id) : In a heap implementation, the elements are stored in an array A such that each parent is guaranteed to be larger than (or equal to) its two children. This ordering is shown in Fig. 1(a), where the circled nodes indicate the *priorities*, the numbers beside the nodes indicate the *ids* and the links indicate the parent-children relationship between the *priorities*. In ASWD,

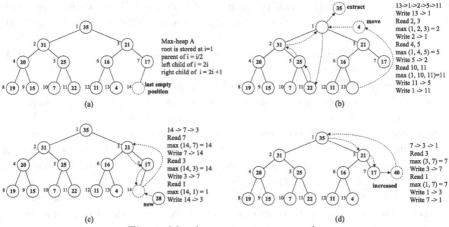

Fig. 1. Max-heap structure example

a *priority* is defined by an EAM value of each coefficient and an *id* is defined in form of an index that indicates the location of each coefficient within a subband.

Extract_Max (id) : The Extract_Max operation removes the highest *priority* element at the root node from the heap and returns the *id* of this element. It is realized by moving the last position node to the root position and searching an appropriate position for this node to keep the heap balanced. As shown in Fig. 1(b), in ASWD, the index of the extracted root node indicates a not-yet-scanned coefficient having maximum EAM among the subband.

Insert_Key (id, priority) : The Insert_Key operation inserts a new element into the heap. As shown in Fig. 1(c), the new node corresponding to a to-be-inserted element is appended to the last empty position at the lowest level and is moved upward until the new node has come to a position where its parent has a lower priority than its own.

Increase_Key (id, priority, offset) : The Increase_Key operation allows to increase the *priority* of an element in the heap. Given the *id* and the *offset* value, the increased node is moved to a new position to maintain a balanced heap. As shown in Fig. 1(d), in ASWD, an increased node is defined by a morphological neighbor EAM of the previously extracted coefficient, it is moved upward until the increased node has come to a position where its parent has a lower priority than its own. In our paper, since the Increase_Key operation is so similar to the Insert_Key operation, we do not consider the latter separately in the rest of the paper, but only Max_Heapify, Extract_Max and Increase_Key operations.

2.4   Related Work

The popularity of heap-based priority queue algorithms has triggered the development of several architectures in recent years. The applications for these architectures range from highly parallelized sorting engine to the pipelined architecture for high-speed queuing network. Although the different hardware architectures proposed for priority queue problems have their advantages, they don't meet current requirements for our application specific heap-based priority queue algorithm employed by ASWD. Bhagwan *et al.* proposed a modified conventional heap architecture with a pipeline priority queue mechanism [11]. In their implementation, the complex memory management is required and the pipelined architecture is not applicable for the recursive calls of Extract_Max and Increase_Key operations. Zabołotny *et al.* proposed an efficient heap sort architecture with a pipelined dual port memory access pattern [12], the efficient implementation allows to sort one element every two clock cycles. However, the architecture only supports pure sorting application, the data access of the pipelined architecture is also restricted to the root node which does not allow to increase the *priorities* of the element in the heap. Suzuki *et al.* implemented a concurrent heap-based queuing solution [13] which segmented the priority memory of the conventional array-based Heap into layers of a binary tree, the operations were parallelized during the extract and insert operations. Nevertheless, in their architecture, by storing the elements of different layers in the separate memories, we are unable to link the *priorities* to its *id* in the entire heap so the EAM-index relationship is unknown during the Extract_Key operation. In the next section, we will present our hardware implementation featuring the self index awareness of the priorities and the multiple memory access along with data concatenation for the priority queue operations.

3   Hardware Implementation of ASWD

We realized a hardware ASWD IP in an embedded Öktem coder SoC implemented on a Terasic DE4-230 board containing a Stratix IV FPGA in [14]. The block diagram is illustrated in Fig. 2. The ASWD IP is coupled to the Nios II processor which manages the system I/O and performs simple control tasks in the SoC, the image data to be processed are loaded from the DDR2 Memory. The Memory Address Decoder allows to initialize the to-be-processed data into the two 4-port on chip memories: id_EAM_combo_memory and id_location_memory, it can also communicate with the two processing modules: Max Heapify and Update Heap during different subband coding. These two modules are connected with both 4-port memories, which are created using FPGA onchip dual port memories running at two times of system speed, in

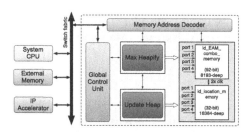

Fig. 2. Architecture of ASWD in Öktem coder SoC

order to accelerate the data comparisons and swaps. The processing module are controlled by a hierarchical finite state machine located in the Global Control Unit. During the Max_Heapify operation, two slave FSMs are implemented for controlling the parallel heapify of the left and right sub-heaps. Once the Max_Heapify operations of both sub-heaps finished, the Master FSM performs the recursive processing of Extract_Max and Increase_Key operations until all the coefficients of the subband have been adaptively scanned. In the Max Heapify module, we perform mainly the Max_Heapify operation, while in the Update Heapify module, we perform the Extract_Max and Increase_Key operations, the details of these operations in the light of our architectural innovations are discussed in the following subsections.

3.1 Index-Aware Heap Structure with Parallel Tree Access

The architecture of the index-aware parallel heap is conceived in the following manner. In the beginning, the coefficient's index standing for the *id* and the corresponding EAM standing for the *priority* are arranged into one data set and stored in an id_EAM_combo_memory. We fix the left half of the data set value at the id_EAM_combo_memory's initial address to zero, as we want to locate two children deriving from the same parent at the same memory address. For instance, as shown in Fig. 3(a), the EAM values at id1 and id2 stored at the same address of id_location_memory (lower-left part of the figure) stand for the two children nodes located at id1 and id2 of the heap (upper part of the figure), and they are derived from the same parent EAM at id0. To be able to track the node's id during the ASWD operations, an id_location_memory (lower-right of the figure) is created to store the position (address) of each node's index located in the heap. The id is used as the id_location_memory's address, while the data stored in the memory indicates each id's position of the heap. Furthermore, we implemented both the id_EAM_combo_memory and the id_location_memory as quad-port memory developed based on the dual-port block memory with a doubled clock and some extra logics, extending the architecture with four memory read/write in one clock cycle, in order to maximize the parallelization.

3.2 Parallelized Max_Heapify Operation

Heapify Step1 : In this step we perform Max_Heapify on the left and right sub-heaps. As shown in Fig. 3(a), the heap is split into left and right sub-heaps (A_l and A_r). The Max_Heapify operation is independent in each sub-heap, so both operations could be executed simultaneously. In the figure example, we start processing Max-Heapify(A_l, 4) and Max-Heapify(A_r, 5) with 4 and 5 representing the ids of the parents of the last nodes in the left and right sub-heaps. During the parallel Max_Heapify, the four ports of the id_EAM_combo_memory are dedicated to the parent and children address of the left and right sub-heaps respectively. Since two children deriving from a parent are located at the same memory address, we are able to fetch a parent and its two children from each sub-heap, that is, 6 nodes simultaneously. After fetching the parents and children

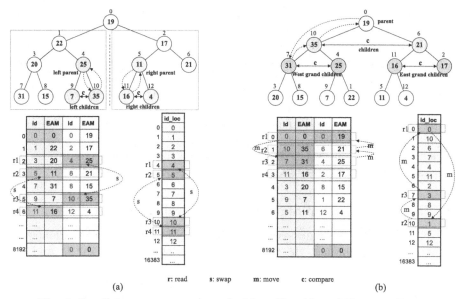

Fig. 3. Parallel tree access pattern for Max_Heapify and Extract_Heap

nodes, we compare their priorities, if the parent violates the heap property, it is swapped with its bigger child. During the swapping, the id and it's corresponding EAM value in a data set of id_EAM_combo_memory are moved together. Meanwhile, the position (address) values stored in the id_location_memory are also swapped according to the swapped nodes in the heap so that the locations of each id are up-to-date. This step is processed recursively until we reach the root node of the left and right sub-heaps.

Heapify Step2 : In this step we perform Max_Heapify on the root node. After the Max_Heapify of the left and right sub-heaps, the sub-heaps A_l and A_r below the root node of A are max-heaps. We continue to process the Max-Heapify$(A, 0)$ as shown in Fig. 3(b), where the four memory ports are dedicated to read the root node (parent) together with it's two children and four grand children in the next two layers. We compare simultaneously the children and grand children in each layer and compare the root node (parent) with the bigger grand child deriving from the bigger child. If a swap is necessary, the nodes are moved to the to-be-inserted position of the id_EAM_combo_memory simultaneously. The position values of the id in the id_location_memory are moved accordingly. The procedure goes through the remaining nodes of the heap until the entire heap is a balanced max-heap.

3.3   Parallelized Extract_Max Operation

The Extract_Max operation is performed on a balanced max-heap, the procedure is similar to step2 of Parallelized Max_Heapify operation. It consists of following two steps.

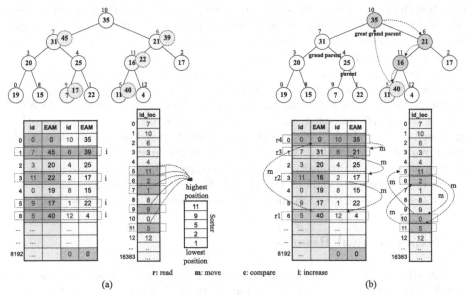

r: read   m: move   c: compare   i: increase

(a)   (b)

Fig. 4. Parallel tree access pattern of heap structure for Increase_Heap

Extract Step1 : Extract the max priority. We swap the root node with the last node of the heap and reduce the array size by one, and we send the original root node as the highest that indicates the coefficient having maximum EAM among the not-yet-scanned coefficients.

Extract Step2 : Heapify the new root node. After moving the last node to the root position, the heap below the new root node is a max-heap. To maintain the heap balanced, we process the Max-Heapify($A, 0$) as shown in Fig. 3(b), which is similar to the step2 of the Max_Heapify operation, thus it can be considered as a special case of the Max_Heapify operation.

3.4 Parallelized Increase_Key Operation

During the Increase_Key operation of ASWD, we increase eight morphological neighbors of the previous extracted node, and move them to the appropriate positions to maintain the balanced heap.

Increase Step1 : Increase priorities and Define the update order. To update the morphological neighbor EAMs, we can identify the 3×3 surrounding nodes of the just picked coefficient within the subband with the help of the id-EAM data set stored in the id_EAM_combo_memory, in addition, we also need to identify the nodes' positions in the heap from the id_location_memory. During the increase, as shown in Fig. 4(a), the four memory ports are dedicated to increase the 4 EAMs at a time until all neighbor nodes are increased. Meanwhile, the position values of the nodes are sent to a parallel insertion sorter [15] composed of an array of cascaded comparators that is able to sort one data every clock cycle and is optimal for small number of data sorting. The nodes whose values have been increased are reordered based on the descending order position values, that is, from the last node position in the heap to the root position in the heap, the reordered nodes are moved to their new positions one after another to avoid violating the already up-to-date nodes.

Increase Step2 : Update the priorities to the new positions. The increased nodes may violate the max heap property so they need to be moved to the new positions. Since the EAM values of the nodes are always increased in ASWD, only "looking up" is needed, the four memory ports are dedicated to read the increased node's value (child) as well as its parent, grand parent and the great grand parent from the three upper layers. After fetching the four values, they are compared simultaneously. If a swap is necessary, the elements are moved to the to-be-inserted positions in the id_EAM_combo_memory simultaneously, the location values of the id in the id_location_memory are moved accordingly.

4   Experimental Results

To investigate the feasibility and efficiency of our parallelized architecture, the ASWD core was developed to communicate with Altera's Avalon bus. The IP and the SoC were validated on a StratixIV GX230KF40C2 FPGA. The implementation was designed to support 32 bit word length for priority and a heap capacity from 1 to 16384 priorities (1 to 15 layers). The resource utilization of each individual modules in ASWD and the total resource utilization are given in Table 2. Values in parentheses stand for the percentage of resource usage over the total Stratix IV FPGA resource. In our hardware implementation, the memory size is fixed to the maximum heap capability needed, i.e., 16384 in ASWD. A distinguishing feature of our architecture is that the heap elements in every layer are stored in an entire block memory, this makes the design being fully scalable for large heap capacity and makes the design being index aware. The four-port RAM requires only small amount of control logic without multiplying the memory usage, it allows to keep the logic to memory ratio reasonably low.

In Fig. 5, according to the number of priorities in the heap, we evaluated the clock cycles needed for the Extract_max operation in the worst case which requires bringing down the node from root position to the lowest layer, as well as the clock cycles needed for the Increase_key operation. The worst case Increase_key operation is considered to be similar as the Insert_key operation, as they both require bringing up the to-be-updated node from the lowest layer

Table 2. FPGA Resource utilization of ASWD

Module	Max Freq.	ALUTs	FFs	Memory bits
Max_Heapify	$153MHz$	3103(1.7%)	1171(0.6%)	0(0%)
Update_Heap	$159MHz$	4491(2.4%)	1749(0.9%)	112(<0.1%)
4-Port RAMs	$396MHz$	1053(0.5%)	636(0.3%)	983132(6.7%)
Total ASWD	$152MHz$	9130(5.0%)	3967(2.2%)	983244(6.7%)

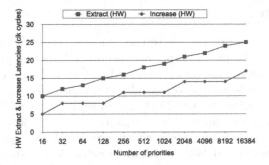

Fig. 5. HW timing requirements for Extract_Max and Increase_Key

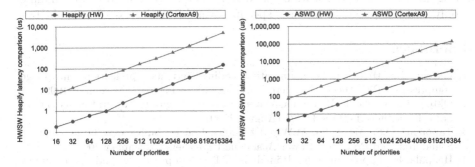

Fig. 6. (a) HW and SW latency comparison for: (a) Max_Heapify and (b) ASWD

to the root position when the updated node's priority is larger than the root node's priority. In Fig. 6, we show the latency of the Max_Heapify operation and the overall latency of the overall ASWD algorithm including the Heapify along with the recursive call of the Extract and Increase operations. We also tested the single threaded software on an ARM Cortex-A9 processor at 666MHz, the input priorities used were the randomly generated integers of 32 bit-width used as unsorted coefficients. According to the two experiments with 16384 random priorities, the 150MHz hardware implementation can run 33x faster than ARM for the Max_Heapify operation, it can run 47x faster than ARM for the overall ASWD. The acceleration obtained by our hardware over the single-threaded software is considered to be a fair comparison, as a multi-threaded implementation using 2/4 cores can only make the software execution 2/4X faster in ideal case.

Finally, the latency of ASWD core running at 150 MHz for the 512 × 512 grayscale lena image were evaluated. The FPGA based hardware execution time was measured to be 43.64 ms using Altera performance counter IP provided by Altera, while the execution time in ARM processor is 1975.11 ms. From the experiments, to process ASWD in the test image consisting of multiple subbands, our implementation provides 45x speedup over the ARM.

5   Conclusion

We presented a novel hardware architecture of an Adaptive Scanning of Wavelet Data scheme called ASWD. It is a specified heap-based priority queue application employed by a wavelet-based image coder called Öktem coder and is dedicated to reorganize the coefficients into a locally stationary sequence. The memory access intensive nature of the ASWD algorithm makes it penalizing for software implementation, a more appropriate implementation is necessary to adapt the design on an embedded system which provides higher performance. We implemented an embedded SoC in Altera Stratix IV FPGA integrating our design for fast prototyping and experiment. By adaptively controlling the index-aware system linked to each key in the queue and the configurable memory access during different ASWD operations, we demonstrated that our hardware running at only 150MHz provided 45 times speedup over ARM Cortex-A9 at 666MHz.

References

1. Öktem, L.: Hierarchical enumerative coding and its applications in image compression. PhD thesis, Tampere University of Technology (November 1999)
2. Öktem, L., Astola, J.: Hierarchical enumerative coding of locally stationary binary data. Electronics Letters 35(17) (August 1999)
3. Taubman, D.S., Marcellin, M.W.: JPEG2000: Image Compression Fundamentals, Standards, and Practice. Kluwer Academic Publishers (November 2001)
4. Haapala, K., Lappalainen, K., Hämäläinen, T.: Microprocessors and Microsystems (2005)
5. Vatolin, D., Moskvin, A., Petrov, O., Trunichkin, N.: JPEG 2000 Image Codecs Comparison (September 2005)
6. Wang, Z., Bovik, A.C., Sheikh, H.R., Simoncelli, E.P.: Image quality assessment: From error visibitily to structural similarity. IEEE Trans. Signal Process 13(4) (April 2004)
7. Vatolin, D., Moskvin, A., Petrov, O., Trunichkin, N.: MSU Video Quality Measurement Tool 3.0 (July 2011)
8. Cormen, T.H., Leiserson, C.E., Rivest, R.L., Stein, C.: Introduction to Algorithms, 3rd edn. The MIT Press (2009)
9. Shapiro, J.M.: Embedded image coding using zerotrees of wavelet coefficients. IEEE Trans. Signal Process 41, 3445–3462 (1993)
10. Servetto, S.D., Ramhandran, K.: Image coding based on a morphological representation of wavelet data. IEEE Trans. Image Proc. 8(9), 1161–1174 (1999)
11. Bhagwan, R., Lin, B.: Fast and scalable priority queue architecture for high-speed network switches. In: INFOCOM 2000, vol. 2, pp. 538–547 (2000)
12. W.M. Zabołotny. Dual port memory based heapsort implementation for fpga. In: SPIE 2011 (2011)
13. Suzuki, M., Minami, K.: Concurrent heap-based network sort engine - toward enabling massive and high speed per-flow queuing. In: IEEE International Conference on Communications, ICC 2009, pp. 1–6 (2009)
14. Bai, Y., Ahmed, S.Z., Granado, B.: FPGA implementation of hierarchical enumerative coding for locally stationary image source. In: FPL, pp. 1–6 (2013)
15. Marcelino, R., Neto, H.C., Cardoso, J.M.P.: A comparison of three representative hardware sorting units. In: Industrial Electronics, IECON 2009 (2009)

A Unified Framework for Over-Clocking Linear Projections on FPGAs under PVT Variation

Rui Policarpo Duarte and Christos-Savvas Bouganis

Imperial College London, United Kingdom
{r.duarte09,christos-savvas.bouganis}@imperial.ac.uk

Abstract. Linear Projection is a widely used algorithm often implemented with high throughput requisites. This work presents a novel methodology to optimise Linear Projection designs that outperform typical design methodologies through a prior characterisation of the arithmetic units in the data path of the circuit under various operating conditions. Limited by the ever increasing process variation, the delay models available in synthesis tools are no longer suitable for performance optimisation of designs, as they are generic and only take into account the worst case variation for a given fabrication process. Hence, they heavily penalise the optimisation strategy of a design by leaving a gap in performance. This work presents a novel unified optimisation framework which contemplates a prior characterisation of the embedded multipliers on the target device under PVT variation. The proposed framework creates designs that achieve high throughput while producing less errors than typical methodologies. The results of a case study reveal that the proposed methodology outperforms the typical implementation in 3 real-life design strategies: high performance, low power and temperature variation. The proposed methodology produced Linear Projection designs that were able to perform up to 18 dB better than the reference methodology.

Keywords: FPGA, embedded multiplier, over-clocking, PVT optimisation, Linear Projection.

1 Introduction

The Linear Projection algorithm, also known known as Karhunen-Loeve Transformation (KLT), is used in many scientific areas to compress data, i.e. face recognition. Additionally, the advent of *big data* and near real-time performance requirements has propelled an increased demand in performance for implementations of this algorithm [5].

The continuous increase of resources and performance in Field-Programmable Gate Arrays (FPGAs), along with low power consumption and highly specialised embedded blocks, has made them attractive to implement the Linear Projection algorithm, which relies on multiplications and additions, with high throughput requirements. In real-life applications, where usually there are hard area requirements, or when the Linear Projection targets a large number of dimensions, unrolling or deeply pipelining the design is unfeasible. Thus, the multiplication is assigned to the embedded multipliers and the convolution is folded. To overcome the performance limitation of the embedded multipliers, which can't be deeply pipelined, the Linear Projection circuit is over-clocked to

D. Goehringer et al. (Eds.): ARC 2014, LNCS 8405, pp. 49–60, 2014.
© Springer International Publishing Switzerland 2014

extreme frequencies beyond those reported by the synthesis tool in order to push further
its overall performance.

Taking into account that synthesis tools rely on models, and don't have information
about the actual device that is being targeted, they are conservative in their estimate.
Notwithstanding, a device can operate at higher clock frequencies, which can be determined via experimentation, still a margin in performance needs to be preserved to
contemplate variation due to process variation and operating conditions (i.e. temperature and voltage). The proposed methodology tries to close this gap by pushing the
performance further into the error-prone region.

Forasmuch as the performance of designs implemented using FPGAs are affected
by Process-Voltage-Temperature (PVT) variation, the same way as any other silicon
device, optimising an over-clocked Linear Projection will depend on the sensitivity of
the design to PVT variation. That fact requires the design on the device to operate
under variation of different conditions simultaneously. To address this problem the proposed methodology supports design strategies with different operating conditions, such
as low-power and high-performance. Moreover, in real-life voltage and clock frequency
are fixed and don't change much over time, whereas temperature is very expensive to
control. In addition, the proposed methodology can optimise designs for graceful degradation over a wide range of temperatures. This means that a single design won't be
optimised for a operating over the worst case temperature, but a set of temperatures.

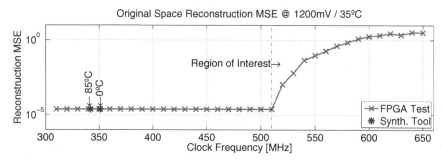

Fig. 1. Mean squared error of the reconstruction of the Linear Projection in the original space *vs*
its clock frequency, as well as the maximum operating clock frequencies provided by the conservative models of the synthesis tools. The region of interest corresponds to the clock frequencies
for which the Linear Projection circuit generates errors when ran on a DE0 board from Terasic.

The proposed framework optimises extreme over-clocking of Linear Projection designs into error-prone operation, designated as *Region of Interest* in figure 1. This figure
shows the evolution of errors with the increase of clock frequency, in a Linear Projection design from a Z^6 space to a Z^3 using the embedded multipliers on the FPGA. It
also shows the maximum clock frequencies reported by the synthesis tool.

A novel methodology is proposed to optimise Linear Projections under a unified
framework for over-clocking, which considers different sources of variation simultaneously. A key step of the proposed framework is the performance characterisation of the
embedded multipliers in a given device when they are clocked with clock frequencies
well above from what is reported by the synthesis tool. The main idea is to have a prior

characterisation of the device with respect to the degradation of the performance of the computational units. This characterisation suits the use of FPGAs because of their reconfigurability property.

The proposed framework automatically selects the best designs to improve the performance of Linear Projection implementations, while minimising errors without the expense of extra circuit resources. The obtained performance information (i.e. errors that are expected at the output of the multipliers) is injected to a Bayesian formulation of the problem in order to obtain the coefficients for the Linear Projection.

This framework uses an error model (for the operating conditions), and later automatically combines this information with high-level parameter selection of the algorithm, generating designs less prone to error, when compared to typical implementations of the KLT algorithm.

The main contributions in this paper are:

- Extension of the characterisation and optimisation frameworks to support embedded multipliers;
- Introduction of the support for PVT variation in the characterisation framework and in the optimisation algorithm;
- Creation of a new error model for the embedded multipliers under a range of operating conditions;
- Optimisation of Linear Projection designs for performance targeting different scenarios (i.e. low power, high performance, temperature variation resilience).

2   Background

Usually the implementation and performance of Linear Projections designs in a digital system is bound to the number of bits used in quantisation and the depth of pipelining. However, these methodologies are unable to cope with the aforementioned operating conditions, consequence of the adopted design strategies, and the intra-die and inter-die variation.

The ever increasing process variation and the fact that circuits need to support different voltages and temperatures makes the designs to operate at lower clock frequencies than the maximum offered by the fabrication process. Synthesis tools use conservative models which set the maximum performance of a circuit below the performance of the worst transistor for the family of the device.

One of the most well known techniques that can be applied to address the problem of performance variability in a Linear Projection design within a device is Razor [13]. It is a generic time-redundant method proposed for Dynamic Voltage Scaling (DVS) of CPUs. More recently, [6] proposed a methodology to recover from errors due to PVT. Both strategies can be applied to any path prone to errors due to time violations, and the recovery is performed at the expense of extra latency, which heavily penalise Linear Projections applications processing streams of data.

In [10] the authors present two strategies to compensate for *intra-die* performance variability by providing a generic characterisation step for the performance of the device followed by a reconfiguration step, where parts of the design are mapped to specific locations of the device given their performance requirements.

A novel approach to improve the performance of Linear Projection designs, using Constant Coefficient Multipliers (CCMs), relied on over-clocking of the design [7]. Notwithstanding this work is restricted to CCMs and doesn't consider different operating conditions demanded by different designs strategies. In this paper, this constraint is lifted to make the proposed framework practical in a wider range of real-life applications. Furthermore, a new optimisation framework that utilises information from a prior characterisation for a Linear Projection design optimisation is presented. It includes a new algorithm for design space exploration that utilises an objective function tuned for the utilisation of embedded multiplier modules within that Linear Projection framework under different operating conditions. Moreover, since the routing inside the embedded multipliers doesn't change, it means that the designs are optimised on a per device basis.

The following sections of this paper detail the proposed methodology to accelerate Linear Projection designs, while being resilient to PVT variation, based on the prior characterisation of the device.

The proposed framework breaks new ground proposing:

- graceful degradation of results at the output of the Linear Projection with the increase in variation of the working conditions;
- a methodology to push forward the performance of embedded multipliers without using extra circuitry;
- a methodology to optimise a design over a set of varying conditions performing better than accounting for the worst case scenario.

3   Linear Projection Revisited

The Linear Projection, also known as KLT, or Principal Component Analysis (PCA), transform is formulated as follows. Given a set of N data $x^i \in R^P$, where $i \in [1, N]$ an orthogonal basis described by a matrix Λ with dimensions $P \times K$ can be estimated that projects these data to a lower dimensional space of K dimensions. The projected data points are related to the original data through the formula in (1), written in matrix notation, where $X = [x^1, x^2, ..., x^N]$ and $F = [f^1, f^2, ..., f^N]$, where $f^i \in R^K$ denote the factor coefficients.

$$F = \Lambda^T X. \tag{1}$$

The original data can be recovered from the lower dimensional space via (2):

$$X = \Lambda F + D \tag{2}$$

where D is the error of the approximation. The objective of the transform is to find a matrix Λ such as the Mean-Square Error (MSE) of the approximation of the data is minimised. A standard technique is to evaluate the matrix Λ iteratively as described in steps (3) and (4), where λ_j denotes the jth column of the Λ matrix.

$$\lambda_j = arg\ max\ \mathrm{E}\{(\lambda_j^T X_{j-1})^2\} \tag{3}$$

$$X_j = X - \sum_{k=1}^{j-1} \lambda_k \lambda_k^T X \tag{4}$$

where $X = [x^1 x^2 ... x^N]$, $X_0 = X$, $\|\lambda_j\| = 1$ and $\mathrm{E}\{.\}$ refers to expectation.

4   Optimisation of Linear Projection Designs for Over-Clocking

In the circuit to implement the Linear Projection design, the data path holds the most critical paths. The main purpose of this work focus on over-clocking embedded multipliers, as they're the components with the largest delay in the data path of the design.

Figure 2 shows a rolled architecture of a circuit to implement the data path of one projection vector from a Z^p to Z^k Linear Projection. This was preferred instead of the unrolled one due to the amount of area taken by it.

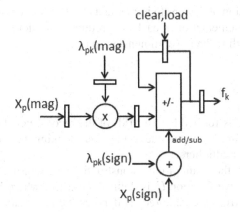

Fig. 2. Schematic of the data path for one projection vector of a Linear Projection circuit

The input stream of the circuit is identified with X_p. The input sample from each dimension is multiplied by the corresponding projection vector λ_{pk}. This multiplication only concerns the magnitude of the input and λ_{pk} values. The inputs and outputs of the multiplier are registered. The output of the multiplier is connected to an adder to do the accumulation. The accumulation sign depends on the signs of the input and λ_{pk}. The output stream is identified with f_k.

The calculation of the projection matrix Λ and its hardware mapping onto FPGAs are often considered as two independent steps in the design process. However, considerable area savings can be achieved by coupling these two steps as shown in [4,3]. The Bayesian formulation presented in [3] considers the subspace estimation and the hardware implementation simultaneously, allowing the framework to efficiently explore the possibilities of custom design offered by FPGAs. This framework generates Linear Projection designs which minimise errors and circuit resources, when compared to the standard approach of the KLT transform application followed by the mapping to the FPGA.

The key idea in [3] is to inject information about the hardware (i.e. in this case about the required hardware resources of a CCM) as a prior knowledge in the Bayesian formulation of the above optimisation problem. In more detail, the proposed framework in [3] estimates the basis matrix Λ, the noise covariance Ψ, and the factors using Gibbs sampling algorithm [8] from the posterior distribution of the variables, having injecting knowledge about the required hardware recourses for the implementation of the CCMs through a prior distribution. Thus, a probability density function is generated for the unknown Λ matrix, which is used to for generation of samples, where the prior distribution tunes this posterior distribution, and thus accommodating the impact the required hardware resources.

[7] provides an extension of the above work for the optimisation of Linear Projection designs using CCMs combating the effects for circuit area as well as performance variation due to over-clocking. This work is focused on the extension of the previous work to support embedded multipliers and PVT variation in the characterisation, error modeling, and generation of designs to implement (1). The framework selects the multipliers used for the implementation of each dot product in (1) along with the coefficients of the Λ matrix that define the lower dimension space.

4.1 Objective Function

The objective function is formed by the MSE of the reconstructed data in the original space, and errors that are produced due to the over-clocking, under PVT variation, of the utilised embedded multipliers.

Let's denote with $\hat{X}$ the result of the reconstruction of the projected data in a matrix form. Then, the objective function U is defined as in (5), where both reconstruction errors and variation errors are captured. E denotes the expectation and Tr the trace operator. The matrix formulation is defined as:

$$U = \mathrm{Tr}\left(\mathrm{E}\left[\left(X - \hat{X}\right)^T \left(X - \hat{X}\right)\right]\right) \tag{5}$$

By expressing the reconstructed data as a function of the Λ matrix, and the variation error with ε such as $\hat{X} = \Lambda(F + \varepsilon)$.

By imposing ε to have zero mean, which is achieved by subtracting a constant in the circuit, and using the fact that the Λ matrix is orthogonal and orthonormal, the objective function is expressed as:

$$\begin{aligned} U &= \mathrm{Tr}\left(\mathrm{E}\left[(X - \Lambda F)^T (X - \Lambda F)\right]\right) + \mathrm{Tr}\left(\mathrm{E}\left[\varepsilon^T \varepsilon\right]\right) \\ &= \mathrm{Tr}\left(\mathrm{E}\left[(X - \Lambda F)^T (X - \Lambda F)\right]\right) + \sum_j \mathrm{var}(\varepsilon_j) \end{aligned}$$

Here j denotes the columns of the Λ matrix. By assuming that the errors at the output of the multipliers are uncorrelated, then the first term in the final expression relates to the approximation of the original data from the Linear Projection without any variation errors, where the second term relates to the variance of the errors at the output of the embedded multipliers due to over-clocking, under PVT variation. Thus, the errors due to dimensionality reduction and variation are captured by one objective function without any need to formulate a problem using a multi-objective function.

4.2 Prior Distribution Formation

The proposed framework utilises information regarding the performance characterisation of the embedded multipliers for a given device and their respective resource utilisation, by suitably constructing a prior distribution function for the coefficients of the Λ matrix. The utilised models for the over-clocking errors, under PVT variation, are described below.

Error Models. The proposed framework utilises the performance characterisation framework for CCMs, introduced in [7] and now extended to support embedded multipliers and capture PVT variation. By executing that framework, a profile of the errors expected at the output of the embedded multipliers when one of the operands is fixed (i.e. representing a coefficient of the Λ matrix) for various frequencies can be obtained. As indicated by the objective function formulation, the objective is to capture the variance of the error at the output of the multiplier which models the uncertainty of the result. As such, a data structure is formed, $Err(m, f, p, v, T)$, that holds information regarding the variance at the output of a multiplier when a stream of data is multiplied by a constant m, the circuit is clocked at frequency f, placed on p coordinates on the FPGA, using core voltage v, and temperature T.

Prior Distribution. The formation of the prior distribution $p(\cdot)$ of the Λ matrix is a key part of the framework as it injects hardware information to the framework for the estimation of the Λ matrix. The aim of the prior distribution is to penalise Λ matrix instances with high errors, due to the use of coefficients that generate high errors due to over-clocking or due to poor description of the original space, by assigning low probabilities to them. As no information regarding the distribution of the coefficients is available on their suitability in representing the original space, this part of the prior distribution is uninformative and results to a flat prior. Thus, the prior distribution reflects solely information about the errors at the output of the over-clocked multipliers as $p(\lambda_{pk}, f, p, v, T) = g(Err(\lambda_{pk}, f, p, v, T))$, where the performance of every coefficient in the Λ matrix is dictated by the targeted clock frequency, the placement on the FPGA, the core voltage, and the temperature of the device; and $g(\cdot)$ denotes a user defined function. In this work, the following $g(\cdot)$ function is selected as it provides good results, without any claim on its optimality.

$$g(Err(\lambda_{pk}, f, p, v, T)) = c_E(1 + Err(\lambda_{pk}, f, p, v, T))^{-\beta} \tag{6}$$

c_E is a constant used to ensure that $\sum_{\lambda_{pk}} g(Err(\lambda_{pk}, f, p, v, T)) = 1$. β is a *Hyper-Parameter* that allows the tuning of the contribution of errors in the prior distribution. $Err(\lambda_{pk}, f, p, v, T)$ is the variance of the error observed from the performance characterisation of the multiplier.

4.3 Design Generation

The proposed framework uses Gibbs sampling [8] to extract, from the design space, a set of designs that minimise the selected objective function U. The resulting designs are the ones that minimise the value of the objective function. The proposed framework estimates each dimension (i.e. column) of the Λ matrix in a sequential manner. The user supplies the targeted dimensions K, the targeted clock frequency f, the coordinates on the FPGA p, the core voltage v, the temperature T, and the β parameter. The pseudo-code of the new version for the optimisation algorithm is given in Alg. 1.

Algorithm 1. Linear Projection Design Unified Framework for Over-Clocking

---

Require: $K \geq 1 \wedge \beta > 0 \wedge f, p, v, T > 0$
Ensure: 1 Linear Projection design
  $X \leftarrow input$ {original data N cases}
  for $d = 1$ **to** K **do**
    Create new empty $Candidate\_Projs$ list
    $prior \leftarrow generate\_prior(\beta, f, p, v, T)$
    $\lambda_d \leftarrow sample\_projection(X, prior)$
    $F \leftarrow (\lambda_d^T \lambda_d)^{-1} \lambda_d^T X$
    $error \leftarrow X - \sum_{j=1}^{d} \lambda_j F$
    $MSE_d \leftarrow \sum \sum error^2 / PN$
    $Proj \leftarrow (\lambda_d, MSE_d)$
    Add $Proj$ to $Candidate\_Projs$ list
    Extract candidate projections {min MSE}
  end for
  return The Linear Projection design with minimum MSE

---

5 Evaluation of Over-Clocked Linear Projections Circuits under PVT Variation

The performance of the proposed methodology was compared contra the performance of the reference design, which is based on a typical implementation of the KLT algorithm. All designs were implemented on a Cyclone III EP3C16 FPGA from Altera [2], attached to a DE0 board from Terasic [11]. The core voltage of the FPGA was provided by a digital power supply PL303QMD-P [1] from TTI. The temperature of the FPGA was set by a thermoelectric cooler placed on top of the FPGA. The temperature controller was calibrated using a digital thermometer from Lascar Electronics [9] and its deviation is below 1 °C.

The aim of this case study is to demonstrate that an optimisation of a Linear Projection design targeting different design strategies, under different operating conditions, using the same framework is achievable. The effectiveness of the framework is demonstrated with a case study implementing a Linear Projection from Z^6 to Z^3. The characterisation of the FPGA, the training of the framework and the test used different sets of data from a uniform pseudo-random distribution, quantised with 9 bits. After synthesis, the tool reported a resource usage of 126 logic cells and 3 9 × 9 embedded multipliers, and a maximum clock frequency of 342 MHz. Examining the timing report revealed that the critical paths belong to the embedded multiplier and the delay for the remaining

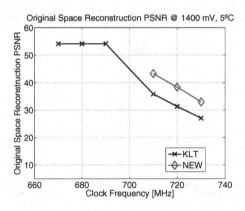

Fig. 3. Comparison of the performance of the two methodologies for the particular case of 1400 mV and 5 °C

components in the data path, i.e. accumulator, and the Finite State Machine (FSM), are out of reach for the selected over-clocking frequencies. The results from the characterisation of the embedded multipliers were verified using Transition Probability from [12]. To better demonstrate the impact of variation for each design strategy only one setting has been changed. The framework supports variation of many operating conditions simultaneously. The results for the reference implementation without information about the characterisation of the device are identified with **KLT**, whereas the results for the proposed framework are identified with **NEW**. They are compared in terms of Peak Signal-to-Noise Ratio (PSNR) of the reconstructed data in the original space.

5.1 Optimisation Targeting Maximum Performance

Optimising a Linear Projection design aiming for the maximum performance implies an increased FPGA core voltage and active cooling of the device. During the test, the device was kept at 5 °C and supplied with 1400 mV, instead of the 1200 mV specified by the manufacturer.

With a clock frequency twice as much as the maximum specified by the synthesis tool for the normal working conditions, the designs generated by the proposed framework exhibited a reconstruction PSNR up to 15 dB better than the KLT designs for the same working conditions, as can be observed in figure 3. On the other hand, if a target PSNR of 30 dB is to be met, then the designs generated by the framework can operate up to 20 MHz higher than the KLT designs.

5.2 Optimisation Targeting Low Voltage

Linear Projection circuits operating under limited power budgets, or battery operated, tend to operate using the least core voltage possible and be without any active cooling components. Figure 3 (left) shows the results for the KLT designs when operating at 35 °C with different FPGA core voltages. This design strategy considered 900 mV as

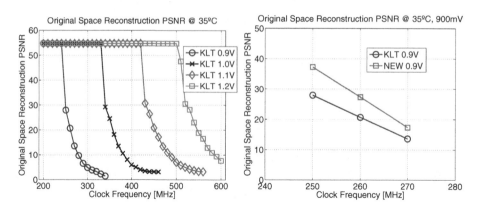

Fig. 4. Performance of the KLT Linear Projection application under different core voltages (left), and a comparison between the two methods for the particular case of 900mV (right)

the minimum core voltage for the FPGA. Figure 3 (right) shows that the designs created by the framework achieve a better PSNR up to 10 dB for the same clock frequency, or for similar PSNR, a clock frequency up to 10 MHz higher than the reference designs.

5.3 Optimisation Targeting Device Temperature Tolerance

It is well established that temperature affects the performance of silicon devices. Implementing Linear Projection designs without any active cooling components, and operating them in environments prone to large temperature variation can compromise their correct functioning. Usually, if an implementation of a Linear Projection has to consider a wide range of temperatures, then it will have to cope with the worst performance of them.

To go beyond with the optimisation methodology, it was considered a scenario where a single design could offer better performance than the reference designs for a range of temperatures, instead of a design per temperature. Seeing that the errors increase with the temperature, optimising a design for the worst-case temperature can restrict the coefficients available to implement the Linear Projection design, hence placing a ceiling on the best reconstruction MSE that a particular design could achieve, even without errors in its data-path.

The new idea is focused on sampling Linear Projection designs using the information from the characterisation of the device at specific temperatures along with its probability to operate under those temperatures. To accomplish this, it was investigated the weighted average of the characterisation errors for a range of operating temperatures in the generation of Linear Projection designs. As follows, the prior distribution from equation (7) is now:

$$g\left(Err\left(\lambda_{pk}, f, p, v, T\right)\right) = \sum_i \alpha_i c_E \left(1 + Err\left(\lambda_{pk}, f, p, v, T_i\right)\right)^{-\beta} \qquad (7)$$

Here i iterates over all contributing temperatures, and $\sum_i \alpha_i = 1$. The different weights represent the significance of the errors at a particular temperature. This

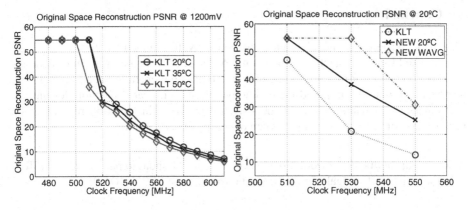

Fig. 5. Performance of the KLT Linear Projection application depending on the temperature of the device (left), and a comparison between the three methods at 20 °C (right)

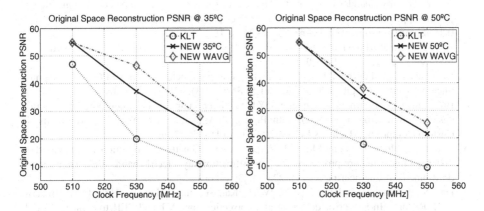

Fig. 6. Performance of the three methods at 35 °C (left) and 50 °C (right)

particular test case used temperatures 20, 35 and 50 °C and $\alpha_{20} = 0.3$, $\alpha_{35} = 0.5$ and $\alpha_{50} = 0.2$. In practice, the proposed framework generates circuit designs per clock frequency, covering all the temperatures within the expected range. They are identified with **NEW WAVG** in the results.

Figure 5 (left) shows the dependency of the performance of the reference Linear Projection circuit with the temperature of the device, with a supply voltage of 1200 mV. Figure 5 (right) shows in detail the comparison between the reference and the optimised designs for a specific temperature and a range of temperatures. Figure 6 holds the results for 35 and 50 °C.

The figures show that the designs generated by the framework always outperformed the KLT designs for all temperatures. Furthermore, at 510 MHz the PSNR is more than 10 dB better than the KLT design, and at 530 MHz the performance of the NEW design at 35 °C is better than the KLT design at 20 °C. The NEW WAVG designs perform significantly better than the NEW ones since they incorporate more information about uncertainty of the results under variation, up to the maximum temperature considered.

6   Conclusion

This paper proposes a novel unified methodology for implementation of extreme over-clocked Linear Projection designs on FPGAs. It couples the problem of data approximation and error minimisation under variation of the operating conditions. It was demonstrated that the proposed methodology optimises Linear Projection designs for performance and resilience simultaneously, by inserting information regarding the performance of the arithmetic units when operating under variation.

Acknowledgments. RPD would like to acknowledge "Fundação para a Ciência e Tecnologia" (Lisbon, Portugal) for the support through grant SFRH/BD/69587.

References

1. Aim & Thurlby Thandar Instruments. The new pl-p series - advanced bus programmable DC power supplies, http://www.tti-test.com/products-tti/pdf-brochure/psu-npl-series-8p.pdf
2. Altera. Cyclone III device handbook, http://www.altera.co.uk/literature/hb/cyc3/cyclone3_handbook.pdf
3. Bouganis, C.-S., Pournara, I., Cheung, P.: Exploration of heterogeneous FPGAs for mapping linear projection designs. IEEE Trans. VLSI Syst. 18(3), 436–449 (2010)
4. Bouganis, C.S., Pournara, I., Cheung, P.Y.K.: Efficient mapping of dimensionality reduction designs onto heterogeneous FPGAs. In: Proc. 15th Annual IEEE Symp. Field-Programmable Custom Computing Machines FCCM 2007, pp. 141–150 (2007)
5. Chu, J.-U., Moon, I., Seong Mun, M.: A real-time EMG pattern recognition system based on linear-nonlinear feature projection for a multifunction myoelectric hand. IEEE Transactions on Biomedical Engineering 53(11), 2232–2239 (2006)
6. Das, S., Tokunaga, C., Pant, S., Ma, W.-H., Kalaiselvan, S., Lai, K., Bull, D.M., Blaauw, D.T.: RazorII: In situ error detection and correction for PVT and SER tolerance. IEEE J. Solid-State Circuits 44(1), 32–48 (2009)
7. Duarte, R.P., Bouganis, C.-S.: High-level linear projection circuit design optimization framework for FPGAs under over-clocking. In: FPL, pp. 723–726 (2012)
8. Geman, S., Geman, D.: Stochastic relaxation, Gibbs distributions, and the Bayesian restoration of images. IEEE Transactions on Pattern Analysis and Machine Intelligence 6(6), 721–741 (1984)
9. Lascar Electronics. El-usb-tc k, j, and t-type thermocouple temperature usb data logger, http://www.lascarelectronics.com/temperaturedatalogger.php?datalogger=364
10. Sedcole, P., Cheung, P.Y.K.: Parametric yield modeling and simulations of fpga circuits considering within-die delay variations. ACM Trans. Reconfigurable Technol. Syst. 1(2), 10:1–10:28 (2008)
11. Terasic Technologies. Terasic DE0 board user manual v. 1.3 (2009)
12. Wong, J.S.J., Sedcole, P., Cheung, P.Y.K.: A transition probability based delay measurement method for arbitrary circuits on FPGAs. In: Proc. Int. Conf. ICECE Technology FPT 2008, pp. 105–112 (2008)
13. Ziesler, C., Blaauw, D., Austin, T., Flautner, K., Mudge, T.: Razor: A low-power pipeline based on circuit-level timing speculation (2003)

Relocatable Hardware Threads in Run-Time Reconfigurable Systems

Alexander Wold[1], Andreas Agne[2], and Jim Torresen[1]

[1] Department of Informatics, University of Oslo, Norway
[2] Computer Engineering Department, University of Paderborn, Germany
{alexawo,jimtoer}@ifi.uio.no, agne@upb.de

Abstract. Run-time reconfiguration provides an opportunity to increase performance, reduce cost and improve energy efficiency in FPGA-based systems. However, run-time reconfigurable systems are more complex to implement than static only systems. This increases time to market, and introduces run-time overhead into the system. Our research aims to raise the abstraction level to develop run-time reconfigurable systems. We present operating system extensions which enable seamless integration of run-time reconfigurable hardware threads into applications. To improve resource utilization, the hardware threads are placed on a fine granularity tile grid. We take advantage of a relocatable module placer targeting modern field programmable gate arrays (FPGAs) to manage the reconfigurable area. The module placer accurately models the FPGA resources to compute feasible placement locations for the hardware threads at run-time. Finally, we evaluate our work by means of a case study that consists of a synthetic application to validate the functionality and performance of the implementation. The results show a reduction in reconfiguration time of up to 42% and more than double resource utilization.

1 Introduction

The design and implementation of field programmable gate array (FPGA)-based systems which use run-time reconfiguration is significantly more complex compared to purely static systems. Run-time reconfigurable systems require careful floorplanning to partition the device into static and reconfigurable regions. In addition, the communication infrastructure that allows for communication between the static and the run-time reconfigurable regions, introduces complexity which increases development time, and introduces run-time overhead into the system. The run-time overhead includes management of reconfigurable resources, reconfiguration time and unused resources due to fragmentation. If the complexity associated with partial run-time reconfiguration is not addressed, the advantages offered may be nullified. It is therefore an attractive proposition to address these challenges in order to allow systems to be implemented at lower cost.

For many years, the implementation of partial run-time reconfigurable systems with many relocatable hardware threads has provided a challenge to engineers. Recently however, improved tools which target partial run-time reconfigurable

D. Goehringer et al. (Eds.): ARC 2014, LNCS 8405, pp. 61–72, 2014.
© Springer International Publishing Switzerland 2014

systems have become available [1, 2]. These tools have simplified the design of reconfigurable systems. In particular, new features enable implementation of systems which allow partially reconfigurable (PR) modules to be relocated at run-time.

Previous work related to both design time aspects and run-time aspects for PR implement a coarse grained tile grid to place the PR modules [3, 4]. As device size and number of PR modules increase, it will be increasingly difficult to maintain resource utilization on a coarse granularity tile grid used in earlier work. This requires a fine granularity tile grid to place the PR modules. Part of the theoretical foundation presented in these publications still applies to modern devices. However, modern FPGAs are both larger and more heterogeneous than earlier devices.

In this work, we present improvements to both the development framework and the run-time environment. We aim to raise the abstraction level for developing such systems. A higher abstraction level has the potential to shorten development time. This requires both a flexible development framework and an operating system to manage the reconfigurable resources at run-time.

Our work targets ReconOS, an operating system and programming model which supports heterogeneous applications [5]. These heterogeneous applications consist of both hardware and software threads. ReconOS provides a unified programming interface for both software and hardware threads. To raise the abstraction level, we hide implementation details related to scheduling and placement of reconfigurable hardware threads behind the operating system's application programming interface (API). This allows the operating system to manage, not only static hardware threads, but also hardware threads which are reconfigurable at run-time.

Relocatable hardware threads are modules which can be placed at different locations in the reconfigurable area during run-time. However, a number of constraints must be met to place a hardware thread. The resources required by the hardware thread must be available at the location, the area must be free (i.e. not used by another hardware thread) and communication has to be routed. To compute placement locations where these constraints are met, we have integrated a module placer into the ReconOS operating system.

The module placer implements a realistic constraint model to accurately model the fabric of the FPGA. Computation of feasible placement locations is based on constraint satisfaction theory [6]. This allows us to implement hardware threads with a complex layout. In addition, the module placer supports multiple alternative layouts for a single hardware thread. Multiple layout variants increase the number of feasible placement locations as reported in [6,7].

In addition, we have implemented a communication infrastructure according to the zero logic overhead concept introduced by Koch et al. [8]. To provide a communication infrastructure between the static and the reconfigurable area, routing of the communication wires is critical. There is no built-in support in the vendor tools to enable fine granularity routing constraints (i.e. mapping of a signal to a physical wire). Therefore, this has to be undertaken with dedicated tools, for example GoAhead [2] and OpenPR [1].

The remainder of the paper is organized as follows: The implementation flow is introduced in the following Section 2. In Section 3, we introduce the run-time environment. This is followed by experimental results in Section 4, and a conclusion in Section 5.

2 Run-time Reconfigurable System Implementation

To implement run-time reconfigurable systems, the design is partitioned into static and dynamically reconfigurable regions. In this work, we have partitioned the device according to the GoAhead floorplan flow presented in [2]. GoAhead works in conjunction with the Xilinx tools by generating placement and routing constraints. The GoAhead flow covers system partitioning and signal-to-wire mapping of wires crossing the boundary of the reconfigurable region. The signal-to-wire mapping is required to implement communication between the regions. In addition, GoAhead supports routing of the clock nets. It is a prerequisite to implement identical clock net routing for the static and partial run-time reconfigurable region.

Subsequent to the essential steps of system partitioning, signal-to-wire mapping and clock net routing, the static design can be implemented independently of the hardware threads. Independent implementation of the static design and the hardware threads is a feature supported in both OpenPR [1] and GoAhead, however not in PlanAhead according to [2]. This is of particular importance in this work, as we implement many hardware threads in small bounding boxes to reduce fragmentation. This significantly increases the tool time to place and route the hardware thread. It is therefore essential to be able to implement multiple hardware threads concurrently.

OpenPR and GoAhead allows design changes to be made to the static design without incurring a reiteration of place and route of the relocatable hardware threads.

2.1 System Partitioning

We aimed to minimize the static region and maximize the run-time reconfigurable areas, since this allows the maximum number of hardware threads to run concurrently. The maximum number of concurrent hardware threads is however restricted to the number of fast simplex link (FSL) ports supported by the MicroBlaze processor. Currently, this is limited to 14 ports.

The static region is not required to have a rectangular shape. For example, it is possible to define reconfigurable areas which are ⬐ and ⬏ shaped in addition to rectangular areas. GoAhead allows definition of placement and routing constraints with a polyomino (e.g. ⬐) shaped layout, and modeling this layout is supported by the module placer.

The size, shape and location of the static region is determined by two factors. Size is determined by the resource requirements. The shape and location

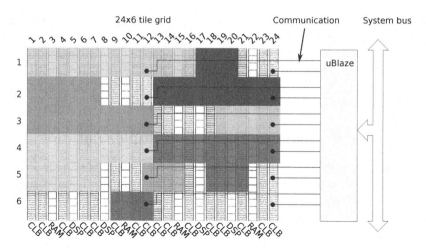

Fig. 1. 8 ReconOS hardware threads placed on a 24×6 tile grid. The placement depicted is computed by the module placer.

is constrained by the IOs to external peripherals. For example, the location of IOs for the PCI-Express interface and memory controller typically reside in the static partition. On the Virtex-6 ML605 evaluation kit, used in this work, the external memory is connected to IOs in the center of the device. In Figure 1, the floorplan of a fully placed and routed design is depicted. To the right of the device depicted in the figure, dedicated interfaces such as high speed serial PCI-Express links are located.

2.2   Relocatable Hardware Threads

We have implemented the run-time reconfigurable area with a fine granularity tile grid, 24×6. 24×6 tiles means the FPGA is divided into a fine granularity grid of 24×6 tiles. However, communication is implemented on a coarser granularity tile grid, 2×6. This allows the implemented hardware threads to have little internal fragmentation. However, unused area between the hardware threads decreases resource utilization for the reconfigurable area. To address this, we support hardware threads with polyomino shapes, as depicted in Figure 1. For example, hardware threads can be of ⌐, ⌐, ⌐ and ⌐ shape. These hardware threads span more than one configuration frame in height, also depicted in Figure 1.

The layout for a hardware threads are defined in GoAhead. GoAhead can be used to generate constraints to allow a hardware thread to be implemented with a particular shape. This forces the Xilinx tools to implement the hardware thread within the defined bounding box. As the Xilinx placer does not support an API to guide the routing decisions, the size of the area defined to implement the hardware thread may be too large or too small. A larger area results in internal fragmentation and a larger bitstream. A smaller area leads to unsuccessful implementation, for example a hardware thread which does not meet timing constraints.

Hardware threads can be made relocatable by modifying the frame address registers (FARs) within the generated bitstreams on the fly during reconfiguration. This is accomplished by storing the addresses where the FARs are located in a list. Since this is done once for each module at design-time, we do not have to parse the entire bitstream at run-time to find the FARs. The FARs are updated to their new values at run-time when the hardware thread position is known.

3   Run-time Environment Implementation

In this section we present our extensions to the ReconOS operating system for the support and management of relocatable hardware threads. The extensions consist of integration of a reconfiguration manager to manage the partial run-time reconfigurable area, and operating system support to schedule hardware threads at run-time. We have encapsulated low level implementation details into a high level thread API. This provides the necessary abstraction level to aid developers to use relocatable hardware threads. The high level API is exposed to the application as a set of system functions to create, suspend, resume and terminate threads.

3.1   ReconOS API Extensions and Scheduling

The ReconOS system function *hwt_create* creates a hardware thread. In Figure 2 API extensions and the life cycle of a hardware thread is depicted. Each hardware thread has a software delegate thread to manage communication with the other threads of the application. Similar to software threads, hardware threads have a thread control block (TCB). The TCB is used by the hardware thread scheduler and contains pointers to the bitstream layout variants, the address of the FSL communication port, and the current scheduling state. The FSL port address is required to allow the hardware thread to communicate with the delegate thread.

The reconfiguration manager is invoked through the hardware thread scheduler to compute a feasible location for the hardware thread's bitstream variants. If a feasible location exists, the FARs in the bitstream are updated and the bitstream is transmitted to the internal configuration access port (ICAP) port of the FPGA. The TCB is updated with the current FSL port address and the scheduling state is set to RUNNING. If a feasible location does not exist for any of the hardware thread layout variants, the scheduling state is set to WAITING. It can then be placed at a later time when the hardware thread constraints are met in the run-time reconfigurable region. We follow the software methodology of adding (hardware) threads to a waiting queue if they cannot be placed. This allows for the creation of more hardware threads than can currently fit into the reconfigurable region.

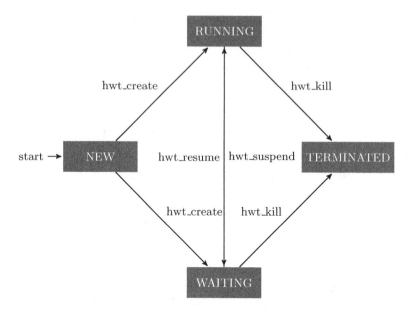

Fig. 2. API extensions to control the life cycle of a hardware thread

Hardware threads can be suspended and resumed through the API functions *hwt_yield* and *hwt_resume*. In this work, we consider a co-operating scheduling strategy of the hardware threads. A co-operative, or run to completion, schedule allows a hardware thread to finish its execution before it is suspended.

When a hardware thread is suspended (*hwt_yield*), the reconfigurable area is marked as unused, and the TCB is updated to reflect the new state. The area can then be used by another hardware thread. If there are threads in the waiting queue, the reconfiguration manager is invoked by the scheduler to compute a feasible placement location for the waiting hardware threads. Hardware threads which have a feasible placement location are placed in the reconfigurable area, and the TCBs are updated with the new FSL port address and state.

Finally, the *hwt_kill* function terminates both, the hardware thread and the delegate thread. The reconfiguration manager is then updated to allow the area to be reused by another hardware thread.

3.2   Reconfiguration Manager

In order to find suitable placements for hardware threads, we integrated a module placer into the ReconOS system. The module placer takes unused area, hardware thread layouts, communication interface and the heterogeneous tile grid into account to compute feasible placement locations. This is accomplished according to the placement model formulated in [6]: A module (hardware thread), M, consist of a sequence of one or more layouts, $M = \{L_1, ..., L_n\}$. A layout, L is a implementation variant, consisting of a sequence of one or more tile resources,

$L = \{R_1, ..., R_n\}$. The tile resource sequence, R, is the arrangement of tiles required by the layout variant. There are different types of tile resources, representing physical FPGA resources such as logic and memory. R is defined as a bounding box, $R(x_0, y_0, x_1, y_1, k)$, in which x and y represent the bounding box coordinates. k is a sequence of elements denoting the type of the tile resource column on the FPGA (e.g. a logic or memory column). Similarly, the run-time reconfigurable area is modeled as a sequence of tile resources, FPGA $= \{R_1, ..., R_n\}$.

To compute feasible placement locations, the constraint solver evaluates each constraint (i.e. unused area, resources). This results in a sequence for each constraint, C. The intersection of all sequences form a sequence, P, of feasible placement locations: $P = \{C_{area} \cap C_{communication} \cap C_{tilegrid}\}$. P is computed by our constraint solver using a branch and bound depth first search function.

An up to date scheduling state of all placed hardware threads in the tile grid is kept by the module placer. This state is updated whenever hardware threads are created, suspended, resumed or terminated. When a hardware thread is to be placed, the module placer is invoked by the hardware thread scheduler. The module placer computes a feasible placement location for one of the hardware thread layout alternatives. The computed placement is then returned to the scheduler which updates the bitstream with the new location and writes the updated bitstream to the ICAP port.

4   Experimental Results

To assess our approach, we have implemented the system presented in the previous sections and performed an experimental evaluation. The experiments have been carried out on a Xilinx ML605 Board. Our implementation supports up to 12 active hardware threads located within a 24×6 tile grid (2×6 for communication). The implemented design is depicted in Figure 3.

We have implemented a benchmark application which consists of hardware and software threads. The application creates 20 hardware threads, 5 for each function listed in Table 1. The hardware threads are scheduled and placed by the operating system. This allows us to verify the correct operation of the system when threads are suspended and resumed. In addition, the application allows us to evaluate the effect of multiple layout variants for the hardware threads on a fine granularity tile grid through experiments rather than simulation.

For comparison, we have also done experiments on two coarser tile grids, 1×6 and 2×6. The height of each tile is a single configuration frame. For the 1×6 tile grid (i.e. slot style), a single tile contains 9920 LUTs (1240 CLBs), 32 BRAMs and 32 DSPs on our XC6VLX-240T FPGA. At this course granularity the tiles are still homogeneous. For the 2×6 tile grid, we have a tile size of 4960 LUTs (620 CLBs), 16 BRAMs and 16 DSPs. Note that our communication infrastructure is implemented according to the zero logic overhead concept for all tile grids - a communication infrastructure that uses only routing resources. Therefore, all other reconfigurable resources in the tiles are available to the the hardware threads. For the 24×6 tile grid (2×6 tile grid for communication), the

Run-time reconfigurable tile grid   Static region

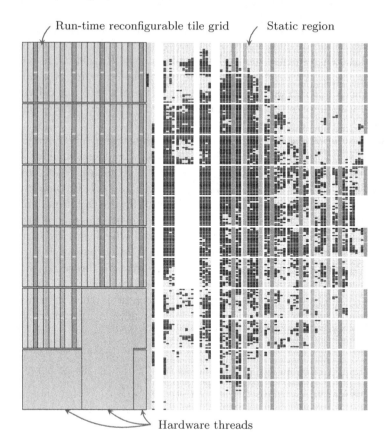

Hardware threads

Fig. 3. Implementation of a the 24×6 (2×6 for communication) tile grid on a Virtex-6 (xc6vlx240t) FPGA. The depicted FPGA fabric is generated from the XDL file of a fully placed and routed system.

tile grid becomes heterogeneous and not every tile contains CLB resources. At this granularity the tile grid contains either 640 LUTs (80 CLBs), 8 BRAMs or 8 DSPs.

4.1 Hardware Thread Implementations

In Table 1, the available hardware thread layout alternatives are listed. The hardware threads were implemented independently of the static system as described in Section 2. The selection of hardware threads include accelerators for computation of square root (SQRT), SHA256 hash function, single precision floating point (FP) addition/subtraction, and fast Fourier transform (FFT).

Resource utilization within the layout bounding box (i.e. the internal fragmentation) is listed as the percentage of the total amount of LUTs used within

Table 1. Relocatable Hardware Threads

Function	Layout	Tile Grid	Tiles	Usage LUTs	LUTs/REGs	Tool Time	Thread Size
SQRT		1×6	1	11%	1162/1390	21m	342KB
SQRT		2×6	1	23%		22m	206KB
SQRT		24×6	5	62%		2h49m	91KB
SHA256		1×6	1	67%	6664/6971	6h24m	392KB
SHA256		2×6	2	67%		6h24m	392KB
SHA256		24×6	19	80%		16h35m	376KB
SHA256		24×6				16h34m	376KB
SHA256		24×6				16h34m	376KB
SHA256		24×6				16h35m	376KB
SHA256		24×6				16h36m	376KB
FP		1×6	1	4%	410/629	22m	209KB
FP		2×6	1	8%		25m	111KB
FP		24×6	4	21%		26m	59KB
FP		24×6	5	21%		21m	73KB
FFT		1×6	1	21%	1996/2737	22m	384KB
FFT		2×6	1	40%		26m	246KB
FFT		24×6	8	62%		6h40m	172KB

the bounding box. A higher utilization is not always possible due to the resource demands of the hardware thread, the granularity of tile grid and routing constraints. For example, hardware threads such as the square root have a high amount of unused resources when implemented on a coarse granularity tile grid. If the hardware thread does not fit on a single tile, two or more tiles are used. For example, the SHA256 hardware thread does not fit in a single 2×6 tile, and therefore requires two 2×6 tiles. The number of tiles listed for the 24×6 grid include BRAM and DSP tiles.

In our work, we have considered layout variants, but not design variants of the hardware threads for the different tile grids. In many cases it is possible to exploit the module design space to better utilize tile resources. For example, various levels of transformations (e.g. loop unrolling and pipelining) can be applied to the SHA256 hashing algorithm to obtain design variants with different resource requirements. In Figure 4, placed and routed layout variants of a functionally equivalent hardware thread is depicted.

We observe that a smaller layout bounding box increase the tool time to implement the hardware thread. In particular the place and route time increases. The tool times as measured on a Xeon X5690 server are listed for each hardware thread, together with the size of the generated bitstream. We also find that a smaller layout bounding box reduce run-time reconfiguration time. This is to be expected, as the resulting bitstream has fewer configuration frames and thus has a reduced size.

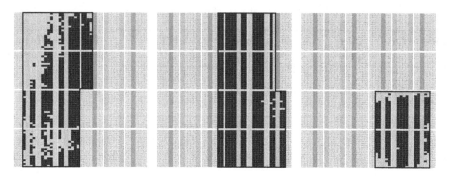

Fig. 4. A hardware thread implemented with multiple layout variants

Table 2. Bitstream Data for all Hardware Threads on Different Tile Grids

Tile Grid	Bitstreams Size	Bitstreams	Average LUT Usage
1×6	6635KB	20	26
2×6	4775KB	20	35
24×6	3855KB	55	56

4.2   Run-time Experiments

In order to evaluate the placement, the application creates 20 hardware threads. Each hardware thread is executed 5 times. After each execution the thread yields, and is removed from the reconfigurable area. If the hardware thread has design alternatives (i.e. the SHA256 and FP), each design alternative is evaluated by the module placer to find one that is feasible.

In Table 2, the hardware thread bitstream data is listed for tile grids of 1×6, 2×6 and 24×6 (2×6 for communication) granularity. On a 1×6 tile grid, a maximum of 6 hardware threads can be executed concurrently. On a 2×6 and 24×6 tile grid, up to 12 hardware threads can be executed at the same time.

A fine granularity tile grid allows significant reduction in the total bitstream size as shown in Table 2. The results show a reduction in bitstream size of up to 42% between a 1×6 and a 24×6 tile grid. Besides reduced storage requirements, the main benefit of this is the decrease in configuration time, which is proportional to the bitstream size. In Table 3, the total bitstream data transferred during execution of the application is listed. On a 24×6 tile grid we have reduced the reconfiguration time by up to 46% compared to a 1×6 tile grid. Using external SPI flash memory at 100MHz, this translates into an improvement from 2.6 seconds (33175KB) down to 1.4 seconds (17800KB).

In addition, we have measured the effect of layout alternatives on resource utilization. While hardware thread layout alternatives consume additional memory

Table 3. Run Time Experiment Results

Tile Grid	Bitstream Data Transferred
1×6	33175KB
2×6	23850KB
24×6	17800KB

for storage, FPGA resources are significantly more expensive than non-volatile memory[1]. It is therefore beneficial to use hardware thread layout alternatives to increase resource utilization, even for hardware thread alternatives which are rarely used.

Through our experiments, we found that even with a course granularity 2×6 communication tile grid, it is possible to achieve improved resource utilization when combined with multiple hardware thread layout alternatives and a fine granularity resource tile grid (24×6).

5   Conclusion

In this work, we have presented our research on integrating support for relocatable hardware threads in the ReconOS operating system. Our aim has been to raise the abstraction level to develop run-time reconfigurable systems. We have achieved this with extensions to ReconOS which encapsulate implementation details into a high level thread API. This allows seamless integration of run-time reconfigurable hardware threads into applications.

To manage the reconfigurable area, we have implemented a module placer targeting modern FPGAs. The module placer accurately models the reconfigurable resources. This is utilized by the operating system to compute feasible placement locations for the hardware threads. The computed placement positions are then used to relocate the hardware threads by updating the frame addresses in the respective bitstreams.

The system floorplan has been created with GOAHEAD, which enables the implementation of a zero logic overhead communication infrastructure. We have used the tool-flow to develop, synthesize, place, and route the hardware threads independently of the static system as well as other hardware threads. Thus, our improvements allow hardware threads to be implemented independently of each other, similar to the threads of a pure software application.

Our experiments were performed on a Virtex-6 device with a implementation that supports a fine granularity 24×6 tile grid and multiple hardware thread layout variants. This combination enables an efficient use of reconfigurable resources at the cost of additional non-volatile memory to store layout variants.

---

[1] The price of a Virtex-6 (xc6vlx195t) FPGA is 2210 Euro, and the price of non-volatile memory (16GB compact flash), 214 Euro. The prices have been obtained from http://de.rs-online.com/web/.

Acknowledgment. This work is funded by THE RESEARCH COUNCIL OF NORWAY as part of the Context Switching Reconfigurable Hardware for Communication Systems (COSRECOS) [9] project, under grant 191156V30, and by the European Union Seventh Framework Programme under grant 257906, as part of the Engineering Proprioception in Computing Systems (EPiCS) [10] project.

References

1. Sohanghpurwala, A.A., Athanas, P., Frangieh, T., Wood, A.: OpenPR: An Open-Source Partial-Reconfiguration Toolkit for Xilinx FPGAs. In: 2011 IEEE International Symposium on Parallel and Distributed Processing Workshops and Phd Forum, Number Xdl, pp. 228–235. IEEE (May 2011)
2. Beckhoff, C., Koch, D., Torresen, J.: Go Ahead: A Partial Reconfiguration Framework. In: 2012 IEEE 20th International Symposium on Field-Programmable Custom Computing Machines, pp. 37–44. IEEE (April 2012)
3. Jara-Berrocal, A., Gordon-Ross, A.: An integrated development toolset and implementation methodology for partially reconfigurable system-on-chips. In: ASAP 2011 - 22nd IEEE International Conference on Application-specific Systems, Architectures and Processors, pp. 219–222. IEEE (September 2011)
4. Wang, Y., Zhou, X., Wang, L., Yan, J., Luk, W.: SPREAD: A Streaming-Based Partially Reconfigurable Architecture and Programming Model. IEEE Transactions on Very Large Scale Integration (VLSI) Systems (99), 1–14 (2013)
5. Lubbers, E., Platzner, M.: ReconOS: An RTOS Supporting Hard-and Software Threads. In: 2007 International Conference on Field Programmable Logic and Applications, pp. 441–446. IEEE (August 2007)
6. Wold, A., Koch, D., Torresen, J.: Enhancing Resource Utilization with Design Alternatives in Runtime Reconfigurable Systems. In: 2011 IEEE International Symposium on Parallel and Distributed Processing Workshops and Phd Forum, Anchorage, pp. 264–270. IEEE (May 2011)
7. Koester, M., Luk, W., Hagemeyer, J., Porrmann, M., Ruckert, U.: Design Optimizations for Tiled Partially Reconfigurable Systems. IEEE Transactions on Very Large Scale Integration (VLSI) Systems 19(6), 1048–1061 (2011)
8. Koch, D., Beckhoff, C., Torresen, J.: Zero logic overhead integration of partially reconfigurable modules. In: Proceedings of the 23rd Symposium on Integrated Circuits and System Design - SBCCI 2010, p. 103. ACM Press, New York (2010)
9. COSRECOS: Context switching reconfigurable hardware for communication systems (cosrecos), `http://www.mn.uio.no/ifi/english/research/projects/cosrecos`
10. EPiCS: Engineering proprioception in computing systems (epics), `http://www.epics-project.eu`

Faster FPGA Debug: Efficiently Coupling Trace Instruments with User Circuitry

Eddie Hung, Jeffrey B. Goeders, and Steven J.E. Wilton

Department of Electrical and Computer Engineering
University of British Columbia
Vancouver, B.C., Canada
{eddieh,jgoeders,stevew}@ece.ubc.ca

Abstract. Prior to fabricating an integrated circuit, designers will often construct FPGA-based prototypes that can test and verify their circuits far more thoroughly than is possible within software simulations, such as by booting an operating system. A key limitation of physical prototypes, however, is the lack of on-chip observability necessary during debug. This paper describes a trace-buffer based platform that can be used to enhance FPGA observability. We use this platform to investigate how best to couple debug instruments with user circuitry, and how the subsequent debug loop — the process of changing the signals or trigger observed when converging on the root-cause of a bug — can be shortened. We demonstrate a working implementation of this platform on Xilinx technology, finding that runtime speedups for each debug loop of 1.2–3.0X (and potentially 5.7–11.2X) can be achieved on industrial benchmarks, when compared to re-instrumenting with vendor tools.

1 Introduction

FPGA prototyping has become an essential tool in the design, verification, and debug of large complex integrated circuits. Mapping a design to one or more FPGAs allows designers to exercise their design far more extensively than is possible using simulation [1]. FPGA prototyping also allows designers to run their design *in-situ*, interacting with other parts of the system, real-world I/O, and embedded software/firmware. Even when simulation is used extensively, many bugs will escape, and FPGA prototyping is the best way to find these bugs.

Observability is a key challenge during FPGA prototyping. Unlike simulation, during prototyping, internal signals can only be observed if they are connected to I/O pins of the FPGA(s), and these I/O pins can be scarce. Worse, it can be difficult to know, at compilation time, which signals will be important to observe, meaning many compilation cycles may be required to track down a difficult-to-find bug. With compile times approaching a day (per FPGA) for the largest designs, this can severely limit debug productivity.

In recent years, there have been significant efforts to increase the observability into circuits mapped onto FPGAs [2,3]. In our research group, we have investigated algorithms for intelligently selecting the most relevant signals to trace [4],

D. Goehringer et al. (Eds.): ARC 2014, LNCS 8405, pp. 73–84, 2014.
© Springer International Publishing Switzerland 2014

incremental routing techniques to connect signals to trace pins at run-time [5], and overlay networks to accelerate the construction of new observation patterns, again at run-time [6]. These previous efforts have been demonstrated primarily using academic routing tools such as VPR [7], although [8] studied its algorithm in the context of a Xilinx device. While these solutions hold the promise for increased debug productivity, they have not yet been evaluated in the context of a complete debug flow and in conjunction with real debug IP, meaning the interactions between our techniques and the rest of the design, validation, and debug infrastructure can only be estimated.

To address this, we have developed a platform which can be used for demonstrating and evaluating alternative debug processes and techniques. In this paper, we describe this platform, and focus on one of the key research questions we encountered during its development — *how should instrumentation best be coupled with user circuitry?* Effective debugging involves adding circuitry or somehow modifying the user circuit, often with the purpose of enhancing visibility. This debug instrumentation circuitry typically consists of trace-buffers, control logic, and pipelining elements, and is often implemented using general-purpose FPGA logic, memory, and routing resources. Any instrumentation needs to be added to a design carefully; ideally, this instrumentation will have as little impact on the user circuit as possible. Minimizing this impact is important; even small changes in the internal timing of the user circuit may obscure or even (temporarily) eliminate bugs that are being sought. Uncovering the root-cause of a bug is impossible if the behaviour changes as new signals are probed. Furthermore, efficiently coupling debug instrumentation can accelerate the turnaround time between debugging iterations.

Specifically, in this paper, we present four different techniques for inserting debug instrumentation into a user circuit. These techniques range from coupling instrumentation to the circuit early in the flow, which requires no additional CAD support but may suffer in that user circuit's quality-of-results may be degraded by the presence of the instrumentation, to a fully incremental flow, in which the user circuit implementation need not be modified as instrumentation is inserted. We then quantitatively compare the first three of these techniques in the context of our platform, which uses the maxflow routing technique from [8] running in conjunction with Xilinx tools and IP. Although we do not present measured results for the final technique, we hope that their inclusion in this paper will motivate others to further develop our techniques, eventually leading to improved debug techniques and, ultimately, increased productivity of designers that use FPGA prototyping systems.

2   Background

Unlike in a software simulation, it is not possible for designers to view the value of any signal in their physical prototype at all timesteps of its operation. Methods of gaining observability into physical prototypes can be divided into two main categories: scan-based solutions and trace-based solutions. Scan-based approaches offer complete observability into a design by providing a snapshot of the values on all state elements, but only once the circuit has been halted. With ASICs, this can be achieved by using scan-chains that are often present for manufacturability, whilst in FPGAs, scan-chains can be implemented using general-purpose resources (the cost of which is prohibitively high [9]) or using device readback techniques [3]. Trigger circuitry is used to halt the clock prior to the scan-out procedure.

In contrast, trace-buffer based solutions operate by recording a small subset of design signals into a set of on-chip memory resources without interrupting normal circuit operation. This on-chip memory can be configured as a circular buffer that continuously samples signals until stopped by the trigger circuit. After recording is completed, the trace-buffer contents are extracted and a history of signal activity can then be presented to the designer. Due to limited on-chip memory, it is only possible to instrument the behaviour of a small number of signals for a small number of clock cycles (both several thousand, at most). Thus, multiple "debug turns" are often necessary — each selecting a different set of trace signals or trigger conditions — to converge on the root-cause of an error.

Typically, modifying the trace instruments between debug turns requires the circuit to be recompiled, which can be a lengthy procedure that hampers designer productivity. Prior work has proposed methods to reduce this overhead, such as by applying trace-specific incremental routing [5], or by building an overlay network that can be rapidly reconfigured with new signals [6]. However, this work only targeted a theoretical FPGA architecture, leaving open the question of their feasibility when applied to a commercial device.

Most recently, [8] presents an incremental-tracing technique that utilizes minimum-cost maximum-flow (MCMF) graph techniques in order to optimally connect design signals to trace-buffers using the fewest number of routing resources. By transforming the trace-buffer routing problem into a single-commodity flow problem (given that the order which user signals connect to trace-buffer ports does not affect their observability) this was shown to be solved optimally. While [8] was evaluated on a real Xilinx routing resource graph with hypothetical IP, in this work, we investigate the practical considerations of using a fully-functioning instrumentation core and demonstrate that it is feasible.

3   Prototype Instrumentation

As described in the previous section, trace-based approaches require inserting additional circuitry (*debug instruments*) to a design in order to enhance the design's observability. These instruments consist of trace-buffers (memories) to store trace data, access logic to transmit the data from the user design to the trace-buffers and to transport the sampled data off-chip, triggering circuitry to coordinate the temporal behaviour of the trace-buffers, and other control logic. Trace compression and filtering circuits are also sometimes used to process data before it is stored in the trace buffers. Together, this instrumentation allows for the collection of "live" signal activity on-chip.

In inserting these instruments, however, it is essential that the instruments do not severely impact the user design, for example, by introducing new

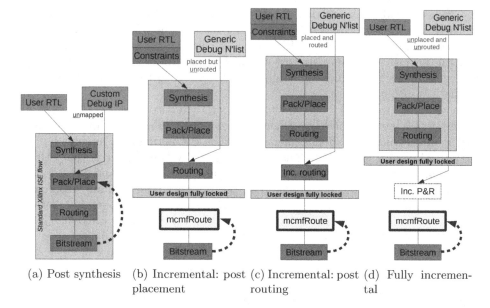

(a) Post synthesis (b) Incremental: post (c) Incremental: post (d) Fully incremen-
                        placement   routing   tal

Fig. 1. Instrumentation methods: dashed arrow indicates the debug loop

critical-paths or by affecting logic optimization. As described in the introduction, changes to the timing behaviour of the circuit may obscure incorrect behaviour, making it more difficult to track down the root-cause of a bug. We have identified a number of ways for FPGA prototypes to be instrumented using trace-based debug IP. This section describes and qualitatively compares these techniques.

The techniques we consider are illustrated by Figure 1. The most basic case, and the case that is currently supported by vendor tools, such as Xilinx PlanA-head, is to instrument the circuit after synthesis (Fig. 1a). Here, the designer would use knowledge of the exposed fault and their intuition to select a set of trace and trigger signals from those present in the synthesized design (though not all signals may be available, as some may have been optimized away) after which the CAD tool would generate a custom debug IP block and integrate this into the user netlist. The compilation procedure would then continue as normal, with both user and debug logic being treated equally. If a designer wishes to change the set of trace/trigger signals, new debug IP would need to be generated, and the design recompiled starting from the packing and placement stage.

Two new approaches evaluated in this paper are shown by Figs. 1b and 1c. In both flows, a predetermined debug core is first pre-compiled and then coupled with the user circuit at different stages of the compilation flow. The advantage of this 'late-coupling' flow is that the debug logic will have a smaller impact on the user circuit, and allow the circuit to be preserved between debug turns. Care is taken to ensure that the placement sites used by both the debug and the user netlists are mutually exclusive, which is enforced through placement (e.g. PROHIBIT) constraints. Once the debug infrastructure has been successfully coupled, our tool — mcmfRoute — is invoked in order to connect the trace/trigger signals of interest to any available port on the debug IP, using only unoccupied routing resources (i.e. it is incapable of ripping-up any existing user nets). Subsequently, should a different set of trace or trigger connections be necessary, only this mcmfRoute stage would need to be rerun.

For the post placement method (Fig. 1b), we couple a placed — but unrouted — debug netlist with the equivalent user netlist after the packing and placement stage. While the two netlists are constrained to mutually exclusive placement sites, the nets in the combined design are routed simultaneously with equal priority. For the post routing method (Fig. 1c), we couple the fully place-and-routed debug netlist with the equivalent user netlist, and perform an additional incremental re-route phase that fixes any routing conflicts. In this manner, user routing would be given topmost priority over all FPGA resources, whilst debug routing is consigned to using the resources that were left behind.

The last method we consider is a fully incremental approach. Here, the placement and routing of the user circuit is performed normally, and the debug IP is inserted into only the unoccupied resources of this design. This is less intrusive than the post placement and post routing methods, which restrict the placement of the circuit. Fig. 1d illustrates this approach.

While the post synthesis approach (Fig. 1a) may have the lowest impact on the maximum clock speed (Fmax) for the circuit under debug, it is also the most intrusive on the circuit and has the highest debug turnaround overhead, given that each new turn requires a fresh place-and-route solution to be computed. For the post placement (Fig. 1b) and post routing (Fig. 1c) methods implemented in this work, this turnaround time can be vastly reduced, at the (one-off) expense of first embedding general-purpose debug IP as part of the initial compilation phase. Subsequently, the instrumented circuit can then be locked (thereby fully preserving all existing routing) and only leftover routing resources be used to build new trace/trigger connections between debug turns.

4   Methodology

To evaluate each of the flows described in the previous section, we integrated them into our prototype framework. Our framework employs the Xilinx design flow (ISE v13.3), ChipScope debug instrumentation cores, our custom debug router (mcmfRoute), and a Virtex-6 ML605 Evaluation Board, which contains the mid-range xc6vlx240t 40nm FPGA device. In this section, we describe this framework and show how we have integrated the coupling techniques within.

4.1   Instrumentation Cores and Flow

A key decision was to employ Xilinx ChipScope instrumentation cores in our platform, rather than create our own instrumentation (however, our techniques are not specific to Xilinx technology). More specifically, in the post synthesis flow, we use Xilinx PlanAhead to generate a custom ChipScope core, tailored

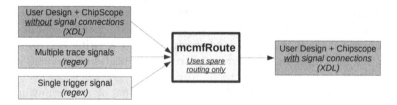

Fig. 2. mcmfRoute tool

to the signals selected for each debug loop, with which to instrument the circuit. For the post placement and post routing approaches, we pre-compile a generic, unconnected ChipScope core (over-provisioned to its widest configuration: 4096 trace ports at 1024 samples, and with 32 trigger ports to provide for maximum routing flexibility).

The ChipScope core is built with verbose placement and timing constraints that restrict the trigger and control logic to a small region in the center of the device, and the trace-buffer RAMs and pipelining registers to the peripheries of the device, in order to minimize any impact on the user circuit. Subsequently, when compiling the user circuit, we use opposing constraints to block these same placement sites from being considered. By applying these constraints, we are able to couple our ChipScope netlist with the user netlist by first converting both into the text-based XDL format, and then merging the resulting files. While the ChipScope core does have priority over the user circuit on these periphery sites, these placement sites will likely not have a significant impact on the user circuit.

While we can use this method to guarantee that no placement conflicts will occur, we cannot (nor wish to) make this same guarantee for routing. During the post routing flow, we are combining two fully routed designs that may use overlapping resources. Conveniently, the Xilinx routing tool (`par`) supports a re-entrant/incremental mode whereby it will accept a partially-routed (or even illegal) netlist and attempt to find a legal solution. We employ this mode in our post routing experiments, but due to the closed-source nature of this vendor tool, we are unable to guarantee that existing user nets are not ripped up. However, as we show in the results, using `par` in re-entrant mode causes significantly fewer nets to be rerouted than for the post placement case.

Unfortunately, Xilinx ISE's placement tool (`map`) does not support a similar re-entrant mode, meaning that we are not currently able to experiment with the fully incremental flow. This is something we would like to rectify in future work by constructing our own incremental placer.

4.2   mcmfRoute

The tool that we use to construct new trace and trigger routing connections between the user circuit and debug core — mcmfRoute — applies many of the techniques first presented in [8], and is summarized by Figure 2. mcmfRoute augments existing work by being wirelength-aware, but it is still incapable of

Table 1. Benchmark / debug core summary (on xc6vlx240t: 150,720 LUTs)

	LEON3:			GSM	Pre-compiled
Utilization	4-core	6-core	8-core	Switch	ChipScope
Logic Slice	50%	65%	81%	42%	+3%
LUT	26%	37%	47%	13%	+3%
FF	10%	14%	17%	29%	+2%
RAM	27%	40%	53%	9%	+27%

optimizing circuit timing due to the lack of knowledge into Xilinx wire delays. While [8] targeted an imaginary debug core using a set of randomly chosen trace signals, mcmfRoute takes as its input an XDL netlist containing a circuit that has already been coupled with trace instrumentation, as well as a set of trace signals and a single trigger signal, described using regular expressions. Although the ChipScope core that we instantiate can support limited trigger operations on buses of up to 32 bits, we make the restriction that mcmfRoute users may only specify one trigger signal; logic operations for reducing any arbitrary trigger event to this single bit is left as an external exercise. The reason for our Chip-Scope core supporting a 32 bit trigger is to provide maximum routing flexibility: instead of allowing the user-specified 1-bit trigger signal to connect to a single trigger port (the routing resources to which may be congested) we can route the trigger to any one of these 32 ports and set the unused ports to "don't care".

5   Results

We evaluate our platform using the four industrial benchmarks shown in Table 1: three variants of a System-on-Chip design, and one GSM switch. Additionally, the resource consumption of our pre-compiled ChipScope netlist (used only for the post placement and post routing flows) is also shown.

Our first experiment involves instrumenting the full-functioning LEON3 SoC design [10] configured with six SPARC cores, a DDR3 memory controller, and supporting peripherals, which occupies 65% of the logic slices on our Virtex-6 FPGA. Table 2 lists the results. Prior to instrumentation, the circuit can be compiled in a total of 2979 seconds, meeting the default 13.333ns clock period constraint (75 MHz). To mimic a debugging scenario, we use regular expressions to select all interface signals from master and slave devices attached to the SoC's internal AHB bus (`ahb[ms].*`), as well as the set of registers controlling all 7 pipeline stages inside the integer unit of the first CPU core (`nosh\.cpu\[0\]\.l3s\.u0/leon3x0/p0/iu/r_.*`). The trigger signal is set to be whenever this core makes a request for a bus transaction (`ahbmo\[0\]_hbusreq`).

Post Synthesis. Instrumenting the design using the post synthesis approach, available natively within Xilinx PlanAhead, incurs a small increase in compile time to 3322s, with the resulting circuit continuing to meet timing regardless

Table 2. Results — LEON3 System-on-Chip (6 core, 13.333ns constraint)

	Uninst.	Post synthesis	This work: Post placement	Post routing
User syn./pack/place (s)	2177	2321	2189	2189
User route time (s)	802	1001	-	802
xdl2ncd time (s)	-	-	90	409
Debug route time (s)	-	-	1098	768
Total compile time (s)	2979	3322	3365	4165
Total routing PIPs	1663K	1677K	1872K	1868K
Routing PIPs diff. (+/-)	-	-	+645K/-628K	+128K/-112K
Recompile time (s)	-	2512	-	-
mcmfRoute time (s)	-	-	315	313
xdl2ncd time (s)	-	-	648	619
Total debug time (s)	-	2512	963	932
Speedup over post syn.	-	1.0X	**2.6X**	**2.7X**
Potential speedup	-	1.0X	**8.0X**	**8.0X**
T_{cpd} debug disabled (ns)	13.328	13.322	13.322	13.328
T_{cpd} debug enabled (ns)	-	13.322	15.032	14.299
Setup violations @ 13.3ns	-	-	8	13
Signals observed	-	2214	2087 (94%)	2087 (94%)

of whether the debug circuitry is enabled or disabled. A total of 2214 signals were matched using regular expressions by PlanAhead. However, the drawback is that the debug loop for this flow is 2512s, which is the time necessary to re-pack, re-place and re-route the entire circuit.

Post Placement. For the post placement flow, the runtime required to couple our pre-synthesized debug instrumentation with the user circuit is comparable to that of post synthesis. Here, each debug loop consists only of re-routing signals to the existing trace-buffers and so can be completed in 963 seconds: 2.6 times faster than for the post synthesis approach. Interestingly, the majority of this turnaround time is consumed by the 'xdl2ncd' conversion step, which involves translating the text-based netlist description back into the proprietary Xilinx binary format (NCD) used by downstream tools, such as timing analysis or bitstream generation, as well as performing a set of verbose design rule checks (DRC). Eliminating this overhead (which would be possible if we had knowledge of Xilinx's binary format) could improve our speedup to as much as 8X.

Two trade-offs exist with this flow when compared to the post synthesis approach. First, the number of signals that exist (and hence, can be traced) post packing/placement is slightly less than those that can be traced post synthesis due to the logic mapping and optimization procedure, though we have observed that generally, registered signals are preserved. Second, whilst a circuit that has been coupled with ChipScope will continue to meet timing when the debug instruments are disabled, enabling these instruments does impact the critical-path delay (T_{cpd}) of the circuit, where trace connections have increased it from 13.322ns to 15.032ns.

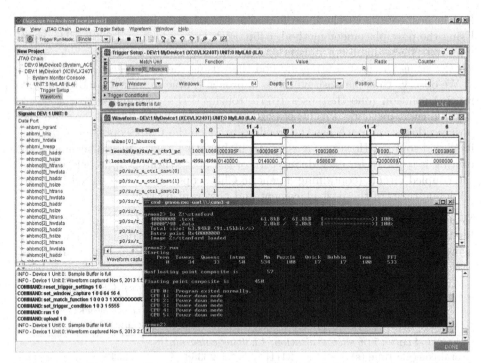

Fig. 3. Functional ChipScope demo: waveforms from an instrumented LEON3 design — rising edges on the CPU0 bus request were used as the multi-window trigger (T), values on program counter and instruction register are shown

The reason for this increase is two fold: a) our debug instrumentation is constrained to be as far away from the user circuit as possible, which minimizes its impact but causes large routing delays, and b) our trace router, mcmfRoute, aims to minimize the *average* wirelength of the circuit, as opposed to minimizing the *worse-case* wirelength of all individual signals [8]. This is evident from timing analysis, which reports that only 8/2087 signals (0.4%) failed to meet the 13.333ns constraint. We believe that this highlights a present limitation of our flow, though one that might not have a huge impact for large ASIC prototypes, where the critical-path delay is often in the region of low MHz — IBM reported 4 MHz (250ns) in [1]. As part of future work, we would like to investigate the possibility of modifying the graph algorithm to consider the worse-case wirelength, as well acquiring real wire delays to make mcmfRoute timing-aware. Presently, using our platform requires either the clock period of the entire circuit to be slowed to this value, or for those connections that violate timing to be ignored.

Post Routing. Lastly, the post routing approach performs similarly to post placement, but has a higher compile time overhead due to its two routing phases. The biggest strength of the post routing approach, however, is that it is less intrusive than the post placement flow. To illustrate this, we used the `xldiff` tool from [11] to measure the number of Programmable Interconnect Points (PIPs) that are different between the original design and the instrumented design.

For the post routing method, our flow added 128K PIPs and removed 112K PIPs. Using the post placement method, 645K PIPs were added and 628K PIPs were removed. These numbers illustrate that the impact on the original design is smaller using the post routing method than using the post placement method.

We observe that the post synthesis approach is able to return a more efficient routing solution (one that uses 1677K routing PIPs), compared to the other instrumented methods which use ~1870K routing PIPs). This is because the post synthesis approach has the freedom to place the ChipScope logic closer to its signal sources. However, it is worth highlighting that a new placement and routing is required for each debug turn of the post synthesis approach, whereas the coupled circuit (containing a generic ChipScope core) is preserved between all debug turns of the post placement and post routing flows.

Working Demo. Figure 3 shows a screen-capture of the ChipScope Pro Analyzer software, when connected to a working 6-core LEON3 design instrumented using the post routing method. The rising edge of the CPU0 bus request was

Table 3. Results — LEON3 System-on-Chip (4 and 8 core), GSM switch

	Uninst.	Post synthesis	This work: Post placement	Post routing
LEON3: 4-core (50% slice utilization, 13.333ns constraint)				
Total compile time (s)	2411	2338	2543	2445
Total debug (mcmfRoute) time (s)		1783 (-)	783 (314)	733 (294)
Speedup over post syn.	-	1.0X	**2.3X**	**2.4X**
Potential speedup	-	1.0X	**5.7X**	**6.1X**
T_{cpd} debug disabled (ns)	13.328	13.326	13.326	13.325
T_{cpd} debug enabled (ns)	-	13.326	14.683	15.300
Setup violations @ 13.3ns	-	-	10	19
Signals observed	-	2071	1947 (94%)	1947 (94%)
LEON3: 8-core (81% slice utilization, 13.333ns constraint)				
Total compile time (s)	3830	4293	4314	5774
Total debug (mcmfRoute) time (s)		3216 (-)	1149 (308)	1087 (286)
Speedup over post syn.	-	1.0X	**2.8X**	**3.0X**
Potential speedup	-	1.0X	**10.4X**	**11.2X**
T_{cpd} debug disabled (ns)	13.327	13.328	13.328	13.324
T_{cpd} debug enabled (ns)	-	13.328	15.674	15.728
Setup violations @ 13.3ns	-	-	35	36
Signals observed	-	2325	2169 (93%)	2169 (93%)
GSM switch (42% slice utilization, 30ns constraint)				
Total compile time (s)	1638	2263	2006	3137
Total debug (mcmfRoute) time (s)		1958 (-)	1626 (294)	1690 (298)
Speedup over post syn.	-	1.0X	**1.2X**	**1.2X**
Potential speedup	-	1.0X	**6.7X**	**6.6X**
T_{cpd} debug disabled (ns)	27.632	23.008	27.140	26.244
T_{cpd} debug enabled (ns)	-	23.008	27.140	26.244
Setup violations @ 30ns	-	-	-	-
Signals observed	-	2049	2049 (100%)	2049 (100%)

selected as the trigger input, and multiple windows of trace data were captured — the waveform viewer (background window) shows the values on the program counter and instruction registers of the register access CPU pipeline stage — when executing the Stanford software test on the SoC (foreground window).

Other Benchmarks. Table 3 shows the results of experiments conducted on two additional variants of the LEON3 design — with 4 cores and 8 cores, and on a GSM switch [12]. As expected, for the smaller 4-core LEON3 design, instrumentation has a smaller impact on the critical-path delay (T_{cpd}) when debug is enabled, than for the larger 6-core and 8-core designs. The speedups achieved also increase as this design scales: from 2.3X (5.7X) for the smallest variant to 2.8X (10.4X) for the largest, but the difference in the number of signals observed is due to the different number of cores attached to the AHB bus. The GSM switch, at a slower constraint of 30ns (33MHz), continues to meet timing both when debug instruments are disabled and enabled. The speedup over post-synthesis for the circuit is not as significant due to the majority of the debug loop (>80%) being consumed by xdl2ncd conversion.

6 Conclusion

When testing FPGA-based circuit prototypes, if an error occurs, the designer needs to rapidly understand the internal behaviour of their circuit in order to debug effectively. Trace-buffer based instruments can offer a limited amount of visibility into on-chip signal activity, but the success of these instruments is dependent on how this additional debug logic is coupled with existing user circuitry. Furthermore, certain instrumentation flows are also amenable to reducing the time required to complete a debug turn, allowing the small subset of signals that are observed to be modified without requiring the whole circuit to be recompiled.

In this paper, we demonstrate a working Xilinx-based platform that can be used to experiment with different methods of coupling debug instruments to user circuits. We describe four different instrumentation flows, and apply our platform to evaluate three of these flows. Results show that adding the debug core to a user circuit using the post placement and post routing methods can have little to no effect on the instrumented circuit when not debugging, but subsequently, allows for the debug loop to be accelerated by 1.2–3.0X. If we could directly manipulate Xilinx binary netlists, our speedups could be as high as 5.7–11.2X.

6.1 Future Work

We believe that a number of improvements can be made to further improve debugging productivity. First, we would like to evaluate the fully incremental debug flow on our platform, which is dependent on access to a high-quality incremental placement tool. We believe this flow would improve the timing of our instrumented circuits significantly, given that we will have the freedom to locate debug logic closer to all signal sources.

Second, we would like to improve the debug instruments used. Through studying ChipScope, we have observed that its control logic utilizes a number of high-fanout high-distance nets in order to drive the address inputs of each trace-buffer, and that the data outputs of these buffers are all reduced through a set of multiplexers before being transported off-chip. We would like to investigate designing our own debug IP, tailored specifically for our coupling flows.

Acknowledgements. This research was supported in part by Semiconductor Research Corporation contract 2010-TJ-2058.

References

1. Sohanghpurwala, A.A., Athanas, P., Frangieh, T., Wood, A.: OpenPR: An Open-Source Partial-Reconfiguration Toolkit for Xilinx FPGAs. In: 2011 IEEE International Symposium on Parallel and Distributed Processing Workshops and Phd Forum, Number Xdl, pp. 228–235. IEEE (May 2011)
2. Poulos, Z., Yang, Y.S., Anderson, J., Veneris, A., Le, B.: Leveraging Reconfigurability to Raise Productivity in FPGA Functional Debug. In: Proc. of the Conf. on Design, Automation Test in Europe, pp. 292–295 (March 2012)
3. Iskander, Y.S., Patterson, C.D., Craven, S.D.: Improved Abstractions and Turnaround Time for FPGA Design Validation and Debug. In: Proc. of the 21st Int'l Conf. on Field Programmable Logic and Applications, pp. 518–523 (September 2011)
4. Hung, E., Wilton, S.J.E.: Scalable Signal Selection for Post-Silicon Debug. IEEE Trans. on Very Large Scale Integration (VLSI) Systems 21, 1103–1115 (2013)
5. Hung, E., Wilton, S.J.E.: Incremental Trace-Buffer Insertion for FPGA Debug. IEEE Transactions on Very Large Scale Integration (VLSI) Systems (accepted for publication April 2013)
6. Hung, E., Wilton, S.J.E.: Towards Simulator-like Observability for FPGAs: A Virtual Overlay Network for Trace-Buffers. In: Proc. of the 21st ACM/SIGDA Int'l Symp. on Field-Programmable Gate Arrays, pp. 19–28 (February 2013)
7. Rose, J., Luu, J., Yu, C.W., Densmore, O., Goeders, J., Somerville, A., Kent, K.B., Jamieson, P., Anderson, J.: The VTR Project: Architecture and CAD for FPGAs from Verilog to Routing. In: Proc. of the 20th ACM/SIGDA Int'l Symp. on Field-Programmable Gate Arrays, pp. 77–86 (February 2012)
8. Hung, E., Jamal, A.-S., Wilton, S.J.E.: Maximum Flow Algorithms for Maximum Observability in FPGA Debug. In: Proc. of the 12th Int'l Conf. on Field-Programmable Technology (December 2013) (to appear)
9. Wheeler, T., Graham, P., Nelson, B.E., Hutchings, B.: Using Design-Level Scan to Improve FPGA Design Observability and Controllability for Functional Verification. In: Proc. of the 11th Int'l Conf. on Field Programmable Logic and Applications, pp. 483–492 (August 2001)
10. Aeroflex Gaisler: GRLIB IP Core User's Manual – v1.3.1 B4135 (August 2013), http://www.gaisler.com/products/grlib/grip.pdf
11. Steiner, N., Wood, A., Shojaei, H., Couch, J., Athanas, P., French, M.: Torc: Towards an Open-Source Tool Flow. In: Proc. of the 19th ACM/SIGDA Int'l Symp. on Field-Programmable Gate Arrays, pp. 41–44 (February 2011)
12. Murray, K.E., Whitty, S., Liu, S., Luu, J., Betz, V.: Titan: Enabling large and complex benchmarks in academic CAD. In: Proc. of the 23rd Int'l Conf. on Field Programmable Logic and Applications, pp. 1–8 (September 2013)

On the Impact of Replacing a Low-Speed Memory Bus on the Maxeler Platform, Using the FPGA's Configuration Infrastructure

Karel Heyse[1,*,**], Dirk Stroobandt[1,**], Oliver Kadlcek[2,**], and Oliver Pell[2,**]

[1] Ghent University, ELIS Department
Sint-Pietersnieuwstraat 41, 9000 Gent, Belgium
{Karel.Heyse,Dirk.Stroobandt}@UGent.be
[2] Maxeler Technologies Ltd.
1 Down Place, London W6 9JH, UK
{okadlcek,oliver}@Maxeler.com

Abstract. It is common for large hardware designs to have a number of registers or memories of which the contents have to be changed very seldom, e.g. only at startup. The conventional way of accessing these memories is using a low-speed memory bus. This bus uses valuable hardware resources, introduces long, global connections and contributes to routing congestion. Hence, it has an impact on the overall design even though it is only rarely used.

A Field-Programmable Gate Array (FPGA) already contains a global communication mechanism in the form of its configuration infrastructure. In this paper we evaluate the use of the configuration infrastructure as a replacement for a low-speed memory bus on the Maxeler HPC platform. We find that by removing the conventional low-speed memory bus the maximum clock frequency of some applications can be improved by 8%. Improvements by 25% and more are also attainable, but constraints of the Xilinx reconfiguration infrastructure prevent fully exploiting these benefits at the moment. We present a number of possible changes to the Xilinx reconfiguration infrastructure and tools that would solve this and make these results more widely applicable.

Keywords: FPGA, HPC, partial reconfiguration, block RAM.

1 Introduction

Large hardware designs often have a number of configuration registers or memories of which the contents are changed only sporadically, e.g. at startup. The conventional way of modifying the contents of these memories is using a low-speed memory bus. Although a low-speed memory bus uses less hardware resources than a high-speed version, it will still introduce long, global connections,

---

* Supported by a Ph.D. grant of the Flemish Fund for Scientific Research (FWO).
** This work was partly supported by the European Commission in the context of the FP7 FASTER project (#287804).

D. Goehringer et al. (Eds.): ARC 2014, LNCS 8405, pp. 85–96, 2014.
© Springer International Publishing Switzerland 2014

contribute to routing congestion and affect the performance of the rest of the design.

A Field-Programmable Gate Array (FPGA) already contains a global communication mechanism in the form of its configuration infrastructure. Although it does not have the same flexibility as a custom bus, it may serve as an excellent alternative for a low-speed bus without the previously listed disadvantages.

This paper focuses on the Maxeler platform [1], a high performance computing (HPC) system consisting of a host CPU and Dataflow Engines (DFE) utilising FPGAs (Section 2). Many of the applications implemented on the Maxeler platform use *mapped memories* or small ROMs and RAMs that can be accessed locally from hardware and globally from the host CPU. Mapped memories are implemented on the FPGA using block RAM (BRAM) primitives so that local access is fast. Global access happens via a low-speed mapped memory controller connecting the host CPU to the mapped memories. In common use, this happens at most every few hundred milliseconds.

In this paper, we investigate the use of partial reconfiguration of block RAMs to replace this low-speed memory bus for global mapped memory access (Section 3). Partial reconfiguration means that the configuration infrastructure of the FPGA is used to change the configuration of a part of the FPGA while the remainder continues to operate without interruption.

Partial reconfiguration is typically used to improve the functional density of designs. This is for instance done by loading and unloading modules as needed [2,3] or by performing dynamic circuit specialisation [4]. This makes it possible to use smaller and cheaper FPGAs to do the same amount of computation as larger FPGAs that do not use partial reconfiguration.

Partial reconfiguration of block RAMs has been proposed in [5] as a way to implement Network-on-Chips on FPGAs with reduced hardware resource cost. In this work, partial reconfiguration is used to transfer data from sender to receiver by temporarily storing the data in a sender block RAM and relocating the configuration bitstream of this block RAM to a receiver block RAM. However, no previous research has ever investigated how partial reconfiguration of block RAMs can be used to improve the routability and maximum clock frequency of applications.

Our experiments on three real-world designs, one financial application and two geoscience applications, have shown that the low-speed memory bus as currently implemented causes routability issues and limits the clock frequency in some designs. In those cases, the use of partial reconfiguration instead of this bus results in higher clock frequencies – up to 8% in our experiments – and thus better quality designs (Section 5). Improvements of 25% and more were also attained, but constraints of the Xilinx configuration infrastructure prevent us to fully exploit these benefits at the moment. In Section 6, we present a number of small improvements to the Xilinx configuration infrastructure and tools that would solve this problem and make these results more widely applicable.

2   Maxeler Platform Background

The Maxeler platform, developed by Maxeler Technologies, is a system for high performance computing consisting of a host CPU and hardware accelerators called Dataflow Engines (DFE) [1]. This section provides an overview of the Maxeler platform and toolchain. It also describes the mapped memory component and the low-speed memory bus by which they are connected.

2.1   Hardware Platform

Maxeler produces several variants of its hardware platform optimised for different computing needs. In general, the platform consists of one or more conventional host CPUs and one or more DFE coprocessors (DFEs) (Figure 1). In the system we study, the DFEs are connected to the CPUs using PCI Express and to each other directly over a custom high-bandwidth MaxRing network.

The host CPUs are used for managing the DFEs, by triggering configuration of the required bitstreams and streaming data to and from the DFEs using DMA streams, and for computations that do not need to be executed in hardware.

The MAX3 DFE used in this work has a large Xilinx Virtex 6 FPGA, called the Compute-FPGA (CFPGA), and a smaller auxiliary Xilinx Virtex 6 FPGA, called Interface-FPGA (IFPGA). This IFPGA is used for managing the PCIe communication between the host and CFPGA and for configuration of the CFPGA via its SelectMap interface. The IFPGA itself is configured from flash memory at startup, while the CFPGA is (re)configured with an application-specific bitstream provided by the host CPU every time a new application is started. The MAX3 also contains 24 GB of DRAM directly accessible from the CFPGA.

2.2   Toolchain

The Maxeler toolchain raises the implementation level for the application developer above the hardware level and thus reduces the development effort for DFE applications.

The part of an application that is accelerated in hardware is called a *kernel*. To implement a kernel on a DFE, the developer has to create a dataflow model of it. This is a description of the logic and arithmetic datapath through which streams of data flow and by which new streams of data are produced.

The description of a complete application for the Maxeler platform consists of three parts: a dataflow model of the kernel(s) in MaxJ (Maxeler's extension of the Java language), a description (also as a dataflow model in MaxJ) of the manager describing how the kernel(s) communicate with the CPU, other DFEs and memory, and the host application that is run on the CPU.

Using the Maxeler toolchain the dataflow model and manager description are compiled into an FPGA configuration bitstream for the hardware accelerator. The host code, in C or any of the other supported languages, is compiled and linked with Maxeler's SLiC and MaxelerOS run-time libraries, which enable it to communicate with the DFEs.

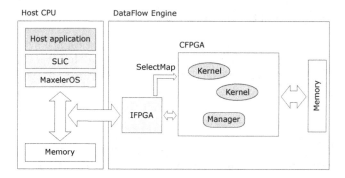

Fig. 1. Maxeler platform with one host CPU and one DFE. The user-defined parts are marked in dark grey.

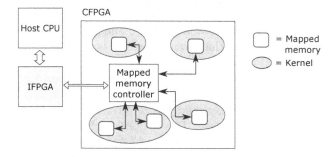

Fig. 2. Mapped memories and the mapped memory controller

2.3 Mapped Memories

Mapped memories are small RAMs or ROMs inside kernels that are implemented using BRAMs and can be accessed with low latency from local hardware. The difference with respect to regular RAMs and ROMs is that mapped memories can also be read and written globally from the host CPU. Mapped memories are therefore often used for configuration data, like filter coefficients, that need to be changed between runs of the application but usually not during the processing of a datastream. Other use cases are 'working memory' that needs to be initialised or of which the final state needs to be retrieved. In common use cases, global access to these memories occurs at most every few hundred milliseconds.

Global access is enabled by a custom low-speed, low-overhead bus and is a lot slower than local access. This 32-bit wide, low-speed bus consists of a mapped memory controller running at 50MHz that is connected in star topology to all the mapped memories (Figure 2). The controller is connected via the IFPGA to the host CPU using Programmed Input/Output (PIO). The mapped memory controller decodes read and write commands received from the host CPU and controls the read and write signals of the different mapped memories.

Because the mapped memory controller is connected to all the mapped memories, which may be spread out over the complete CFPGA, it can become

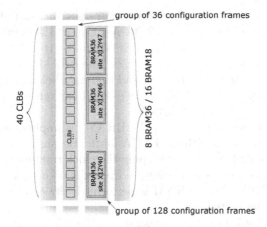

Fig. 3. Groups of configuration frames and stacks of BRAMs and CLBs

a routing bottleneck. Also the long, device spanning connections from remote mapped memories to the typically centrally located mapped memory controller can cause timing issues that are hard or impossible to resolve.

3   Implementation of Mapped Memories Using Partial Reconfiguration

The Xilinx Virtex 6, used in the MAX3, supports configuration readback and partial reconfiguration of a small portion of the FPGA while the rest of the FPGA remains operational. Because the contents of the BRAMs are also part of the FPGA's configuration, this feature can be used to read and write BRAMs.

By using partial reconfiguration of BRAMs to read and write the mapped memories, the use of the mapped memory controller can be avoided and the long, timing-sensitive connections can be removed.

In this section we will first provide more details about partial reconfiguration of BRAMs, then describe the changes made to the hardware, compilation toolchain and run-time libraries.

3.1   Partial Reconfiguration of BRAMs

Partial reconfiguration and configuration readback are done by sending special bitstreams from the host CPU to one of the FPGA's configuration interfaces: JTAG, SelectMap or ICAP (Internal Configuration Access Port) [6]. This bitstream contains the commands to read or write a specific portion of the FPGA's configuration.

The minimum granularity by which the FPGA configuration can be accessed, i.e. the smallest unit of data with its own address, is a configuration frame (2592 bits). Together, a group of frames describes the configuration of a section of the

FPGA's resources (Figure 3) [7]. A group of 36 frames, for example, describes the configuration of a partial column of CLBs. A group of 128 frames describes the contents of a partial column or stack of 8 BRAM36s or 16 BRAM18s, since each BRAM36 can also be split into two BRAM18s. The BRAMs that are described in the same group of configuration frames, and therefore belong to the same stack, have the same X coordinate and the same Y coordinate after integer division by 8 for a BRAM36 or by 16 for a BRAM18.

The configuration infrastructure of the BRAMs is implemented in hardware by sharing read/write ports with the FPGA fabric. Because of this it is unsafe to use a BRAM in the FPGA fabric – keeping the clock running and enable signal active – while readback of its configuration frames is taking place. As a result, if configuration readback of one BRAM is performed, the complete BRAM stack containing it must be halted.

According to [8,5] it is possible to mask specific BRAM36s (but not BRAM18s) during reconfiguration so that their configuration is not overwritten. Our experiments seem to imply that if a BRAM is masked in this way, and only then, it is safe to use it in the FPGA fabric while reconfiguration of its frames is happening. Unfortunately, no similar masking function is available for configuration readback.

3.2   Configuration Interface

To enable communication between the host CPU and the FPGA's configuration port the *ICAPStreamingBlock* is implemented on the CFPGA. This block, operating at 60MHz, connects the ICAP to two PCI Express streams, one in each direction. The ICAPStreamingBlock receives a combined bitstream and command stream from the host CPU. The bitstream is passed to the data port of the ICAP and the command stream sets the ICAP control signals and tells the ICAPStreamingBlock whether data is expected on the output port of the ICAP. This output data is then streamed back to the host CPU.

Alternatively, this functionality could be implemented on the IFPGA, which is already connected to the SelectMap configuration interface. Previous work has shown that the IFPGA can be used to partially reconfigure the CFPGA[9], but it is currently only able to (re)configure the FPGA and not to perform configuration readback. Adding readback support is straightforward engineering but we have not implemented this as part of this work since it would require significant development time and it is possible to assess the impact on the CFPGA without this feature being operational.

3.3   Changes to the Compilation Toolchain

We adapt the compilation toolchain so that partial reconfiguration can be used to perform global access of mapped memories. The underlying implementation of the global access method is transparent to the developer of the DFE and it is simple to switch between the original and new access method using the *UseMicroreconfigMem* option in the MaxJ description of the kernel (Figure 4).

```
optimization.pushUseMicroreconfigMem(true);
Memory<DFEVar> ram = mem.alloc(type, size);
ram.mapToCPU("mapped_ram_name");
optimization.popUseMicroreconfigMem();
DFEVar x = ram.read(addr);
```

Fig. 4. Instantiating a mapped memory with global access implemented using partial reconfiguration

The compilation toolchain disconnects these mapped memories from the mapped memory controller and extracts the placement and port width of the BRAMs so that this information can be used by the run-time libraries.

Instead of Xilinx Coregen, we have implemented our own mechanism for composing large memories from BRAM primitives. This is done because the exact way Coregen combines BRAMs to form larger memories is not documented and this information is required to map the contents of the mapped memories to the correct parts of the FPGA's configuration. This information is also exported for use by the run-time libraries.

3.4   Changes to the Run-Time Libraries

Instead of passing the read and write commands from the host code to the mapped memory controller, the MaxelerOS run-time library must now interpret these commands and translate them into the necessary reconfiguration and readback actions.

First, it must find out in which physical BRAM(s) a memory element is stored (Figure 5) and calculate the corresponding configuration frame addresses. This is done using the information that was exported by the compilation toolchain.

To perform a read operation on a BRAM, a special readback bitstream is sent to the FPGA's configuration interface causing the contents of the BRAM's configuration to be sent back. The mapping of the contents of the BRAM to the configuration bits is then reversed to extract the requested element. If a memory element is spread out over multiple BRAMs this procedure is repeated for each BRAM.

For a write operation we need to take into account that it is not possible to update a single memory element because a reconfiguration always updates at least a full BRAM36 (or 2 BRAM18s). Therefore, to correctly perform a write operation the relevant portion of the current configuration of the BRAM must be obtained, modified locally on the host CPU and then written back to the FPGA.

Because the contents of a mapped ROM will only be written from the host CPU and not locally on the FPGA, it is sufficient to keep a local mirror of the BRAMs' configurations on the host CPU to know their current configuration at all times. This local mirror must be updated in sync with the configuration of the FPGA.

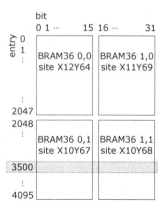

Fig. 5. Large block memory combining 4 BRAM36s (port width: 16 bits). The first 16 bits of element 3500 are stored in element 1452 of the BRAM on site X10Y67, the last 16 bits in element 1452 of the BRAM on site X10Y68.

For a mapped RAM the only way to know the current configuration of the BRAM is to perform a configuration readback. It is important that the contents of the BRAM do not change between the readback and reconfiguration operations because such an update would be lost.

Global access to mapped memories often happens in batches; a large part of a mapped memory is read or written at the same time. To improve efficiency, multiple accesses to the same mapped memory that affect the same configuration frames are grouped together so that the number of configuration readback and reconfiguration operations is reduced.

4   Challenges: Partial Reconfiguration Constraints

In this section we discuss how the constraints imposed by the configuration infrastructure, introduced in Section 3.1, affect applications on the Maxeler platform. We recall that during configuration readback the complete stack of BRAMs that is being read cannot be used and during reconfiguration only the BRAMs that are masked can be used.

Write operations to ROM mapped memories, which do not require a configuration readback, can therefore be performed safely as long as only BRAM36 primitives are used for their implementation and the other BRAMs are masked during reconfiguration.

In contrast to write operations on ROMs, read and read-modify-write operations on RAM mapped memories require that the complete stack of BRAM primitives containing the BRAM to be accessed is halted. For applications on the Maxeler platform it may be safely assumed that BRAMs from the same kernel as the mapped memory will be halted when the mapped memory is being accessed, but no assumptions about other BRAMs can be made. This will be a common case in many scenarios where part of a chip must continue running while another part is paused for reconfiguration. Placement constraints must therefore be used to prevent other BRAMs being placed in the read back stacks. In general, (automatic) floorplanning could be used to achieve this, previous experiments by Maxeler have shown that overly aggressive floorplanning has significant detrimental effects on maximum clock frequency, so we do not believe this to be a feasible option.

An alternative method using multiple iterations of Place & Route (P&R) has also been tested. In this method each incremental P&R run adds constraints (LOC and PROHIBIT) based on previous runs until the location constraints for reconfigurable BRAMs are met. This also had an unacceptable impact on the clock speed of anything but the smallest applications. This is not entirely unexpected because, for the same reason as the problems with floorplanning in general, large numbers of constraints are known to make it harder to find a feasible P&R solution.

While ROM mapped memories using partial reconfiguration can be used on the Maxeler platform, no feasible solution has been found for RAMs for realistically sized applications. In Section 6 we propose a number of changes to the configuration infrastructure and Xilinx tools that would make it possible to use RAM mapped memories on the Maxeler platform and other platforms with similar constraints. Note that on certain other platforms the location constraints may be resolved using floorplanning or circumvented by stopping all BRAMs.

5   Evaluation: Clock Frequency Benefits

5.1   Evaluated Applications

We have evaluated the proposed method on one financial application related to price prediction of financial derivatives and two geoscience applications related to detecting underground oil and gas reserves based on acoustic reflections. We will call them FINAN, GEO1 and GEO2. The evaluated designs are real-world applications developed by Maxeler and its customers.

Table 1. Description of the applications

	Logic	DSP	BRAM	Mapped memories
FINAN	87%	81%	51%	36 x 624 elem. x 32 bit
GEO1	69%	22%	50%	27 x 50 elem. x 23 bit
GEO2	70%	59%	70%	6 x 2002 elem. x 17 bit + 3 x 1024 elem. x 18 bit + 33 x ≤128 elem. x 18 bit

Table 1 contains a summary of the resource utilisation and mapped memories of each application. All three applications use only ROMs and these have values which are loaded at the start of each compute job (once every few minutes to hours).

All applications additionally contain 2 small mapped memories that cannot be implemented with partial reconfiguration so the mapped memory controller has to be retained. Even though the mapped memory controller cannot be removed, the routing bottleneck is resolved by disconnecting the majority of the mapped memories from the controller.

5.2   Maximum Clock Frequency

Table 2 contains the maximum clock frequencies for the three applications in different configurations. The "Conventional" column contains the maximum clock frequencies using the conventional implementation of mapped memories, the "ICAP" and "SelectMap" columns show the maximum frequencies using partial reconfiguration. For the values in the "SelectMap" column, the IFPGA is used to perform partial reconfiguration via the external SelectMap configuration port of the CFPGA (Section 3.2) instead of the "ICAP" interface and ICAP-StreamingBlock on the CFPGA itself. This is currently not functional but it is straightforward to see how it would operate.

In the ROM cases, the use of partial reconfiguration improves the maximum clock frequency of GEO2 by about 8% and leaves the other applications unchanged (SelectMap). The introduction of the ICAPStreamingBlock, however, causes a reduction of the maximum clock frequency of about 10% for GEO1. The reason for this is that the ICAP and DDR memory controller both are constrained to the same, congested area of the FPGA. The use of the SelectMap configuration interface would alleviate this problem.

In the RAM cases we assume, for the sake of the experiment, that the mapped memories are RAMs instead of ROMs and that the placement constraints for RAMs (Section 4) do not exist. In these applications the primary use of RAMs is for providing debug visibility, however other applications would also use RAMs in production mode. The conventional implementation of mapped RAMs causes extra routability issues and increases the advantage of the proposed method. For GEO1 we now see a frequency increase of 13-25% and for GEO2 we find that while it was impossible to meet the minimal timing constraints using the conventional method, a clock frequency of 130MHz can now be attained.

Because in this experiment we are ignoring the placement constraints for partially reconfigurable RAMs, the result of this experiment can currently not

Table 2. Maximum clock frequency (MHz). Items with * are currently not functional.

	Conventional	Partial reconfiguration	
		ICAP	SelectMap*
GEO1 (ROM)	100	90 (0.90)	100 (1)
GEO1 (RAM)*	80	90 (1.13)	100 (1.25)
GEO2 (ROM)	130	140 (1.08)	140 (1.08)
GEO2 (RAM)*	< 80	130 (> 1.63)	130 (> 1.63)
FINAN (ROM)	180	180 (1)	180 (1)
FINAN (RAM)*	180	180 (1)	180 (1)

be used in practice, however this experiment illustrates the potential benefits of this approach if modest improvements were made to the partial reconfiguration mechanism of the FPGA (as we discuss in Section 6). We successfully ran all the applications in ROM mode.

The relatively high clock frequency of the FINAN application is not affected by the method used to implement the mapped memories. This shows that not in every application the mapped memory controller is a routing bottleneck. There is currently insufficient data to make conclusions about which type of applications will benefit the most from the proposed implementation method. Our preliminary findings, however, show that applications that require a larger effort to solve the original P&R problem with low-speed bus generally benefit more.

Experiments have shown that read and write speeds of mapped memories implemented using partial reconfiguration (read: 2-14 Mbit/s, write: 1-10 Mbit/s) remain in the same order of magnitude as with the conventional implementation (read: 2-4 Mbit/s, write: 7-14 Mbit/s). The difference is of small importance because the read and write times are very small compared to the total execution time.

The solutions using partial reconfiguration used at most 1% more logic resources and 2% more BRAM resources than the conventional implementations. The additional resources were needed for the ICAPStreamingBlock and in some cases because BRAM18 primitives had to be replaced by BRAM36 primitives. We believe that this hardware cost is acceptable for an 8% speed improvement.

6   Recommendations

In this section we make a number of recommendations for possible changes to the FPGA configuration infrastructure and P&R tools that would make the proposed method more widely applicable.

Configuration readback of a BRAM can currently only be done when all the BRAMs in the stack containing it are halted or unused (Section 4). This can be achieved by locking the BRAM to a specific location and prohibiting the other BRAMs in the same stack from being used, by shutting down all the BRAMs on the FPGA during configuration readback or, if floorplanning is used, by turning off all the BRAMs in the region containing the BRAM to be read. For many applications, including the ones implemented on the Maxeler platform, these are infeasible solutions. We present three possible ways to solve this problem.

A first possible solution is to change the Placement & Routing algorithm so that it does not place the BRAMs of which we want to read back the configuration in the same stacks as BRAMs that we do not wish to halt during reconfiguration. As has been shown, a work-around method using multiple passes of the existing P&R tools is insufficient, but an integrated algorithm might achieve better results. We present the option because it is the only solution that does not require changes to the physical FPGA architecture.

A second option would be read masking – a straightforward extension of the existing write masking. This would allow independent configuration readback of

BRAMs even if they are located in the same stack. Because the configuration infrastructure already supports write masking, we believe that it would be feasible to implement the same for readback operations in future FPGA architectures.

Alternatively, the bits of the BRAMs in the configuration frames can be rearranged so that data of only one BRAM is stored in each frame, as opposed to the current situation where content from multiple BRAMs is striped across multiple frames.

Finally, we recommend to provide more possible locations to place the ICAP port than the currently available two options, which are located close together. This would help to avoid the routing congestion caused by logic modules that need to be constrained to the same region.

7   Conclusion

We have proposed a method to access block memories on FPGAs using partial reconfiguration and configuration readback. The use of this method removes the need for the low-speed memory bus that is conventionally used for this purpose. Using three real-world applications, we have shown that a maximum clock frequency improvement of up to 8% is possible because of this. The proposed method can currently be applied to all applications of which the block memories only need to be written. We have proposed a number of small improvements to the Xilinx configuration infrastructure and tools that would make it possible to achieve clock speed improvements of 25% and more when block memories need to be read as well as written.

References

1. Pell, O., Mencer, O., Tsoi, K.H., Luk, W.: Maximum Performance Computing with Dataflow Engines. In: High-Performance Computing Using FPGAs, pp. 747–774 (2013)
2. Beckhoff, C., Koch, D., Torresen, J.: GoAhead: A Partial Reconfiguration Framework. In: IEEE 20th Annual International Symposium on Field-Programmable Custom Computing Machines (FCCM), pp. 37–44 (2012)
3. Xilinx: Partial Reconfiguration User Guide (2010)
4. Bruneel, K., Heirman, W., Stroobandt, D.: Dynamic Data Folding with Parameterizable FPGA Configurations. ACM Transactions on Design Automation of Electronic Systems (TODAES) 16(4), 43:1–43:29 (2011)
5. Shelburne, M., Patterson, C., Athanas, P., Jones, M., Martin, B., Fong, R.: MetaWire: Using FPGA Configuration Circuitry to Emulate a Network-on-Chip. In: International Conf. on Field Programmable Logic and Applications, pp. 257–262 (2008)
6. Xilinx: Virtex-6 FPGA Configuration User Guide (2012)
7. Xilinx: Virtex-5 FPGA Configuration User Guide (2012)
8. Xilinx: XAPP290 Difference-Based Partial Reconfiguration, 1–11 (2007)
9. Cattaneo, R., Pilato, C., Mastinu, M., Kadlcek, O., Pell, O., Santambrogio, M.: Runtime Adaptation on Dataflow HPC Platforms. In: NASA/ESA Conference on Adaptive Hardware and Systems (AHS), pp. 84–91 (2013)

Towards Dynamic Cache and Bandwidth Invasion

Carsten Tradowsky[1], Martin Schreiber[2], Malte Vesper[1], Ivan Domladovec[1], Maximilian Braun[1], Hans-Joachim Bungartz[2], and Jürgen Becker[1]

[1] Institute for Information Processing Technology, Karlsruhe Institute of Technology
{tradowsky,becker}@kit.edu,
{malte.vesper,ivan.domladovec,maximilian.braun}@student.kit.edu
[2] Scientific Computing in Computer Science, Technische Universität München (TUM)
{martin.schreiber,bungartz}@in.tum.de

Abstract. State-of-the-art optimizations for high performance are frequently related to particular hardware parameters and features. This typically leads to optimized software for execution on particular hardware configurations. However, so far, the applications lack the ability to modify hardware parameters either statically before execution of a program or dynamically during run-time.

In this paper, we first propose to utilize the flexibility of underlying invasive hardware to adapt to the needs of the software. This enables us to ask for more than just processing power by, e. g., requesting particular cache parameters that correspond to certain application properties. The adaptive hardware architecture therefore is able to dynamically reconfigure itself dependent on the availability of the resources in order to achieve an optimized working point for each application scenario. Secondly, we present requirements for dynamical scheduling of computing resources to resource-competing applications. This becomes mandatory to account for memory-access characteristics of concurrently executed applications. We propose consideration of such characteristics with bandwidth-aware invasion.

With this novel approach, we are able to show that dynamic hardware and software co-design leads to improved utilization of the underlying hardware resulting in higher throughput in means of efficiency such as application-throughput per time-unit.

Keywords: invasive computing, adaptive, application-specific microarchitecture, reconfigurable cache, compute-bound, memory-bound, HPC.

1 Introduction

Invasive computing is regarded as the paradigm of building a platform that has a multitude of heterogeneous resources. It allows for dynamic allocation and utilization depending on the resources' availability to solve various computing problems. Due to additional and changing demands of both hardware and software requirements, respective changes have to be considered for each of those

D. Goehringer et al. (Eds.): ARC 2014, LNCS 8405, pp. 97–107, 2014.
© Springer International Publishing Switzerland 2014

building blocks of the invasive hardware and software architecture. Both up-coming sections discuss the different views on dynamic adaptive hardware and software.

1.1 Dynamic Adaptive Software

Following the trend towards many-core systems and extrapolating the number of cores exceeding one thousand during the next decades, dynamically chang-ing resources get mandatory for energy-efficiency, throughput optimizations and further upcoming requirements like reliability or security. This leads to several new demands to the application developer to be able to express this changing resource demands.

Applications should provide information on their requirements, targeting at improved application- and memory-throughput, real-time requirements, energy efficiency, etc. Different application scenarios such as multi-resolution image pro-cessing and dynamic adaptive hyperbolic simulations [1,6] set up the require-ments from static resource requirements towards dynamic resource scheduling. With such dynamically changing requirements of applications, further referred as different *phases*, it would be beneficial for applications making particular hardware sets available to other applications or deactivating them for energy efficiency reasons. With memory expected to be one of the main bottlenecks in a few years, dynamic reconfigurable memory related components such as caches and memory bandwidth is our main focus for this work.

Running only a single program on a particular number of cores, numerical applications such as a matrix-matrix multiplication (MMul) are typically (a) optimized to a particular cache-line size *during compile time*, (b) are *not able to consider changing cache-line sizes* and (c) are *not able to adapt the hardware to their requirements*. To our knowledge, those dynamic optimizations so far target only non-adaptive hardware resources in current HPC studies[1].

1.2 Dynamic Adaptive Hardware

Adaptive application-specific processors lead to higher efficiency by dedicated support of applications [9]. E. g., *i*-Core provides enhanced flexibility within the microarchitecture itself by enabling the application developer's interaction with the microarchitecture [19].

In addition to the standard setting of the hardware, the software developer should provide extra input to further parametrize the *i*-Core. This enables the application developer to pass on its knowledge about the application to the *i*-Core in order to achieve an optimized processor configuration. We refer to this as resource aware programming, which can as well include configurations oo caches.

To our best knowledge, a parametrizable cache was not considered so far. This constraints the degree of freedom when defining the sizes of, e. g., the dedicated level one caches in an optimized manner.

2 Related Work

2.1 Dynamic Adaptive Memory

In the classical model of an n-way associative cache, parameters such as line length, degree of associativity and number of sets exist. These parameters are coupled by the total cache size and thus constrained by available chip resources. Until now, most evaluations on memories have only been done using special simulators and models neither considering silicon implementation possibilities nor overhead. This is necessary for invasive computing since one of the key points is resource sharing between several concurrent independent computational problems.

For this work, the approach presented in [10] and [13], to tune the cache for inner loops before the start of each run seems appealing and will be used to get an overview of the benefits of adaptation. At first glance, it seems obvious that the highest associativity (fully associative cache) would yield best performance since the forced cache misses can be minimized. However, the gain by increasing associativity diminishes vastly after four or eight while the hardware expenditure keeps rising [5,20]. Another side effect of increasing the set size is mapping larger memory area to the set. This reduces the benefit of having more possible locations for element storage. With a variable fixed cache size, decreasing this cache size by deactivating particular sets is expected to yield power benefits but should only be considered with negligible impact on application's performance.

In this work, we consider a fixed cache size as a given number of sets being defined by line length and associativity. The three performance related keys compensating reduced cache size are *prefetching*, *dense storage* and *temporal locality*. While prefetching exploits local spatiality by pre-emptive loading of data, dense storage refers to storing a particular amount of data in a small memory area. A third effect to be exploited is temporal locality, which refers to data usually being accessed multiple times in a short time frame. On the one hand, cache-oblivious algorithms (e. g., matrix multiplication [8] and dynamic adaptive simulations [3,18]) are likely to benefit of dynamic adaptive caches optimized to their particular demands. On the other hand, algorithms not being able to exploit the access locality (e. g., dot product), would improve the performance of cache-oblivious algorithms by sharing the cache resources with them.

Existing work on reconfigurable caches [14,7] uses only simulation models so far and thus stays on the hypothetical side from the hardware point of view. Besides these parameters, there are further additions to a cache that leverage the same effects introduced above. They include cache-assists (prefetch buffer, victim cache) and way management.

Prefetch Buffer: A prefetch buffer[10] is a FIFO, into which data following the location of the last miss is loaded. On the next miss the prefetch buffer will be queried before the request goes to a lower memory hierarchy level.

Victim Cache: In case of replacement, the data being replaced is stored in a small fully associative cache, which is searched in case of a miss. This is a mixture of temporal and spatial locality and works by increasing the virtual cache density. An evaluation of reconfigurable combinations of a victim cache and prefetch buffer is given in [10].

Way Management: Way management [11] introduces control bits for every line and assumes a mixed instruction and data cache. The control bits decide whether a way is writable for data or for instructions. Thus the size of the instruction and data cache can be changed and parts of the memory can be shared. Furthermore, some data can be frozen in cache by locking the line completely.

Replacement Strategies: Different replacement strategies [12] appear to be almost orthogonal to the parameters of line length and associativity. However, there are corner cases where different replacement strategies yield better results.

2.2 Application Requirements for Dynamic Memory

Without knowledge of applications and their performance, no appropriate run-time decisions can be undertaken to optimize the hardware resources towards software requirements. In order to differentiate between particular requirements of applications, we start with taxonomy of representative state-of-the art algorithms with respect to the memory-related requirements.

Bandwidth Limited Applications: Typical memory access patterns for bandwidth limited applications are streams, stencils and in general a relatively small computation / memory access (CM) ratio for current architectures. Considering a *dot product* [16] under the assumption that the sum is kept in a register, two vector components have to be loaded followed by two computations of multiplication of both values and adding the result to the value in the register with $CM = 2 : 2 = 1$. *Stencil operations* are frequently used in image processing for border detection and scientific computing for iterative solvers [4]. Considering a simplified sparse 2D stencil operation computing second order derivatives with a stencil size 3x3, five values have to be loaded, each followed by a multiplication with the stencil value assumed to be available in a register and an add operation. Using blocking techniques for cache-reutilization and assuming a single boundary-data for blocks of size $\sqrt{S} \times \sqrt{S}$ still stored in cache, this leads to CM $= 6 : 5 \approx 1.2$

Compute Bound Algorithms: We consider numerical quadrature of a computational intensive function [2]. With frequent evaluation of such functions with $n \gg 1$ instructions with higher order quadrature formula, those computations are clearly compute bound due to avoidance of data access assuming that all instructions to evaluate the function fit into L1 instruction-cache.

Latency Bound Algorithms: Unpredictable access to memory occurs especially with interactively driven computations such as steering, image editing as well as spatial-residual aware iterative solvers [17]. Since the access occurs randomly, those algorithms are unlikely to fully exploit cache features. Those classes of unpredictable algorithms depend on the dynamically changing memory access patterns itself. Therefore no clear statement on memory dependency can be given and those algorithms are not further evaluated in this work.

3   Dynamic Scheduling and Adaptive Hardware

We propose a novel approach to reconfigure particular parts in hardware, which so far was only statically exploitable to the software developers. Currently, the concept involves a model of cache tiles. Depending on control signals, these tiles either form larger memory sections for deeper ways or are used in parallel as different ways. Each tile incorporates the control logic and can store tags. The implementation of replacement strategies and the cache assistant is considered as orthogonal.We consider it reasonable to store line associated management information in the tiles, since this memory grows automatically with the addition of tiles and its connections are managed more naturally if the tiles are dynamically assigned to different cores in a later step.

Our partitioning of the cache puts the actual memory of data and management information in one module and control logic like fetch on miss and replacement in another. This hides the choice on reconfiguring the number of ways or size from the control module and sets up new tasks: deciding where to put the reconfiguration management, the logic ensuring that the data is in the right places after changing the size or associativity. On the one hand, it should be fairly general. On the other hand, detailed knowledge about the memory layout could help to speed up the implementation. Cache coherency will have to be covered once we cross the single-core boundary. This will open up new degrees of freedom, such as partly shared caches or dynamical redistribution of cache, which is one of the main reasons why we consider re-sizing.

Runtime reconfiguration leads to the issue of changing data layout in the cache, introducing the need to reorder data before continuing. Reconfiguration is shown to be a feasible process and provides a solution that flushes half the cache and realigns the remaining entries in cache for a change in associativity [15]. It is claimed that one would need a buffer of half the cache size to fully reorder entries in the cache on an associativity increase [14]. We expect to circumvent this with our tile approach.

We present an extension of the invasive programming constructs with support of invadable memory hierarchy. This leads to modification of the cache within the processor depending on application-specific requirements. With dynamically changing number of resources for invasion, interfaces have to be provided by the application developer for distributed memory and by an invasion-safe programming style on shared memory systems to assure stability. For our invadable memory hierarchy, changing resources do not change the reliability as long as the cache-coherency among processors is guaranteed. The worst-case scenario is a severe slowdown, but no stability issues. Due to optimizations on requested hardware layouts, no multiplexing of the claimed resources is allowed.

4   Case Study on Potentials of Cache and Bandwidth-Aware Invasions

We first present a case study of varying cache parameters on representative algorithmic kernels. Secondly, we present required extensions of resource managers for concurrently executed memory- and compute-bound applications.

4.1   Variation of Cache Parameters

For this case study, we use an inner-loop blocked matrix-matrix multiplication (MMul). During the execution of the benchmark, the cache is invalidated after each run of the outer loop. For evaluation, we use a Xilinx XUPV5-lx110t prototyping board. We use the Gaisler Leon3, which has two sets of $8\,kB$ ($16\,kB$) of instruction cache and four sets of $4\,kB$ ($16\,kB$) of data cache. This enables the use of different cache parameters that can be defined at design time. Our *baseline* for comparisons with parametrizable caches is given by this basic configuration.

Parametrizable Instruction-Cache: On the one hand, the program size of numerical cores such as MMul and stencil operations is typically small while on the other hand, the code binary of functions demanding many different computations integrated typically by numerical quadrature is by far larger. Consequently, this underlines the potential of changing the cache sizes. As a case study, we disable one set and halved the instruction cache and benchmarked the blocked MMul. This had only minor impact to the program's execution time with a variance of less than $1\,\%$ relative to the baseline. This provides us with additional memory resources that can be *assigned to the data cache* or deactivated for *energy efficiency*.

Parametrizable Data-Cache: Applications optimized for spatial-local access such as the blocked MMul and stencil operations target at exploiting data caches in an optimal way. Efficiency for such algorithms is gained by cache-oblivious access of the matrix-matrix multiplication data for particular cache-parameters. Additionally to the complete execution time, we compare the performance of every outer loop's iteration to the baseline of the default configuration.

At first, the cache size is kept constant at $16\,kB$. This just leaves two options for variation: the number of sets with respective adjustments of the set size. Fig. 1 (left) shows halved number of sets (2) and doubled set size ($8\,kB$). We see a slight overall efficiency gain (approx. $3\,\%$), however, more importantly, we can see that different input data to the MMul is handled very well. In Fig. 1 (right), a single set with a $16\,kB$ set results in increased efficiency (approx. $7\,\%$) relative to the baseline. Especially the 40 block-size and 384 matrix-size input benefit from the change in cache parameters.

Secondly, we half the size of the data cache. One option is to half the set size to $2\,kB$ per set (see Fig. 2, left) or the other option is to half the number of sets down to two (see Fig. 2, right). As we compare the two results, almost the same relative performance for the application is achieved in both settings. In contrast to our first results, modifications of cache parameters did not affect the

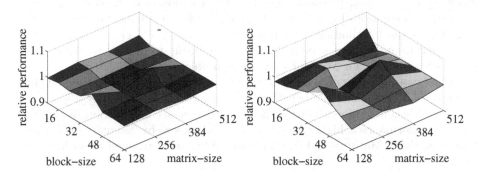

Fig. 1. Relative performance using a $16\,kB$ data cache consisting of two sets with $8\,kB$ per set (left) and one set with $16\,kB$ (right)

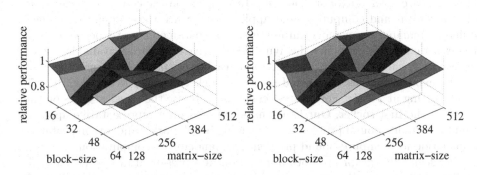

Fig. 2. Relative performance using a $8\,kB$ data cache consisting of four sets with $2\,kB$ per set (left) and two sets with $4\,kB$ (right)

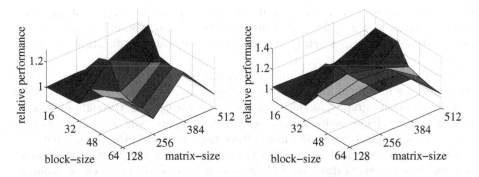

Fig. 3. Relative performance using a $32\,kB$ data cache consisting of four sets with $8\,kB$ per set (left) and a $64\,kB$ data cache consisting of four sets with $16\,kB$ per set (right)

efficiency of particular problem sizes, by the reduction of cache size. However, the performance drops by less than 20% compared to a standard execution. We expect that the information on performance change play a crucial role for the dynamical resource management. It is very promising to be able to change the cache set parameter for MatMul with larger problem sizes.

At last, we make potential additional cache resources available to the MatMul application. Fig. 3 shows the benefits of this approach. Interestingly, the application still benefits differently from the change in cache configuration. While the relative performance is higher for the 24 & 32 block size by 256 matrix-size configuration (left), MatMuls on larger matrices only benefit from a further increase of the set size (right).

4.2   Intermixing Bandwidth- and Compute-Bound Applications

Concurrently executed applications with different characteristics with respect to CM ratios have to be considered in an orthogonal way by the resource manager on a software level. Therefore, our next test case is on the concurrent execution of bandwidth- and compute-bound applications. Since these applications have different demands on memory parameters, those parameters are expected to lead to further efficiency gain once the dynamic adaptive hardware is available, e.g. by deactivating cache or statically reassigning cache sets to applications.

The experiments are conducted on a four-socket Intel(R) Xeon(R) CPU E7-4850 running at $2\,GHz$. For our test cases, we only use the physical cores on the CPU on the first socket. Our benchmark is based on a representative application for memory-bound problems, a streaming benchmark[1], and a representative application for compute-bound problems, a mandelbrot[2] computation.

The scalability graphs of both applications are presented in Fig. 4. The scalability of the representative memory-bound application almost reaches its peak with six cores due to the overloaded memory bus. For our representative compute-bound application, the scalability is almost linear for all ten cores.

Next, we consider the concurrent execution of one memory- and one compute-bound application. We pin each application to an exclusive set of cores. The description and results for the concurrent execution of our considered applications are given in Fig. 4. They indicate, that the memory-bound application is independent to the concurrently executed compute-bound application and vice versa.

Considering the application's optimal throughput being directly related to the scalability, we find the optimal throughput by searching the extrema of the sum of both scalability graphs, as shown in Fig. 5. For the optimal throughput in our benchmark, two cores should be assigned to the memory-bound application and the remaining eight cores to the mandelbrot for maximizing the throughput.

However, this optimal application throughput is *only valid if at most one bandwidth-bound application has to be considered*. In case of two memory-bound

---

[1]   http://www.cs.virginia.edu/stream/, C-ver., *Add* BW, N=50 mio, NITER=2.

[2]   http://www.cs.trinity.edu/~bmassing/CS3366/SamplePrograms/OpenMP/
mandelbrot-omp-by-rows.c, exec. with $maxiter = 2048$, $(x, y) = (0, 0)$, $size = 1$.

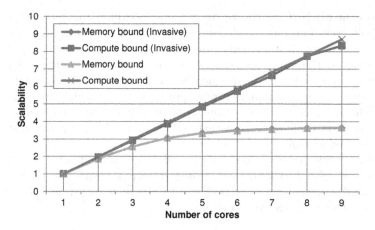

Fig. 4. Scalability of memory-bound application (streaming benchmark) and compute-bound application (mandelbrot). The *invasive* versions are executed concurrently: If n cores are assigned to the memory-bound application, then $10 - n$ cores are assigned to the compute-bound application. Both applications almost do not influence each other.

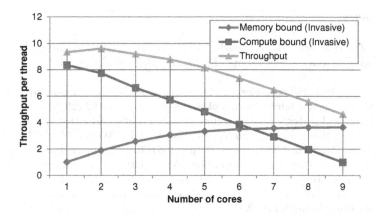

Fig. 5. Searching optimal distribution of cores to applications. The theoretical optimal throughput is given for assigning two cores to the bandwidth- and eight cores to the compute-bound application.

applications, a concurrent execution of both applications would influence the throughput and thus invalidate their scalability graphs. This yields requirements for information on memory characteristics which can then be utilized on software and hardware level for optimizations and is part of our ongoing research.

5   Conclusion and Future Work

We present an approach that exploits parameterization of cache parameters and computing resource parameters on hardware and software level. In contrast to the state-of-the-art HPC hardware, we are able to exploit this parameterization to the application developer and offer an optimized application-specific hardware and software realization. This moves away from today's way of application programming, as the developer needs to be aware of the underlying hardware configuration and resources. Consequently, we are able to show a relative performance increase on an adaptive prototyping system, on which we dynamically change cache parameters. Furthermore, concurrently executed applications with different bandwidth characteristics extend invasive scheduling parameters for more efficient execution.

For future work, we plan to simulate and experimentally evaluate the presented concept. Also, further details of the hardware realization will be specified and evaluated. Another complex task will be the demonstration and complete integration into a single System-on-Chip.

Acknowledgement. This work was supported by the German Research Foundation (DFG) as part of the Transregional Collaborative Research Center "Invasive Computing" (SFB/TR 89).

References

1. Bader, M., Bungartz, H.-J., Gerndt, M., Hollmann, A., Weidendorfer, J.: Invasive programming as a concept for hpc. In: Proc. of the 10h IASTED Int. Conf. on Par. and Dist. Comp. and Netw. (2011)
2. Brechmann, E.C., Schepsmeier, U.: Modeling dependence with c-and d-vine copulas: The r-package cdvine. Journal of Statistical Software 52 (2012)
3. Bungartz, H.-J., Mehl, M., Weinzierl, T.: A Parallel Adaptive Cartesian PDE Solver Using Space–Filling Curves. In: Nagel, W.E., Walter, W.V., Lehner, W. (eds.) Euro-Par 2006. LNCS, vol. 4128, pp. 1064–1074. Springer, Heidelberg (2006)
4. Bungartz, H.-J., Riesinger, C., Schreiber, M., Snelting, G., Zwinkau, A.: Invasive Computing in HPC with X10. In: X10 Workshop, X10 2013 (2013)
5. Damien, G.: Study of different cache line replacement algorithms in embedded systems. PhD thesis, KTH (2007)
6. Gerndt, M., Hollmann, A., Meyer, M., Schreiber, M., Weidendorfer, J.: Invasive computing with iomp. In: Specification and Design Languages, FDL (2012)
7. Gordon-Ross, A., Vahid, F.: A self-tuning configurable cache. In: Proceedings of the 44th Annual Conference on Design Automation, DAC (2007)
8. Heinecke, A., Trinitis, C.: Cache-oblivious matrix algorithms in the age of multi- and many-cores. In: Concurrency and Computation: Practice and Experience (2012)
9. Henkel, J., Bauer, L., Hübner, M., Grudnitsky, A.: *i*-Core: A run-time adaptive processor for embedded multi-core systems. In: International Conference on Engineering of Reconfigurable Systems and Algorithms (2011)
10. Ji, X., Nicolaescu, D., Veidenbaum, A., Nicolau, A., Gupta, R.: Compiler Directed Cache Assist Adaptivity. In: High Performance Computing (2000)
11. Malik, A., Moyer, B., Cermak, D.: A low power unified cache architecture providing power and performance flexibility (poster session). In: Proceedings of the 2000 International Symposium on Low Power Electronics and Design (2000)

12. Marty, M.R.: Cache Coherence Techniques for Multicore Proc. PhD thesis (2008)
13. Nicolaescu, D., Ji, X., Veidenbaum, A.V., Nicolau, A., Gupta, R.: Compiler-directed cache line size adaptivity. In: Chong, F.T., Kozyrakis, C., Oskin, M. (eds.) IMS 2000. LNCS, vol. 2107, p. 183. Springer, Heidelberg (2001)
14. Nowak, F., Buchty, R., Karl, W.: A Run-time Reconfigurable Cache Architecture. In: International Conference on Parallel Computing: Architectures, Algorithms and Applications (2007)
15. Nowak, F., Buchty, R., Karl, W.: Adaptive Cache Infrastructure: Supporting dynamic Program Changes following dynamic Program Behavior. In: Proceedings of the 9th Workshop on Parallel Systems and Algorithms, PASA (2008)
16. Ogita, T., Rump, S.M., Oishi, S.: Accurate sum and dot product. SIAM Journal on Scientific Computing 26 (2005)
17. Rüde, U.: Mathematical and computational techniques for multilevel adaptive methods. Society for Industrial and Applied Mathematics (1993)
18. Schreiber, M., Bungartz, H.-J., Bader, M.: Shared memory parallelization of fully-adaptive simulations using a dynamic tree-split and -join approach. In: IEEE Int. Conf. on High Performance Comp, HiPC (2012)
19. Tradowsky, C., Thoma, F., Hubner, M., Becker, J.: Lisparc: Using an architecture description language approach for modelling an adaptive processor microarchitecture (best work-in-progress (wip) paper award). In: 7th IEEE International Symposium on Industrial Embedded Systems, SIES (2012)
20. Zhang, C., Vahid, F., Najjar, W.: A Highly Configurable Cache Architecture for Embedded Systems. In: 30th Annual Int. Symp. on Computer Architecture (2003)

Stand-Alone Memory Controller
for Graphics System

Tassadaq Hussain[1], Oscar Palomar[1], Osman S. Ünsal[1], Adrian Cristal[1],
Eduard Ayguadé[1], Mateo Valero[1], and Amna Haider[2]

[1] Barcelona Supercomputing Center
[2] Unal Center of Education Research and Development
first.last@bsc.es, amna@ucerd.com

Abstract. There has been a dramatic increase in the complexity of
graphics applications in System-on-Chip (SoC) with a corresponding
increase in performance requirements. Various powerful and expensive
platforms to support graphical applications appeared recently. All these
platforms require a high performance core that manages and schedules
the high speed data of graphics peripherals (camera, display, etc.) and
an efficient on chip scheduler. In this article we design and propose a SoC
based Programmable Graphics Controller (PGC) that handles graphics
peripherals efficiently. The data access patterns are described in the program memory; the PGC reads them, generates transactions and manages
both bus and connected peripherals without the support of a master core.
The proposed system is highly reliable in terms of cost, performance and
power. The PGC based system is implemented and tested on a Xilinx
ML505 FPGA board. The performance of the PGC is compared with
the Microblaze processor based graphic system. When compared with
the baseline system, the results show that the PGC captures video at 2x
of higher frame rate and achieves 3.4x to 7.4x of speedup while processing images. PGC consumes 30% less hardware resources and 22% less
on-chip power than the baseline system.

1   Introduction

Graphics systems are now being used in different engineering sectors such as
artificial intelligence, robotics, telecommunication, etc. Hand-held devices, such
as personal digital assistants (PDAs), or cellular phones have embedded cameras
and most of them have mega-pixel image sensor cameras and interactive applications such as symbol recognition, etc. As the image resolution of these devices
grows, application specific and high-performance hardware are required to run
complex graphics code.

In this work, we intend to design a low-power and high-performance bus controller called the Programmable Graphics Controller (PGC) for FPGA based
SoC. The PGC resides in on-chip *Bus Unit* and holds data transfer patterns and
control instructions in its program memory. The PGC provides on-chip and off-
chip bus interconnects and controls data transfer without the support of complex

D. Goehringer et al. (Eds.): ARC 2014, LNCS 8405, pp. 108–120, 2014.
© Springer International Publishing Switzerland 2014

bus matrix, DMA and master processor. The PGC reduces the master/slave arbitration delay, bus switching time, balances the work load and gives a promising interconnection approach for multi-peripherals with the potential to exploit parallelism while coping the memory/network latencies. PGC bus scheduler provides low-cost and simple control that arranges multiple bus access requests and communicates with integrated processing units. We integrated dedicated hardware accelerators in the design as they have low footprint and low power consumption and gives high performance computation. The PGC supports multi-peripherals (camera, display) and processor core without support of the master cores and operating system. The integration of PGC with peripherals facilitates the graphics system to overcome wire (interconnection) and memory read/write delays and improves the performance of application kernels by arranging complex on-chip data transfers.

2   Related Work

Rowe et al. [1] proposed an FPGA based camera system for sensor networking applications. The design dealt with an 8-bit microprocessor and FPGA based hardware accelerator to capture and process the images. The system does not support high resolutions due to limited RAM and can process 2 frame per second. Petouris et al. [2] proposed an architecture that is used to implement and test advanced image processing algorithms. The system gives control to the user to control camera system through LCD panel and the system maintains contact with a PC through a JTAG interface for storing the images on it. The design is evaluated on Altera's DE2 development board and is designed to be a low cost proposal for academia. Murphy et al. [3] proposed a low cost stereo vision system on an FPGA, based on the census transform algorithm. The design uses a camera projection model to represent the image formation process that occurs in each of the two cameras which is suitable for independent vehicles for agricultural applications. The PGC system does not require a master core to manage the graphics system. The data movement is controlled by an on-chip scheduler at higher frame rate which reduces the power and cost of system. A light weight 16-bit processor core is also proposed in the design to perform basic image processing.

Matthew proposed an optical imaging system [4] having multiple high sensitivity cooled CCD cameras. The system gives desired representation of point source metastases and other small injuries. Shi et al. [5] presented a camera that can not only see but also perform recognition called Smart Camera. The proposed camera system recognizes simple hand gestures. The camera was built using a single chip of FPGA as processing device. The PGC system has ability to read data from multiple image sensors and provide it to processing core in arranged formate. The PGC bus management allows the processing core to perform computation (recognition, transformation, etc) on run-time video at higher frame rates. 16-bit or 32-bit processing cores can be used to perform complex algorithms.

To solve the on-chip bus bandwidth bottleneck, several types of high-performance on-chip buses have been proposed. The multi-layer AHB (ML-AHB)

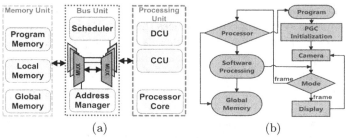

Fig. 1. PGC : (a) Internal Structure (b) Flowchart

bus-matrix proposed by ARM [6] has been used in may SoC designs due to its simplicity, the good architecture and low power. The ML-AHB bus-matrix interconnection scheme provides parallel access paths between multiple masters and slaves in a system. Hussain et al. [7,8,9,10] discussed the architecture of a memory controller and its implementation on a Xilinx Virtex-5 in order to establish a fast communication with the host. The PLB crossbar switch (CBS) from IBM [11] allows communication between masters on one PLB and slaves on the other. The CBS supports concurrent data transfers on multiple PLB buses along with a prioritization method to hold multiple requests to a generic slave port. Like other on-chip Bus Units, AHB (ML-AHB) and PLB (CBS) use a master core that manages on-chip bus transactions. The PGC controls processing units and manages data transfer between them without support of complex bus-matrix and processor core. This reduces request/grant time and bus arbitration time. Moreover, the support for strided and scatter/gather data transfers allows the PGC system to manage complex data transactions.

3   PGC Graphics System Specification

In this section, we describe the specification of PGC system and design its architecture. The section is further divided into four subsections: *Overview of PGC System*, the *Processing Units*, the *Memory Unit* and the *Bus Unit*.

3.1   Overview of PGC System

The PGC graphics system architecture is pipelined from the sensor chip over the wire to the processing chip. The PGC inner architecture is shown in Figure 1(a), which shows the interconnection with the processing units and memory. The system uses a combined hardware/software solution that includes hardware accelerators and a RISC processor core. The camera control unit (CCU) and display control unit (DCU) are custom hardware accelerators and control the camera sensor and the display unit respectively. The *Local Memory* holds the CCU/DCU data for basic image/video processing using the *Processor Core*. To store high resolution images the *Global Memory* is integrated. The *Program Memory* is used to hold CCU/DCU program description and data transfer information. Depending upon the data transfer the *Address Manager* takes single or

Table 1. Graphics System: Use Case, Mode of Operations

Use Case	Processing	Pixel $_{Depth}$	Resolution	frame/sec (fps)
Video Mode				
Single-Camera Video	With/Without	24-bit	VGA = 640×480	variable up to 150
Dual-Camera Video	With	24-bit	VGA = 640×480	variable
Snapshot Mode	With/Without	24-bit	QSXGA = 2560×2048	1

multiple instructions from *Program Memory* and schedules the data movement for *CCU* and *DCU*. The PGC *Scheduler* handles the concurrent bus request by the CCU and DCU and rearranges multiple bus access requests and arbitrates data transfer without creating bus contention.

We define two use cases of graphic system (shown in Table 1); the *Video Mode* and the *Snapshot Mode*. The *processing* step is used to perform filtering, compression, transformation, etc. on the input image. Each use case has two variants: with-processing and without-processing. The resolution of *Video Mode* is selected to fit in *Local Memory* of the target device. In our current design, the *Video Mode* supports up to 640×480 image resolution. It reads multiple frames (images) per second (*fps*) from the camera sensor and transfers them to display unit. The *Video Mode* is further divided into two modes. The *Single-Camera Video* uses a single image sensor and *Dual-Camera Video* supports two image sensors. The *Snapshot Mode* of operation takes a still image from the image sensor, performs software processing if required and writes to *Global Memory*. The *Snapshot Mode* supports a maximum resolution of 2560×2048 with 24-bit pixels (16 Mega colors) depth.

The working operation of the PGC system is shown in Figure 1(b). The program memory of PGC is initialized during programming-time. The program memory holds the instructions of CCU/DCU program registers and data transfer. During initialization, the PGC programs the CCU and DCU according to the different use cases (*Video Mode* or *Snapshot Mode*).

3.2 Processing Unit

The PGC supports two types of cores: the *Application Specific Accelerator Core* and the *RISC Core*.

Application Specific Accelerator Core: Camera Control Unit (*CCU*) and Display Control Unit (*DCU*) *Application Specific Accelerator Cores* are used in the design to control camera and display units respectively. The *CCU* grabs raw data from Image sensor, processes it and transfers it to the system via on-chip bus. The major function blocks of *CCU* are Camera Interface Front-End, Image Signal Processor, Color processing, Scaling, Compression, and Bus controller. Each *CCU* block has memory mapped internal registers that can be initialized and programmed by the processor core. The *DCU* is used to control and display image data on LCD panel. The *DCU* supports LCD 16bpp up to 24bpp colors and user defined resolution from VGA to QSXGA. Programming is done by register read/write transactions using a slave interface. The *DCU* consumes 425 registers and 312 LUTs on a V5-Lx110T FPGA device.

RISC Core: A low power and light weight RISC processor core is used to provide programmability, flexibility and software data processing. The processing core changes the features by programming the PGC system using a software API. The API can be used to correct design errors, update the system to a new graphic standard and add more features to the graphics system. The proposed processor core has 16-bit data bus, 16-general purpose registers, custom instruction set, non-pipelined Load/Store access, hardwired control unit, 64KBytes address space 16 interrupts and memory mapped I/O. 1KBytes of memory is allocated for display and camera control units using chip select. On a V5-Lx110T FPGA device, the core uses 481 registers, 1496 LUTs and 4 Brams.

3.3   Memory Unit

The PGC graphics system memory [12] is organized into two sections: the *Local Memory* and the *Global Memory*.

Local Memory: The *Local Memory* is used to support run-time video processing. It also reduces wire delay, data access latency and provide parallel read/write accesses to the processing core. The memory is shared between processor, CCU and DCU. During *Video Mode*, two frames buffers are required: one for processing and other for displaying. Each VGA frame has 900KBytes of size therefore 2MBytes of *Local Memory* are reserved. To save the image in *Snapshot Mode* we use *Global Memory*.

Global Memory: The slowest type of memory in the graphics system is *Global Memory* and is accessible by the whole system. The *Global Memory* has SDRAM, SD/SDHC cards, etc. interfaces to read/write data. Even though the PGC system has an efficient way of accessing *Global Memory* that best utilizes the bandwidth, it still has substantially higher latency with respect to the *Local Memory*.

3.4   Bus Unit

Two buses are used in the graphics system which are the *Graphics Bus* and the *System Bus*. The *Graphics Bus* is used for internal communication between the processing units and *Local Memory*. The *System Bus* is used to communicate with external peripherals such as global memories. Both buses can operate in parallel. This section is further divided into three subsections: *Bus Specification*, *Bus Control Unit* and *Bus Interconnect Network*.

3.4.1   Bus Specification

It is important to calculate the required data-rate for each *use case* before selecting and configuring the *Bus Unit*. This section is further divided into three subsections: *Graphics Bus Specification*, *System Bus Specification* and *Bus Usage*.

Graphics Bus Specification: The clock of the camera and display is directly synchronized with the output data hence define the bandwidth of *Graphics Bus*. The actual theoretical data rate of the *Graphics Bus* (GBB) is the total bandwidth of master sources (shown in Figure 2(a)). For example, during *Video Mode*

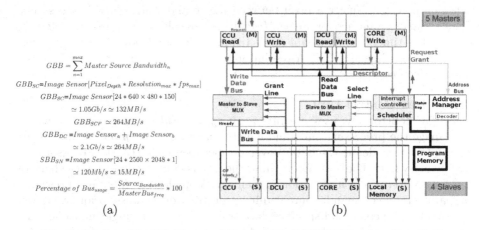

$$GBB = \sum_{n=1}^{max} Master\ Source\ Bandwidth_n$$

$$GBB_{SC} = Image\ Sensor[Pixel_{Depth} * Resolution_{max} * fps_{max}]$$

$$GBB_{SC} = Image\ Sensor[24 * 640 \times 480 * 150]$$

$$\simeq 1.05Gb/s \simeq 132MB/s$$

$$GBB_{SCP} \simeq 264MB/s$$

$$GBB_{DC} = Image\ Sensor_a + Image\ Sensor_b$$

$$\simeq 2.1Gb/s \simeq 264MB/s$$

$$SBB_{SN} = Image\ Sensor[24 * 2560 \times 2048 * 1]$$

$$\simeq 120Mb/s \simeq 15MB/s$$

$$Percentage\ of\ Bus_{usage} = \frac{Source_{Bandwidth}}{Master Bus_{freq}} * 100$$

(a)   (b)

Fig. 2. (a) Graphics Bus Required Bandwidth (b) PGC Graphics Bus Unit

(without-processing) the PGC reads streaming data from CCU and writes directly to DCU. For *Video Mode* with-processing, the PGC takes video frames from CCU, writes them to *Local Memory* for processing and then transfers the processed frames to DCU. In this case the PGC operates CCU and DCU in parallel, therefore the bandwidth of the *Graphics Bus* is the sum of CCU and DCU data-rates. For dual camera, the PGC takes two video frames and transfers them to CCU. The required *Graphics Bus* bandwidth (shown in Figure 2(a)) with single camera without processing and with processing is given by the formula GBB$_{SC}$ and GBB$_{SCP}$ respectively. Figure 2(a) also presents the bandwidth of dual camera GBB$_{DC}$. The *Local Memory* provides high bandwidth and has 2 cycles of latency for an individual transfer. The *Bus Latency* contains the on-chip/off-chip memories read/write and on-chip bus delays. The *Graphics Bus* manages multiple read/write access transactions in a single transfer and pipelines the multiple stream, thus reducing the overhead of *Local Memory*$_{Latency}$ and improving the bus performance. After calculating bus bandwidth and considering the different use cases we selected a bus with 100 Mhz of clock speed and 32 bit-width.

System Bus Specification: The *System Bus* manages data transfers during *Snapshot Mode*. The PGC reads data from image sensor and writes it to *Global Memory*. The bandwidth requirements of *System Bus* for *Snapshot Mode* are given by the Formula (SBB$_{SN}$) (shown in Figure 2(a)).

Bus Usage: The PGC *Graphics Bus* has 400 MB/s of bandwidth, so it takes 10 nsec to transfer 1 pixel (32bit). For example, the graphics bandwidth for video of 30 *fps* (without-processing) is 9 Mega pixels per second. This means that given the formula *Percentage of Bus*$_{usage}$ (shown in Figure 2(a)) each pixel takes 111 nsec and occupies *Graphics Bus* for 9% of its time.

For *Video Mode* with-processing, the *Graphics Bus* takes 111 nsec to transfer one pixel from CCU to *Local Memory*, and it takes the same time to transfer it to DCU. Similarly *Video Mode* needs 18 Mega pixels of bus bandwidth, that takes 56 nsec to transfer a pixel between image and display accelerators. The display camera interface for *Video Mode* utilizes graphics for approximately 14% of total bus time. The *Snapshot Mode* requires bus bandwidth of 5 Mega pixels to transfer one image (QSXGA resolution without-processing) from CCU to the *Global Memory*.

3.4.2   Bus Control Unit

The PGC control unit uses *program memory, scheduler* and *address manager*, to manage the processing units and memory units. The *program memory* holds *descriptors* that define the data movement between CCU/DCU, processor core and memory unit. The *descriptors* allow the programmer to describe the shape of memory patterns and its location in memory. A single *descriptor* is represented by parameters: command, source address, destination address, priority, stream and stride. The command specifies data transfers between single/multiple masters and single/multiple slaves. The address parameters also specify the master and slave cores. The priority describes the selection and execution criteria of data transfer by a master core. It also defines the order in which memory accesses are entitled to be processed. Stream defines the number of pixels to be transferred. Stride indicates the distance between two consecutive memory addresses of a stream. PGC manages a complex data transfer protocol using single or multiple *descriptors*. Each *descriptor* transfers a strided burst, by using multiple *descriptors* the PGC transfers more complex data. C/C++ function calls are provided to define a complex pattern in software.

The PGC bus *scheduler* along with *address manager* (shown in Figure 2(b)) arrange requests coming from single or multi-bus masters and arbitrate master processing units. A *bus master* provides address and control information to initiate read and write operations. A *bus slave* responds to a transfer that is initiated by the masters core. The *address manager* holds the address and control information of *bus slaves*. The *scheduler*'s *interrupt controller* reads requests from master cores and routes them to the slave. The *address manager*'s *decoder* determines for which slave a transfer is destined for. The PGC bus holds two types of status registers: the source status and the slave status registers. The status registers indicate the state of each master and slave, such as request, ready, busy and grant. The *scheduler* and *address manager* administer the status register of master and slave cores respectively. The PGC *scheduler* emphasizes on priority and incoming requests of the master core. At compile-time a number of priority levels are configured for each data transfer. At run-time the *scheduler* picks a master core to transfer data, only if it is ready to run and there are no higher priority data patterns that are ready. If same priorities are assigned for more than one data pattern, the PGC scheduler executes them in first-in first-out (FIFO) order.

At run-time, a master core generates a request, the *interrupt controller* reads the request and updates its status registers. The *scheduler* reads data transfer information of the master and slave cores from program memory and transfer slave core information to *address manager*. The PGC *address manager* decodes the address of each transfer and provides a select signal for the slave that is involved in the transfer and provides a control signal to the multiplexers. A single master-to-slave multiplexer (MUX) is controlled by the scheduler. The master-to-slave MUX multiplexes the write data bus and allocate data bus for a single master after getting the response signal from the slave-to-master MUX. A slave-to-master MUX multiplexes the read data bus and response signals from the slaves to the master. Multiple master-to-slave and slave-to-master multiplexers can be added to implement a multi-layer Bus Unit. The PGC Bus Unit can be programmed up to eight layer bus which requires eight pairs of master-to-slave and slave-to-master multiplexers.

3.4.3 Bus Interconnect

To connect the graphics components together, a bus interconnection is described (shown in Figure 2(b)). We select a double layer Bus Interconnect (System Bus and Graphics Bus) for the design due to its design simplicity and low power consumption. Each layer is controlled by a pair of master-to-slave and slave-to-master multiplexers. The PGC scheduler and address manager control the pairs of multiplexers. The PGC Bus Interconnects can be configured according to the requirements of hardware accelerator, master and slave ports. The System Bus has a simple design that uses a single master and slave port. The bus is used to read/write high resolution image to global memory.

The Graphics Bus is employed to provide high speed link between the CCU, DCU, processor and Local Memory components. Current PGC Graphics Bus has 5 Masters and 4 Slaves therefore the Bus Unit is configured accordingly. The proposed Bus Unit provides standard communication protocol and implements the features required for high-performance.

4 Experimental Framework

In this section, we describe and evaluate the PGC based graphics system. In order to evaluate the performance of the PGC system, the results are compared with a generic graphics system managed by the MicroBlaze processor. The Xilinx Integrated Software Environment and Xilinx Platform Studio are used to design the graphic systems. The power analysis is done by Xilinx Power Estimator (XPE). A Xilinx ML505 [13] development board is used to test the systems. For the implementation of graphics system the THDB-D5M Camera and the TRDB-LTM LCD Touch Panel by Terasic have been chosen. This section is divided into two subsections: the MicroBlaze based Graphics System and the PGC based Graphics System.

4.1 MicroBlaze Based Graphics System

The FPGA based MicroBlaze system is proposed (Figure 3 (a)) to operate graphics system. The design (without CCU & DCU) uses 9547 flip-flops, 11643 LUTs and 51 BRAMs in a Xilinx V5-Lx110T device. The system architecture is further divided into the Processor Core and the Bus Unit.

The Processor Unit: Two MicroBlaze cores [14] are used in the graphics system which are the Master core and the Graphics Core. The Master core is used to program, schedule and manage the system components. The camera and display hardware scheduling and data memory management are controlled by Graphics processor. Both cores use local memory Bus (LMB) [15] to link with local-memory (FPGA BRAM) that offers single clock cycle access to the local BRAM.

The Bus Unit: In the design, a Processor Local Bus (PLB) [16] provides connection between peripheral components and microprocessors. The PLB has 32 bit-width and is connected to a bus control unit, a watchdog timer, separate address read/write data path units, and an optional DCR (Device Control Register) slave interface that provides access to a bus error status registers. Bus is configured for single master (MicroBlaze) and multi slaves. The PLB provides maximum of 400 MBytes of bandwidth while operating at 100Mhz and 32-bit width, with byte enables to write byte and half-word data.

4.2   PGC Based Graphics System

The PGC based graphics system is shown in Figure 3(b) having components similar to the MicroBlaze based graphic system. The implementation details of PGC based graphics system are addressed in Section 3. The main difference between PGC and MicroBlaze based system is that PGC system takes instructions during initialize-time and at run-time it manages and schedules data transfer without the support of the processor. The processor core and *System Bus* remain free for the use cases which do not involve processing. The design (without CCU and DCU) uses 5547 flip-flops, 6643 LUTs and 35 BRAMs in a Xilinx V5-Lx110T device.

5   Results and Discussion

This section analyzes the results of different experiments conducted on the different graphic systems. The experiments are classified into four subsections: *Bus Performance, Snapshot Mode Performance, Applications Performance* and *Area & Power.*

5.1   Bus Performance

To measure the bus performance, the graphic systems are executed on *Video Mode* (without-processing) having fixed resolution (640×480) and variable frame

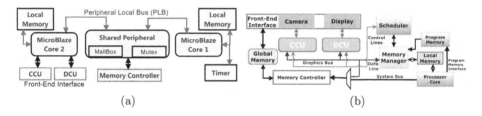

(a)   (b)

Fig. 3. Graphics System: (a) MicroBlaze Core System (b) PGC System

rate (*frame per second - fps*). The image sensor is programmed to transfer variable frames (*fps*) and each frame has VGA quality. Inside DCU we integrated a controller that detects video frame rate, the speed at which frames are coming. A hardware timer is added to the on-chip bus controller that measures clocks used to transfer frames between master to slave peripherals. This section discusses results for *Single-Camera Bus Bandwidth* and *Multi-Camera Bus Bandwidth*.

5.1.1   Single-Camera Bus Bandwidth

In this section, we compare the bus performance of graphic systems while using single image and display units. Figure 4 shows the on-chip data bus transfer speed of PGC and Microblaze systems for different video frame rates. A single THDB-D5M image sensor is used. It can operate up to 150 *fps* with VGA resolution. The X-axis presents video of different *fps*. The Y-axis shows measured bandwidth for different videos frame rates. To measure the bandwidth we calculate the time to transfer video from CCU to DCU. Theoretically the PLB and the graphic bus support video of VGA quality more than 100 *fps*. In practice there are on-chip bus arbitration and request grant time delays. By using the PGC system, the results show that the system manages video for higher *fps*. While the MicroBlaze based graphic system supports video up to 40 *fps*, with higher *fps* the video starts flicking. The system uses a separate processor core that manages the data movement of CCU and DCU. The PGC allows graphics system to operate *Video Mode* up to 85 *fps*. The PGC resides in on-chip bus unit and has direct interconnection with CCU and DCU. The PGC *control unit* controls the CCU and DCU without the intervention of processor core which reduces the master/slave request/grant time.

5.1.2   Multi-camera Bus Bandwidth

A multi-camera graphics system can be used for 3D-graphics using geometric transformation and projection plane [17]. In this section, two THDB-D5M image sensors are used that generate two separate, simultaneous video streams and apply *Alpha blending* application that evaluate the performance of system. Each camera is operating at VGA color resolution. The video of dual image sensors is

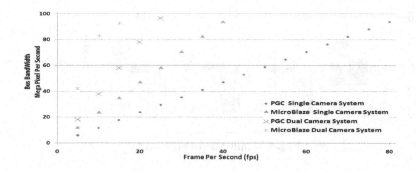

Fig. 4. Single and Dual Camera Systems: Bandwidth For Different Frame Rate

combined into a single stream, processed by graphics core and then displayed. The key issue of the dual-camera system is receiving the images synchronously, in the right format and on the right bus. The graphic system sends the configuration data to both image sensors and ensure that they are properly configured and synchronized. Once both sensors are set up and synchronized, both sensors begin to transmit image data. The graphic system looks for the appropriate control characters so it recognizes the start of the frame and start of line for each sensor. The PGC system performs it by looking for a control character and sequence of sensors commands. *Alpha blending* is applied to give a translucent effect to the incoming video stream. The application blends the color value of the consecutive pixels of image sensors of the same position. This blending is done according to the alpha value associated with the pixel. The alpha value represents the capacity of the given pixel. After blending, the result color value is updated to the frame buffer of the DCU. Results show (Figure 4) that PGC system handles dual camera system and support system up to 30 fps. The MicroBlaze based dual-camera graphics system supports videos only up to 15 *fps*. The PGC on-chip *scheduler* and *decoder* update multi-camera information in status register. This allows both cameras to synchronize without using extra clocks.

5.2   Snapshot Mode Performance

In this section the performance is measured by executing PGC and MicroBlaze systems in *Snapshot Mode*. During *Snapshot Mode* the system reads one still image of QSXGA resolution from CCU using *Graphics Bus* and writes it to *Global Memory* using *System Bus*. The MicroBlaze based system and PGC take 22.17M and 7.07M clocks respectively to transfer an image. The *Snapshot Mode* results show that the PGC system achieves 3.1x of speed compared to MicroBlaze based system. The PGC directly controls the *Graphics Bus, System Bus, CCU* and *Global Memory*, therefore it takes less clocks to read data from *CCU* to synchronize different units, transfer data from *Graphics Bus* to *System Bus* and write data to *Global Memory*. The MicroBlaze based system uses a separate bus controller that controls bus system and a DMA controller that transfers data from *CCU* to *Global Memory*.

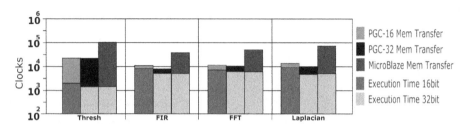

Fig. 5. Application Performance

5.3   Applications Performance

In this section we execute some application kernels that perform image processing. The image is saved in *Global Memory* (SDRAM), the processor core reads the 4KBytes image, performs computation and then writes it back to *Global Memory*. To achieve low power the application kernels are executed by the 16-bit core on PGC system. Alternatively, a 32-bit MicroBlaze core is also used with PGC system to get higher performance. Figure 5 shows time (clock cycles) to process application kernels. The X and Y axis represent application kernels and number of clock cycles, respectively. The Y-axis has logarithmic scale. Each bar represents the application kernel's execution time with 16/32 bit cores and memory access time. By using the PGC system with 16-bit and 32-bit cores, the results show that thresholding (Thresh) applications achieve 4.6x and 4.7x of speedup respectively over the MicroBlaze graphics system. This application kernel requires single pixel element and very few operations, therefore it achieves almost the same performance on 16-bit and 32-bit cores. The FIR application has streaming data access pattern and perform multiplication and addition. The PGC 16-bit and 32-bit cores achieve 3.4x and 4.7x of speedup respectively. The FFT application kernel reads a 1D block of data, perform complex computation and writes it back to *Global Memory*. This application achieves 4.4x and 4.8 of speedup. The Laplacian application processes over 2D block of data and achieve 5.2x and 7.4x of speedup. The PGC places access patterns on *program memory* at program-time and are programmed in such a way that few operations are required for generating addresses at run-time. The MicroBlaze based system uses multiple load/store or DMA calls to access complex patterns. The speedups are possible because PGC is able to manage data transfers with a single *descriptor*. At run-time, PGC takes *descriptor* from *program memory* and manages them, whereas the baseline system is dependent on the processor core that feeds data transfer instructions. The stand-alone working operation of PGC removes the overhead of processor/memory system request/grant delay.

5.4   Power

In comparison with on-chip power in a Xilinx V5-Lx110T device, the Microblaze based system dissipates 3.45 watts and the PGC system 2.7 watts. Results show that PGC system consumes 30% fewer slices than the Microblaze system. While comparing on-chip power of Microblaze graphics system with the PGC, results show that PGC system consumes 22% of less on-chip power.

6   Conclusion

With the increase of image resolution the graphics system demands a low power, low cost and high performance architecture. In this paper we have suggested a Programmable Graphics Controller (PGC) for low cost and low power graphics system. The system takes high resolution images and supports video at higher frame rate without the support of a processor. The PGC system provides strided, scatter/gather and tiled access pattern that eliminates the overhead of arranging and gathering address/data. In the future, we plan to execute some complex and high performance image processing applications which include image recognition, image transform and image compression.

Acknowledgments. We thankfully acknowledge the support of Microsoft Research though the BSC-Microsoft Research Centre, the European Commission through the HiPEAC-3 Network of Excellence, the Spanish Ministry of Education (TIN2007-60625 and CSD2007-00050), the Generalitat de Catalunya (2009-SGR-980) and Unal Center of Education Research and Development.

References

1. Rowe, A., et al.: Cmucam3: an open programmable embedded vision sensor. In: International Conferences on Intelligent Robots and Systems (2007)
2. Petouris, M., et al.: An fpga-based digital camera system controlled from an lcd touch panel. In: International Symposium on Signals, Circuits and Systems, ISSCS (2009)
3. Murphy, C., et al.: Low-cost stereo vision on an fpga. In: 15th Annual IEEE Symposium on Field-Programmable Custom Computing Machines, FCCM (2007)
4. Lewis, M.A., et al.: A multi-camera system for bioluminescence tomography in preclinical oncology research. Diagnostics (2013)
5. Shi, Y., Tsui, T.: An FPGA-based smart camera for gesture recognition in HCI applications. In: Yagi, Y., Kang, S.B., Kweon, I.S., Zha, H. (eds.) ACCV 2007, Part I. LNCS, vol. 4843, pp. 718–727. Springer, Heidelberg (2007)
6. AMBA 4 AXI (2013), http://infocenter.arm.com/help/index.jsp?topic=/com.arm.doc.ihi0022e/index.html
7. Tassadaq, H., et al.: Recongurable memory controller with programmable pattern support. In: 5th HiPEAC Workshop on Reconfigurable Computing, WRC (2007)
8. Tassadaq, H., et al.: PPMC: A Programmable Pattern based Memory Controller. In: 8th International Symposium on Applied Reconfigurable Computing, ARC (2012)
9. Tassadaq, H., et al.: PPMC: Hardware Scheduling and Memory Management support for Multi Hardware Accelerators. In: 22nd International Conference on Field Programmable Logic and Applications, FPL (2012)
10. Tassadaq, H., et al.: APMC: Advanced Pattern based Memory Controller. In: 22nd ACM/SIGDA International Symposium on Field-Programmable Gate Arrays, FPGA (2014)
11. IBM CoreConnect. PLB Crossbar Arbiter Core (2001)
12. Tassadaq, H., et al.: Implementation of a reverse time migration kernel using the hce high level synthesis tool. In: International Conference on Field-Programmable Technology, FPT (2011)
13. Xilinx University Program XUPV5-LX110T Development System, http://www.xilinx.com/univ/xupv5-lx110t.htm
14. Embedded Development Kit EDK 10.1i. MicroBlaze Processor Reference Guide
15. Xilinx LogiCORE IP. Local Memory Bus (LMB) (December 2009)
16. Embedded Development KitEDK 10.1i. MicroBlaze Processor Reference Guide
17. Hartley, R., et al.: Multiple view geometry in computer vision, vol. 2. Cambridge Univ. Press (2000)

Evaluating High-Level Program Invariants Using Reconfigurable Hardware*

Joonseok Park[1] and Pedro C. Diniz[2]

[1] Computer and Information Engineering
Inha University, Incheon, Rep. South Korea
joonseok@inha.ac.kr
[2] Univ. of Southern California / Information Sciences Institute
Marina del Rey, CA, USA
pedro@isi.edu

Abstract. There is an increasing concern about transient errors in deep sub-micron processor architectures. Software-only error detection approaches that exploit program invariants for silent error detection incur large execution overheads and are unreliable as state can be corrupted after invariant check points. In this paper we explore the use of configurable hardware structures for the continuous evaluation of high-level program invariants at the assembly-level. We evaluate the resource requirements and performance of the proposed hardware structures on a contemporary reconfigurable hardware device. The results, for a small set of kernels codes, reveal that these hardware structures require a very small number of resources and are fairly insensitive to the complexity of the invariants thus making the proposed hardware approach an attractive alternative to software-only invariant checking by integrating them in traditional processor architectures.

1 Introduction

The sheer scale of multicore systems and their need to cooperatively perform aggregate large scale computations expose their brittleness to transient failures. While much progress has been done in protecting regular structures such as storage with either pairing techniques for the correction of single memory bit errors and dual error detection (SECDED) most internal processor structures (logic and even register file) are largely unprotected. Silent data corruption (SDC) in register files and L1 data caches (deemed too expensive to protected via current storage protection practices) are notoriously nefarious as a single even transient error in these structure will quickly "spread" to cache memories and registers.

In this paper we explore an alternative approach that evaluates program invariants using configurable hardware structures and thus avoids the execution

* Supported in part by the National Science Foundation under Award CCF 1255949 and by the Semiconductor Research Corp. under contract 2013-TJ-2425. This work was also partly supported by Basic Science Research Program by the National Research Foundation of Korea funded by the Ministry of Education (2011-0024909).

D. Goehringer et al. (Eds.): ARC 2014, LNCS 8405, pp. 121–132, 2014.
© Springer International Publishing Switzerland 2014

penalties of software-only invariant checking. The proposed approach has the benefit of constant monitoring of the values of the variables involved in an invariant, thus preventing further state corruption as soon as an error is detected. These benefits, however, come at the added cost of additional hardware for invariant evaluation, but more importantly, they require the accurate mapping of high-level program variables to hardware registers and the tracking of this mapping at run-time. This paper thus makes the following specific contributions:

1. Describes an algorithm for the mapping of high-level program invariants to assembly-level invariants that can be directly evaluated in hardware. This algorithm can be used in a compiler to map program invariants to hardware.
2. Describes the architecture of configurable hardware structures for the evaluation of such invariants.
3. Evaluates the implementation complexity and expected performance of the proposed hardware structures for a small set of kernel codes.

The experimental results reveal that the proposed hardware structures when mapped to contemporary Field-Programmable Gate Arrays (FPGAs) devices require a very small number of resources. Furthermore, the hardware structures are fairly insensitive to the number of clauses in the explored program invariants. Both these features, make the proposed structures an attractive alternative to software-only invariant checking, by their integration with traditional processor architectures in the form of reconfigurable logic.

The remainder of this paper is structured as follows. The next section provides a simple example illustrating the use of invariants in detecting abnormal computation behavior. Section 3 describes how to map high-level program invariants to their corresponding assembly-level representation that can be evaluated in custom hardware. Section 4 presents experimental results for a set of kernel codes and section 5 describes related work. Finally, we conclude in section 6.

2   Using Invariants for Silent Error Detection

We now present an example of the use of invariants for the detection of silent errors in a processor's logic and internal storage. As this example illustrates the implementation of this approach requires an interaction between program analyses and compiler-level register allocation for tracking the values of high-level variables. We focus on the invariants associated with the program variable i commonly used in the definition of for loop constructs in a language such as C. At a high level, a compiler, or in its absence a programmer, can derive a correctness invariant that would assert the variable i can never assume a value larger than a specific constant value and can never be negative.[1]

To evaluate such an invariant in hardware one must track which hardware registers will hold and at what points of the execution, the values of i. The

---

[1] While the presence of transient errors would not ensure that i would assume monotonic behavior, it would at least detect clearly abnormal execution behaviors.

key knowledge for this mapping can be captured the computation's Control-Flow-Graph (CFG) using Static Single-Assignment (SSA) form which explicit represents the flow of values between variables as illustrated in figure 1(a). The example highlights the values of the loop control variable, i, across the execution of blocks $block_0$ through $block_4$. Figure 1(b) depicts the same CFG after a register allocation phase where ϕ nodes of the SSA representation have been instantiated with real registers in this example using the MIPS $t8 and $t9 registers and taking into account the live ranges of each of the variables names.

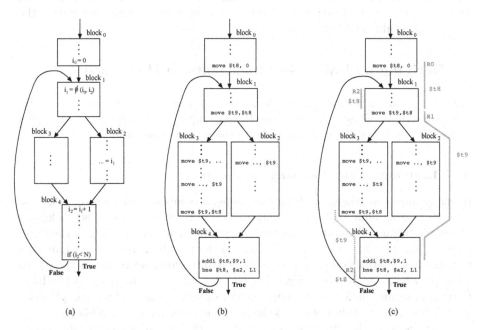

(a)   (b)   (c)

Fig. 1. Example: (a) CFG representation. (b) SSA representation. (c) Tracing of values for variable i and the associated CFG sections and registers.

Given this assembly-level representation there are three main observations about tracking of the value of the i variable:

1. Depending on the aggressiveness of the compiler optimizations the loop control variable might not even be mapped to any field of the enclosing procedure activation record. As such, at run-time there are variables that might not be mapped to virtual address.
2. A variable might be mapped to distinct live ranges as well as distinct registers. In this particular example one of i's live ranges is mapped to the $t8 register whereas another is mapped to the $t9 register.
3. Values of the register $t9 in $block_3$ are not related to the variable i.

In order to track and use the values of the variable i at run-time an implementation must be able to detect the start and the end of each of the traces of live ranges of the variables to validate output of a hardware logic block that used the value of i for the evaluation of an invariant.

Figure 1(c) depicts the same CFG as Figure 1(b) but indicating which CFG section or regions (labelled R0 through R2) and which register the implementation needs to trace the value of, to capture the run-time value associated with the variable i. Notice that in some CFG sections as is the case of the $block_3$ no values are associated with i and the checking of the values of registers \$t8 and \$t9 can be effectively postponed to the beginning of $block_4$ thus eliminating the need for an additional tracing region.

3   Deriving and Mapping Invariants to Hardware

We focus on the derivation of simple invariants from a selected set of programming constructs. These invariants can be automatically derived using tools such as Houdini [1], or directly by relying on programmer annotations.

3.1   Loop and Array Indexing Invariants

In many loop constructs, such as `for` loops, a compiler can perform symbolic analysis to determine that the loop upper bound is constant (although unknown at compiler time). This is the case with common `for` loop constructs of the form: `for(i = 0; i < n; i++){ ... }` where the loop body includes no assignments to variable n. Here a compiler can safely derive the logic invariant (i >= 0) && (i < n) whenever the control reaches the statements in the body of the loop. Furthermore, and under the assumption of no assignments to i[2] the compiler can even derive hardware that observes the monotonic behavior of i. While out of the scope of the work described in this paper, the derivation of more sophisticated invariants and the corresponding hardware structures is clearly within reach of the techniques and approach presented here.

Associated with loop constructs, programmers commonly use array variables with statically known indexing bounds. Also, when relying on common dynamic memory allocation routines such as `malloc` once allocated the sizes of these arrays often remain unchanged throughout the execution. Even if allocated dynamically a compiler can generate code that tracks the size of arrays saving that information to be used at run-time for array indexing bounds checking. Irrespective of the allocation scheme, the array bounds checking[3] can be captured by an invariant with the same structure as the loop invariant described above.

---

[2] A simple condition that compilers performing loop induction variable recognition and strength reduction can check.

[3] Software array bounds checking has been the subject of intense research, in particular the minimization of the overhead it incurs (as it relies on additional instructions). The approach presented here can in fact eliminate this overhead.

3.2   Mapping Invariants to Assembly: SSA and Live Ranges

The mapping of high-level program invariants to the assembly instructions that manipulate the corresponding values, requires knowledge about which register(s) will hold the values of which program variables and when, *i.e.* when in the execution of the code is this binding of variables to registers valid. In this context a compiler must capture the following information:

- Live Range Start Address: Relative PC address offset from the beginning of the procedure where the invariant needs to begin holding.
- Live Range End Address: Relative PC address offset from the beginning of the procedure where the invariant still needs to hold.
- Mapped Register that holds the value of the variable v.
- Invariant to be evaluated possibly making explicit reference to other registers (corresponding to other high-level variables) or symbolic constants.

The issue with the starting and ending PC address offsets relates to the fact that it is possible for two or more live ranges of a given variable to overlap as at a control-flow joint-point a variable can be mapped to the same register while originating from multiple locations within a procedure.[4] As the example in section 2 illustrates, the mapping of a variable values to registers is directly (and almost trivially) derived from the SSA representation after register allocation.

A subtle but important consequence of the potential assignment of different registers to the same high-level program variable and of the fact that the same invariant might be *splitted* across branches of a given web (possibly even disjoint) is that a single high-level invariant may have to be cast as the union of invariants whose evaluation logic although the same, is active in distinct CFG regions and possible using different registers. This is the illustrative case of the invariant illustrated in figure 1.

3.3   Translation to Hardware

The translation of invariants to hardware follows a simple mapping of its logic clauses using common numerical operations + or − and the trivial translation to hardware of bit-level operations and, or and not. Special attention is given to minimization or even elimination of arithmetic operations as they can lead to slower hardware implementations. For example the predicate (i < 16) && (i > 0) can be implemented by logic that checks that all upper 28 bits of a $32 - bit$ integer representation are 0 and in its lower 4 bits at least one bit is non-zero. The figure 2(a) below depicts the implementation of this predicate that does not require any subtraction operator.

In other cases, however, as for instance with the predicate (i < j) the use of a subtractor is required as shown in figure 2(b). In this case, the compiler can, nevertheless combine the knowledge that both i and j values are less than a specific

---

[4] In the compiler parlance multiple live-ranges form a *web* itself associated with a single register which can have multiple starting and ending points.

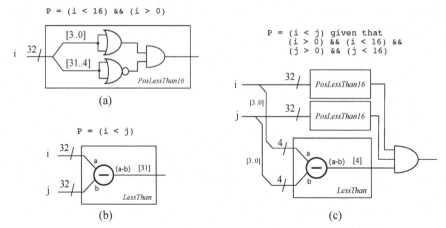

Fig. 2. Example of hardware implementation Predicates: Example of predicate (i > 0) && (i < 16) without subtraction operation (a); Example of predicate (i < j) with generic subtraction operator; Exploiting values ranges of both i and j (c)

constant to fold that information in the predicate evaluation and thus reduce the size of the subtractor circuit used. The combined example in figure 2(c) shows the use of the additional clauses (i < 16) and (j < 16) commonly resulting from the use of the loop control variables i and j in nested loops.

3.4 System Architecture and Invariant Checker Circuit

At a high-level we envision an architecture where a configurable *Invariant Checker* circuit is coupled to a processor execution pipeline via the register file wherefrom the values used to evaluate the invariant clauses are drawn (as depicted in figure 3(a)). In this illustrative architecture the *Invariant Checker* is composed a single program invariant logic block, itself structured as three independent logic sub-blocks that evaluate its predicates or clauses.

The evaluation of an invariant is activated by recognizing the CFG region of interest (bounded by the live ranges' start/end PC offset values). If the program's execution moves into the CFG region of interest, the Invariant Logic block will continuously track the corresponding clauses via the values of the hardware registers defined by the mapping of high-level program variables to assembly. If a violation of an invariant is detected (corresponding to one or more of its clauses evaluating to **false**) the hardware records the value of the program counter register (PC). Other state of interest, such as the contents of ancillary registers, of the main processor can obviously also be recorded.

3.5 Reconfigurable Invariant Logic Block

The base architecture of an Invariant Logic block, depicted in figure 3(b), is organized into three main blocks, namely the *FSM* (and its address registers), one or more *Clause Logic* blocks and as *Register Selector* block as described next.

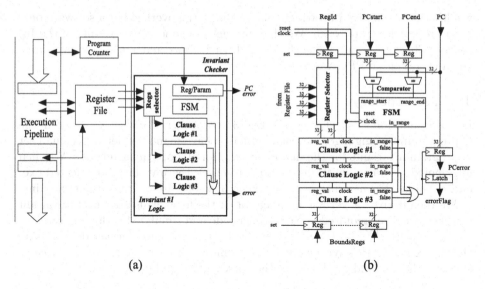

(a)   (b)

Fig. 3. Overall system architecture with an Invariant Checker circuit for a single program invariant with 3 logic clauses (a); Architecture of an Invariant Logic block (b)

- **Register Selector**: This block selects which registers should have their values tested against the clause logic blocks.
- **FSM**: This finite-state-machine (FSM) block detects the starting address value and the ending address value corresponding to a CFG region where an invariant (and its clauses) should be evaluated. By not enforcing all the addresses in a traced region to be consecutive, a FSM allows for the continued activation of invariants across control flow (jumps).
- **Clause Logic**: These blocks directly implement the logic of each of the invariants' clauses. As many clause logic blocks can refer to the same variable, and hence the same register, the reuse of logic of this block is possible.

The output of a Invariant Checker is an *error flag* alongside the PC that is recorded when a violation of an invariant is detected. While the structure of the FSM and Register Selector blocks is well defined, the structure a clause logic block is dictated by the needs in terms of inputs and operators of each invariant. In practice, however, these blocks includes a range of comparators, arithmetic operators of combined with simple boolean logic gates as illustrated in the examples in section 3.3.

4 Experiments

We now report on the evaluation the implementation complexity, in terms or hardware resources and performance, of the Invariant Checker circuit described in section 3. For this evaluation we relied on a set of high-level program invariants for three basic code kernels. After a brief description of each kernel we describe the derived invariants and evaluate the overhead of a software-only invariant checking approach. We then present implementation results of the Invariant Checker circuit for each of the kernel codes and respective invariants when targeting an FPGA device.

4.1   Methodology

In this evaluation we used a set of three (3) simple kernel codes developed in the C programming language. For each kernel we have manually derived a small set of program invariants for the main computational loops in each code.[5] We then augmented each code with instructions to check the invariants at selected execution points thus measuring the overhead of a software-only invariant checking.

We then derived a Verilog specification of the logic clauses for each Invariant Checker circuit as required in each kernel code and simulated it (for correctness) using ModelSim[TM]. Lastly, we synthesized each Invariant Checker design using the Xilinx ISE[TM]14.3 synthesis tool targeting a Virtex-6[TM]FPGA [2] device to evaluate the size and clock rate of the corresponding implementation.

4.2   Sample Set of Codes and Derived Invariants

The 3 kernels codes used in our evaluation are as follows:

- **InsertSort**: This is the basic insertion sort algorithm of $65,536$ integer values, structured as a doubly nested loop. We derived two invariants over the loops control variables requiring the iteration space to be "triangular".
- **FFT**: This kernel computes a one-dimensional in-place single-precision floating-point Fast Fourier Transform for a vector of length 16. We derived two integer invariants that bound the array access and loop iterations.[6]
- **BFS**: This kernel computes the breath-first-search number associated with the nodes of a 32-node directed graph. The algorithm uses a *worklist* algorithm over an array. We derived two invariants checking the scanning of the *worklist* array to be monotonic, *i.e.* the two index pointers move in ascending order, one always trailing the other.

4.3   Overhead of Invariants in Software

We analyzed the execution of each of the kernel codes and observed their overhead in terms of the additional source code compiler-inserted instructions as well as actual executed instructions using the Intel®VTune Amplifier XE 2013[TM] performance tool on an Intel i7-2600 machine clocked at 3.4 GHz.

The results are depicted in table 1 where v denotes a program variable (subscript distinguishes between variables and hence registers); K denotes a compile-time known constant (different from either 0 or 1) and N denotes a symbolically

---

[5] Omitting invariants in initialization sections of the codes.

[6] We deliberately ignored predicates involving floating-point values as extreme cases such as *NaN* are detected in common floating-point unit implementations.

Table 1. Synopsis of kernel invariants and software-only execution overhead

Kernel Code	Number of Invariants	Structure of Invariant	Number of Variables	Execution Overhead (%)
InsertSort	2	$[(v_0 >= 0)$ and $(v_0 < K)]$ $[(v_1 >= 1)$ and $(v_1 <= N)]$	3	9.3
FFT	1	$[(v_0 > v_1)$ or $(v_2 <= N)]$	4	0.5
BFS	1	$[(v_0 >= N)]$	2	2.04

constant value (run-time constant). Except for small or compile time known constants, all other invariant inputs require a register reference when implemented in hardware. This number of registers is also indicated in the table. Lastly, the table includes the invariant checking overhead as a percentage of additionally executed instructions with respect to the software version without any invariant checking. To reduce sample size sensitivity we profiled $10K$ executions of the **BFS** and **FFT** kernels and report the average execution overhead for 5 runs of each code and using the -O compiler flag option.

As shown, the instruction execution overhead, while not being overwhelming in two of the three codes, is also non-negligible, in particular for the **InsertSort** as the invariants are evaluated at every internal loop iteration. Moreover, this overhead figure corresponds to the entire execution of each kernel code and not just the function or loop in which the invariant instructions were inserted as the latter overhead figure is bound to be higher.

4.4   Implementation Results on an FPGA

Table 2 presents FPGA implementation results of the Invariant Checker circuits for the three kernel codes as presented in table 1. The table indicates for each implementation design the number of Flip-Flop elements (FFs); the number of Look-Up Tables (LUTs) and the maximum frequency at which each design can be safely clocked. The current set of designs are implemented using 32-bit register sizes. In these results we used the Xilinx ISE 14.3 Synthesis tool targeting a Xilinx Virtex-6 FPGA [2] (xc6vlx75t-2ff484), with *area reduction* as the design goal. As a reference, the target FPGA has $46,560$ LUTs and $93,120$ FFs. No DSP-48 blocks were used so not to bias the designs that requires arithmetic operators for the evaluation of the invariants and make the results as device-family independent as possible.

Overall, the sizes of the Invariant Checkers are very small exhibiting low numbers of LUTs (tiny portions of a large Virtex-6 FPGA). The designs clock rate, however are fairly low, in particular if an effective integration with a modern execution pipeline is desired (see discussion section below).

Table 2 also includes a **combined** design where we have merged all the invariants for the three kernels codes so as to evaluate the impact on an increasing number of clause and invariant checker circuits. As can be observed the increase of the *combined* design over the largest of the individual designs is very small,

Table 2. FPGA implementation results for Invariant Checkers (32 bits)

Kernel Code	Number of FFs	Number of LUTs	Clock Rate (MHz)
InsertSort	165	67	140.7
FFT	233	195	103.9
BFS	165	96	123.8
Combined	236	295	84.4

suggesting that the logic blocks in each Invariant Checker circuits are a small fraction of the overall design.

4.5   Discussion

Overall the results elicit the following observations. First, the structure of an Invariant Checker circuit is simple and easily parametrizable. An invariant and its clauses can be easily mapped to custom logic using a simple logic mapping scheme. Second, the Invariant Checker circuits, even for a modest set of invariants (the *combined* design has 4 logic invariant circuits) are small with respect to the overall resources capacity of a modern FPGA device. This suggests that the inclusion of a reconfigurable array (even of modest size) as a configurable region in a common processor is feasible. Lastly, however, the attained clock rate of the designs is very modest and clearly not on par with existing processor execution pipelines, in itself a major drawback, happening the effective integration of an Invariant Checker circuit with a modern processor. One possible alternative to the fine-grain FPGA-like fabric explored here, would be the use of circuit using a coarse-grain Programmable Logic Device (PLD) style of architecture. Internally, such PLD architecture would contain fixed blocks such as the FSM and Register Selector as hard macros onto which coarse-grain field-programmable components such as comparators, adders and zero/sign detectors of various bit-widths would be connected. While not as flexible as the fine grain FPGA-style of configurable logic, this PLD-style of architecture would allow better and more predictable and higher clocking performance.

5   Related Work

The growing interest of reconfigurable architectures and the expected increase in transient transistor failure rates have prompted numerous researchers to develop various techniques to ameliorate the potential impact of these failures. We focus here on intra-design techniques for transient errors that are complementary to both techniques for the detection of permanent faults (*e.g*, [3]) or techniques that rely on the re-programming of the device (either partially or totally) from a "golden" copy of the base design in what is commonly known as *scrubbing* [4].

Traditional techniques for detecting and correcting soft errors rely on hardware spatial replication and voting in the form of triple modular redundancy (TMR). TMR can detect and correct a single error at the expense of a substantial hardware and energy penalty. To mitigate the spatial impact of TMR researchers have combined hardware and software protection. As an example, Cuenca *et. al* [5] describe the hardening in a soft-microprocessor of a small subset of architecture components, such as the program counter, register file, and stack pointer thus hardening some of the components in hardware (via TMR) and others in software (via SWIFT-R [6]). Other techniques combine duplication of resources with temporal redundancy, named Duplication-with-Compare with Concurrent-Error-Detection (DWC-CED) [7].

Other approaches have focused exclusively on software-level techniques at various levels of abstraction. Reinhardt *et. al* [8], have proposed *simultaneous and redundantly threaded* (SRT) processors exploiting the multiple hardware contexts of a symmetric multiprocessor architecture for fault detection where redundant copies of a program's execution execute on independent threads. Performance overhead is reduced by loosely synchronizing the threads, and eliminating cache misses and branch mis-speculations in the checking thread. At a lower level of granularity, Oh *et. al* [9] proposed *EDDI* where instructions of a computation are replicated and the values compared to detect errors. These instructions are duplicated and interleaved to maximize available ILP when executed on a superscalar architecture. While this approach provides error detection on any architecture, regardless of hardware support, the duplication of program flow incurs an average 89.3% performance penalty for the benchmarks tested. Rather then duplicating instructions, other authors have focused on techniques that address control-flow errors, by devising minimal invading code insertion schemes (using the notion of signatures) [10] that indicate a faulty control flow in itself a reflect of an unspecified internal error. While this approach only protects control flow errors, its overhead is extremely low for non control-intensive computations.

While previous efforts include many points of contact with the work presented in this paper, there are subtle but important differences. First, and rather than relying on software-only instruction-based evaluation of invariants at specific points of the execution, our approach relies on the continuous evaluation of invariants using the hardware registers that hold the variables values. Second, the proposed architecture (the Predicate Processor) relies on reconfigurable hardware logic and can thus be configured to suite the specific needs of the invariants for a given code. Lastly, and unlike other instruction-based methods, the proposed approach requires a close interaction between the compiler (in particular with its register allocation phase) so that program-level variables can be mapped to registers. Lu *et. al* [11] described an approach similar to ours but where they explicitly rely on the mapping of variables to the activation records of each procedure onto the stack and thus cannot handle the continuous or instantaneous checking of invariant violation that occurs in optimized code or code where the values of the variables are not explicitly written to storage or when these values live exclusively in registers and are never mapped to external processor storage.

6   Conclusion

As transient errors will become the norm rather than the exception, architectures will have to incorporate error detection and possibly correction capabilities to mitigate their effects. In this paper we explore the use of reconfigurable hardware structure for the evaluation of high-level program invariants used to detection abnormal program behavior. We described a mapping approach for these high-level program invariants to assembly-level invariants that can be directly evaluated in hardware and described the architecture of a hardware Invariant Checker circuit to directly evaluate them. Implementation results on a contemporary FPGA device, albeit limited, suggest that even for a modest number of program invariants the proposed hardware structures require a small amount of resources and are fairly insensitive to the number of invariant clauses.

References

1. Flanagan, C., M. Leino, K.R.: Houdini: An Annotation Assistant for ESC/Java. In: Oliveira, J.N., Zave, P. (eds.) FME 2001. LNCS, vol. 2021, pp. 500–517. Springer, Heidelberg (2001)
2. Xilinx Corp., Virtex-6^{TM} Series FPGAs: Overview (2012), http://www.xilinx.com/support/documentation/data_sheets/ds150.pdf
3. Yu, S.-Y., McCluskey, E.: Permanent Fault Repair for FPGAs with Limited Redundant Area. In: Proc. of the IEEE Intl. Symp. on Defect and Fault-Tolerance in VLSI Systems. IEEE Computer Society, Los Alamitos (2001)
4. Heiner, J., Sellers, B., Wirthlin, M., Kalb, J.: FPGA Partial Reconfiguration via Configuration Scrubbing. In: Proc. of the 2009 Intl. Conf. on Field Programmable Logic and Applications (FPL), pp. 99–104 (2009)
5. Cuenca-Asensi, S., Martinez-Alvarez, A., Restrepo-Calle, F., Palomo, F., Guzman-Miranda, H., Aguirre, M.: A Novel Co-Design Approach for Soft Errors Mitigation in Embedded Systems. IEEE Trans. on Nuclear Science 58(3) (2011)
6. Reis, G., Chang, J., Vachharajani, N., Rangan, R., August, D.: SWIFT: Software Implemented Fault Tolerance. In: Proc. of the Intl. Symp. on Code Generation and Optimization, pp. 243–254 (March 2005)
7. Kastensmidt, F., Neuberger, G., Carro, L., Reis, R.: Designing and Testing Fault-tolerant Techniques for SRAM-based FPGAs. In: Proc. of the 1st Conf. on Computing Frontiers, pp. 419–432. ACM, New York (2004)
8. Reinhardt, S., Mukherjee, S.: Transient Fault Detection via Simultaneous Multi-threading. Computer Architecture News 28(2), 25–36 (2000)
9. Oh, N., Mitra, S., McCluskey, E.: ED4I: Error Detection by Diverse Data and Duplicated Instructions. IEEE Trans. on Comp. 51(2) (February 2002)
10. Vemu, R., Abraham, J.: CEDA: Control-Flow Error Detection Using Assertions. IEEE Trans. on Computers 60(9), 1233–1245 (2011)
11. Lu, H., Forin, A.: Automatic Processor Customization for Zero-Overhead Online Software Verification. IEEE Trans. Very Large Scale Integr. Syst. 16(10), 1346–1357 (2008)

Automated Data Flow Graph Partitioning for a Hierarchical Approach to Wordlength Optimization

Enrique Sedano[1]*, Daniel Menard[2], and Juan A. López[1]

[1] ETSI Telecomunicación (UPM)
Avenida Complutense, 30
28040 Madrid, Spain
{esedano,juanant}@die.upm.es
[2] INSA/IETR
20, Avenue des Buttes de Coësmes
35708 Rennes, France
daniel.menard@insa-rennes.fr

Abstract. Modern automatic analytical methods for studying range and accuracy in fixed-point systems are gradually replacing the traditional bit-true fixed-point simulations used in Word-Length Optimization (WLO) problems. But these models have several limitations that must be overcome if they are going to be used in real world applications. When targeting large systems, the mathematical expressions quickly become too large to be handled in reasonable times by numerical engines. This paper proposes adapting the classical Fiduccia-Mattheyses partitioning algorithm to the WLO domain to automatically generate hierarchical partitions of the systems to quantize. This is the first time this type of algorithms are used for this purpose. The algorithm has been successfully applied to large problems that could not be addressed before. It generates, in the order of minutes, maneuverable sub-problems where state-of-the-art models can be applied. Thus, scalability is achieved and the impact of the problem size as a constraint is minimized.

1   Introduction

In an industry where time-to-market is critical and the efficient implementation of Digital Signal Processing (DSP) systems can make the difference between success and failure, an optimized conversion of floating-point system descriptions to fixed-point implementations in a fast and reliable way still remains an open issue. The WLO is an iterative process whose objective is to optimize the integer and fractional Finite Word-Length (FWL) of the variables in the system so that

---

* Research by Enrique Sedano was partly supported by a PICATA predoctoral fellowship of the Moncloa Campus of International Excellence (UCM-UPM, CIEMAT) and by the Spanish Ministry of Education and Science under project TEC2009-14219-C03-02.

D. Goehringer et al. (Eds.): ARC 2014, LNCS 8405, pp. 133–143, 2014.
© Springer International Publishing Switzerland 2014

the implementation cost is minimized under certain performance constraints. To do this, a large number of wordlength combinations from large solution spaces must be evaluated.

The increasing size and complexity of DSP systems make classical approaches based on bit-true fixed-point Monte-Carlo simulations impractical due to the excessive computation times. As an alternative, several analytical models have been developed in the past years [1, 2, 3, 4]. These models are several orders of magnitude faster than the simulation-based approaches, but the range of systems they can accurately model is smaller. In order to be more accurate in complex systems, the analytical models are gradually becoming more complex. Added to the increment in the number of operations and the uncertainties required to evaluate such systems, it leads to large and complex mathematical equation systems that even modern computers have difficulties to solve in reasonable times. Consequently, analytical approaches that attempt to be used in real world industrial applications must not only be as general as possible but also scalable.

Up to now, there are few models that have addressed the issue of scalability [4, 5]. And even in these, the process is performed mainly by hand. In this paper, an algorithm to automatically perform a hierarchical decomposition of systems is presented. It iteratively applies an adapted classical algorithm from the netlist partitioning literature [6] to divide complete system descriptions into maneuverable clusters of operations that can be mathematically analyzed without exceeding the computational and memory limits of nowadays computers. Thus scalability is achieved and systems can be analytically modeled regardless their size. The main contributions of this work are:

- An iterative algorithm to carry out the hierarchical partitioning of a system, including the specification of the cost function, balance and stop criterions. It is the first time that an automated procedure of this type is used to deal with the problem of scalability in the WLO literature. Up to now, partitioning has been mostly made by hand.
- The introduction of a simple yet effective Single Source Directed Hypergraph model to represent the system to be partitioned.
- The demonstration of the suitability of adapting classical netlist partitioning algorithms to the WLO problem through several experimental results.

The rest of the paper is organized as follows. Section 2 presents a brief overview of the analytical approaches for range and accuracy evaluation and graph partitioning. The partitioning problem is formulated in Section 3 and the implemented algorithm is detailed in Section 4. Section 5 collects the experimental results, and Section 6 draws the conclusions of the work.

2   Related Work

2.1   Automatic Quantization

The process of transforming the floating-point specification of a system into its fixed-point implementation requires careful range and accuracy evaluation in order to avoid over- and underflows and keep quantization errors within reasonable bounds. The most traditional approach to this analysis is to carry out bit-true fixed-point simulations that suffer from exceedingly long execution times. To overcome this limitation, several analytical models have been developed. Their objective is to obtain the required metrics for range and precision analysis through mathematical models.

In [1], the authors present an analysis of the system based on the perturbation theory approach where quantization errors are considered small deviations from the infinite precision values. This approach is valid while none of the operators in the circuit present strong non-linearities. When studying Linear Time-Invariant (LTI) systems, Affine Arithmetic (AA) [2, 7, 8] has proven to be a reliable and fast method to model range and quantization noise. It adequately cancels the linear dependencies of the uncertainties in the system, but it is not able to retain temporal correlation after non-linear operations. Modified Affine Arithmetic (MAA) has been proposed as a solution to this issue for computer graphics applications [3].

However, in the literature only a few of them have recently dealt with the problem of scalability. In [4] a hierarchical decomposition of the problem is proposed. In this approach, the decomposition of the complete system into a hierarchy of subsystems is performed so each region can be handled independently and, in the wordlength optimization stage, a divide and conquer strategy is applied. Nevertheless, the hierarchical decomposition is done by hand. A different approach is introduced in [5, 9], where Polynomial Chaos Expansion (PCE) is used to study the dynamic range and numerical accuracy of the systems.

The present work introduces a novel algorithm that performs a hierarchical decomposition of the Data Flow Graph (DFG) fast and automatically, achieving scalability in order to apply existing dynamic range and accuracy evaluation techniques. The objective is to isolate strongly non-linear operators and to generate partitions with a reduced number of inputs while the number of edges interconnecting the subgraphs is minimized. The algorithm is independent from the analytical model used, so after partitioning the DFG any of the methods previously described can be used to perform range and precision analysis.

2.2   Graph Partitioning Algorithms

Graph partitioning has been widely used in the placement and routing stages, where millions of transistors have to be handled while tight timing constraints must be met. Only by dividing the netlists into smaller entities the logic-level and physical-level tools can manage the vast number of components involved. Thus, the literature related to netlist partitioning is extensive and varied. They range from move-based iterative improvement algorithms [10, 6] to geometrical and mathematical abstractions of the problem [11, 12], and from top-down approaches [6, 13] to bottom-up ones [14]. A complete survey of methods and formulations used in graph partitioning is found in [15].

The objective of partitioning is to find suitable subgraphs with minimal interconnection (cutset) between them. It is possible to find recent and advanced partitioning methods based on genetic algorithms [16], but for the aim of this work only move-based iterative improvement algorithms will be taken into account. Since the optimization problem itself is already a very time-consuming task, it is imperative to minimize the time dedicated to additional tasks. On this behalf, move-based iterative algorithms offer reasonably good results in minimal times.

Kernighan and Lin (KL) [10] initially proposed a bisection heuristic where a series of passes are iteratively performed. An advantage of this procedure is that it can escape from local minima because in each pass all movements are considered, even those with negative gains. Its major drawback is that the execution time of the algorithm is between $\Theta(n^2 \log n)$ and $\Theta(n^3)$ depending on the implementation.

A KL-inspired but much faster algorithm is introduced by Fiduccia and Mattheyses (FM) in [6]. Although the main idea is similar to the one in [10], the execution is reduced to linear time. This is mainly achieved due to the use of the *bucket list*, a specialized data structure with constant access time to the node with the highest gain and fast update time for the gains after each move. Additional information about the highest gain non-empty bucket is also held in the *bucket list*, so the access time is linear. Also, the number of elements to have in each partition is relaxed by introducing a *balance condition* that allows a certain degree of variation between the partition sizes. During the execution passes only those moves that do not violate the balance condition are allowed. Nowadays this algorithm remains as the standard against every new heuristic is compared.

The FM algorithm is further improved [17], by introducing gain vectors as sequences of potential gains corresponding to future possible moves. The FM algorithm, along with this improvement, is extended in a straightforward way in [18] to allow multiple-way partitioning. An important feature of this work is that, again, an efficient management of the data structures leads to a linear increase of the execution time with respect to the number of partitions.

3   Definition of the Problem

The input for the partitioning algorithm are DFGs, with a set $I = \{i_1, i_2, \cdots, i_n\}$ of independent inputs that relate among them through $F = \{f_1, f_2, \cdots, f_j\}$ operations, to generate $O = \{o_1, o_2, \cdots, i_k\}$ outputs. The information is propagated from the inputs to the outputs as defined by the set $E = \{e_1, e_2, \cdots, e_m\}$ of directed edges, where $e_p \in (I, F) \cup (F, F) \cup (F, O) \cup (I, O)$. To simplify the formulation of the problem, the DFG is defined following the notation in [15] as $G = (V, E)$ where $V = I \cup F \cup O$. The elements in F can be classified as smooth or un-smooth operators. Smooth operators display a linear behavior for noise computations even if they are non-linear and time variant and hence can be treated analytically. Un-smooth operators are not continuous or differentiable functions of their inputs, such as decision operators and modulus operators.

Following the ideas of the hierarchical partitioning described in [4], a decomposition of a given DFG is valid if it satisfies the following requisites:

- All un-smooth operators are isolated in different individual partitions in the first level of decomposition.
- The number of inputs to each of the final subsystems are balanced (within a degree of variation).
- The number of inputs to each of the final subsystems is less than a certain established value.

Due to the characteristics of this problem, it must be taken into account that each cut implies a new input in the subgraph that includes the node in which the cut edge incides. This will be discussed in depth in Section 4.2.

The problem is formalized as follows:

Given a graph $G = (V, E)$ with weighted nodes and two parameters s (partition size) and b (balance condition),

Find a multi-level, hierarchical partitioning of G where $G^{p-1} = \bigcup_{i=0}^{q} G_i^p$ and $\forall i, j, i \neq j, G_i^p \cap G_j^p = \emptyset$, being G^n a subgraph of level n and G_m the m-th partition of a graph. Un-smooth operators must be kept in the first level of the hierarchy in partitions that contain only one instruction at a time. For the rest of partitions, the difference in number of inputs per subgraph with less than or equals to s inputs (counting the ones generated by the cut edges) must be below b and, for each level, the number of edges crossing between partitions (the cutset size, C_s) must be minimized.

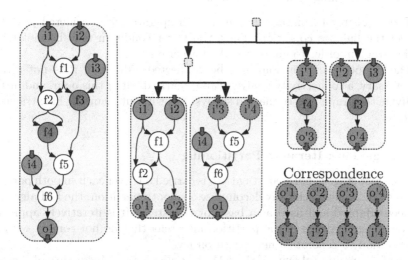

Fig. 1. Example of the hierarchical decomposition of a DFG

Figure 1 shows an example of a valid decomposition. On the left side the original DFG is presented. Dark grey nodes with an arrow are inputs or outputs, depending on the direction of the arrow. Nodes in white are smooth operators, and the ones in red are un-smooth ones. On the right side a decomposition of the DFG is shown assuming each partition can contain a maximum of 3 (± 1) inputs. Nodes with dotted lines are new inputs and outputs generated during the partitioning process, and the corresponding connections among them is indicated in the lower right box with the red background.

4   Partitioning Algorithm

Given the requisites specified in the previous section, the partitioning algorithm is divided in two main stages. This section presents the implementation details and the basic considerations for both of them. The pseudocode for the complete partitioner is found in Algorithm 1.

4.1   Stage One: Un-smooth Operators Handling

In this case, the first condition of a valid partitioned DFG is that the un-smooth operators are kept in the first level of the hierarchy, each of them in a different subsystem that holds them as the only operation. For the scope of this work, it is assumed that a list of such operators is available, and thus a single pass over the DFG is enough to identify and isolate all of them.

By doing this, a DFG with n un-smooth operators will be partitioned into $n + 1$ subsystems in the first level; one for each of these operators (un-smooth partitions) and another where the rest of the operations from E are kept (smooth partition). Two things must be noted here:

1. The requisite of isolating the un-smooth operators is considered prioritary over the balance condition. Thus, the latter condition may be violated at this stage in order to guarantee the former one.
2. The smooth partition may not be connected. Although it is not strictly necessary, a connectivity analysis can be carried out at this point and further divide the graph into connected subsystems without incurring in extra cutset costs.

4.2   Stage Two: Iterative Partitioning

Once the first stage is finished, stage two is carried out over each smooth partition just created. To hierarchically decompose a smooth partition, the FM algorithm has been adapted and used as a base for this stage. It is iteratively applied to each of the subsystems in the partition hierarchy that do not comply with the stop criterion to generate a new partition level.

One of the main problems of the FM algorithm is that the quality of the solution strongly depends on the initial partition, which is generated randomly. This issue is overcome by running several passes of the FM partitioning, each of them with a different initial state, and using only the best (i.e. the one that minimizes the cost function) of the obtained final partitions. Given the fast execution time of the FM algorithm, this can be done a large number of times (N_{test}) without incurring into excessive overall execution times. Some authors have already suggested this type of solutions to obtain as good results with iterative improvement algorithms as with more refined schemes such as Simulated Annealing [19].

DFG Representation. It is common to use hypergraphs [20] when solving partitioning problems with the FM algorithm. Assuming that an hyperedge includes all the edges that connect a node with its successors, a *Single Source Directed Hypergraph (SSD Hypergraph)* is defined. Each hyperedge is represented as a list of the edges in the structure and an indicator of which of them is the source. The graph is redefined as $\hat{G} = (V, \hat{E})$, where $\hat{E} = (\hat{e}_1, \hat{e}_2, \cdots, \hat{e}_k)$. Each $\hat{e}_i = (v_s, L_d)$ being L_d the list of all v_d that verify $(v_s, v_d) \in E$. If the list is empty no hyperedge is generated (i.e. there are no hyperedges with elements from O as source).

This representation allows the identification of the direction of the edges with minimal memory occupation. The detection of whether an hyperedge belongs to a given cutset is done by checking if any of the nodes from the list is not in the same partition as the source. Since cutting an edge generates new nodes in the graph, the SSD Hypergraph notation permits a fast identification of the type of node that has to be added to each partition by just checking the position of the source.

Cost Function. The objective of the partitioning algorithm is to obtain a well-balanced number of inputs in each partition while minimizing C_s. To this end, only the input nodes are given a non-zero weight. This allows the free movement of any other node in the graph that may produce a reduction in the cutset size.

It must be taken into account that it is necessary to include new inputs and outputs to the partitions when an hyperedge is cut, so the corresponding terms and coefficients from the analytical expressions can be included in the models. The partition that holds the source node of the cut hyperedge gets one more output while the number of inputs of the other one is increased in one. Thus, the resulting subsystems will have different number of inputs and outputs depending on the final cutset.

Considering all of the above, the cost function for a given partition G_m^p is the number of inputs to the graph plus the number of cut SSD Hyperedges that incide in the partition. The expression of the cost is as follows:

$$f_{cost}(G_m^p) = |I_m| + |\hat{e}_i \rightarrow \hat{e}_i \in cs(G^{p-1}) \wedge src(\hat{e}_i) \notin V_m^p|$$

being I_m the inputs to the partition, V_m^p the list of nodes of G_m^p, $cs(G^{p-1})$ the list of hyperedges cut in the partition of the parent level of G_m^p and $src(\hat{e}_i)$ the source node of the hypernode $\hat{e}_i$.

Balance and Stop Criterions. The **balance criterion** considered for the present algorithm differs from the one proposed in [6]. In our case, the allowed deviation is set as a function of the total number of inputs of the graph (in the experiments in Section 5 a 20% of the size of I was used) while keeping the *largest cell size* as its lower bound.

The **stop criterion** depends exclusively on the analytical model that is going to be applied to the subsystems to evaluate the dynamic range and accuracy. Depending on its formulation and implementation, the number of uncertainties (i.e. inputs of the DFG) that can be handled in reasonable times by the numerical

Algorithm 1. Hierarchical partitioning pseudocode

```
// Stage One
for all F_i in F do
   if F_i is un-smooth then
      partitions ← new_partition(F_i);
   else
      smooth_ops ← F_i;
   end if
end for
partitions ← new_partition(smooth_ops);
// Stage Two
for each P_k ∈ partitions not complying stop criterion do
   for i = 1 → N_test do
      FM_trials ← Fiduccia_Mattheyses(P_k);
   end for
   // partitions_to_add are two subgraphs
   partitions_to_add ← best_partition(FM_trials);
   set_as_children_of(partitions_to_add, P_k);
   partitions ← partitions_to_add;
end for
```

engines may vary. Thus, the iterative partitioning stops when the number of inputs in the partitions is such a value that the analytical model can handle at once.

5   Experimental Results

This section presents the results of the experiments carried out on a number of different graphs. They include an example extracted from the teager benchmark [21], a simple 2-order IIR filter, a 29-order FIR filter and a pipelined version of a large Computer Fluid Dynamics (CFD) algorithm. To represent the quantization noise, Additive White Noise Source (AWNS) inputs have been added to each operation in the system as in [2], thus greatly incrementing the total number of operations and inputs in the DFGs. The properties of the different benchmarks are presented in Table 1, where **NNod** is the number of nodes of the graph, **NEdg** the number of edges and **NInp** the number of inputs of the graph. The functional version of the code was written in C++ and the experiments were carried out in an Intel Core 2 Q9400 running at 2.66 GHz with 6 GB of RAM.

In order to show the behaviour of the algorithm when the initial number of nodes is large in relation to the number of inputs that comply with the stop condition, the maximum number of inputs per final partition has been set to $s = 5$ in all the experiments. For the present set of benchmarks N_{test} has been set to 256. As stated before, it is the first time a netlist partitioning algorithm is used to split a DFG hierarchically in order to solve the scalability problem of analytical approaches. To evaluate the quality of the presented solution, it is compared to a random partitioner. The stage one is executed unmodified in

Table 1. Benchmarks properties

Value	Teager	IIR-2	FIR-29	CFD
NNod	25	116	172	1585
NEdg	27	117	171	1795
NInp	10	40	58	614

Table 2. Results of the proposed algorithm (100 runs each)

Value	Teager		IIR-2		FIR-29		CFD	
	Rand	FM	Rand	FM	Rand	FM	Rand	FM
ACS	4,33	1,62	4,22	1,49	4,25	1,72	–	1,87
ACS AD	0,30	0,19	0,17	0,12	0,04	0,08	–	0,02
MCS	13,43	2,35	35,96	4,8	85,24	12,27	–	103,16
MCS AD	1,52	0,45	3,48	1,01	4,82	1,72	–	5,23
FPS	8,92	9,56	8,5	11,05	8,53	9,59	–	8,38
FPS AD	0,53	0,9	0,35	0,61	0,09	0,32	–	0,08
NLvl	46,89	3,32	31,9	5,08	26,81	6,79	–	11,27
ExT	1,21	0,174	7,783	1,725	120,57	6,375	–	557,147

order to isolate non-smooth operators in the first partition level, but in stage two the destination partition for each node in the graph is decided randomly. In this case the partitioning for each level is also run $N_{test} = 256$ times and only the best solution per level is used. No balance criterion is considered.

To obtain a better measure of the results, the partitioning algorithm has been executed 100 times for each DFG. The results of the experiments, shown in Table 2, collect the average results from all the executions. The absolute deviation values for some of them is also presented to demonstrate that, even though the quality of the solution of the FM partitioning is dependent on the initial random partition, the method presented in this paper generates homogeneous solutions through several executions.

The following values are presented in Table 2:

- **ACS**: Average Cutset Size through all the levels in the partitioned graph (in number of hyperedges).
- **ACS AD**: ACS Absolute Deviation.
- **MCS**: Maximum Cutset Size through all the levels in the partitioned graph (in number of hyperedges).
- **MCS AD**: MCS Absolute Deviation.
- **FPS**: Average Final Partitions Size (in number of nodes).
- **FPS AD**: FPS Absolute Deviation.
- **NLvl**: Number of Levels generated by the partitioner.
- **ExT**: Execution Time (in seconds).

It can be observed in the results that both the average and maximum cutset sizes are notably reduced compared to the results of the random partitioning.

Also the greatest improvements can be noticed in the number of levels (and consequently, of partitions performed) and in the execution times. Performing a single random partition is faster than using the FM algorithm, but the necessity of doing a larger number of partitions causes longer overall execution times. It can be noticed that the final partitions size (i.e. the size of the partitions in the leafs of the hierarchical partitioning tree) is larger in the case of the proposed algorithm. Obviously, having a smaller number of partitions means that the number of instructions per partition must be larger. There are no experimental results for the random partitioning of the CFD algorithm because the large number of generated partitions caused the system to run out of memory during runtime.

The results show that the objective of carrying out the partitioning with fast execution times is fully achieved. While for small sized problems the algorithm runs in about one second, large benchmarks like the CFD are solved in a few minutes. It can also be noted that the obtained results are consistent between executions, being the deviations in cutset sizes and number of levels considerably small. This proves that the proposed approach deals with the dependency of the initial solution issue in an effective way, significantly reducing its impact in the final partitioning results.

6   Conclusion

A two-stage automated hierarchical partitioning algorithm for DFGs that are going to be processed during the quantization and wordlength optimization stage of VLSI design has been proposed. Aiming for low execution times without loss of solution quality, it has been developed using an adapted version of the Fiduccia-Mattheyses netlist partitioning algorithm and generates solutions that comply with the requirements established by previous works. The algorithm steps, the cost function and the balance and stop criterions are specified, and an effective Single Source Directed Hypergraph representation is introduced. The algorithm has been applied to a variety of systems to prove its validity and fast execution time. When compared to a random partitioning, cutset sizes are, on average, $2,7$ times smaller, the number of levels are between 4 and 14 times less and solutions are obtained between one and three orders of magnitude faster. It is the first time that an algorithm of this type is applied to address the problem of scalability in analytical approaches to system modeling, and the feasibility of adapting netlist partitioning algorithms to the domain of DFG partitioning for wordlength optimization has been effectively demonstrated.

References

[1] Shi, C., Brodersen, R.W.: A perturbation theory on statistical quantization effects in fixed-point DSP with non-stationary inputs. In: Proceedings of the 2004 International Symposium on Circuits and Systems, ISCAS 2004, vol. 3, p. III–373. IEEE (2004)

[2] López, J.A., Caffarena, G., Carreras, C., Nieto-Taladriz, O.: Fast and accurate computation of the round-off noise of linear time-invariant systems. IET Circuits, Devices & Systems 2(4), 393 (2008)

[3] Shou, H., Lin, H., Martin, R.R., Wang, G.: Modified affine arithmetic in tensor form for trivariate polynomial evaluation and algebraic surface plotting. Journal of Computational and Applied Mathematics 195(1-2), 155–171 (2006)

[4] Parashar, K., Rocher, R., Menard, D., Sentieys, O.: A Hierarchical Methodology for Word-Length Optimization of Signal Processing Systems. In: 23rd International Conference on VLSI Design, pp. 318–323. IEEE (2010)

[5] Esteban, L., López, J., Sedano, E., Hernandez-Montero, S., Sanchez, M.: Quantization analysis of the infrared interferometer of the tj-ii stellarator for its optimized fpga-based implementation. IEEE Transactions on Nuclear Science 60, 3592–3596 (2013)

[6] Fiduccia, C., Mattheyses, R.: A linear-time heuristic for improving network partitions. In: 19th Conference on Design Automation, pp. 241–247 (1982)

[7] López, J.A., Sedano, E., Esteban, L., Caffarena, G., Fernández-Herrero, A., Carreras, C.: Applications of Interval-Based Simulations to the Analysis and Design of Digital LTI Systems. In: Cuadrado-Laborde, C. (ed.) Applications of Digital Signal Processing. Number i, 1st edn., pp. 279–296. InTech (2011)

[8] Sarbishei, O., Radecka, K., Zilic, Z.: Analytical Optimization of Bit-Widths in Fixed-Point LTI Systems. IEEE Transactions on Computer-Aided Design of Integrated Circuits and Systems 31(3), 343–355 (2012)

[9] Esteban, L., López, J.A., Sedano, E., Sánchez, M.: Quantization Analysis of the Infrared Interferometer of the TJ-II for its Optimized FPGA-based Implementation. In: IEEE 18th Real Time Conference, RTC 2012, Berkeley, California, USA (2012)

[10] Kernighan, B., Lin, S.: An Efficient Heuristic Procedure for Partitioning Graphs. The Bell System Technical Journal 49(1), 291–307 (1970)

[11] Hall, K.M.: An r-Dimensional Quadratic Placement Algorithm. Management Science 17(3), 219–229 (1970)

[12] Tsay, R.S., Kuh, E.: A unified approach to partitioning and placement (VLSI layout). IEEE Transactions on Circuits and Systems 38(5), 521–533 (1991)

[13] Bui, T.N., Moon, B.R.: Genetic algorithm and graph partitioning. IEEE Transactions on Computers 45(7), 841–855 (1996)

[14] Johnson, E.L., Mehrotra, A., Nemhauser, G.L.: Min-cut clustering. Mathematical Programming 62, 133–151 (1993)

[15] Alpert, C.J., Kahng, A.B.: Recent directions in netlist partitioning: a survey. The VLSI Journal on Integration 19(1-2), 1–81 (1995)

[16] Kim, J., Hwang, I., Kim, Y.H., Moon, B.R.: Genetic approaches for graph partitioning: a survey. In: Proceedings of the 13th Annual Conference on Genetic and Evolutionary Computation, pp. 473–480. ACM (2011)

[17] Krishnamurthy, B.: An Improved Min-Cut Algonthm for Partitioning VLSI Networks. IEEE Transactions on Computers C-33(5), 438–446 (1984)

[18] Sanchis, L.: Multiple-way network partitioning with different cost functions. IEEE Transactions on Computers 42(12), 1500–1504 (1993)

[19] Johnson, D.S., Aragon, C.R., McGeoch, L.A., Schevon, C.: Optimization by Simulated Annealing: An Experimental Evaluation; Part I, Graph Partitioning. Operations Research 37(6), 865–892 (1989)

[20] Berge, C.: Graphs and Hypergraphs. Elsevier (1976)

[21] Mathews, V.J., Sicuranza, G.L.: Polynomial Signal Processing. Wiley (2000)

Partitioning and Vectorizing Binary Applications for a Reconfigurable Vector Computer

Tobias Kenter, Gavin Vaz, and Christian Plessl

Department of Computer Science,
University of Paderborn, Germany
{kenter,gavin.vaz,christian.plessl}@uni-paderborn.de

Abstract. In order to leverage the use of reconfigurable architectures in general-purpose computing, quick and automated methods to find suitable accelerator designs are required. We tackle this challenge in both regards. In order to avoid long synthesis times, we target a vector coprocessor, implemented on the FPGAs of a Convey HC-1. Previous studies showed that existing tools were not able to accelerate a real-world application with low effort. We present a toolflow to automatically identify suitable loops for vectorization, generate a corresponding hardware/software bipartition, and generate coprocessor code. Where applicable, we leverage outer-loop vectorization. We evaluate our tools with a set of characteristic loops, systematically analyzing different dependency and data layout properties.

Keywords: Heterogeneous System, Binary Acceleration, Outer-Loop Vectorization.

1 Introduction

Numerous studies have shown that FPGAs can accelerate a wide range of applications by up to several orders of magnitude compared to general-purpose CPUs. However, until now they are solely regarded as a special-purpose compute platform. For this to change, two fundamental challenges must be met. On the one hand, general-purpose computing platforms shine by their ability to execute virtually any workload with a relatively good performance. In order to achieve this, a general-purpose FPGA platform needs to incorporate a reasonable CPU for any tasks that perform badly on FPGAs. With Xilinx Zynq, Altera Cyclone/Arria and Intel Stellarton such platforms are emerging for the embedded and mobile market. Architecturally, the Convey HC-1 platform we target can be regarded as their counterpart for the desktop and server market, with an Intel Xeon CPU and an FPGA-accelerator in the two respective sockets of a server mainboard. The second, more pressing challenge is the design process for FPGA platforms. Traditionally, a huge implementation effort and long synthesis times are required to harvest the performance of FPGAs. Over the last couple of years, High Level Synthesis (HLS) toolflows like Catapult C, Xilinx Vivado (formerly AutoPilot), and bambu have started to gain more and more

D. Goehringer et al. (Eds.): ARC 2014, LNCS 8405, pp. 144–155, 2014.
© Springer International Publishing Switzerland 2014

traction. They promise reduced design effort by producing FPGA designs from high-level source code in C or similar syntax. They generate state machines to execute the control flow and custom data paths for the computations. Typically, HLS tools require user interaction to specify where and to what extent those techniques are to be applied. Afterwards, the designs still need to undergo the entire time-consuming synthesis process for FPGAs.

One way to avoid this long synthesis process is to utilize a set of prepared configurations for the FPGA that can then be programmed for a specific application with relatively low effort. This can be a Coarse Grained Array structure, which can be configured with far fewer configuration bits than the underlying FPGA. Another approach is to implement a softcore processor with specific features, which enable the acceleration of a class of problems. The so called Vector Personality for the Convey HC-1 follows this latter approach and features an instruction set with large vector instructions, which enable it to internally profit both from pipelining and parallel execution. It serves as a coprocessor which can most efficiently work on vectorizable loops and leaves sequential or control-dominated code on the x86 host processor. We found that targeting this architecture with the Convey Compiler required significant effort in refactoring the source code and annotating it with pragmas. Yet the generated vector code was not performing anywhere as good as manually written assembly code [10]. In particular, we found outer-loop vectorization to be an important feature the Convey Compiler was lacking.

In this work we present a new toolflow based on LLVM, which addresses those issues. It works on the LLVM intermediate representation (IR) of non-annotated source code, identifies hotspots to move to the coprocessor and performs suitable vectorization. Where the problem dimensions are unknown at compile time, it inserts runtime decisions for selecting the best execution path. The toolflow integrates some existing LLVM and Convey Compiler tools, but most of the partitioning related aspects, as well as the vectorization and coprocessor code generation are new contributions for this work.

The compelling features of our presented work are threefold. Firstly, the unguided acceleration process requires no additional expertise and manual development effort. As such, even a platform that initially has limited market penetration and correspondingly limited support from application developers can be put to good use. Secondly, the toolflow works on binary applications in the form of LLVM IR. Even though this is no machine code, it is a binary format in which applications can be distributed or it can be generated from machine code [2]. Thus, the toolflow can even be applied in scenarios where source code is not available [8]. Thirdly, we target a platform that we architecturally consider as a prototype for general-purpose desktop or server systems with FPGA acceleration, combining a state-of-the-art CPU with an FPGA accelerator.

In the remainder of this paper, we first refer to related work and introduce our targeted hardware platform. Then we present details about our approach and toolflow, before discussing the results, conclusion and outlook.

2   Related Work

In this section, we present related work on the Convey HC-1 platform and its Vector Personality, then discuss approaches of binary acceleration on embedded FPGA platforms and finally give a brief overview of the compiler background on the vectorization strategies we follow.

The fundamentals of the Convey HC-1 system architecture and its capability to implement instruction set extensions and custom personalities have been described in the works of Brewer [6] and Bakos [4]. The work by Augustin et al. [3] studies the suitability of the Convey HC-1 for kernels from linear algebra and compares the performance to CPUs and GPUs. Their work also uses the Vector Personality and Convey Compiler infrastructure, as well as the work by Meyer et al. [12]. They port a stencil computation application to the Vector Personality and compare both results and development flow with an OpenMP parallelization. In our previous work, we investigated the pragma-guided compilation approach and theoretical performance data of the Vector Personality [10]. Our current work differs from the all this related work by offering a new, unguided toolflow embedded into the LLVM compiler infrastructure and working on its IR code representation.

Other projects in this field of binary acceleration try to include a full synthesis process into that process. This limits them to small embedded systems or soft core CPUs [5] with additional restrictions on a simplified FPGA fabric [11] or a coarse grained array structure [5] as reconfigurable target platform, or on custom instructions as acceleration target [7]. By targeting an instruction-programmable architecture on an FPGA, we avoid the costly synthesis phase and thus can target a general-purpose and high performance computing platform with large FPGAs. In contrast to those related embedded projects, our system has a non-uniform memory access (NUMA) architecture with a shared address space, but physically distinct memory locations having different throughput and latency properties.

Our source of speedup comes from vectorization of loops that enable large vectors. The foundations of automated loop vectorization driven by data dependency analysis were established by Allen and Kennedy [1]. In their source-to-source compilation system they apply loop interchange and then vectorize inner loops or entire loops nests that are fully vectorizable from the innermost loop on. Later on, the vectorizing Fortran compiler by Scarborough et al. [15] also featured direct outer-loop vectorization, like Ngo's [13] compiler framework integrated into the "Cray Fortran-90 compiling system". More recently, outer-loop vectorization has also gained interest for SIMD architectures with short vector units [14]. In contrast to the systems those compilers target, our system is heterogeneous. It has a host CPU, which delivers high performance for sequential code and even contains short SIMD units itself, which can be used without synchronization overhead or data movement into a distinct memory location. The large vector unit on the coprocessor offers a richer vector instruction set, e.g. indexed load and store operations and variable length vectors. It can boost performance specifically when large vectors can be derived from the loops.

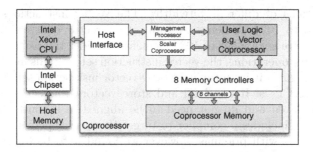

Fig. 1. Coprocessor Architecture

3   Convey HC-1 Platform and Vector Personality

In this section, we introduce the Convey HC-1 hardware platform, give a brief overview of the different ways to configure its FPGAs, specifically with the Vector Personality and introduce the basic tool flow to target the Vector Personality.

A schematic overview of the Convey HC-1 architecture [6] is presented in Figure 1. At its heart, the Convey HC-1 is a dual socket server system, where one socket is populated with a Intel Xeon CPU while the other socket is connected to a stacked coprocessor board. The two boards communicate using the Intel Front-Side Bus (FSB) protocol. Both processing units have their own dedicated physical memory, which can be transparently accessed by the other unit through a common cache-coherent virtual address space. The coprocessor consists of multiple, individually programmable FPGAs. One FPGA implements the infrastructure that is shared by all coprocessor configurations. These functions include the physical FSB interface and cache coherency protocol as well as configuration and execution management for user programmable FPGAs. For implementing the application-specific functionality, four high-density Xilinx Virtex-5LX330 FPGAs are available.

A distinctive feature of the HC-1 architecture is the availability of a fast multi channel memory interface, which provides the application engines with access to 8 independent memory banks through 8 dedicated memory controllers with an aggregated bandwidth of 80 GB/s. In our system configuration, custom-made scatter-gather modules are installed, which allow accessing memory efficiently in 8-byte data blocks, while standard modules are optimized for 64-byte blocks. The user logic FPGAs can be configured with so-called *Personalities*, that need to implement interfaces to the management processor and scalar coprocessor as well as to the memory controllers. Users can create their own specialized personalities or use those provided by Convey, which exist for a number of specific tasks like graph traversal or local string alignment, and as the general-purpose *Vector Personality*.

The Vector Personality provides the functionality of a vector coprocessor that executes programs targeting its vector instruction set. The Personality we target is optimized for single-precision floating point operations and also supports integer operations of different bitwidths. The vector instructions are implemented for up to 1024 elements. A total of 64 vector registers are available and each can store such a set of 1024 elements. Besides the usual element-wise arithmetic vector operations, the vector instruction set contains memory instructions that distinguish it from typical SIMD vector instruction set extensions for general-purpose CPUs. It can load and store vectors where the elements are individually indexed and do not need to be aligned in a continuous memory location. Convey includes a compiler to target this vector personality by annotating source code with pragmas, however we found it to be limited to simple array data structures, which often requires significant code adaptations besides adding the vectorization pragmas.

4   Approach

In this section, we first present our overall toolflow to generate heterogeneous executables for CPU and coprocessor. After this general overview, we discuss in more detail the extraction of code parts for execution on the coprocessor, the actual vectorization and our support for runtime checks to guide the execution and data movement.

4.1   Toolflow for Heterogeneous Executables

Since we use and extend the LLVM compiler infrastructure in this project, we use its terminology. In particular, a module denotes the top level compilation unit, e.g. an entire program or a library that will be linked with the main executable later. A module contains a set of functions which consist of basic blocks. Control flow between basic blocks is denoted by edges. Figure 2 depicts our overall toolflow for generating heterogeneous binaries for execution on the host CPU and coprocessor. We start with LLVM IR code, which we generated for our tests in Section 5 with the clang compiler frontend. In our *PartitionPass*, we then split the module into code that is to remain on host and code that is to be executed on the coprocessor. The details of this phase will be presented in Subsection 4.2. The *PartitionPass* also includes the planning of a vectorization strategy described in Subsection 4.3 and the inclusion of runtime decisions as detailed in Subsection 4.4. The modified host code is then translated by the LLVM backend to x86 assembly code. Note that, where applicable, this will generate short vector instructions for the host CPU's SIMD units.

For generating the interface between the host and coprocessor code, we use the Convey Compiler to match Convey's calling conventions and to avoid reimplementing that functionality. For that purpose, the *PartitionPass* additionally emits a .cpp file containing stubs of all the functions we want to implement on the coprocessor along with their signature of arguments. We also generate pragmas indicating to the Convey Compiler that those functions are to be executed on the coprocessor. The Convey Compiler then generates an x86 function entry, which contains a runtime check for availability of the coprocessor and puts all

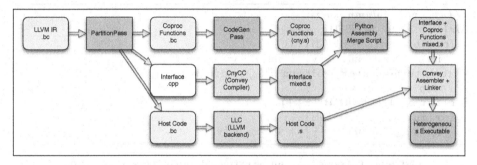

Fig. 2. Toolflow for generating heterogeneous binaries; blue: our implementation; yellow: Convey Compiler infrastructure; green: LLVM infrastructure

arguments properly on the coprocessor stack. Then control is handed over to the coprocessor entry of this function, where arguments are loaded from the stack into coprocessor registers.

From the code extracted for the coprocessor, we generate vectorized coprocessor assembly code in our *CodeGenPass* following the vectorization strategy determined by the *PartitionPass*. With the help of a Python script we then merge this code with the headers including function arguments of the function stubs compiled by the Convey Compiler. Finally we assemble and link the generated assembly and object files, again using the Convey Compiler tools.

4.2   Code Extraction

We want to identify parts of the code that can be executed on the coprocessor and are likely to yield a speedup. This subsection focuses on the feasibility whereas the performance depends on the outcome of the subsequently described steps.

On our platform, the control flow between host CPU and coprocessor is based on function calls. The only way to transfer control from the CPU to the coprocessor is to call a function that is compiled for the latter; the only regular way to transfer control back is to return from the called function. The coprocessor may call other coprocessor functions but it can not call functions on the host. The following process identifies coprocessor suitable code regions in two phases, before the actual extraction starts.

In the first phase, we identify all function calls to libraries on the host CPU, e.g. I/O, as direct incompatibilities. The basic blocks containing these calls can not be moved to the coprocessor, except for a few selected functions, for which we can generate coprocessor code directly, e.g. a `std::min()` with appropriate data types can be directly translated into assembly functions later. In the second phase, we search for indirect incompatibilities, where function calls inside the compilation module point to functions that need to be at least partially executed on the host. We repeat this second phase until no new incompatibilities are detected. The outcome of these two phases are functions that can be entirely moved to the coprocessor and functions that are only partially coprocessor feasible.

```
//Integral column sums
for(int x=0; x<WIDTH; x++)
  for(int y=1; y<HEIGHT; y++)
    im[x][y] = im[x][y] + im[x][y-1];
writeIntermediateResult(im); // call with IO
//Integral row sums
for(int x=1; x<WIDTH; x++)
  for(int y=0; y<HEIGHT; y++)
    im[x][y] = im[x][y] + im[x-1][y];
```

Listing 1.1. Loops that can be extracted for coprocessor execution

For those latter functions, we want to extract the basic blocks that can be executed on the coprocessor into new functions. For this extraction to be possible, a set of blocks must have a single entry edge and a single exit edge [9]. Some sets of basic blocks may not have this property, but can be transformed to satisfy it. In particular this is the case if they have a single basic block as target for all entry edges and a single basic block as source for all exiting edges. As such, all loops in any nesting level have this property. As speedups are only expected from vectorizing loops, we restrict our toolflow to extract only sets of basic blocks that form a loop. We proceed from outer to inner nested loops, so if all basic blocks of an outer loop are marked as coprocessor feasible, the outer loop gets extracted, otherwise inner loops are tested in the order of their nesting level. We use LLVM's refactoring capabilities to perform this extraction after a suitable loop is detected.

Listing 1.1 shows a simple code example where this function splitting is required. After the first vectorizable loop nest, some intermediate result is written to a file, before a second vectorizable loop nest follows. Our toolflow will extract the two loop nests into two new coprocessor functions, leaving the calls to those functions along with the other call inside the original function on the host. Note that we chose the source code listing just for illustration purposes, whereas internally our tools operate on LLVM IR.

4.3   Vectorization

The vectorization phase checks for two important conditions on each loop nest level. Firstly, dependencies between loop iterations are detected, which would prevent vectorization of this loop. The example from Listing 1.1 computes integral line and column sums respectively, thus the inner loop from the first loop nest and the outer loop from the second loop nest have dependencies, leaving the respective other loop for vectorization. Secondly, the dimensions of the loops are checked, whether they permit any speedup. As heuristic, we use an iteration count of 100, when plain array data structures are detected and 500, when following pointers to inner dimension, as threshold below which vectorization often isn't sufficient to allow speedups on the coprocessor. When the iteration count of loops is constant, this decision can be made at compile time. However,

```
1  for( int  x=0;  x<WIDTH;  x+=VL_max)
2    VL = min(VL_max,  WIDTH-x)
3    for( int  y=1;  y<HEIGHT;  y++)
4      im[x:x+VL][y] = im[x:x+VL][y] + im[x:x+VL][y-1];
```

Listing 1.2. Vectorized pseudo-code for horizontal integral sums

often those counts can only be determined at runtime, which will be covered in Subsection 4.4.

When the conditions for vectorization specify, that only an outer loop can be vectorized, many compilers, including the Convey Compiler will try to interchange the loop nests and afterwards vectorize the inner loop. Depending on the compute and data access pattern, this may be inefficient, or infeasible, e.g. if the loops are not perfectly nested. Therefore we prefer to vectorize the outer loop directly.

Listing 1.2 illustrates the outer-loop vectorization of the first loop nest from Listing 1.1 in C-like syntax, where a [x:y] statement indicates, that the elements from x to y will be processed in parallel. The outer loop is strip-mined: it now increments by the size of the vector registers VL_max. The actually used vector size VL is computed in line 2, because in the last iteration, there will often be less than VL_max elements left.

Our toolflow does not actually produce code like shown in this listing, but rather the *PartitionPass* plans vectorization and marks the identified loops for vectorization. When mapping the LLVM IR instructions to Convey coprocessor assembly code, the *CodeGenPass* then replaces all instructions involving the induction variable of the vectorized loop, in this case x, by corresponding vector instructions. This can in turn require to vectorize further instructions and variables, even if they are scalars independent of x. We support this scalar expansion, but no vector code generation of reduction operations.

In this simple example, loop exchange with inner-loop vectorization would easily be possible as well. However we can note, that the computation of VL with outer-loop vectorization is executed only $\frac{WIDTH}{VL_{max}}$ times, whereas after loop interchange and inner-loop vectorization it would take place in the inner loop $HEIGHT * \frac{WIDTH}{VL_{max}}$ times. Additional benefits can be exploited when loop-invariant instructions from the inner loop can be moved to the outer loop. For example an address calculation or pointer load for an outer dimension of an array, like im[x:x+VL] in Listing 1.2 can be moved to the outer loop, which may not be possible after a loop interchange.

Note, that the pattern of vectorized memory operations is independent of the decision between outer-loop vectorization and inner-loop vectorization after loop interchange. In this example, assuming C-like row-major order, vectorization requires strided or indexed loads, which impose an overhead compared to continuous loads. When manually optimizing an application for vectorization, adapting the data layout, also combined with tiling, can be a major source of speedups. However for our automated acceleration approach, we leave the data layout unchanged.

4.4   Runtime Decisions

When the iteration space of a loop nest is known at compile time and promises speedups according to our heuristic threshold, we statically replace the execution on the host with execution on the coprocessor. However, often the iteration space depends on concrete input data to an application or on unknown function arguments when accelerating a library. In many of those cases, the iteration space can be determined at runtime of the program at the entry of the actual loop. In this case, we generate code to compute the iteration space before executing the actual loop, using LLVM's ScalarEvolution analysis. Then we add a comparison instruction to compare this value to the threshold for coprocessor execution. If the threshold is not met, a branch instruction will point to the original entry of the loop on the host, otherwise to a new basic block where we generate data movement statements and a call to the according coprocessor function. If the iteration space can not be computed at this point, e.g. when following a linked list, execution will remain on the host.

For achieving best performance on the NUMA architecture of our platform, data should be migrated to the physical memory location where it is most frequently accessed. Therefore we insert calls to Convey's data movement API to transfer data to coprocessor memory, before transferring control to the coprocessor. For these data movement statements, we need the data space of the accessed data structures. Similar to the iteration space, it can either be statically computed at compile time, dynamically at runtime before execution of the loop or it is uncomputable at this point. If it is computable, we add the according data movement statements, either with static size arguments or with runtime computed size arguments. After the coprocessor function execution, similar statements could move the data back to host memory. However, we would need to analyze the further control flow of the application to determine whether the next intensive data access will happen on the host or the coprocessor. Currently we don't support this, so we optimistically assume that typically the runtime relevant code sections will be executed on the coprocessor and leave the migrated data in coprocessor memory. Thus, subsequent coprocessor loops working on the same data will still have calls to migrate data to coprocessor memory, but will need very little time because no data actually needs to be moved.

5   Evaluation

We evaluate our approach by comparing the performance achieved after applying our toolflow and running on host CPU and coprocessor to the baseline performance when compiling to pure host code with the clang backend and executing only on the host CPU. Our entire toolflow just adds a few seconds to the default clang compilation time. In order to assess the impact of different dependency patterns, vectorization strategies and data layouts systematically, we designed a synthetic loop test suite, where we gathered a number of compute patterns which we observed during our practical work with the Convey Compiler (e.g. in [10]) and considered vectorizable. We generate variants of each pattern, one allowing direct inner-loop vectorization (denoted as *Inner*) and one requiring loop interchange or outer-loop vectorization (denoted as *Outer*). The horizontal and vertical integral sums from Listing 1.1 form one of these pairs. Additionally, for each of these loops, we generate one data layout which is *Favorable* for vectorization by enabling continuous vector loads and one *Transposed* layout, which requires strided or indexed vector loads. Some loops have no dependencies but pose other challenges like conditionals and are classified as as *Independent*.

Orthogonal to that distinction, we also vary the data access structure where possible: multi-dimensional data structures are either put into a continuous *Array* or are accessed by following a *Pointer* for every dimension to a dynamically allocated memory location. Accordingly, we group our total of 38 benchmark loops into five times two groups in Table 1. The 32 loops with dependencies can be found in their corresponding line of either column *Inner* or column *Outer* and in order to enable a different point of view they are contained again either in column *Favorable* or in column *Transposed*. Additionally, there are four *Independent Array* loops and two *Independent Pointer* loops.

Table 1. Observed speedup for different groups of loops

Loops	Inner	Outer	Favorable	Transposed	Independent
Array	8.82	9.16	13.59	4.39	12.49
Pointer	2.62	2.64	3.43	1.83	5.28

Table 1 summarizes the average speedups of our toolflow compared to pure host execution for each group. The iteration spaces and data spaces are designed so that the vectorizable loops execute for 5000 sequential iterations on host or 5 iterations on the coprocessor after vectorization, where one iteration is using less than the maximum possible width of 1024 vector elements. All measurements are performed with data already present in coprocessor memory, which is close to the practical performance if our optimistic data movement strategy works out. We see that *Array* data structures allow speedups of more than one order of magnitude for independent loops and almost one order of magnitude for dependent loops. Even *Pointer* data structures can be accelerated by making extensive use of indexed vector loads. However, sequences of a pointer load followed by a dependent data load seem to have a relatively stronger performance impact on the coprocessor than on the host CPU. Thus for the *Pointer* loops, we achieve only 5x on the independent loops and 2.5x on loops with dependencies. Outer-loop vectorization instead of loop interchange yields slightly better speedups. Grouping the same *Inner* and *Outer* benchmarks with dependencies into whether their data layout is *Favorable* for vectorization or *Transposed*, we see that all groups still show some speedups even with ill-suited data layout. However, the right data layout allows three times or two times better speedups, for arrays and pointers respectively.

When, in contrast to the presented measurements, all data needs to be moved to the coprocessor before execution of the loop, this adds on average 59% of the original CPU runtime to the overall runtime of the loop. For these measurements, we applied the rather pessimistic scenario that the entire data structure is only iterated once. In that case, 22 investigated loops still yield a speedup with their first invocation, 13 need two or more invocations to overcome transfer times and 3 have a slowdown even without data movement.

When testing the Convey Compiler on the same benchmark in its fully unguided mode, which is intended mainly for finding possible vectorization candidates, it produces wrong results, probably due to some unsafe optimizations. When properly guided by some pragmas like Convey's toolflow suggests, it can vectorize only the 20 loops with array data structures. When comparing the runtimes after applying our toolflow to those from the Convey Compiler, in 9 of those loops, we are faster between $2.88x$ and $10.05x$, mostly because our more direct vectorization approach allows higher data reuse. For 7 loops, the runtimes are almost identical (speedups of $1.00x$ to $1.06x$). In 4 examples, we have slowdowns of 0.44 to 0.49, because we miss a data reuse opportunity by a loop interchange the Convey Compiler performs.

6   Conclusion

We have presented an automated, unguided acceleration process for binary applications targeting a heterogeneous platform with an FPGA-based coprocessor. Our toolflow introduces decisions made at application runtime and beats existing pragma-based tools in versatility and in many cases in performance. This shows that acceleration with FPGAs can be achieved without costly design or synthesis processes, which may open new practical uses for FPGAs in general-purpose computing.

For moving code to the coprocessor, we currently use a threshold for the required degree of exploitable parallelism that is based on general observations. In future work, we would like to refine that decision process by including some automated profiling for loops with different problem sizes into our toolflow. A bigger goal on the horizon is to exploit the fast acceleration process by moving it from compile time as presented here to the actual runtime of the program, e.g. by running the program in LLVM's just-in-time execution engine and then accelerating applications fully transparently to the user.

Acknowledgement. This work was partially supported by the German Research Foundation (DFG) within the Collaborative Research Centre "On-The-Fly Computing" (SFB 901) and the European Union Seventh Framework Programme under grant agreement no. 610996 (SAVE).

References

1. Allen, J.R., Kennedy, K.: Automatic loop interchange. In: Proc. ACM SIGPLAN Symp. on Compiler Construction, SIGPLAN 1984, pp. 233–246. ACM (1984)
2. Anand, K., Smithson, M., Elwazeer, K., Kotha, A., Gruen, J., Giles, N., Barua, R.: A compiler-level intermediate representation based binary analysis and rewriting system. In: Proc. ACM European Conference on Computer Systems (EuroSys), EuroSys 2013, pp. 295–308. ACM (2013)
3. Augustin, W., Heuveline, V., Weiss, J.-P.: Convey HC-1 hybrid core computer – the potential of FPGAs in numerical simulation. In: Proc. Int. Workshop on New Frontiers in High-performance and Hardware-aware Computing (HipHaC). KIT Scientific Publishing (March 2011)
4. Bakos, J.D.: High-performance heterogeneous computing with the Convey HC-1. Computing in Science and Engineering 12(6), 80–87 (2010)
5. Bispo, J., Cardoso, J.M.P., Monteiro, J.: Hardware pipelining of runtime-detected loops. In: 2012 25th Symposium on Integrated Circuits and Systems Design (SBCCI), pp. 1–6 (2012)
6. Brewer, T.M.: Instruction set innovations for the Convey HC-1 computer. IEEE Micro 30(2), 70–79 (2010)
7. Grad, M., Plessl, C.: On the feasibility and limitations of just-in-time instruction set extension for FPGA-based reconfigurable processors. Int. Journal of Reconfigurable Computing, IJRC (2012)
8. Happe, M., Meyeraufder Heide, F., Kling, P., Platzner, M., Plessl, C.: On-the-fly computing: A novel paradigm for individualized IT services. In: Proc. Workshop on Software Technologies for Future Embedded and Ubiquitous Systems (SEUS). IEEE Computer Society Press (June 2013)
9. Johnson, R., Pearson, D., Pingali, K.: The program structure tree: computing control regions in linear time. In: Proc. ACM SIGPLAN Conf. on Programming Language Design and Implementation (PLDI), PLDI 1994, pp. 171–185. ACM (1994)
10. Kenter, T., Schmitz, H., Plessl, C.: Pragma based parallelization – trading hardware efficiency for ease of use? In: Proc. Int. Conf. on ReConFigurable Computing and FPGAs (ReConFig), pp. 1–6. IEEE Computer Society (December 2012)
11. Lysecky, R., Stitt, G., Vahid, F.: Warp processors. ACM Transactions on Design Automation of Electronic Systems (TODAES) 11(3), 659–681 (2004)
12. Meyer, B., Schumacher, J., Plessl, C., Förstner, J.: Convey vector personalities – FPGA acceleration with an OpenMP-like programming effort? In: Proc. Int. Conf. on Field Programmable Logic and Applications (FPL) (August 2012)
13. Ngo, V.N.: Parallel loop transformation techniques for vector-based multiprocessor systems. PhD thesis (1995) UMI Order No. GAX94-33091
14. Nuzman, D., Zaks, A.: Outer-loop vectorization: revisited for short SIMD architectures. In: Proc. Int. Conf. on Parallel Architecture and Compilation Techniques (PACT), PACT 2008, pp. 2–11. ACM (2008)
15. Scarborough, R.G., Kolsky, H.G.: A vectorizing Fortran compiler. IBM Journal of Research and Development 30(2), 163–171 (1986)

Enhanced Radiation Tolerance of an Optically Reconfigurable Gate Array by Exploiting an Inversion/Non-inversion Implementation

Takashi Yoza and Minoru Watanabe

Electrical and Electronic Engineering
Shizuoka University
3-5-1 Johoku, Hamamatsu, Shizuoka 432-8561, Japan
tmwatan@ipc.shizuoka.ac.jp

Abstract. To date, optically reconfigurable gate arrays (ORGAs) have been developed to realize highly dependable embedded systems. ORGAs present many beneficial capabilities beyond those of field programmable gate arrays (FPGAs): The most important is that an ORGA can be reconfigured using an error-included configuration context that has been damaged by high-energy charged particles. The radiation tolerance of an ORGA is extremely high. Moreover, if an inversion/ non-inversion implementation architecture is introduced to an ORGA, the configuration dependability of the ORGA for radiation can be increased drastically. This paper therefore presents a demonstration of the enhanced radiation tolerance of an optically reconfigurable gate array achieved by exploiting the inversion/ non-inversion implementation.

1 Introduction

Currently, field programmable gate arrays (FPGAs) are widely used for embedded systems [1][2]. Moreover, FPGAs are anticipated for use in high-radiation environments such as space environments or nuclear power plants because such systems cannot be repaired easily. If FPGAs can be used for such environment systems, then the system can be repaired remotely with the remaining functioning components and can be restarted remotely, even if the system malfunctions because of total dose effects.

A radiation-tolerant FPGA always includes error checking and correction (ECC) for configuration SRAM. For that reason, the FPGA is tolerant for a single-bit error [3]–[5]. However, under a radiation-rich environment, several high-energy charged particles are incident to the configuration SRAM simultaneously. In such cases, the ECC cannot repair numerous errors, thereby leading to fatal errors.

Therefore, optically reconfigurable gate arrays (ORGAs) that can execute a more robust configuration than FPGAs have been developed recently [6]–[9]. In an ORGA, a configuration procedure is executed optically. At that time, a majority voting operation is executed automatically. An ORGA's configuration context consists of bright points and dark points corresponding respectively to binary state H and binary state L. Bright points of binary state H can be generated with a summation of numerous in-phase waves while dark points of binary state L can be generated with a correction of waves with

D. Goehringer et al. (Eds.): ARC 2014, LNCS 8405, pp. 156–166, 2014.
© Springer International Publishing Switzerland 2014

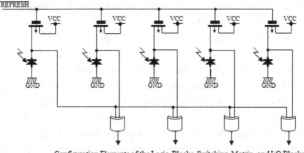

Configuration Elements of the Logic Blocks, Switching Matrix, and I/O Blocks

Fig. 1. Circuit diagram of an inversion/ non-inversion dynamic optical configuration circuit including four configuration bits

various phases. Finally, the bright points and dark points are received on a photodiode array along with a threshold operation. The mechanism is the same as that of a majority voting operation. In ORGAs, the configuration procedure becomes very robust since the number of majority voting operations is extremely high.

In addition, an ORGA's programmable gate array is also robust [10]. An ORGA can support high-speed dynamic reconfiguration using numerous reconfiguration contexts. In fact, the reconfiguration frequency can reach the operation clock frequency of a programmable gate array. In this case, multi-function units can be decomposed to single function unit because the function change can be executed by reconfiguring its programmable gate array. As a result, many-modular redundancy over triple-modular redundancy (TMR) can be realized. Therefore, the ORGA's programmable gate array is also extremely robust.

However, if an inversion/ non-inversion implementation architecture is incorporated into an ORGA, then the configuration dependability of the ORGA for radiation can be increased drastically. This paper therefore presents a demonstration of enhanced radiation tolerance of an optically reconfigurable gate array by exploiting an inversion/ non-inversion implementation.

2   Configuration Dependability of an ORGA

An ORGA optical system comprises laser sources, an optical holographic memory, and a programmable gate array VLSI. The holographic memory can store numerous reconfiguration contexts. The reconfiguration contexts in the holographic memory are addressed by a laser diode array. The diffraction pattern from the holographic memory can be received as a reconfiguration context on a photodiode-array that is implemented in a programmable gate array of an ORGA-VLSI. Since the diffraction pattern is generated by the summation of numerous light waves from a holographic memory, the configuration procedure on an ORGA is extremely robust against radiation.

Here, an optical reconfiguration circuit for ORGAs is discussed. An ORGA-VLSI has many configuration circuits for receiving a configuration context. The configuration circuit has two roles: detection of a configuration context pattern and execution of a threshold operation. Numerous optical light waves from a holographic memory are added to each photodiode. Then a threshold operation is executed on each photodiode. The photodiode operation means a majority voting operation.

The photodiode circuit detects a bright point of binary state H or a dark point of binary state L. Here, dark points of binary state L are generated by a collection of numerous waves having various phases. Since the pixel data of a holographic memory are always damaged randomly by high-energy charged particles, they almost never affect the light intensity of the dark bits. However, the bright bits are sensitive to damage of a holographic memory because the number of in-phase waves to generate a bright bit is lower than the number of waves with various phases to produce a dark bit. Therefore, to increase the ORGA's configuration dependability, first, the dependability of bright bits or binary state Highs have only to be considered. The ORGA's configuration dependability can be discussed only by the dependability of bright bits or binary state Highs. The following inversion/ non-inversion configuration method can increase the dependability of bright bits.

3   Inversion/Non-inversion Configuration Method on ORGA

According to the property of holographic memories, the number of in-phase waves to generate a bright bit or binary state H depends on the number of bright bits included in a configuration context. As increasing the number of bright bits, the number of overlaps of the transparent area of one bright bit and opaque areas for the other bright bits are also increased. The overlapped area becomes an intermediate value between the transparent condition and the opaque condition. Along with the increase in the number of bright bits, the overlapped area is also increased so that the number of holographic memory pixels corresponding to in-phase waves to generate each bright bit is decreased. Therefore, to increase the dependability, the reduction of the number of bright bits or binary state highs is extremely important. The inversion/ non-inversion configuration method can decrease the number of bright bits or binary state highs.

A new ORGA-VLSI has an inversion/ non-inversion configuration circuit. Figure 1 portrays the circuit diagram of the inversion/ non-inversion dynamic optical reconfiguration circuit including four configuration bits. The configuration circuit consists of charge-integrated photo-circuits and exclusive OR gates. A one-inversion control photo circuit is also implemented. The output is connected to a port of exclusive OR gates. Another ports of the exclusive OR gates are connected to the four configuration circuits. Therefore, if the control photo-circuit receives light, then the outputs of the four configuration circuits are flipped. However, when the control photo-circuit never receives a light, the outputs of four configuration circuits are sent directly as configuration information. If the architecture can be used, then we can generate any four-bit configuration pattern using two or fewer bits of binary state highs. When the grouping number of configuration context bits is larger than that, the effect of the bright bit reduction is also decreased. Consequently, in this case, we have chosen four configuration bits as one group.

Here, the reduction efficiency of the number of bright bits of the inversion/ non-inversion configuration method is calculated. It is assumed that configuration contexts are given continuously for an ORGA-VLSI and that they uniformly include all possible patterns. For example, regarding four-bit configuration, all possible patterns indicates 16 patterns of "0000", "0001"..., and "1111". Under such a condition, first, the reduction efficiency of the number of bright bits in a configuration context of conventional ORGAs is estimated. The average number of '1' s corresponding to laser irradiation is calculated by counting bit '1' of all possible vectors and dividing it by $N2^N$ of the summation of bits of all possible vectors, as in the following equation.

$$\kappa_{ORGA} = \frac{\sum_{r=1}^{N} r \cdot {}_N C_r}{2^N N} = \frac{1}{2},$$ (1)

Therein, ${}_N C_r$ is a combination. The average number of writing '1' s corresponding to laser irradiation is calculated by counting the '1' bits of all possible vectors and dividing it by $N2^N$ of the summation of bits of all possible vectors, as in the following equation.

$$\kappa_{new} = \frac{\sum_{r=1}^{[\frac{N}{2}]} r \cdot {}_N C_r}{2^N N} + \frac{\sum_{r=[\frac{N}{2}+1]}^{N} (N - r + 1) \cdot {}_N C_r}{2^N N}$$ (2)

The first term in the right side of the upper Eq. (2) is identical to Eq. (1). In this case, an inversion bit γ_{N+1} is equal to 0. In addition, the second term in the right side of upper Eq. (2) is applicable to the case in which the inversion bit γ_{N+1} is equal to 1. In the case of four configuration bits, the average number of bright bits can be decreased from 2.0 of conventional ORGAs to 1.5625. Using this inversion/ non-inversion dynamic optical configuration method, in the case of four bits, about 22% of bright bits are removable. Consequently, the configuration dependability can be increased using this method.

4   VLSI Design

A new optically reconfigurable gate array VLSI (ORGA-VLSI) chip which can support the inversion/ non-inversion configuration was designed and fabricated using 0.18 μm standard complementary metal oxide semiconductor (CMOS) process technology, as shown in Fig. 2. A transmission gate and a photodiode cell were designed as custom cells. The gate array design was synthesized by combining such custom cells and standard cells and using a logic synthesis tool (Design Compiler; Synopsys Inc.). Then, a place and route for the synthesized gate array design was executed using Astro (Synopsys Inc.). Finally, the ORGA-VLSI was fabricated at Rohm's manufacturing facility. The specifications are presented in Table 1. Voltages of the core and I/O cells were designed respectively using 1.8 V and 3.3 V. Photodiodes were constructed between an N-Well and a P-substrate. The junction area of a photodiode was designed as 4.40 μm $\times$ 4.45 μm. The photodiode cells are arranged at 30.08 μm horizontal intervals and at 30.24 μm vertical intervals. This design incorporates 10,322 photodiodes. To increase the photodiode sensitivity, a refresh transistor and an optical amplifier connected to a photodiode were designed to be as small as possible to reduce the load capacitance and drain capacitance.

Fig. 2. Photograph of a 0.18 μm CMOS process highly sensitive optically differential reconfigurable gate array VLSI

Table 1. Specifications of ORGA-VLSI supporting the inversion/ non-inversion configuration

Technology	0.18 μm double-poly 5-metal CMOS process
Chip size	5.0 × 2.5 [mm]
Supply Voltage	Core 1.8V, I/O 3.3V
Photodiode size	4.40 × 4.45 [μm]
Photodiode response time	< 5 ns
Sensitivity	2.12×10^{-14} J
Distance between Photodiodes	h.=30.08, v.= 30.24 [μm]
Number of Photodiodes	10,322
Number of Logic Blocks	80
Number of Switching Matrices	90
Number of Wires in a Routing Channel	8
Number of I/O blocks	8 (32 bit)
Gate Count	2,720

The gate array of the ORGA-VLSI uses an island style. The basic functionality of a gate array is fundamentally identical to that of currently available field programmable gate arrays (FPGAs). In all, 80 optically reconfigurable logic blocks (ORLBs), 90 optically reconfigurable switching matrices (ORSMs), and 8 optically reconfigurable I/O blocks (ORIOBs), which include 4 programmable I/O bits, were implemented in the

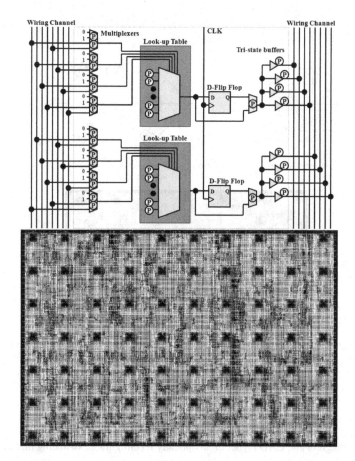

Fig. 3. Block diagram and CAD layout of an optically reconfigurable logic block (ORLB)

gate array. The respective ORLBs, ORSMs, and ORIOBs are programmable block-by-block through 69, 49, and 49 optical connections. Each block can be reconfigured block-by-block. The total gate count is 2,720.

Optically reconfigurable logic block. The block diagram and CAD layout of an optically reconfigurable logic block are presented in Fig. 3. Each optically reconfigurable logic block consists of 2 four-input one-output look-up tables (LUTs), 10 multiplexers, 8 tri-state buffers, and 2 delay-type flip-flops with a reset function. The input signals from the wiring channel, which are applied through some switching matrices and wiring channels from optically reconfigurable I/O blocks, are transferred to LUTs through eight multiplexers. The LUTs are used for implementing Boolean functions. The outputs of an LUT and of a delay-type flip-flop connected to the LUT are connected to a multiplexer. A combinational circuit and sequential circuit can be chosen by changing the multiplexer, as in FPGAs. Finally, outputs of the multiplexers are connected to the wiring channel again through eight tri-state buffers. In all, 69 photodiodes are used for programming an optically reconfigurable logic block. The optically reconfigurable logic

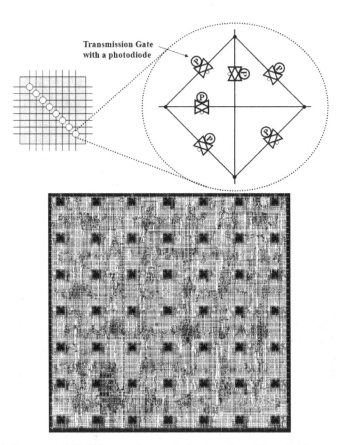

Fig. 4. Block diagram and CAD layout of an optically reconfigurable switching matrix (ORSM)

block can be reconfigured perfectly in parallel. The cell size is $288.00 \times 192.48 \ \mu m^2$. Such an optically reconfigurable logic block design is based on a standard cell design, except for the custom designs used for the transmission gate cells and photodiode cells.

Optically reconfigurable switching matrix. The block diagram and CAD layout of the optically reconfigurable switching matrix are portrayed in Fig. 4. Its basic construction is the same as that used by Xilinx Inc. Four-directional switching matrices with 48 transmission gates were implemented in the gate array. Each transmission gate can be regarded as a bi-directional switch. A photodiode is connected to each transmission gate; it controls whether the transmission gate is closed or not. The four-direction switching matrices can be programmed as 49 optical connections. The cell size is 197.76 $\times$ 192.48 μm^2. Such an optically reconfigurable switching matrix was designed using custom cells of photodiode cells and transmission gate cells, except for some buffers. The switching matrix never includes the inversion/ non-inversion configuration method since the number of bright bits is always small so that it is not necessary the inversion operation.

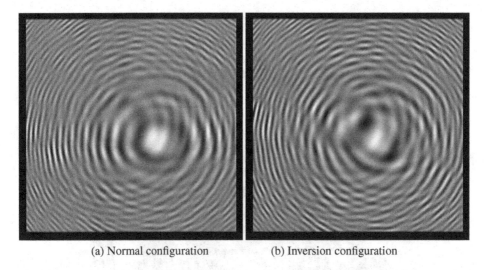

(a) Normal configuration   (b) Inversion configuration

Fig. 5. Holographic memory patterns of a NAND circuit consisting of 300×300 pixels

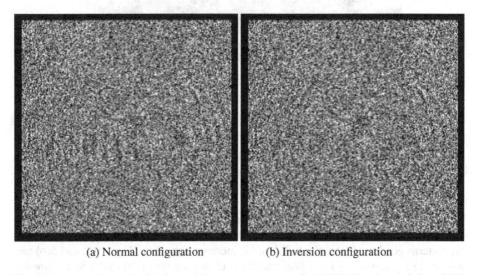

(a) Normal configuration   (b) Inversion configuration

Fig. 6. Impulse-noise-applied holographic memory patterns of a NAND circuit consisting of 300 $\times$ 300 pixels

5   Experimental System and Results

An ORGA optical system comprises a laser source, an optical holographic memory, and an ORGA-VLSI, as shown in Figs. 7(a) and 7(b). As holographic memory, a liquid crystal spatial light modulator (LC-SLM) was used. The light source was a 532 nm 300 mW laser (torus 532; Laser Quantum). The LC-SLM was a projection TV panel

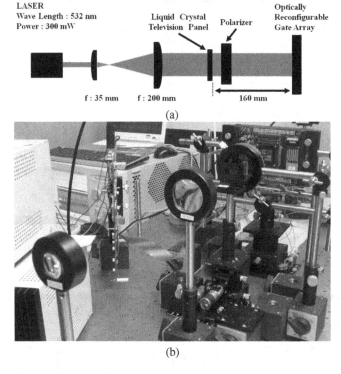

Fig. 7. Experimental system

(L3D07U-81G00; Seiko Epson Corp.): a 90° twisted nematic device with a thin film transistor. The panel consists of 1,920 × 1,080 pixels, each of which is 8.5 × 8.5 μm^2. The new ORGA-VLSI was placed 160 mm distant from the LC-SLM.

Here, a simple three-input NAND circuit was implemented onto the ORGA-VLSI. The original holographic memory pattern of the NAND circuit is presented in Fig. 5(a). Also, the holographic memory pattern of the NAND circuit using the inversion/ non-inversion configuration is presented in Fig. 5(b). The CCD-captured configuration context patterns generated from the holographic memory patterns of Figs. 5(a) and 5(b) are presented respectively in Figs. 8(a) and 8(b). Using the new ORGA-VLSI to support the inversion/ non-inversion configuration, the number of bright bits on a configuration context of NAND circuit was reduced from 16 to 12.

We applied impulse noise for the original holographic memory patterns of Fig. 5(a) and 5(b). The impulse-noise-applied holographic memory patterns are depicted in Fig. 6(a) and 6(b). In the original holographic memory, correct configuration procedures can be executed up to 64,800 impulse-noises. However, in the inversion configuration holographic memory, correct configuration procedures were confirmed up to 68,400 impulse noises. Therefore, the radiation tolerance can be improved drastically. The inversion/ non-inversion configuration is useful to increase the dependability of ORGA with only a small increase in hardware.

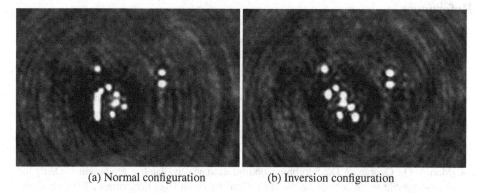

(a) Normal configuration   (b) Inversion configuration

Fig. 8. CCD-captured configuration context images of a NAND circuit generated from original holographic memory patterns

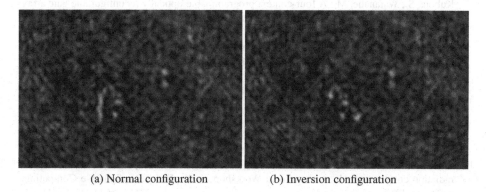

(a) Normal configuration   (b) Inversion configuration

Fig. 9. CCD-captured configuration context images of a NAND circuit generated from noise-applied holographic memory patterns

6   Conclusion

This paper has presented a proposal of a more advanced method for increasing the radiation tolerance of ORGAs by exploiting an inversion/ non-inversion implementation. It was demonstrated that the use of an inversion/ non-inversion implementation reduces the number of bright bits on a configuration context so that the radiation tolerance can be increased to 106 %. This advanced method for increasing radiation tolerance, which exploits an inversion/ non-inversion implementation, is expected to be useful to increase the reliability of ORGAs in a radiation environment.

Acknowledgments. This research was supported by the Ministry of Education, Science, Sports and Culture, Grant-in-Aid for Scientific Research (B), No. 24300017. The VLSI chip in this study was fabricated in the chip fabrication program of VLSI Design and Education Center (VDEC), the University of Tokyo in collaboration with Rohm Co. Ltd. and Toppan Printing Co. Ltd.

References

1. Khalil-Hani, M., Eng, P.C.: FPGA-based embedded system implementation of finger vein biometrics. In: IEEE Symposium on Industrial Electronics & Applications (ISIEA), pp. 700–705 (2010)
2. Sterpone, L., Violante, M.: An Analysis of SEU Effects in Embedded Operating Systems for Real-Time Applications. In: IEEE International Symposium on Industrial Electronics, pp. 3345–3349 (2007)
3. Bonacini, S., Faccio, F., Kloukinas, K., Marchioro, A.: An SEU-Robust Configurable Logic Block for the Implementation of a Radiation-Tolerant FPGA. IEEE Transactions on Nuclear Science 53(6), 3408–3416 (2006)
4. Martin, Q., George, A.D.: Scrubbing optimization via availability prediction (SOAP) for reconfigurable space computing. In: IEEE Conference on High Performance Extreme Computing (HPEC), pp. 1–6 (2012)
5. Hjortland, E., Chen, L.: Fault-tolerant FPGAs by online ECC verification and restoration. In: IEEE Region 5 Conference, pp. 91–93 (2006)
6. Kubota, S., Watanabe, M.: A four-context programmable optically reconfigurable gate array with a reflective silver-halide holographic memory. IEEE Photonics Journal 3(4), 665–675 (2011)
7. Nakajima, M., Watanabe, M.: Fast optical reconfiguration of a nine-context DORGA using a speed adjustment control. ACM Transaction on Reconfigurable Technology and Systems 4(2) (2011)
8. Seto, D., Nakajima, M., Watanabe, M.: Dynamic optically reconfigurable gate array very large-scale integration with partial reconfiguration capability. Applied Optics 49(36), 6986–6994 (2010)
9. Morita, H., Watanabe, M.: Microelectromechanical Configuration of an Optically Reconfigurable Gate Array. IEEE Journal of Quantum Electronics 46(9), 1288–1294 (2010)
10. Shirahashi, Y., Watanabe, M.: Dependability-increasing method of processors under a space radiation environment. In: International Workshop on Applied Reconfigurable Computing, p. 218 (2013)
11. Watanabe, M., Nakajima, M., Kato, S.: An inversion/non-inversion dynamic optically reconfigurable gate array VLSI. World Scientific and Engineering Academy and Society Transactions on Circuits and Systems 8(1), 11–20 (2009)

Hardware-Accelerated Data Compression in Low-Power Wireless Sensor Networks

Andreas Engel[1] and Andreas Koch[2]

[1] LOEWE Research Center AdRIA, Darmstadt
[2] Embedded Systems and Applications Group, Technische Universität Darmstadt

Abstract. In wireless sensor networks, the actual transmission of collected data is often the most energy-consuming operation. Frequently, it is worthwhile to spend energy aggregating the raw sensor data on the node to reduce the transmission effort. For many cases, lossless data compression can be employed as a general data aggregation method, as incompressible data (noise) generally does not carry any information worth transmitting. Nevertheless, the energy spent for data compression must be traded-off against the energy saved for transmitting the compressed data. In this work, sensor data of two real-life applications is compressed using a hardware-accelerator of the heterogeneous HaLOEWEn sensor node. The benefits of providing the node with a reconfigurable compute unit is demonstrated by comparing its energy consumption with that of of a purely software-based implementation.

Keywords: reconfigurable computing, wireless sensor network, data compression, heterogeneous architecture, low-power mode.

1 Introduction

Wireless Sensor Networks have been the subject of intense research [11]. In these distributed monitoring applications, the data gathered by the sensor nodes usually has to be forwarded to a central base station for final processing or storage. As the radio transceiver is the major power consumer of a wireless sensor node, even computationally intensive decentralized data aggregation methods can result in a reduction of the overall energy consumption of the sensor node. This is a major concern for the typically battery-powered sensor nodes.

In many applications, no specialized high-level data aggregation scheme (e.g., actual feature extraction) can be applied. Instead, all of the sensor data has to be forwarded to the base station. In these cases, lossless data compression can be employed as a more general form of data aggregation. However, efficiency can sometimes be improved by considering an application-specific system model in the compression scheme, e.g., the nature of rotating machinery. Generally, a trade-off between the compression quality and complexity of the underlying data model has to be found. When monitoring slowly changing environmental conditions, differential encoding has often proven useful.

D. Goehringer et al. (Eds.): ARC 2014, LNCS 8405, pp. 167–178, 2014.
© Springer International Publishing Switzerland 2014

While reducing the communication demands and energy consumption of the sensor nodes, data compression comes at the cost of encoder and decoder complexity. As the decoding is typically performed at the (often mains-powered) base station, the decoder complexity is not a major concern, thus this work focuses on encoding.

To improve the compression quality, many encoders first collect a block of data to analyze its statistical nature before compressing the block with the appropriate settings. This two-pass strategy increases the memory capacity required on the node as well as the latency between data acquisition and transmission. The block size, and thus the gains in compression quality, may be limited by the amount of available memory or real-time requirements in latency-sensitive applications. In addition, both encoder passes require a certain amount of computation time and energy, which must be amortized by the reduced communication effort. Moving operations from software to specialized hardware blocks can often reduce energy consumption and thus offers an attractive option to improve the computation vs. transmission energy balance on a sensor node.

In this work, data acquired by two different monitoring applications is losslessly compressed by a heterogeneous sensor node incorporating a low-power FPGA-based reconfigurable compute unit and a microcontroller-based radio system-on-chip [4]. The energy required for data transmission as well as for software and hardware implementations of the encoding are compared to demonstrate the benefits of hardware-accelerated data compression.

The remainder of this article is organized as follows: Section 2 gives a brief overview of software- and hardware-based data compression in WSN. In Section 3, the sample applications are introduced and a variety of compression schemes is applied to the raw sensor data to find the trade-off between compression quality and encoder complexity. Section 4 details the hardware-accelerated implementation of the most appropriate compression scheme before evaluating the energy reduction of the proposed method in Section 5. Section 6 concludes this work and looks out to further research.

2   Related Work

Fundamentally, we distinguish between generic data compression, applicable to almost all kinds of sensor data, and compressive sensing [3]. The latter assumes highly specific properties in the input signals and is not addressed in this work.

Data compression in WSN was investigated frequently in the last decade [7]. For example, an LZW-compressor was implemented on an MSP430 MCU to analyze the effect of reduced data rates on the end-to-end packet delay in a multi-hop network [2]. The energy savings achievable by an nonlinear adaptive pulse code modulator running on the ARM processor of a Beagle Board were investigated in [6]. However, these authors erroneously considered the compression ratios achieved directly as energy savings, completely ignoring the energy required for the encoding. This gross simplification was not used in [9], where run-length and adaptive Huffman encoding were implemented on the AVR MCU of a Mica2 mote. The energy for encoding was determined solely by simulations and datasheet-specifications, using just synthetic data streams with guaranteed statistical properties as inputs.

Hardware-accelerated data compression in context of wireless sensor networks focused mainly on lossy image compression in visual surveillance networks, such as the JPEG compression on an Altera EP2C35 FPGA [12], or the identification of relevant image sections using a Xilinx Virtex II FPGA [8]. In addition to not compressing losslessly, these investigations aimed at reducing the required data rate to the throughput limits of the wireless transmission channel, instead of minimizing overall system energy consumption. The acceleration of a second order ADPCM compressor on a Xilinx XC4000 device was proposed in [1], but did not report any energy requirements.

The use of hardware accelerators for lossless data compression under energy constraints, which is the focus of this work, has not been studied extensively before.

3   Characteristics of Monitoring Applications

To investigate the potential and difficulties of compressing sensed data, two different applications were examined. The first one, neural activity in primates, is delay constrained, while the second one, condition monitoring of heavy industrial machinery, is computationally expensive due to multiple parallel data channels.

3.1   Evaluation of Compression Algorithms

As a baseline for our work, we examined the fundamental efficiencies of various compression *algorithms* for the applications, using off-the-shelf software implementations running on a non-energy constrained x86 processor.

In both cases, 8192 samples of each data stream were split into blocks of different size and fed into the compression algorithms listed in Table 1 with their specific run-time options. Static overhead (e.g., file headers) generated by these tools was disregarded when calculating compression ratios.

Table 1. Compression algorithms and options used in further evaluation

codec	options	version	codec	overhead
BZIP2	-9	1.0.6	RLE + BWT + MTF + Huffman	24 B
RAR	-m5 -en	5.00	proprietary	55 B
ZP	c3	1.00	context modeling + arith. coding	221 B
MP4ALS	-7e	RM23	adapt. linear prediction + Rice	34 B
FLAC	-8	1.3.0	adapt. linear prediction + Rice	8292 B
ALAC	ffmpeg	0.8.7-6	adapt. linear prediction + Rice	0 B

In addition to using these off-the-shelf encoders, a custom forward-adaptive differential pulse code modulation (ADPCM-APF) compressor was implemented to allow a fine-grained trade-off between encoder complexity and compression ratio. Here, the first M samples of a sample-block $(x_1, \ldots, x_N)$ are transmitted uncompressed. The successive samples x_i are mapped to a prediction error

$$d_i = x_i - \sum_{k=1}^{M} a_k x_{i-k} \qquad M < i \leq N \tag{1}$$

for the linear predictor of order M with coefficients $a_1, \ldots, a_M \in \mathbb{R}$. The classical approach of using an encoder based on a static first-order ($M = 1$) predictor and $a_1 = 1$ is referred to in the following as *DPCM* scheme.

For the forward adaptive predictor, which is referred to as a *ADPCM* scheme, the predictor coefficients $a_1, \ldots, a_M$ are not static but fitted to the current sample block by calculating the autocorrelation values for the block:

$$r_k = \frac{s_k}{N-k} \qquad \text{with} \qquad s_k = \sum_{i=1}^{N-k} x_i x_{i+k} \qquad 0 \leq k \leq M \tag{2}$$

These values are then used to build a system of linear equations, whose solution results in prediction coefficients that minimize the variance of the prediction error sequence $(d_1, \ldots, d_N)$ [10]. This is important for the downstream Rice encoder, which maps the error value sequence to an actual bit stream, aiming for short bit representations for each error value. We will use Rice encoding in both the *DPCM* and *ADPCM* schemes.

As an initial step for Rice encoding, the sequence of signed difference (prediction error) values d_i is converted to a sequence of unsigned values p_i by a simple transformation:

$$p_i = \begin{cases} 2d_i, & \text{for } d_i \geq 0 \\ -2d_i - 1, & \text{for } d_i < 0 \end{cases} \tag{3}$$

The values p_i are then encoded into Rice-form bit sequences

$$R_K(p_i) = \texttt{concat}\left(U(\tfrac{p_i}{2^K}), B_K(p_i \bmod 2^K)\right) \tag{4}$$

with K being the Rice parameter that balances the widths of a zero-terminated unary code U and the binary block code B_K in a bit-wise concatenation. Precise predictions ($p_i < 2^K$) can thus be represented by $K + 1$ bits. Infrequently occurring larger prediction errors, caused by unforeseen spikes, can still be expressed losslessly by exploiting the variable length unary code. In our experiments, K was statically chosen for each data channel and not adapted to each sample block, in contrast to the audio encoders listed in Table 1.

3.2   Neural Activity in Primates

At the German Primate Center in Göttingen, the neural activities of primates solving different tasks are measured by a micro-electrode inside the probands brains. As the apes have to move freely over a wide testing area, wired instrumentation is impractical and thus the sensor data sampled with 16 bit resolution

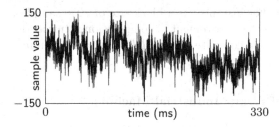

Fig. 1. 8192 samples of neural activity data (min = -155, max = 169, mean = 6.3, stddev = 45.5)

Table 2. Statistical characteristics of 8192 samples of machinery condition monitoring data

channel	1	2	3
min	-3872	-4156	-22466
max	5203	13104	16307
mean	110	2919	-3339
stddev	1213	2374	13041

at a frequency of 24.414 kHz (see Figure 1) has to be transmitted wirelessly. The resulting data rate of 391 kbit/s exceeds the capability of the popular IEEE 802.15.4 protocol, on which many recent low power radio transceivers are based. The captured data stream thus has to be compressed by about 50 % before it can actually be transmitted by an IEEE 802.15.4 transceiver.

Based on the received neural data, the variable penetration depth of the microelectrode is controlled remotely by an operator at the control station. In order to allow timely interactive manipulation of the probe depth, the maximum end-to-end latency is thus restricted by the human response time of about 100 ms. Thus, the maximum block size used by a two pass encoder may not exceed 2, 400 samples at 24.414 kHz.

The compression ratios (compressed data size / uncompressed data size) achieved by applying the compression algorithms from Section 3.1 are shown in Figure 2. As expected, the compression ratios of all encoders improve with increasing block sizes. With the exception of *MP4ALS*, the predictive audio encoders clearly outperform the dictionary-based compression schemes. Given the audio-like characteristics of the neural activity data, this in itself is unsurprising. However, the additional encoder complexity necessary for adapting the higher order linear predictor coefficients in the algorithms used in *MP4ALS*, *ALAC* or *FLAC* does not improve the compression ratios significantly compared to the

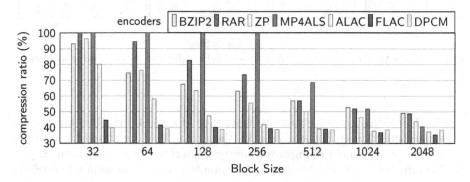

Fig. 2. Reduction of neural activity data achieved by various compression schemes

static first-order *DPCM* predictor. For instance, at a block size of 2048 samples, the *FLAC* encoder achieves only a 3 % improvement in compression ratios at the cost of double the execution time when compared to the *DPCM* encoder running on the same platform.

3.3   Condition Monitoring of Heavy Industrial Machinery

The second application deals with detecting damage or fatigue of the rotating parts of very large industrial machines. This condition monitoring is used to schedule inspection/maintenance intervals before unanticipated major damage leads to high repair costs and downtime of the machinery. Since the monitoring algorithms observe long-term trends in the acquired data, this application is latency insensitive. Note that the sensor nodes are located on heavily vibrating parts of the machine, which would quickly wear out fixed cable connections, thus making low-power wireless communication preferable.

The raw data streams are gathered from a three channel MEMS sensor sampled at 1 kHz with a resolution of 16 bit per channel. Table 2 shows some statistical characteristics of the captured signals[1].

The compression algorithms described in Section 3.1 were applied to each channel separately. The resulting overall compression ratios are shown in Figure 3. Again, the predictive audio codecs are most appropriate. At a block size of 2048 samples, *FLAC* produces results 6 % smaller than *DPCM*. As in Section 3.2, this improvement comes at the cost of double the execution time for *FLAC*.

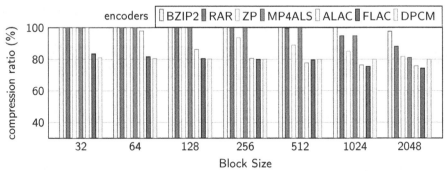

Fig. 3. Reduction of condition monitoring data achieved by various compression algorithms

The *ADPCM* scheme is examined separately. Figure 4 quantifies the impact of the prediction order. For small blocks, the size of the stored prediction parameters exceeds the benefit of improved compression ratios due to the reduced prediction error variance. For blocks of 2048 samples, the compression ratio strictly

---

[1] Actual waveforms cannot be shown here for confidentiality reasons.

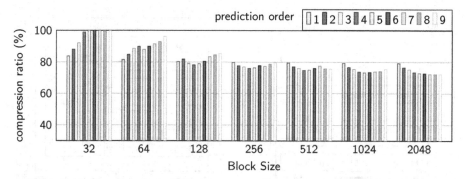

Fig. 4. Impact of prediction order on *ADPCM* compression ratio

decreases with the prediction order and a break even point for best energy efficiency can be derived from the platform specific power draw for computation and transmission. Thus, adaptive prediction should be used for condition monitoring if the target platform supports storing a sufficient amount of samples (recall that there are three data channels, and double-buffering may be necessary for parallel sampling and encoding).

In conclusion, the adaptive schemes reached the best compression ratios for larger sample blocks, while static *DPCM* proved superior on small blocks. Thus, for delay-sensitive applications or memory-constrained platforms, the simple *DPCM* scheme should be applied. In all other cases, *FLAC* can improve the compression ratio of *DPCM* by about 5 %. Note that *FLAC* is just a combination of *ADPCM* with an extensive search for the optimal prediction order. For data sources with known characteristics, a static selection of the prediction order may be sufficient. The adaptation of prediction coefficients in *ADPCM* only becomes worthwhile, if the further data size reduction of 5 % over *DPCM* can be achieved with less energy than required to transmit the just *DPCM*-compressed data. For this reason, we also examine the energy efficiency of a hardware implementation of the *ADPCM* algorithm.

4   Hardware-Accelerated Data Compression

In Section 3, (adaptive) differential pulse code modulation combined with Rice coding was identified as a balanced trade-off between compression quality and run-time effort for the investigated data streams. However, the low-power micro-controllers typically used in wireless sensor nodes may be overburdened even by these simpler algorithms, particularly by the adaptive compression scheme.

In [4], the HaLoMote architecture was proposed to energy-efficiently perform more compute-intensive distributed tasks even on low-power wireless sensor nodes. This heterogeneous architecture combines a micro-controller-based radio system-on-chip (MCU), responsible for handling wireless protocols and system management, with a reconfigurable compute unit (RCU) for the hardware-acceleration

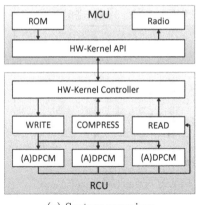

(a) System overview

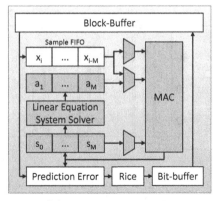

(b) Compression Module

Fig. 5. Hardware-software interaction of the heterogeneous sensor node (a) and hardware-accelerated data compression (b)

of complex computations. The current implementation, called HaLOEWEn, employs a TI CC2531 RF-SoC as MCU and a Microsemi AGL1000 FPGA as RCU. This section describes the hardware implementation of the $(a)DPCM$ algorithms on the HaLoMote reconfigurable architecture.

Figure 5a gives an overview of the proposed implementation. The RCU can hold multiple hardware (HW) kernels performing different algorithmic functions. A communications API allows the MCU to interact with individual kernels [5]. The HW-Kernel controller starts the execution of HW-Kernels, manages data input and output, and reports execution completion. It is driven by the MCU via a bit-parallel interface through the application-independent API. For the data compression application, three HW-Kernels were implemented. The *WRITE* kernel distributes a sample stream to the compression modules, each processing one data channel. In practice, this sample stream will be generated by sensors attached to the RCU. For better reproducibility of results, our experiments below will process a prerecorded sample stream, read from the MCU code memory.

The compressed data stream generated by the compression modules is then sequentialized by the *READ* kernel and passed back to the MCU, which transmits it wirelessly. The HaLOEWEn radio stack allows parallelizing the radio transmission with the data transfer from the RCU to the MCU. Thus, the MCU duty cycle is not stretched by the communication task. This is important for the energy efficiency of the system (shorter duty cycles allow longer ultra-low-power sleep phases). Finally, the *COMPRESS* kernel controls the compression modules and tracks the number of generated output bytes.

Figure 5b shows the implementation of the compression module, instantiated once for each data channel. It contains a block buffer using on-chip RAM to hold the sample stream and compressed data stream. This in-place compression architecture allows to compress larger data blocks in memory-constrained systems (the on-chip RAM of the low-power FPGA used is limited to just 144 kbit).

However, it requires a compression ratio *smaller* than 100 % (i.e., compression actually *reduces* the data size) for each prefix of each sample block in the sample stream. This constraint is achievable for both the primate neural activity as well condition monitoring scenarios, where the spikiness of data is limited by the inertia of the underlying biochemical and mechanical systems.

The shaded modules of Figure 5b are used only in the adaptive prediction. For the simple static first-order *DPCM* compression, the block buffer is read once (retrieving uncompressed data), with the last sample x_{i-1} also being retained in a sample FIFO to calculate the prediction error as required by Equation 1. This prediction error is passed to the Rice coder to produce the bit sequence described by Equations 3 and 4. This bit sequence is sliced into bytes and written back to the block-buffer (now in compressed form) by a bit-buffer module.

For the adaptive *ADPCM* compression scheme, an additional coefficient optimization pass precedes the compression pass. During this pass through the block-buffer, the autocorrelation sums s_k of Equation 2 are accumulated. To this end, a time-multiplexed multiply-accumulate unit (MAC) is supplied with the appropriate operands from the sample FIFO $(x_i, \ldots, x_{i-M})$ and the accumulator set $(s_0, \ldots, s_M)$. At the end of the pass, the autocorrelation sums s_k computed in the accumulators are used to generate the linear equation system that has to be solved to retrieve the prediction coefficients $(a_1, \ldots, a_M)$. As a trade-off between prediction accuracy and the time and energy spent to calculate the coefficients and the prediction values, fixed point arithmetic was chosen. The resulting coefficients are stored in Q4.12 format. To conserve FPGA area and energy, we chose $M = 1$ for our experiment, which simplifies the linear equation system solver to just

$$a_1 = \frac{r_1}{r_0} = \frac{s_1 \cdot N}{s_0 \cdot N - s_0} \tag{5}$$

By restricting the block size N to a power of two, the remaining integer division can be performed sequentially in 16 clock cycles. In each step of the subsequent compression pass, the prediction coefficients have to be multiplied with the corresponding prior value(s) from the sample FIFO to accumulate the prediction of the next sample (Equation 1). The MAC unit and one of the autocorrelation sums is reused for these calculations, which are performed in parallel with the bit-buffering of the Rice code of the previous prediction error.

5   Experimental Evaluation

The hardware-accelerated data compression design described in Section 4 was synthesized for the Microsemi IGLOO AGL1000V2 FPGA using Synplify Pro H-2013.03M-1 with retiming. The block buffer size of the compression modules was fixed at 2048 samples. As shown in Table 3, the design is primarily limited by the available memory and restricted to four channels at the given block size. Even so, some area remains for implementing higher order predictors.

To demonstrate the energy efficiency of the hardware-accelerated data compression, the measurement setup shown in Figure 6 was used. The HaLOEWEn sensor node is supplied by an external 3 V voltage source to power its internal

Table 3. Synthesis results for the Microsemi IGLOO AGL1000V2 device

channels	scheme	BRAM	Core Cells	max Frequency
1	DPCM	8 (25 %)	1681 (7 %)	19.2 MHz
1	ADPCM	8 (25 %)	6728 (27 %)	10.5 MHz
3	DPCM	24 (75 %)	4419 (18 %)	22.4 MHz
3	ADPCM	24 (75 %)	14088 (57 %)	10.7 MHz

components. The MCU drives the RCU into its low power flash freeze mode as long as no hardware-accelerated computations are required. For precise time measurements, an external trigger is asserted by the MCU when a compute task starts and is recorded by an oscilloscope. The average current drawn by the system during the task execution is measured by an Agilent 34411A multimeter, which provides a resolution of 3 µA at a sampling frequency of 50 kHz.

For comparison with the hardware-accelerated encoders described in Section 4, the *DPCM* and *ADPCM* compression schemes were also implemented on the TI CC2530 MCU of the HaLOEWEn sensor node to estimate the energy consumption of a conventional microcontroller-based sensor node. The software was compiled by the Small Device C-Compiler (SDCC) v3.3 with speed optimizations enabled. The energy required for transmitting the uncompressed data stream is used as the baseline measurement. Each transmitted packet carries a maximum of 116 payload bytes.

As indicated in Figure 5a, a block of 2048 prerecorded sensor samples per channel, stored in the MCUs code memory, is used as the data source. The software implementations of the compression schemes operate directly on this data block. For the hardware-accelerated compressors, the process of moving the samples from the MCU to the RCU is *not* included in the measurements, as we assume that in practice, the sensors would be directly attached to the RCU.

Table 4 shows the results for processing the neural data described in Section 3.2. Both *DPCM* and *ADPCM* compression reduce the data size down to 38.5 %, making the simpler *DPCM* algorithm a better choice for this application. The *DPCM* execution on the MCU takes more than double the 61.2 ms required for transmitting the compressed data stream. The MCU thus has to be kept active beyond the pure transmission time of the prior packet in order to perform the compression of the current packet. As the current drawn by the system during compression exceeds the current drawn in low-power mode by about 120 times,

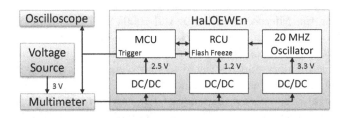

Fig. 6. Measurement setup

Table 4. Energy to compress/transmit 2048 samples of neural data (Sec. 3.2)

		compression			compression + transmission				
		duration	current	energy		duration	current	energy	
scheme	on	[ms]	[mA]	[µJ]	bytes	[ms]	[mA]	[mJ]	[%]
none					4096	158.8	41.5	19.77	**100.0**
DPCM MCU		132.2	11.8	4680	1577	184.6	21.6	11.96	60.5
ADPCM MCU		249.4	11.8	8829	1577	310.4	17.5	16.30	82.4
DPCM RCU		1.4	10.7	45	1577	62.6	41.9	7.87	39.8
ADPCM RCU		2.6	10.7	83	1577	63.8	41.3	7.90	40.0

Table 5. Energy to compress/transmit 3×2048 samples of condition data (Sec. 3.3)

		compression			compression + transmission				
		duration	current	energy		duration	current	energy	
scheme	on	[ms]	[mA]	[µJ]	bytes	[ms]	[mA]	[mJ]	[%]
none					12288	474.4	41.6	59.21	**100.0**
DPCM MCU		531.0	11.9	18957	9836	912.0	24.3	66.48	112.3
ADPCM MCU		906.0	11.9	32344	9732	1281.0	20.6	79.17	133.7
DPCM RCU		1.6	10.7	51	9836	381.6	42.5	48.62	82.1
ADPCM RCU		2.9	10.7	93	9732	378.9	42.4	48.15	81.3

the longer duty cycles lead to deteriorated overall energy efficiency. In contrast, for the hardware-accelerated implementations, RCU to MCU data movement occurs in parallel to the ongoing data transmission. The very short execution time of the compression stretches the duty cycle before going back to sleep only marginally, leading to an almost complete translation of compression ratio into system-level energy savings (38.5 % ratio vs. 39.8 % energy for *DPCM*).

Processing of the condition monitoring data discussed in Section 3.3 is evaluated in Table 5. Here, the adaptive predictor improves the compression ratio over *DPCM* such that a complete radio packet is saved. On the MCU, however, compressing the three data channels takes so much time, that the energy required cannot be amortized over the transmission savings, instead leading to an efficiency deterioration. The hardware-accelerated encoders fare much better: Since all channels can be compressed in parallel, the total execution time only slightly increases over that of the single channel encoder used in Table 4. As before, the encoders using the RCU convert nearly all of the data volume savings into actual energy savings.

6   Conclusion and Future Work

In this work, lossless data compression was used to aggregate collected sensor data before transmitting it wirelessly to a data sink (central node). The trade-off between compression quality and encoder complexity was analyzed for two different types of real-world sensor data. To this end, differential compression with a linear predictor and a downstream Rice encoder has been implemented on a Microsemi IGLOO FPGA and a TI CC2530 microcontroller. While the software compressor did reduce the overall energy consumption of compression and transmission for data compression ratios of 40 %, it did not succeed for compression ratios of only 80 %. The hardware-accelerated encoder, however, achieved almost perfect efficiency converting space savings due to compression into actual energy savings. Since for some data streams, such as the condition monitoring application, adaptive encoding yields improved efficiency, future work will evaluate the gains possible using higher-order adaptive predictors.

References

1. Boonyakitmaitree, C., Nandhasri, K., Ngarmnil, J.: A low computational predictor coefficient algorithm for adpcm implementation of portable recording devices. In: The 2004 47th Midwest Symposium on Circuits and Systems, MWSCAS 2004, vol. 3, pp. iii-187–iii-190 (2004)
2. Deng, X., Yang, Y.: Online adaptive compression in delay sensitive wireless sensor networks. IEEE Transactions on Computers 61(10), 1429–1442 (2012)
3. Donoho, D.: Compressed sensing. IEEE Transactions on Information Theory 52(4), 1289–1306 (2006)
4. Engel, A., Liebig, B., Koch, A.: Feasibility analysis of reconfigurable computing in low-power wireless sensor applications. In: Koch, A., Krishnamurthy, R., McAllister, J., Woods, R., El-Ghazawi, T. (eds.) ARC 2011. LNCS, vol. 6578, pp. 261–268. Springer, Heidelberg (2011)
5. Engel, A., Liebig, L., Koch, A.: Energy-efficient heterogeneous reconfigurable sensor node for distributed structural health monitoring. In: Morawiec, D.A., Hinderscheit, J. (eds.) Conference on Design and Architectures for Signal and Image Processing (DASIP), Electronic Chips & Systems design Initiative (2012)
6. Kasirajan, P., Larsen, C., Jagannathan, S.: A new data aggregation scheme via adaptive compression for wireless sensor networks. ACM Trans. Sen. Netw. 9(1), 5:1–5:26 (2012)
7. Kimura, N., Latifi, S.: A survey on data compression in wireless sensor networks. In: Proc. Int. Conf. Information Technology: Coding and Computing, ITCC 2005, vol. 2, pp. 8–13 (2005)
8. Ngau, C., Ang, L.M., Seng, K.: Low memory visual saliency architecture for data reduction in wireless sensor networks. IET Wireless Sensor Systems 2(2) (2012)
9. Reinhardt, A., Christin, D., Hollick, M., Steinmetz, R.: On the energy efficiency of lossless data compression in wireless sensor networks. Proc. IEEE 34th Conf. Local Computer Networks, LCN 2009, 873–880 (2009)
10. Sayood, K.: Introduction to Data Compression. Morgan Kaufmann (2005)
11. Yick, J., Mukherjee, B., Ghosal, D.: Wireless sensor network survey. Comput. Netw. 52, 2292–2330 (2008)
12. Zhiyong, C., Pan, L., Zeng, Z., Meng, M.: A novel fpga-based wireless vision sensor node. In: Proc. IEEE Int. Conf. Automation and Logistics ICAL (2009)

OCP2XI Bridge: An OCP to AXI Protocol Bridge

Zdravko Panjkov[1], Juergen Haas[1], Martin Aigner[1], Herbert Rosmanith[1,2],
Tianlun Liu[1], Roland Poppenreiter[1], Andreas Wasserbauer[1],
and Richard Hagelauer[1,2]

[1] Intel Mobile Communication (IMC), Danube Mobile Communications Engineering
Zdravko.Panjkov@intel.com
[2] Institute for Integrated Circuits, Johannes Kepler University Linz

Abstract. The modern SOC design contains many IP cores with different communication protocols. Improving the bridging and signal translation between these protocols has become a critical factor for the performance of the whole system. In this paper we will address the bridging of two well defined protocols, the Advanced Extensible Interface (AXI) and the Open Core Protocol (OCP). This bridge supports pipelined and multiplied transactions from both AXI and OCP interface. In comparison to related work our bridge offers simpler implementation and handling while containing full protocol functionality. The bridge is implemented and verified in a modern SystemC regression environment with large functional coverage. FPGA emulation is done on Versatile Express board using the CPU board as a main emulation controller. The result shows that the bridge is covering full protocol functionality and that maximal FPGA frequency is acceptable for a wide range of applications.

Keywords: AXI, OCP, FPGA.

1 Introduction

With the increase in process integrity and frequency, the amount of different protocols used in SOC increased substantially. The result is that the configurability and reusability of the chip protocol to the different bus types has become a dominant factor.

In the past, the widely accepted bus protocol was AMBA AHB [1], which facilitates single and burst transactions by using shared multiplexer architecture. The multiplexer architecture performs well with a limited number of IP cores, but with the increase number of cores the amount of transactions increased to more than one transaction at the time which is not supported by the shared architecture. Precisely for this reason two new protocols have been developed: the first is an Advanced extensible Interface (AXI) protocol, and the second is an Open Source Protocol (OCP).

The Open Core Protocol organization (OC-IP) started work in 2001 on something that would eventually become an OCP protocol [2]. OCP-IP aim was to

D. Goehringer et al. (Eds.): ARC 2014, LNCS 8405, pp. 179–190, 2014.
© Springer International Publishing Switzerland 2014

create a standardized interface and thus simplify the SOC's integration problems. The most important benefit of the OCP is its flexibility and configurability. OCP can be configured as a simple peripheral core, a high performance microprocessor or a chip subsystem.

AXI was first launched in 2003 with AMBA 3 architecture [3]. A protocol defines five separated channels with a separate set of signals for each channel. The interface is not restricted by the internal bus architecture so the designer can integrate different IP's by direct connection or by bus infrastructure between them.

This paper presents our experience and methodology with designing, verifying and emulating the bridge between OCP and AXI protocols. Verification is done in a state of the art SystemC verification environment with a wide range of cases and with high functional coverage. For emulation, the bridge is synthesized for Xilinx Virtex6 FPGA, which is part of the Versatile Express board. The entire verification environment is ported and implemented on Versatile Express board which gave a significant increase in verification speed. We showed that this bridge can handle many real time applications such as high definition images, different types of data or even a slow stream transmission.

The key contributions of this paper are:

- The paper presents the design of a full-featured OCP to AXI bus bridge, which is verified in the SystemC verification environment.
- The paper presents our FPGA synthesis methodology for OCP to AXI bus bridge and the porting of whole SystemC verification environment to an emulation board.
- The paper demonstrates how the above bridge can handle real time application directly on FPGA emulation board.

The remainder of the paper is organized as follows. Section 2 reviews related work and provides backward information on the bus bridge. Section 3 describes our experience in designing the bridge. Section 4 describes the verification environment used to verify protocol bridge. Section 5 presents emulation board and procedure to create an emulation environment. Section 6 present results, functionality and performance of the synthesized bridge. Section 7 concludes.

2   Related Work

There are commercially available software tools and solutions for protocol bridging.

The most used software tools are the Sonics Express [4] and Arteries FlexNoC [5]. Sonic Express provides a high bandwidth bridge between AXI and OCP protocols with the capability of crossing clock, power and physical boundaries. Arteries FlexNoC can implement a bridge between any combination of AMBA, AXI, AHB, APB and OCP protocols. The only problem of these tools is their price and usually quite complicated GUI which adds additional complexity.

Beside software tools there are also commercial IP solutions. MIPS-Imagination offers OCP to AXI Bridge [6]. The MIPS IP is relatively specialized as it only allows the connection of OCP 32 bit width interface to AXI bus. This makes sense because the bridge was developed for MIPS32 processor but it is not applicable in any different solution. Xilinx offers many different protocol bridges as part of the Xilinx Platform studio [7], including AHB2AXI, AXI2APB, AXI2PLB. However, the OCP2AXI bridge is not supported.

There are many applications where protocol bridging plays an important role. In applications such as sound, graphic and network the peripheral component interconnect (PCI) has to be connected to the AMBA bus throw AHB-PCI bridge/adapter [8][9][10]. In the SoC test techniques the AHB-APB bridge is extensively adopted to adjust different protocol speeds [11][12][13].

It is true that commercial tools offer a form of bridging but additional complexity and the introduction of a new tool is not always desirable in modern design. However solutions both scientific and commercial do not offer a functional OCP to AXI Bridge.

3   Hardware Design of the On-chip Bridge

The OCP to AXI bridge connects two protocols with different functionality. The bridging involves mapping the inputs and outputs of the OCP slave to the inputs and outputs of AXI master. The signals coming from OCP master are inputs to OCP2AXI bridge which are then converted into AXI signals and delivered to AXI master.

Figure 1 shows the block scheme of OCP2AXI bridge, with key components highlighted. The bridge consists of:

- OCP slave
- OCP to AXI kernel
- AXI master
- AXI Downsizer

Because we can't directly connect AXI and OCP interfaces we developed our own intermediate interface which can be easily translated to both OCP and AXI

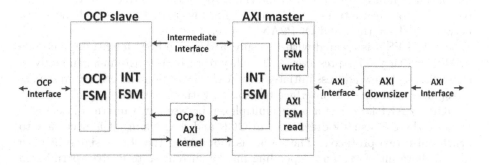

Fig. 1. Block scheme of OCP to AXI bridge

interfaces. The interface preserves all key features of both protocols but without specialized optimization of one particular protocol.

The intermediate interface consists of read and write channels with one common address channel (see Figure 2). Both read and data channels have similar interface with one FIFO's input for better handling of different protocol timing. Address channel covers all other protocol functionality, including out-of-order transaction, multiple transactions, and burst size. The interface is designed to provide a quick way to implement a lightweight interface between OCP and AXI interface. Finite state machine (intermediate FSM) is developed to implement functionality of intermediate interface and to serve as slaves for OCP/AXI protocol. The intermediate interface does not support specific optimizations such as separate read/write transaction for AXI protocol or configurable interface of OCP protocol.

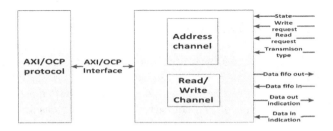

Fig. 2. Block diagram of intermediate interface

The OCP slave design applies a translation of the OCP interface signals to intermediate interface signals. The intermediate FSM is capable of executing translation but we still needed to generate handshake signals for OCP side of the bridge. Simple OCP FSM is implemented to control the flow of each OCP transaction and to generate signals as OCP slave interface (MCmd, MAddr, MData). The OCP FSM supports burst, pipelined, out-of-order transaction and its output is delivered to intermediate FSM.

The AXI master design is responsible for the reverse translation form the intermediate interface to the AXI interface. Again the intermediate FSM is implemented to execute translation and AXI FSM is created to handle hand shake between AXI interface and OCP2AXI bridge.

The AXI FSM is created with two subs FSMs, one FSM for reading and one FSM for writing. This preserves AXI ability to read and write independently of channels. Each new address initiates new AXI transaction and AXI FSM expect a response from the AXI interface to proceed with a next transaction.

OCP to AXI kernel is a time multiplexer between two intermediate FSM. Because there is usually differences in OCP and AXI timing it is necessary to synchronize two protocols. The kernel is monitoring the status signal of both intermediate interfaces and depending on the current state it gives permission for the next read/write transmission.

The AXI Downsizer is responsible for the downsizing data width of 256, 128, 64 to 32. This is a design from Xilinx [14] and it is offered as part of their ISE tool. Reason for implementing AXI Downsizer is necessity to simulate and emulate 32 data width within our verification/emulation environment while DSP design used as driver is designed with configurable OCP data width.

4 RTL Simulation of the Bridge

We used RTL simulation as the primary approach to debug RTL modifications until the whole design became stable enough. Once the design became stable to allow basic transactions we proceeded to more sophisticated levels of verification.

For sophisticated verification we developed SystemC verification environment. The environment contains a large number of high quality regression tests with high coverage over a large functional domain. Figure 3 shows the block design of the verification environment. The environment consists of four parts:

– OCP driver/monitor
– AXI random access memory (RAM)
– OCP2AXI Bridge
– System C environment

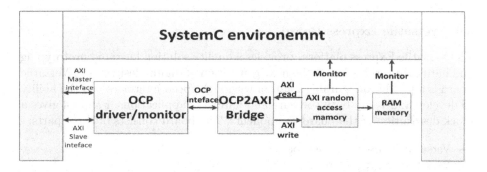

Fig. 3. Block design of the verification environment

The OCP driver/monitor is essentially an IMC DSP processor. The DSP was developed in our group during previous project and it has an OCP interface with adjustable bit data width (from 32 to 256 data bit width). With a limited interface optimization the DSP becomes precisely what we needed for this verification procedure. The DSP gives great controllability and visibility which can be easily combined with verification environment. It is relatively easy to create a wide range of input vectors and to cover almost all functionality of the OCP interface.

AXI random access memory is developed to support the AXI side of the bridge and it consists of two designs. The first design is the Xilinx AXI BRAM Controller which is a soft IP core designed as an AXI endpoint slave and the master device to local RAM [15]. The second design is a RAM with a regular interface, the RAM is a simple concurrent design with variable matrix as its basis.

The verification environment is a state of the art environment developed using the SystemC language. The SystemC language is an advanced set of C++ libraries that provides an event driven simulation [16]. The environment is successfully used in many different projects including previously mentioned DSP project. The environment has complete control over DSP which allows a wide variety of different OCP regression tests. These regression tests could be run over a couple of days in our ModelSim batch mode transaction pool.

During designing even after small changes it was necessary to rerun the whole regression pool to be sure that change did not affect any other bridge functionality. In case of new functionality it was necessary to develop a new test case which would cover new functionality. Until the whole design was not working properly we did not start the next step (synthesis). Even when everything was working correctly in simulation, we still continued to use simulation flows to ensure that the synthesis tool chain performs correctly.

5   FPGA Emulation of the OP2XI Bridge

RTL simulation is a basic methodology for verifying and debugging RTL design. The main problem of RTL simulation is its limited speed, one second of real time is usually around a couple of days in the simulator. To improve verification of real time situations we used the Versatile Express board as emulation environment.

5.1   Versatile Express Board

The Versatile Express platform provides a quality solution for rapid prototyping and hardware verification of the next generation of digital designs [17]. Versatile board is a highly configurable solution with high speed interfaces and the ability to develop and verify both software and hardware applications. Figure 4 gives a block description of the board components. The board consists of three parts:

– Versatile Express Motherboard
– Versatile Express CoreTile
– Versatile Express LogicTiles

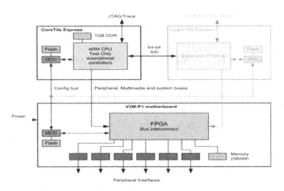

Fig. 4. Versatile Express board, block description

The motherboard has been specially designed to support future generations of software development. The board envelops all the necessary interfaces and peripherals for development of any new digital designs or graphic engine.

The CoreTile is delivered with different types of processor cores (Cortex-A15, Cortex-A9, Cortex-A7 and Cortex-A5) and it is mainly used as a CPU for the whole environment.

The LogiTile is delivered with a choice of different types of FPGAs and with capabilities to stack up to four boards one on top of each other. The board enables rapid prototyping, software/hardware codesign, verification and hardware driver development alongside a CoreTile CPU. This greatly reduces bring-up time and testing of IP design in parallel with software driver.

5.2   Synthesis Tool Flow

Most of our RTL design is coded in Verilog language so at the beginning we chose Xilinx Ise [18] as main synthesis tools. Xilinx Ise is relatively cheap and easy to use but does not support all features and languages available on the market. Unfortunately some part of our design is written in System Verilog which is not supported in XILINX Ise so it was necessary to find a different solution.

We had two solutions to either use Synplify Pro [19], or to use new Xilinx Vivado [20] suit. Both tools are high performance, cost effective FPGA synthesis tool with the ability to interpret System Verilog syntax.

The Vivado Design Suite implements all steps necessary for the FPGA bit generation (synthesis, mapping and placement) in one tool. Synplify Pro synthesis software is the industry standard FPGA tool and its unique Behavioral Technology performs optimization at a highest level. It is important to notice that in the case of Synplify Pro we still needed to use Xilinx Ise for mapping and placement.

In this case we have chosen a Synplify Pro not just for its optimization abilities but also because of good customer and time proven reviews. Compared to Synplify Pro Vivado Design Suit is a relatively a newcomer to the field and it is still necessary to pass the test of time.

Cshel scripts are created to control synthesis procedure. Synplify Pro interprets the RTL files and creates the edf file. Xilinx ISE collects the edf files and implements mapping and placement. In Table 1 you can see the synthesis results.

Table 1. Synthesis results

Device	Xlinx Virtex 6 xc6vlx760	%
Slices:	79.940 out of 948,480	8
LUTs:	82,027 out of 474,240	17
RAM36:	122 out of 720	16
RAM18:	17 out of 1440	1
IOB:	635 out of 1200	52
MAX. FREQ:	27.083 MHz	

5.3   Emulation on Versatile Express Board

The whole Versatile Express board is connected by an AXI interface [21] so the only way to send data between LogicTile board and CoreTile board is through the AXI bus.

LogicTile environment. The AXI bus was delivered as a basic driver for the LogicTile board. The problem was that the basic driver has only one AXI master for the emulation environment while in our case we needed at least two masters and one slave. For the generation of additional interfaces we used Xilinx Platform Studio [22] which enables easy generating of additional AXI interfaces. Figure 5 (a) presents a LogicTile environment which consists of AXI bus with connections to Logic Tile Fash DRAM memory, processor and emulation environment.

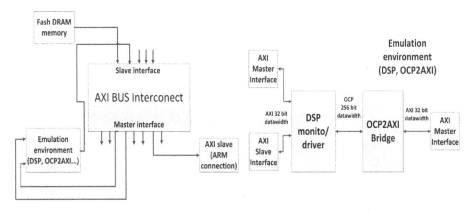

Fig. 5. Top system design (a) LogicTile environment (b) Emulation environment

Emulation environment (DSP, OCP2AXI...). During emulation development we tried to reuse as much of RTL simulation as possible knowing that we can greatly improve functional coverage and also simplify our development process. Figure 5 (b) shows the block design of the emulation environment. The environment consists of:

- DSP processor
- OCP2AXI bridge
- Emulation environment

Both DSP and OCP2XI bridge are described in previous chapters.

The emulation environment consists of two AXI master interfaces and one AXI slave interface. The first AXI master is connecting the OCP2AXI bridge with flash DRAM memory (see Figure 4) enabling collecting data from the bride output. The second master interface transfers data between DSP and flash DRAM memory delivering input date to the DSP. The AXI slave is giving the CPU full control over DSP design.

During emulation individual functionality or even entire blocks can be separately verified. This was enabled by DSP design which has nearly the same functionality as in RTL simulation. The CPU is used to control the DSP from outside of FPGA using Linux drivers and partially ported SystemC verification environment.

Drivers for CPU core. The Core Tile board is delivered with Boot Monitor which is a standard application built on CPU platform library. The library handles the system initialization and provides basic I/O subsystem that supports simple drivers [23]. Unfortunately this was not enough to enable communication between CPU AXI interface and FPGA environment design on LogicTile boards.

In order to run the bridge core in the FPGA emulation board, we installed Linux image and developed two Linux drivers to enable delivering and collecting data from the design. Figure 6 presents Linux driver which consists of two components.

– Direct memory driver
– DSP driver

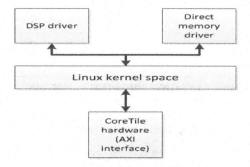

Fig. 6. CPU Linux driver design

The direct memory driver is responsible for delivering data to the flash DRAM memory located on the LogicTile board Figure 4. Its function is to provide necessary service to direct memory access so that data can be sent without any problems. This data will be used during a transaction as input/output data to the AXI interface of the bridge.

DSP driver is partly redesigned DSP control from SystemC environment. The driver controls the DSP AXI interfaces from CPU giving similar DSP controllability as in RTL simulation.

Beside these two drivers, the almost entire verification environment is ported and translated from the SystemC language to CSHELL scripts. For porting we extract SystemC functionality and optimized it for CSHELL scripts. It was not possible to use the whole environment because in simulation we had full visibility while in emulation only a small subset of signals was extracted by Xilinx ChipScope [24].

6   Results

For emulation and verification we used images of different sizes and definition. Besides images we also used many different types of data but images remain the

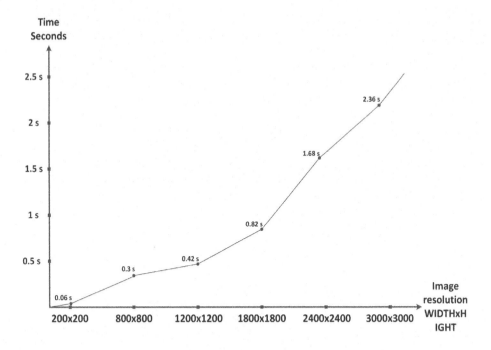

Fig. 7. Evaluation results

best and the simplest way to measure the quality of the bridge. Figure 7 presents
an execution time for different image sizes on FPGA emulation board. The Y-
presents size/resolution of images and the X-presents execution time.

We also tried to use the live stream for system emulation but unfortunately
the max frequency is too low to support this feature (see table 1). The system
can only process around 3 images per second, (this greatly depends on image
quality) and for live stream you need at least 20 images per second.

The benefits of the RTL simulation environment such as high functional coverage, large number of tests and relatively long regression run are implemented in
the emulation environment. Emulation still adds large speed increase so almost
all simulation tests are rerun in less than a couple of hours. Table 2 presents a
functional coverage results.

Table 2. Presents a functional coverage results

Design	Branch %	Conditions %	STMT %	Toggled %
OCP slave	91.176	94.737	96.00	96.585
OCP2AXI kernel	95.277	93.888	87.821	92.223
AXI master	90.887	96.551	90.221	98.002
AXI Downsizer	92.222	93.367	89.032	96.988

Our OCP2AXI bridge preserves all instructions and functionality of both protocols. Table 3 (a) presents protocol specifications which are supported in the bridge.

Table 3. Result tables: (a) Supported protocol specification (b) Synthesis report of the stand alone OCP2AXI Bridge

AXI interface	OCP interface	Device	Xlinx Virtex 6	%
Separate address and	Small set of	Slices:	79.940 of 948,480	1
data channel	mandatory signals	LUTs:	82,027 of 474,240	1
Unaligned data	Configurable address	RAM36:	122 of 720	0
transfers	and data width	RAM18:	17 of 1440	0
Limited burst transactions	Burst transfers	IOB:	635 of 1200	52
Separate read and	Inclusion of sideband	MAX. FREQ: 83.773 MHz		
write channel	signals			
Multiple addresses	Pipelined transfers			
Out-of-order transac.	Out-of-order transac.			

As explained in synthesis section, the max frequency of the system on FPGA is 27 MHZ (see table 1). This is a relatively low frequency, especially knowing that the bridge is not a large design. The reason for low frequency is coming from a complicated emulation environment. DSP is probably a synthesis overhead but it would be rather complicated to create dedicated OCP driver with the same emulation purpose and functional coverage. The synthesis results of the stand alone bridge are presented in Table 3 (b). The results are extracted from the bridge alone synthesis report and they represent the real capability of a bridge. From this report it is obvious that a stand alone bridge can handle real time applications like live streaming.

7   Conclusion

In this paper we presented our experience in designing, verifying and emulating an OCP to AXI bridge. The described design technique provides an easier implementation of the protocol bridge for modern digital design. Verification and emulation is done using a modern regression environment with large coverage and long test execution.

The proposed OCP to AXI bridge improves SOC integrations by allowing connection and reuse of IP's with different on-chip protocols. Furthermore it is also possible to connect two different bus protocols with almost no functional or bandwidth loss. Our FPGA emulation based on the Versatile Express board demonstrates that the bridge can be successfully used in many different real time situations such as live stream, high-definition images, and data transfer.

For future design we plan to optimize the emulation environment by designing a specific OCP driver and monitor so that we do not need to use IMC DSP as a driver. With this improvement the maximal frequency should increase from 27 MHz to approximately 50 MHz which would enable sending a high definition live stream through an FPGA board.

References

1. AMBA AHB interface, http://infocenter.arm.com/help/ index.jsp?topic=/com.arm.doc.ddi0203f/I1054045.html
2. Open Core Protocol International Partnership (OCP-IP), http://www.ocpip.org/
3. AMBA Open Specifications, http://www.arm.com/products/system-ip/amba/ amba-open-specifications.php
4. Sonics Express, http://sonicsinc.com/products/
5. Arteris FlexNoC Interconnect IP, http://www.arteris.com/
6. MIPS-Imagination BusBridge3 Module, http://www.imgtec.com/mips/mips-busbridge3.asp
7. Xilinx Platform studio, http://www.xilinx.com/ise/embedded/edk_ip.htm
8. Zhonghai, W., Yizheng, Y., Jinxiang, W., Mingyan, Y.: Designing AHB/PCI bridge ASIC. In: Proceeding of the 4th International Conference on ASIC, pp. 578–580 (2001)
9. AMBA-AHB PCI Bridge IP Introductory Document PLDA Ltd., http://www.plda.com/
10. ARM PrimeCell External Bus Interface (PL220), ARM, ARM DDI 0249B (2002), http://www.arm.com
11. Song, J., Yi, H., Han, J., Park, S.: An efficient SoC test technique by reusing on/off-chip bus bridge. Journal IEEE Transactions on Circuits and Systems 56(3), 554–565 (2009)
12. Lin, C., Liang, H.: Bus-oriented DFT design for embedded cores. In: Proc. IEEE Asia-Pacific Conf. on Circuits and Systems, pp. 561–563 (2004)
13. Song, J., Min, P., Yi, H., Park, S.: Design of Test Access Mechanism for AMBA-Based System-on-a-Chip. In: IEEE VLSI Test Symmposium, pp. 375–380 (2007)
14. Xilinx data-width conversion Downsizer, http://www.xilinx.com/products/ intellectual-property/axi_interconnect.htm
15. AXI BRAM Controller, http://www.xilinx.com/products/ intellectual-property/axi_bram_if_ctlr.htm
16. SystemC, http://www.accellera.org/activities/ committees/systemc-language/
17. Versatile Express Product Family, http://www.arm.com/products/tools/ development-boards/versatile-express/index.php
18. ISE WebPACK Design Software, http://www.xilinx.com/products/ design-tools/ise-design-suite/ise-webpack.htm
19. Synplify Pro, http://www.synopsys.com/Tools/Implementation/ FPGAImplementation/FPGASynthesis/Pages/SynplifyPro.aspx
20. Vivado Design Suite, http://www.xilinx.com/products/design-tools/vivado/
21. Example LogicTile Express 13MG design for a CoreTile Express A15x2, http://infocenter.arm.com/help/index.jsp?topic=/ com.arm.doc.dai0305a/index.html
22. Xilinx Platform Studio, http://www.xilinx.com/tools/xps.htm
23. Versatile Express Boot Monitor, http://infocenter.arm.com/help/topic/ com.arm.doc.dui0465f/DUI0465F_boot_monitor_trm.pdf
24. Xilinx ChipScope, http://www.xilinx.com/tools/cspro.htm

FPGA Implementation of a Video Based Abnormal Action Detection System with Real-Time Cubic Higher Order Local Auto-Correlation Analysis

Kaoru Hamasaki, Keisuke Dohi, Yuichiro Shibata, and Kiyoshi Oguri

Nagasaki University, 1-14 Bunkyo-machi, Nagasaki 852-8521, Japan

Abstract. In this paper, we show FPGA implementation of a real-time video-based abnormal action detection system, which is a key basic function of applications such as security systems and monitoring systems for nursing elderly people. Our system extracts Cubic Higher order Local Auto-Correlation (CHLAC) features from input video frames and detects abnormal actions with a subspace method based on Candid Covariance-free Incremental Principal Component Analysis (CCIPCA). Empirical experiments demonstrate our system works well at 62.5 fps, which is limited by a camera device. The system implemented on the FPGA is estimated to achieve up to 240 fps, which corresponds to 8.6 times speedup compare to software execution on a PC. It is also shown that the FPGA implementation is more than 20 times energy efficient than the software execution.

1 Introduction

Abnormal action detection is an important and useful image recognition technique for a wide range of application fields. As a powerful feature extraction method for abnormal action detection, Otsu *et al* proposed Cubic Higher order Local Auto-Correlation (CHLAC)[1][2] and they applied the Candid Covariance-free Incremental Principal Component Analysis (CCIPCA)[3] method to compute a subspace of normal action patterns.

The CHLAC feature is extension of HLAC feature. Although abnormal action detection systems with HLAC[4] have been proven to achieve a high performance, real time CHLAC feature extraction is difficult for software-based implementation when large size images are processed with a real-time rate [5]. In this paper, we propose FPGA implementation of a real-time video-based abnormal action detection system with the CHLAC and CCIPCA methods. The design employs deep-pipelined stream computing approach, which is known to be able to efficiently exploit parallelism in real-time image processing with reduced energy consumption[6–8].

The contributions of this paper are as follows: (1) Real-time stream-based FPGA implementation of the CHLAC feature extraction method is shown. (2) A full system including a learning mechanism with CCIPCA as well as camera input interface is implemented on a single FPGA chip without using external memory. (3) The implementation demonstrates to achieve not only higher performance but also higher energy efficiency compared to software implementation.

D. Goehringer et al. (Eds.): ARC 2014, LNCS 8405, pp. 191–196, 2014.
© Springer International Publishing Switzerland 2014

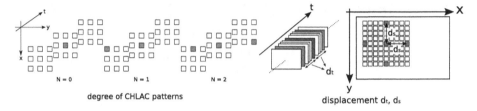

Fig. 1. CHLAC feature

2   Abnormal Action Detection

Our image recognition process is divided into three stages: preprocessing, feature extraction and discrimination. In preprocessing, smoothing and binarization are applied to normalize a given input video sequence and interframe differences are calculated. Next, we extract CHLAC features from the normalized interframe difference images. Then, in the discrimination step, we calculate how far away the given input feature is from normal action patterns in the CHLAC feature space. Here, a subspace method with the CCIPCA algorithm is used. In this section, we describe these algorithms.

2.1   CHLAC Feature

The Cubic Higher order Local Auto-Correlation (CHLAC) is a feature widely used for action detection systems owing to position invariance and an additive property[2]. The CHLAC feature is a multi-dimensional vector defined in a spatiotemporal space consisting of a sequence of binarized interframe differences. Elements of a CHLAC feature vector is autocorrelation of pixels in the spatiotemporal space. The N-th autocorrelation function $x^N(a_1, \ldots, a_N)$ is expressed as:

$$x^N(a_1, \ldots, a_N) = \int f(r)f(r + a_1) \ldots f(r + a_N)dr \tag{1}$$

where r is a reference point in the spatiotemporal space, a_i is a displacement from the point r, and $f(r)$ is a pixel value of the point r. This multiple integration is defined on the space direction and the time direction. The interval of integration for the space directions covers a whole area of the frame and the interval of the time direction spans time $t - W$ to t. Since the interframe difference images have been binarized, $f(r)$ takes a value of 0 or 1. The number N is called a *degree* of the CHLAC pattern (Fig.1).

The displacement a_i in the CHLAC definition has a constraint. Since the autocorrelation is defined in the spatiotemporal space of the sequence of the interframe difference images, a_i has three axises: the x-axis and the y-axis within a frame and the t-axis along the time domain. Then, the CHLAC constraint on the displacement vectors is denoted:

$$a_i = (d_s a_{ix}, d_s a_{iy}, d_t a_{it}) \quad \begin{cases} a_{ix}, a_{iy}, a_{it} \in \{0, 1, -1\} \\ \|a_i\| \neq 0 \end{cases} \tag{2}$$

where d_s and d_t are distance coefficients in space and time domains, respectively. Thus, the number of the restricted a_i vectors is $3^3 - 1 = 26$. When we set $0 \leq N \leq 2$, the number of combinations of a_i becomes 251, eliminating the same vector patterns with parallel translation. These are corresponding to elements of a CHLAC feature vector.

Fig. 2. Overview of the detection system

2.2 CCIPCA

The Candid Covariance-free Incremental Principal Components Analysis (CCIPCA) is an incremental method for principal component analysis which does not need to solve an eigenvalue problem directly.

Here, the eigenvector is updated as a sum of the weighted last estimated eigenvector and input data by

$$v(n) = \frac{n-1}{n}v(n-1) + \frac{1}{n}u(n)^t u(n)\frac{v(n-1)}{\|v(n-1)\|}. \qquad (3)$$

While this equation estimates only the first dominant eigenvector, we typically need some other eigenvectors for principal component analysis. In this case, we can utilize an orthogonally projected input series:

$$u_{i+1}(n) = u_i(n) - {}^t u_i(n)\frac{v(n)}{\|v(n)\|}\frac{v(n)}{\|v(n)\|}. \qquad (4)$$

3 Implementation

An overview of our implementation is shown in Fig.2. The architecture was designed based on a deeply pipelined stream processing structure, where input image data is fed through sequentially-connected filter modules.

3.1 CHLAC Extraction Module

The process of the CHLAC feature extraction consists of two steps: 1) extraction of a CHLAC feature vector from input; and 2) integration of the CHLAC feature vectors in time-domain (Fig.3).

In the CHLAC feature vector extraction step, the binarized pixels of interframe differences are stored in frame buffers. Given a displacement in the time dimension d_t, a total of $2d_t$ frame buffers for full-size difference images and one frame buffer for a partial difference image are needed. Each frame buffer is consisted of registers and BRAMs with $(2d_s+1)\times(2d_s+1)$ of a window. At every clock, 27 pixels, one for a reference point and 26 for surrounding points, are fetched from frame buffers. Then, the 251 CHLAC patterns of comparisons are performed on the pixels in parallel. The number of pixels which matched with each CHLAC pattern is counted by independent 251 accumulators. Repeating this operation until the last pixel in the valid region of a frame is processed, a partial sum of a CHLAC feature vector in space-domain $x_s(t)$ is obtained as the output of the accumulators. These processes are performed in a pixel-by-pixel manner.

In the CHLAC feature vector integration step, a series of W partial sums is accumulated in time-domain to obtain a CHALC feature vector $x(t)$. To reduce the latency and resource utilization, we used the following recursive relationship:

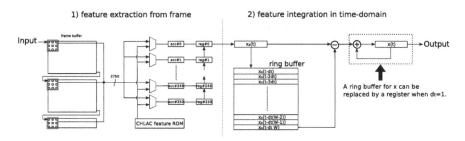

Fig. 3. Frame buffers for CHLAC extraction with $d_t = 1$

$$x(t) = x_s(t) + \sum_{i=1}^{W} x_s(t - d_t i) - x_s(t - d_t W)$$

$$= x_s(t) + x(t - d_t) - x_s(t - d_t W). \tag{5}$$

Eq. (5) requires only two vector addition operations regardless of the integration width W and the displacement d_t. Therefore, we equipped two ring buffers which can keep d_t vectors for x and $(d_t W - 1)$ vectors for x_s.

With this architecture, the time-domain accumulation is performed as follows: (1) $x(t - d_t)$ and $x_s(t - d_t W)$ are read from the ring buffers, respectively; (2) $x(t)$ is computed by Eq. (5); (3) $x(t - d_t)$ and $x_s(t - d_t W)$ on the ring buffers are replaced by $x(t)$ and $x_s(t)$, respectively; (4) Indexes of the two ring buffers are put forward, respectively.

3.2   CCIPCA Module

The CCIPCA module in this implementation computes up to five base vectors $v_1 \sim v_5$. Since a computation of v_i is dependent on the result of computation of v_{i-1}, each computational process of v_i needs to be performed sequentially. Each computation of v_i consists of two steps, computation of u_i and computation of v_i with the use of u_i; the latter depends on the former.

Both Eq. (3) and (4) can be separated into two steps: calculation of an inner product of vectors and the others. The computation of Eq. (3) and (4) excluding the inner product can be generalized as follows:

$$z = C_0 x + \frac{C_1}{C_2} y \tag{6}$$

where C_0, C_1 and C_2 are scalar values, x and y are input vectors and z is an output vector of the computation, respectively. We call this computation a *kernel* of CCIPCA. The CCIPCA computation for the five base vectors can be break down into 10 inner product operations and 10 kernel computations.

The kernel module is implemented in a fully-pipelined manner. All the operators in the module are for single precision floating point numbers. Both input and output vectors form a stream, where new output result is generated every clock cycle.

The operations of the inner products can be overlapped with an immediate predecessor kernel calculation because the output stream of the kernel module can be connected to the input stream of the inner product module. Fig.4 illustrates pipeline scheduling of the kernel and inner product modules.

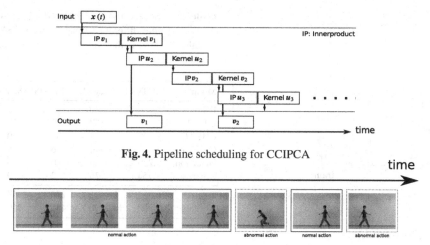

Fig. 4. Pipeline scheduling for CCIPCA

Fig. 5. Test video for experiments

4   Evaluation

The system was mapped on a Xilinx KC705 board equipped with a Kintex-7 XC7K325T FPGA. The input video frames were fed by an Omnivision Technologies OV9620 camera device. To compare the performance, we also implemented the same functionality in software on a Linux PC with a 3.40-GHz Intel Core-i7 2600K processor with 16-GB DDR III-1066 memory by C++ (for feature extraction) and Octave (for CCIPCA and projection computation). The parameters for the CHLAC extraction we employed were $d_s = 10, d_t = 1, W = 20$.

In this experiment, we used a 2099-frame VGA video sequence which contains three action patterns: walking leftward, walking rightward, and stumbling. In this video, a person performs 7 actions shown in Fig.5. We used the first 2 normal actions for learning.

Fig.6 plots the detection results as a distance of CHLAC feature from the normal actions. There are 7 peaks which corresponding to the input actions. Among them, we can clearly distinguish the 5-th and 7-th peaks from the others as abnormal actions. In addition, the FPGA implementation and the software implementation produced the almost the same distance results. This suggests the use of single precision floating arithmetic in the FPGA implementation did not negatively affect the detection results.

While the frame rate of the software implementation was 28.1 fps, our FPGA implementation worked at 62.5 fps. This was limited by the camera device that we used this time. If a faster camera device is available, our system is estimated to achieve 240.3 fps, considering that the maximum operating frequency of the FPGA circuit was 96.13 MHz.

The resource usage of each module is illustrated in Table1. The Block RAM usage was relatively high, since both of the Diff module and the CHLAC extraction module utilized frame buffers. However, energy consumption of our FPGA implementation was 384.82 J, while that of the software implementation was 7416.46 J, highlighting the efficiency of the deep pipelined structure of the FPGA implementation.

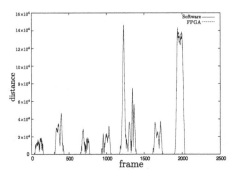

Fig. 6. Detection results

Table 1. Resource usage. Diff module calculates interframe difference images and DTSM module binarizes the interframe difference images.

Module	LUTs	Slice Regs	BRAMs	DSP48Es
Diff	80	50	128	0
DTSM	6,694	3,577	2	17
CHLAC	9,128	5,402	37	0
CCIPCA	3,487	3,640	6	16
Detection	6,239	8,166	0	26
Others	754	576	2	0
Total	26,382	21,411	175	59
Available	203,800	407,600	445	840

5 Conclusion

The empirical experiments revealed that the presented architecture achieved a throughput of 62.5fps taking the advantage of streamed processing without accessing external memories. Theoretical analysis suggests the implementation is able to achieve the throughput of 240fps, which corresponds to 8.6 times speedup compared to software execution. It was also shown that the FPGA implementation is more than 20 times efficient than the software in terms of energy efficiency. Our future work includes evaluation of detection accuracy in more details considering practical applications.

References

1. Otsu, N.: Towards flexible and intelligent vision systems-from thresholding to CHLAC. In: IAPR Conference on Machine Vision Application, pp. 430–439 (2005)
2. Nanri, T., Otsu, N.: Unsupervised abnormality detection in video surveillance. In: IAPR Conference on Machine Vision Applications, pp. 574–577 (2005)
3. Weng, J., Zhang, Y., Hwang, W.S.: Candid covariance-free incremental principal component analysis. IEEE Trans. on Pattern Analysis and Machine Intelligence 25(8), 1034–1040 (2003)
4. Ishii, I., Sukenobe, R., Yamamoto, K., Takaki, T.: Real-time image recognition using hlac features at 1000 fps. In: Proceedings of the 2009 International Conference on Robotics and Biomimetics, pp. 954–959 (2009)
5. Shiraki, T., Saito, H., Kamoshida, Y., Ishiguro, K., Fukano, R., Shirai, T., Taura, K., Otake, M., Sato, T., Otsu, N.: Real-time motion recognition using chlac features and cluster computing. In: Proceedings of the 3rd IFIP International Conference on Network and Parallel Computing, pp. 50–56 (2006)
6. Dohi, K., Yorita, Y., Shibata, Y., Oguri, K.: Pattern compression of FAST corner detection for efficient hardware implementation. In: Proc. IEEE 21st Int. Conf. Field Programmable Logic and Applications, pp. 478–481 (September 2011)
7. Negi, K., Dohi, K., Shibata, Y., Oguri, K.: Deep pipelined one-chip FPGA implementation of a real-time image-based human detection algorithm. In: Proc. Int. Conf. Field-Programmable Technology, pp. 1–8 (December 2011)
8. Dohi, K., Hatanaka, Y., Negi, K., Shibata, Y., Oguri, K.: Deep-pipelined FPGA implementation of ellipse estimation for eye tracking. In: Proc. IEEE 22st Int. Conf. Field Programmable Logic and Applications, pp. 458–463 (2012)

A Synthesizable Multicore Platform for Microwave Imaging

Pascal Schleuniger and Sven Karlsson

DTU Compute
Technical University of Denmark
{pass,svea}@dtu.dk

Abstract. Active microwave imaging techniques such as radar and tomography are used in a wide range of medical, industrial, scientific, and military applications. Microwave imaging devices emit radio waves and process their reflections to reconstruct an image. However, data processing remains a challenge as image reconstruction algorithms are computationally expensive and many applications come with strictly constrained mechanical or power requirements. We developed Tinuso, a multicore architecture optimized for performance when implemented on an FPGA. Tinuso's architecture is well suited to run highly parallel image reconstruction applications at a low power budget. In this paper, we describe the design and the implementation of Tinuso's communication structures, which include a generic 2D mesh on-chip interconnect and a network interface to the processor pipeline. We optimize the network for a latency of one cycle per network hop and attain a high clock frequency by pipelining the feedback loop to manage contention. We implement a multicore configuration with 48 cores and achieve a clock frequency as high as 300 MHz with a peak switching data rate of 9.6 Gbits/s per link on state-of-the-art FPGAs.

1 Introduction

Active microwave imaging techniques such as radar and tomography are used to detect, locate, and analyze objects. Microwave imaging systems consist of synchronized radio transmitters and receivers that emit radio waves and process their reflections to reconstruct an image of an object. Radar systems deliver high quality pictures of a scene independent of light and weather conditions and tomography is able to visualize internal structures of the body. Therefore, microwave imaging is used in a wide range of medical, industrial, scientific, and military applications including diagnostic medicine, baggage inspection, environmental monitoring, surveillance, and reconnaissance. An output image is reconstructed from reflected data that is interpreted as a set of projections. Often a very high number of operations is required to reconstruct the output image because each pixel must analyze hundreds of these reflections. Given the large amount of data and the parallel structure of image reconstruction applications, graphic processing units, GPUs, are well suited for this type of data processing.

D. Goehringer et al. (Eds.): ARC 2014, LNCS 8405, pp. 197–204, 2014.
© Springer International Publishing Switzerland 2014

However, for many applications with strict mechanical or power requirements GPUs may not be an appropriate solution and custom embedded systems need to be designed.

The production and design costs for application specific integrated circuits, *ASICs*, continue to rise making ASICs only feasible for very high production volumes. Field programmable gate arrays, *FPGAs*, on the other hand, have a high unit cost but essentially no setup cost. Due to this, FPGAs are increasingly being used in low and medium volume markets. The logic integration of FPGAs has reached a point where multiple processor cores, dedicated accelerators, and a large number of interfaces can be integrated on a single device. As many modern microwave imaging systems successfully use FPGAs for signal processing already, we aim to integrate the data processing in the same device. We propose and advocate for a multicore system because it raises the abstraction level for the application programmer without facing the current performance drawbacks of high-level synthesis [4]. Moreover, mapping an application to multicore system significantly reduces development effort over a fully custom FPGA implementation [2].

We developed Tinuso, a processor architecture optimized for a high throughput on modern FPGA architectures. Our current hardware implementation, the Tinuso I core, can be clocked as high as 376MHz on a Xilinx Virtex 6 and consumes less hardware resources than a similar MicroBlaze configuration [7]. In a case study, we have shown how to map the POLARIS synthetic aperture radar, SAR, application on a Tinuso multicore system on a Xilinx Virtex-7 consuming only about 10 watt [6].

In this paper, we evaluate Tinuso's communication structures and analyze the scalability. We make the following contributions:

- We describe the design and implementation of a generic packet switched, 2D mesh on-chip network optimized for FPGA implementation.
- To attain a high data rate, we optimize routing scheme and flow control mechanism for high clock frequency and low latency. We apply a look-ahead routing scheme to simplify decode and arbitration logic in the router. We pipeline the feedback loop to manage contention to reduce the routing delay in the time-critical path of the design.
- We evaluate the network-on-chip, *NoC*, by measuring the network latency of random traffic and compare it to a baseline implementation without pipelined feedback loop to manage contention.
- To evaluate the scalability of the system we compose multicore systems and derive the maximum clock speed. On a multicore system with 48 processor cores we reach a clock frequency of 300 MHz with a peak switching data rate of 9.6 Gbits/s per link on state-of-the-art FPGAs.

2   Related Work

MARC is a many-core approach to reconfigurable computing that allows programmers to easily express parallelism through a high-level programming language [2]. MARC enables efficient high performance computing for applications expressed in C or C++ by exploiting FPGA specific resources such as distributed block memories and DSP blocks. In contrast to Tinuso, MARC implements a heterogeneous multicore architecture with a central processing core and high number of arithmetic processing cores.

MoCReS is a router architecture that applies virtual cut-through flow-control to transfer packets across multiple clock domains [1]. The router uses a FIFO buffer, implemented as block RAM, to transfer data across clock domains. It allows for operating multiple routers on independent clock frequencies and prevents the slowest router from restricting the operating frequency of the network. This is of particular interest for heterogeneous systems where processing elements operate at different clock frequencies. The MoCReS router operates at a clock frequency as high as 357MHz on a Xilinx Virtex 4 device. However, the performance of this network design is limited by a latency of at least 7 cycles per hop. In contrast, our router is designed to operate at the same clock frequency as the processor cores to avoid latencies in synchronization buffers.

DESA is a distributed elastic switch architecture presented by Roca et.al. [5]. The interconnect is composed of a collection of independent switching modules, called AC-modules. The fine-grained decomposition of the network in AC-switching modules allows for various network topologies and leads to better mapping on the FPGA. The design is evaluated by comparing to a mesh interconnect that consists of routers with a single pipeline stage. The evaluation shows that the DESA design increases the clock frequency by 50% while consuming about the same amount of resources as the baseline implementation. Nevertheless, the increased clock frequency comes at the cost of an additional pipeline stage, which increases the latency by one clock cycle per network hop. Tinuso allows for much higher clock frequencies than the single pipeline stage router used for the DESA evaluation. Therefore, Tinuso achieves lower network latency for low network loads while DESA performs better at higher network loads.

Lu et. al. introduce a generic router architecture optimized for FPGA implementation [3]. It supports network topologies such as ring, 2D mesh, 3D cube, and hybrid configurations. They apply a look-ahead routing scheme and pipeline the router design to attain a high clock frequency. A router with five ports and a 32 bit data-path width utilizes about 700 LUTs and can be clocked as high as 220MHz on an Altera Stratix III device. Tinuso requires more hardware resources than a 2D mesh implementation of the proposed architecture. However, Tinuso allows for a higher clock speed and a lower latency of only 1 clock cycles per hop.

3   System Overview

We aim for a system as shown in Figure 1 to integrate signal and data processing of microwave imaging applications in a single FPGA device. The image reconstruction application is mapped to a number of parallel processing elements that communicate over an interconnect with a memory controller.

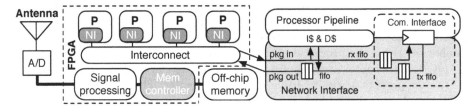

Fig. 1. System overview of a multicore data processing unit

We use instances of the Tinuso processor architecture as processing elements. Tinuso is a lightweight architecture with a small instruction set that can easily be extended. It is a three operand, load-store architecture with a fixed instruction word length of 32-bits. The single issue, in-order pipeline is optimized for a high instruction throughput when implemented on an FPGA. For example, Tinuso uses pipelined cache and register file accesses, which results in a fast and deep pipeline. Given the high instruction throughput, the small hardware footprint, and the ability to extend the design, Tinuso is an attractive choice for multicore systems. Figure 1 shows the internals of the network interface. Its primary task is to connect a processor core to a router and to translate cache misses into memory request messages.

4   Router Architecture

Typically, an FPGA consists of a two-dimensional array of logic elements called configurable logic blocks, *CLBs*, that are interconnected by horizontal and vertical routing channels. We argue for a 2D mesh network topology as it maps well to the FPGA architecture. The network consists of a number of routers that are connected through unidirectional links. A router has five bidirectional ports, namely, North (N), East (E), South (S), West (W), and Home (H).

Figure 2 shows the block diagram of the router and the state diagram of an input port. We have implemented a wormhole router with a backpressure flow-control mechanism and only use flip-flops at the output to attain a latency of one cycle per hop. We decided for an XY routing scheme because it is deterministic, deadlock-free and simple to implement.

Data packets are broken into a sequence of flow control digits, *flits*. The network supports packets that consist of a header flit and an arbitrary number of data flits. To keep the communication overhead low, all routing information is encoded in a single header flit. Each data link includes a status signal that indicates whether the data is valid or not.

The state machines of the router input ports remain in the idle state until a packet arrives. The destination node is extracted from the header flit and an output port is selected following the routing scheme. If multiple flits arrives at the same time and aim for the same output resource, the arbiter applies a round-robin

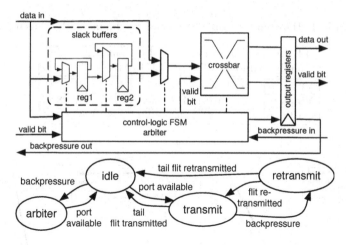

Fig. 2. Router block diagram and control state diagram

scheme to decide which one will proceed. In cases where the desired output port is not available the flit is retained in slack buffers and the backpressure signal is set. The backpressure signal propagates up-stream to stall the data flits until the desired output port is available.

We implement the router architecture as behavior-level description in VHDL as it is shorter, easier to adapt, and less error prone than descriptions at a lower level. Moreover, behavioral-level designs are independent of the technology and can easily be migrated to alternative platforms. We identified the time-critical path of the design in the decode logic in the idle state. The decode logic extracts the destination address of the header flit and determines an output port according to the XY routing scheme. If the header flit only contains the coordinates of the destination node, costly comparison operations are necessary to determine the route of the packet. Therefore, we apply look-ahead routing to simplify the time-critical path by computing the output port in the previous network hops. The proposed router architecture requires the ability to retransmit flits if contention occurs. We use a backpressure flow control mechanism to manage contention. It was necessary to pipeline the backpressure feedback loop to reduce the routing delay in the time-critical path of the design. As a consequence, a backpressure signal that reports contention arrives with a delay of two clock cycles. Hence, the slack buffers store the last two transmitted flits and the router retransmits them when the backpressure signal is released. While this leads to a higher system clock frequency, it slightly rises the network latency when contention occurs because data need to be retransmitted.

Other networks that are optimized for FPGA implementation typically use buffers implemented as block RAMs [8,3,1]. We use CLBs to implement the buffers because block RAMs slow down the design or require a pipelined router design with an additional clock cycle latency.

Table 1. Hardware resource usage and maximum clock frequency

FPGA Family	Speed Grade	16 bit link LUTs	MHz	24 bit link LUTs	MHz	32 bit link LUTs	MHz
Virtex 7	-3	683	437	913	428	1121	394
Virtex 6	-3	679	412	903	372	1097	347
Spartan 6	-3	753	223	1031	208	1299	204

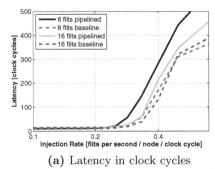

(a) Latency in clock cycles

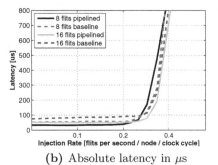

(b) Absolute latency in μs

Fig. 3. Latency vs. packet injection rate of a 4x4 2D mesh network

5   Results

We evaluate the proposed network in two steps. First, we derive clock speed and
hardware resources of various router configurations and measure the network latency of random traffic. Second, we evaluate the scalability of Tinuso multicore
systems. Table 1 lists hardware resources and maximum clock speed of a single
router implementation on various Xilinx FPGA families based on Xilinx ISE
14.6 "place and route report". The proposed design scales well with the data
link width as a 16 bit router consumes about 60% of the hardware resources
of a 32 bit implementation. To evaluate the network latency we use a VHDL
simulator on multicore setups consisting of 4x4 nodes to measure the average
network latency of random packets for various injection rates. We run experiments with 32 bit link width and a fixed packet size of eight and sixteen flits. To
get unbiased results, we warm the network and run up to 50 iterations per test
point. We compare the latency of a Tinuso network with a baseline router implementation without pipelined feedback loop to manage contention. The baseline
router is simpler as it only requires a single slack buffer but the backpressure
feedback loop restricts the clock frequency of the design. Figure 3a shows average
latencies for various injection rates. The latency of the baseline implementation
is lower when contention occurs because of the smaller slack buffer fewer flits
need to be retransmitted. We observe a very low latency up to an injection rate
of 0.3 flits per node per cycle. At higher injection rates high contention occurs
and latencies become unacceptable long. In Figure 3b we derive the absolute

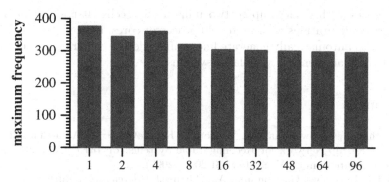

Fig. 4. Scaling of Tinuso multicore systems

latency in μs. We scale the latency with the maximum clock frequency of 304 MHz for the Tinuso router and 164 MHz for the baseline implementation. The maximum frequency of the multicore system is lower than the clock speed of a single router implementation because it includes routing delays between the routers. The Tinuso network performs better at low injection rates but there are situations at high contention where the latency in the network with the baseline router is lower. To evaluate scalability, we populate the network nodes with Tinuso processor cores to compose multicore systems of various size and derive the maximum clock frequency on a Virtex 7 device. Figure 4 shows the results of the placed and routed designs. With increasing system size it becomes more difficult for the tools to map the design on the FPGA fabric. Designs with more than 4 processor cores require floor-planning in Xilinx PlanAhead to attain an acceptable clock speed. We assign local area constraints (Pblocks) to the processor cores and let the Xilinx toolchain find a performance optimized placement for the network. However, for very large systems with more than 64 processor cores the tools report a high system frequency after synthesis but the tools are not able to map the design efficiently and report slow place and route results.

6   Conclusion

In this paper, we motivated synthesizable multicore platforms for microwave imaging systems. We described the design, implementation and evaluation of communication structures for Tinuso multicore systems. The proposed router architecture uses wormhole switching and a backpressure flow control mechanism to attain a latency of one clock cycle per hop. We optimized routing scheme and flow control mechanism for high system clock frequency. We measured the network latency of random traffic and compared it to a baseline router implementation. We showed that a pipelined feedback loop to manage contention leads to significantly higher clock speed and a lower network latency at low injection rates. For a Tinuso multicore system we attain a maximum clock frequency of 300 MHz on a Xilinx Virtex 7 device. However, as we scale the system, the Xilinx tools increasingly have problems to map the design efficiently. Xilinx's Virtex 7 family comes with devices up to two million logic cells that allow for Tinuso multicore configurations with up to 480 processor cores. Hence, we currently explore how to automatically generate fine-grained design constraints to efficiently support the placement for very large systems.

References

1. Janarthanan, A., Swaminathan, V., Tomko, K.: MoCReS: An Area-Efficient Multi-Clock On-Chip Network for Reconfigurable Systems. In: IEEE Computer Society Annual Symposium on VLSI, ISVLSI 2007 (2007)
2. Lebedev, I., Shaoyi, C., Doupnik, A., Martin, J., Fletcher, C., Burke, D., Mingjie, L., Wawrzynek, J.: MARC: A many-core approach to reconfigurable computing. In: Conference on Reconfigurable Computing and FPGAs, ReConFig (2010)
3. Lu, Y., McCanny, J., Sezer, S.: Generic Low-Latency NoC Router Architecture for FPGA Computing Systems. In: Conference on Field Programmable Logic and Applications, FPL 2011 (2011)
4. Papakonstantinou, A., Liang, Y., Stratton, J., Gururaj, K., Chen, D., Hwu, W.: Multilevel granularity parallelism synthesis on FPGA. In: Symposium on Field-Programmable Custom Computing Machines FCCM (2011)
5. Roca, A., Flich, J., Dimitrakopoulos, G.: DESA: Distributed elastic switch architecture for efficient networks-on-fpgas. In: Conference on Field Programmable Logic and Applications, FPL (2012)
6. Schleuniger, P., Kusk, A., Dall, J., Karlsson, S.: Synthetic aperture radar data processing on an fpga multi-core system. In: Conference on Architecture of Computing Systems ARCS (2013)
7. Schleuniger, P., McKee, S.A., Karlsson, S.: Design principles for synthesizable processor cores. In: Conference on Architecture of Computing Systems ARCS (2012)
8. Sethuraman, B., Bhattacharya, P., Khan, J., Vemuri, R.: LiPaR: A light-weight parallel router for FPGA-based networks-on-chip. In: Great Lakes Symposium on VLSI, GLSVLSI (2005)

An Efficient Implementation of the Adams-Hamilton's Demosaicing Algorithm in FPGAs

Jalal Khalifat, Ali Ebrahim, and Tughrul Arslan

{J.Khalifat,A.ebrahim,T.Arslan}@ed.ac.uk

Abstract. Demosaicing is the process of reconstructing a full color image from incomplete samples generated by typical image sensors. This paper discusses the Adams-Hamilton's demosaicing algorithm and presents a high-performance and cost-effective implementation of the algorithm in Field Programmable Gate Arrays (FPGAs). The paper also presents a proposed demosaicing hardware architecture which increases the number of pixels processed in a single clock cycle by using efficient pipelining. Images obtained from our FPGA implementation are compared to images obtained from standard software demosaicing functions. Our proposed hardware *architecture is shown to outperform previous hardware implementations of the algorithm. Our architecture is capable of processing up to 419 MPixels/s.*

Keywords: Adams-Hamilton, FPGAs, Demosaicing, PSNR , HD, Bayer CFA.

1 Introduction

Most of the commercial portable devices, which capture digital images such as digital cameras and mobile phones, use an array of filters on top of the image sensors. In the case of RGB images format, each pixel record is produced by a sensor overlaid with one type of color filter. This arrangement results in an incomplete image samples with two missing colors from each pixel. Using Color Filter Array (CFA), sensors produce a two-dimensional array of pixels each representing a single color: red, green or blue. Many types of color filter arrays are used in digital capturing devices. The most common type is the Bayer color filter array [1]. The Red-Green-Green-Blue (RGGB) arrangement of the Bayer color filter array is shown in Fig.1a). In this arrangement, the filters are 50% green, 25% red and 25% blue. Half of the sensors are coupled with filters for the green color, the color for which the human eye is more sensitive.

To construct a full RGB image, demosaicing algorithms are used to interpolate missing red, green and blue sub-pixels from the surrounding pixels. Different algorithms have different image qualities and vary in term of computation demand. Bilinear interpolation is the simplest algorithm that interpolates missing colors using symmetric bilinear interpolation from the nearest neighbors of the same color by finding the average color from two or four of the matched surrounding sub-pixels.

A huge number of Demosaicing algorithms have been patented. Some of them, such as the Freeman's algorithm [2], use a median filter added to the bilinear interpolation to

D. Goehringer et al. (Eds.): ARC 2014, LNCS 8405, pp. 205–212, 2014.
© Springer International Publishing Switzerland 2014

reduce the noise and artifacts produce by bilinear interpolation. Other algorithms exploit the spatial correlation principle such as Adams-Hamilton's algorithm demonstrated in [3], and the asymmetric interpolation scheme using color discontinuity equalization demonstrated in [4].

Most of the demosaicing algorithms are implemented and tested using software-based environments. This type of implementation causes a huge reduction in the performance as they execute instructions sequentially. On the other hand, hardware implementation could process the algorithm faster as they use parallel computing concept. Few research works discuss the implementation of demosaicing algorithm in hardware-based environments, but most of them use the bilinear interpolation [5][6] and [8], which adds zipper effects and artifacts to the images produced. Other implementations use customized algorithms such as the algorithm in [9]. In [5] the algorithm was verified using Altera's Cyclone II FPGA. In [6], the implementation uses the same algorithm with HD images. However, no details are given on how data are passed to/from memory. In [7], the author implemented the Freeman's algorithm using a dual-core architecture with coarse-grained dynamically reconfigurable processors that provide throughput of up to 241Mpixel/s.

This paper presents a novel hardware implementation of Adams-Hamilton's algorithm which utilizes efficient pipelining in Field Programmable Gate Arrays (FPGAs). The design of the different components of the data path is discussed and analyzed. This paper also presents a brief introduction of the algorithm and discusses its benefits compared to other algorithms. Moreover, implementation results are compared to other similar designs.

The rest of the paper is organized as follows. In Section 2, we explain the background of Adams-Hamilton's algorithm. In Section 3, we show the architecture of the system and design components. In Section 4, we show the experimental results. Finally, Section 5 concludes the paper.

2   Adams-Hamilton's Demosaicing

Adams-Hamilton's algorithm is considered one of the edge-based algorithms that exploit the spatial correlation principle by interpolating along the edges and not across them. This technique reduces color artifacts and zipper effects to the regions with edges not like the other type of algorithms which disregard directional information. Moreover, averaging the pixels across an edge will decrease the sharpness at edges.

The algorithm is divided into two steps; firstly, the green color plane is interpolated, and then the red and blue planes are interpolated. G missing pixels can be interpolated vertically, horizontally or using the two directions based on specific classifiers to choose the interpolation direction as depicted in Fig. 1b) and Fig. 1c). In the case of G pixels in B positions, the same equations are used as R positions replaced with B.

Once the G color plane is interpolated, the algorithm starts interpolating the red and blue colors. In this estimation, a window of 3x3 needed as depicted in Fig. 1b and1c. This step is categorized into three different cases: Case 1 is when the nearest neighbors to (R or B) are in the same column. Case 2 is when the nearest neighbors to

(R or B) are in the same row and case 3 is when the nearest neighbors to the (R or B) are at the corners. In cases 1 and 2, the missing (R or B)s are in G locations as shown in Fig. 1b). The classifiers used to estimate the missing colors are as follow: Equation 1 for nearest neighbor in the same column and Equation 2 in the same row.

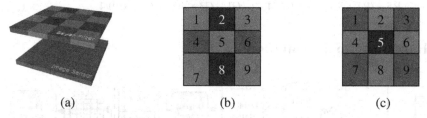

(a)   (b)   (c)

Fig. 1. (a) Bayer Filters and sensors (a) pixel estimation case 1 and 2 (b) pixel estimation case 3

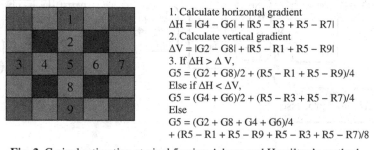

1. Calculate horizontal gradient
$\Delta H = |G4 - G6| + |R5 - R3 + R5 - R7|$
2. Calculate vertical gradient
$\Delta V = |G2 - G8| + |R5 - R1 + R5 - R9|$
3. If $\Delta H > \Delta V$,
$G5 = (G2 + G8)/2 + (R5 - R1 + R5 - R9)/4$
Else if $\Delta H < \Delta V$,
$G5 = (G4 + G6)/2 + (R5 - R3 + R5 - R7)/4$
Else
$G5 = (G2 + G8 + G4 + G6)/4$
$+ (R5 - R1 + R5 - R9 + R5 - R3 + R5 - R7)/8$

Fig. 2. G pixel estimation at pixel 5 using Adams and Hamilton's method

$$B5 = (B2+B8)/2 + (-G2+2G5-G8)/2 \tag{1}$$

$$R5 = (R4+R6)/2 + (-G4+2G5-G6)/2 \tag{2}$$

Case 3, when the missing R pixel part in B locations as the case depicted in Fig. 1c) or missing B pixel part in R locations. The nearest neighbors are at the corners of the 3x3 window. Classifiers composed of Laplacian second-order terms for the green data and gradients for the chroma data are used. These classifiers are sensing the high spatial frequency information present in the pixel neighborhood in the negative diagonal (DN) and positive diagonal (DP) directions as shown in Equations (3) and (4) for the case of missing R pixel part in B locations, and based of the classifiers, the direction of interpolation determined as shown in Equations 5, 6, 7.

$$DN = |R1 - R9| + |G5 - G1 + G5 - G9| \tag{3}$$

$$DP = |R3 - R7| + |G5 - G3 + G5 - G7| \tag{4}$$

If DN > DP,

$$R5 = (R3 + R7)/2 + (- G3 + 2G5 - G7)/2 \tag{5}$$

Else if DN < DP,

$$R5 = (R1 + R9)/2 + (- G1 + 2G5 - G9)/2 \tag{6}$$

Else

$$R5 = (R1 + R3 + R7 + R9)/4 + (- G1 - G3 + 4G5 - G7 - G9)/4 \tag{7}$$

3   Hardware Implementation

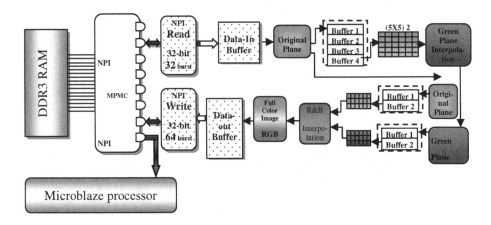

Fig. 3. System implementation

Our implementation of the Adams-Hamilton's demosaicing is illustrated in Fig. 3. As the images processed line by line from left to right, a set of data buffers employed for each line. The implemented system designed to process images of size 1920x1080 pixels where 1920 is the width. A shift window of sizes 5x5 and 3x3 are used in G interpolation and R&B colors interpolation stages respectively.

The system designed to process two pixels in one clock cycle using an efficient pipelining scheme, as the data input is designed to accept 2 bytes (pixels) and the processes are parallelized in the data path. This technique will double the performance but will increase the resources required. Each input pixel (byte) is converted to 3 bytes which limits the number of pixels processed in one clock cycle.

3.1   Data Buffering

The size of the FIFO is 1914 bytes as the image width is 1920 and the remaining six bytes are located in the shift registers where the window is located. Block memories (BRAMs) are used to design FIFOs for each line in the shift window. For the green interpolation stage, Fig. 4 shows the four FIFOs contain the image lines under process and the registers where the actual window is located. The red and blue interpolation uses the same structure but uses two FIFOs instead of four. P22 and P23 are the locations of pixels processed at each clock cycle. In each clock cycle, a shift operation occurs by shifting the bytes in registers 1 and 2 to the next row buffer and bytes in registers 3 and 4 to registers 1 and 2 and finally the most significant two bytes in the same row buffer to registers 5 and 6. Inside the buffer, if the data of the image is still coming, the write address and read address are incremented when a shift operation occurs; otherwise, the read address is incremented only until the two addresses are equal, which means the end of the image data.

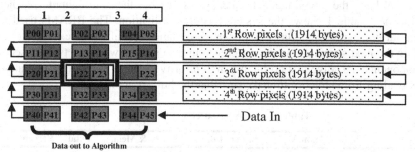

Fig. 4. Buffers of G interpolation stage

3.2   Image Interpolation

In each clock cycle, the content of registers 1 to 6 is sent to the hardware design of the equations mentioned in section 2, for both sets of equations, the G interpolation stage and the R & B interpolation stage. The design is divided into two parts:

1. Even rows: In these rows, the received six bytes ordered in the form RGRGRG. The algorithm interpolates the missing colors in the middle locations where the pixels RG are located. For the G interpolation stage, only the first Green pixel is interpolated as the second is contained in the original data. However, for the R & B interpolation stage, the B part is unknown in the first pixel and the B and R parts are unknown in the second pixel.
2. Odd rows: In these rows, the received six bytes are ordered in the form GBGBGB. The design in these rows acts as it acts in the even rows case, but interpolates different colors as the location of each color is changed. In G stage, the green color part is missing in the second pixels in the odd rows. On the other hand, the red and blue color parts are missing in the first pixel while the red color part is missing in the second pixel.

3.3   Memory Interface

The Xilinx Native Port Interface (NPI) [10] is used to connect the system to the DDR memory through the Xilinx Multi Port Memory Controller (MPMC) [10]. Two ports of the MPMC are dedicated, one for reading and the other for writing. Due to the difference in data size between the NPI part and the demosaicing system, two blocks in the middle named Data_In and Data_out are implemented to convert the size of data from the NPI form to the system form and vise versa. A Microblaze processor is used to control data transfer from memory side and number of burst required.

4   Experimental Results

4.1   Performance and Utilization

The above architecture was implemented on Xilinx ML605 boards with a Virtex-6 XCE6VLX240T FPGA chip. The maximum operation frequency is 209.6 MHz but the system was tested at a frequency of 200MHz due to the limitation in memory interface. When the maximum frequency is used, the throughput reaches 419.2Mpixel/s. Table 1 shows the system resource utilization. The BRAMs used in "Data in buffers" and "Data out" components are mainly to buffer the extra data not yet sent to the next stage, due to the difference in data size between the two consecutive components. To solve this problem a high priority given to the writing operation over the reading from memory to make sure that the buffers are not full.

Table 1. System resource's utilizstion

Resources	Data in B.	Ham Alg.	Data out B.	Mblaze & Mem.	Total	Percentage
Slices	101	1003(2.6%)	202	3163	4469	11%
RAMB36s	15	8 (2%)	36	29	88	21%

The latency of the design equals to the time needed for 2940 clock cycles as the data passes through two different set of FIFOs to process the data. The first FIFO needs around 1940 clock cycles and the second 960 clock cycles. The other logics need around 40 clock cycles. The time measured to process the whole image of size 1920x1080 is equal to 8.53 ms including the memory interface timing. This system can process around 117 frames per second. The design can perform better than the designs proposed in [6][7] in terms of execution time and average throughput as shown in Table. 2 for images of size 1920x1080.

Table 2. Demosaicing performance comparison

Resources	Multi-core DR Freeman [7]	FPGA bilinear implementation [6]	Bilinear Inter. Architecture for Vision Systems [11]	Our Implementation
Execution time (ms)	8.92	13.82	-	8.53
Throughput (Mpix./s)	232.2	150	250	419.2

4.2   Image Analysis

Fig. 5b) shows the constructed images using the implemented system, which are originally in raw format as shown in Fig. 5a). To measure the quality of constructed images, a set of images are modified and mosaiced by removing two colors from each pixel to construct images as the one produced by the digital camera's sensors. The position of the colors determines the type Bayer pattern. RGGB Bayer patterned images are produced and then passed to the implemented system stages. The reconstructed images are compared with the original RGB images by taking the Peak Signal to Noise Ratio (PSNR) between the two images.

PSNR is used to measure how closely the constructed image fits the original one. In our case, a set of three images are mosaiced using Matlab. The three Bayer patterned images are passed to the implemented system and PSNR values are calculated for the constructed images to show the algorithm quality. Table 3 shows both the PSNR values for the images using the implemented system and for the same images reconstructed using the function demosaic from Matlab's image processing toolboxes. The results show that our system can achieve similar quality to the one achieved by the gradient-corrected linear interpolation algorithm used in the default demosaic function in Matlab.

Table 3. PSNR for different images vs Matlab

Image	PSNR of the implemented system images (dB)	PSNR of images using demosaic's Matlab function (dB)
Image1 (Woman)	34.214	34.562
Image2 (Battle)	41.931	36.361
Image3 (Green mountains)	31.254	32.458

(a)   (b)

Fig. 5. (a) Raw Bayer images; (b) Constructed images

5   Conclusion

In this paper, we have presented an Adams-Hamilton demosaicing implementation based on FPGAs. The implementation is highly cost effective and real time approach to image demosaicing as the system can process images of size 1920x1080 within 9ms. The results have demonstrated that the architecture provides higher throughput than similar designs implemented in hardware. The system used number of data buffers to buffer the unprocessed data prior the processing units and to form processing windows of size 3x3 and 5x5. We have used the Xilinx NPI with MPMC cores to interface the system to the DDR3 RAM memory. The architecture achieved a clock speed of 210MHz on a Xilinx Virtex-6. We have also presented image analysis on number of images produced by the system and compare them with the original RGB images. The measured PSNR values range between 30dB and 42dB.

References

1. Bayer, B.E.: Color imaging array. U.S. Patent No. 3,971,065 (July 1976)
2. Freeman, W.T.: Median filter for reconstruction missing color samples. U.S. Patent No. 4,724,395 (1988)
3. Hamilton, J.F., Adams, J.E.: Adaptive Color Plane Interpolation in Single Sensor Color Electronic Camera. U.S. Patent, No. 5629734 (1997)
4. Nguyen, T.: System and method for asymmetrically demosaicing raw data images using color discontinuity equalization. U.S. Patent No. 0,167,602 A1 (2002)
5. Fuentes, I.O.H., Bravo-Zanoguera, M.E., Yanez, G.G.: FPGA Implementation of the Bilinar Interpolation Algorithm for Image Demosaicking. In: International Conference on Electrical, Communications, and Computers (CONIELECOM), pp. 25–28 (2009)
6. Jair, G.L., Miguel, A.A., Julio, W.V.: A Digital Real Time Image Demosaicking Implementation for High Definition Video Cameras. In: Electronics, Robotics and Automotive Mechanics Conference (CERMA), pp. 565–569 (2008)
7. Zhao, X., Yi, Y., Erdogan, A.T., Arslan, T.: Dual-core reconfigurable demosaicing engine for next generation of portable camera systems. In: Conference on Design and Architectures for Signal and Image Processing Conference (DASIP), pp. 289–294 (2010)
8. Rani, K.S., Hans, W.J.: FPGA implementation of bilinear interpolation algorithm for CFA demosaicing. In: International Conference on Communications and Signal Processing (ICCSP), pp. 857–863 (2013)
9. Karloff, A., Muscedere, R.: A low-cost, real-time, hardware-based image demosaicking algorithm. In: IEEE International Conference on Electro/Information Technology (EIT), pp. 146–150 (2009)
10. DS643: LogiCORE IP Multi-Port Memory Controller (MPMC) (v6.03.a), Xilinx Inc. (March 2011)
11. Fahmy, S.A.: Generalised Parallel Bilinear Interpolation Architecture for Vision Systems. In: International Conference on Reconfigurable Computing and FPGAs (ReConFig), pp. 331–336 (2008)

FPGA Design of Delay-Based Digital Effects for Electric Guitar

Pablo Calleja, Gabriel Caffarena, and Ana Iriarte

University CEU-San Pablo,
Urb. Monteprincipe, 28668, Madrid, Spain
`pablocallejaibanez@gmail`
`gabriel.caffarena@ceu.es`
`http://biolab.uspceu.com`

Abstract. In this paper we address the hardware design of delay-based audio effects. The paper focuses on the fixed-point hardware implementation of the effects *delay*, *flanger* and *chorus*. This work aims at providing a proof-of-concept for the application of reconfigurable devices in real-time audio processing. The results yield that FPGA devices enable for the simultaneous application of a high number of digital effects using a high sampling rate and providing a very low latency.

Keywords: Audio, Delay, DSP, Fixed-Point.

1 Introduction

Early electric guitar players sought for a distinctive sound by selecting different types of guitars or varying the amplifiers' settings. Later on, guitar pedals were created to generate a wide range of audio effects (e.g. echo, distortion, etc.). Digital processing allows increasing the complexity and subtlety of these effects. Real-time digital processing of audio signals is commonly implemented using processor-based approaches: computers with specialized software or stand-alone solutions based on DSP (digital signal processors) [1]. The former leads to high latencies for complex processing, making it inappropriate for real-time playing. The latter provides reduced latencies, though the number of effects that can be chained together is limited. Reconfigurable hardware provides a high level of parallelism, difficult to beat by other approaches that rely on software. Their main drawbacks are long development time and reduced flexibility. These might be overcome by the fact that professional sampling rates as well as extremely low latencies can be offered.

There are scarce published works on the use of FPGA devices [2] for real-time audio processing, and in general they do not focus on the implementation process. In this paper we present an up-to-date implementation of some digital effects, putting the stress on hardware design. Delay-based effects are used since they conform some of the most fundamental guitar effects.

D. Goehringer et al. (Eds.): ARC 2014, LNCS 8405, pp. 213–218, 2014.
© Springer International Publishing Switzerland 2014

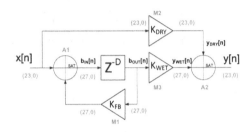

Fig. 1. Block diagram of delay-based effects

2 Delay-Based Audio Effects

Fig. 1 shows the block diagram for the delay-based audio effects [3]. The figure contains the name of the inner variables, and the the the fixed-point formats in grey (see subsection 3.3). There are 2 adders (A_i), a D-tap buffer and 3 multipliers (M_i) involved in the processing.

The output signal $y[n]$ has the following expression:

$$y[n] = k_{dry} \cdot x[n] + k_{wet} \cdot (x[n-D] + k_{fb} \cdot y[n-D]). \tag{1}$$

Parameter $k_{dry} \in [0,1]$ controls the level of $x[n]$ at the output, $k_{wet} \in [0,1]$ controls the amount of echo, and parameter $k_{fb} \in [-1,1]$ determines the amount of feedback in the system. Finally, parameter D sets the separation in samples of the repeated echoes.

Table 1 shows the different parameter configurations for the three delay-based effects. Note that effects *flanger* and *chorus* have a time-variant delay generated by an oscillator, so the oscillation frequency f_{OSC} is required. Also, the delay range is specified in milliseconds and not in samples.

Table 1. Effects' parameters

Effect	D_{min} (msec)	D_{max} (msec)	k_{wet}/k_{dry}	k_{fb}	f_{osc} (Hz)	Memory size[1] (samples)
Delay	> 0.0	$\approx 5 \cdot 10^3$	$(0.0, 1.0]$	$(-1.0, 1.0)$	0.0	$\approx 5 \cdot 10^6$
Chorus	> 5	$[7, 40]$	0.5	0.0	$[0.02, 5.0]$	$\approx 4 \cdot 10^3$
Flanger	0.0	$[7, 10]$	0.5	$(-1.0, 1.0)$	$[0.02, 5.0]$	$\approx 10^3$

[1] With respect to a sample rate of $f_s = 88$ ksps.

2.1 Delay

The *delay* effect generates one echo or more of the input signal. The user can control the time separation of echoes with parameter D, as well as the presence or not of feedback in the system. If the delay is too short, then, there is no way to distinguish the echoes from the original signal, and, interesting audio effects are produced (e.g. the sound becomes metallic). Typical delays range from half a second to several seconds so a buffer with several thousand of taps will be required (see Table 1).

2.2   Chorus

The effect *chorus* modifies the guitar sound so it seems that several instruments are playing simultaneously. The time-variant delay produces a Doppler effect, which in fact varies the frequency of the guitar signal. Table 1 shows that there is a lower and upper limit to the delay, and that the delays are very short. Thus, the frequency changes are subtle and also the hardware requirements for the buffer are low. Finally, note that feedback is set to 0.

2.3   Flanger

The *flanger* effect is also based on a time-variant delay, but this time there is feedback and the lower limit for D is fixed to 0. The audio sensation is similar to the whoosh of a plane [3]. The range of D is small, so the buffer requirements are, again, not too restrictive.

3   Hardware Design

The hardware design of the effects must comply with different goals in mind: i) the effects must be parameterizable; ii) high-quality audio is targeted setting the precision to 24 bits and the sampling rate f_s to 88 ksps; iii) fixed-point design must be optimized so the quality degradation is controlled and the final hardware cost is low; iv) real-time must be accomplished, minimizing latency; and, iv) effect chaining must be supported.

FPGA devices are suitable for all these points. They enable for the implementation of multiple-wordlength arithmetic circuits, which is essential for optimized fixed-point implementations. Also, they are specially suitable for pipelining and parallelization, which leads to real-time processing for high sampling rates and eases effects chaining. The high amount of memory resources (LUTs and flip-flops) supports parameterization.

In this work we target Altera devices, concretely the Cyclone IV family, but the applied methodology can be extended to other families of Altera devices, and to other manufacturers' FPGAs.

3.1   Handling Memories for Buffering

Cyclone-IV devices provide three types of memory: flip-flops (bit), 4-input LUTs (2^4 bits), and memory blocks (2^{13} bits).

The variable-delay buffer is implemented using a circular buffer. Given a memory with M words, a counter is used to generate the write addresses (A_{WR}), so each incoming datum ($b_{IN}[n]$) is stored. The delay signal ($b_{OUT}[n]$) is created by reading from the address $A_{RD} = |A_{WR} - D|_M$. The *delay* has a fixed value for D, so it is stored in a register, while for *flanger* and *chorus*, D is the output of the oscillator.

Delay requires an external memory, so an SRAM controller must be added. The other two effects can make use of the $M9K$ inner memory blocks.

3.2   Parameterizable Coefficients

The parameter multiplications are implemented with a generic multiplier, a shift operation and a truncation. It was decided to use 8-bit parameters with a fixed scaling of 2^{-8}, so the range is $[0, (2^8 - 1)/2^{-8}]$ and they can be stored in registers. The shift and truncation operations can be implemented in hardware for free. Next section analyses the truncation error.

3.3   Fixed-Point Issues

The circuits are developed using fixed-point arithmetic in order to obtain a reduced area as well as good performance [4,5].

First, it is necessary to select the number of integer bits for each signal in our circuit. A positive number of integer bits implies a most significant bit (MSB) located to the left of the fractionary point. The MSB must be such that the probability of overflow is minimized. Next, it is necessary to select the position of the LSBs, which might result in a truncation, thus, introducing an underflow error which is propagated towards the output. The errors must be controlled so the overall quality of the application does not degrade.

Overflow Error. The range of a signal $s[n]$ is bounded as follows [6]:

$$
\left(range\,(x[n]) \sum_{i=0}^{\infty} |h_s[i]| \right)^{1/2} \leq range\,(s[n]) \leq range\,(x[n]) \sum_{i=0}^{\infty} |h_s[i]|, \quad (2)
$$

where h_s is the impulse response from the input of the system to signal $s[n]$.

The range of signal b_{in} is computed considering the worst-case ($k_{fb} = \frac{2^8-1}{2^8}$, $k_{wet} = k_{dir} = 1$) and $D = 1$. To minimize resources, the left side of expression (2) was considered, which resulted in adding 4 extra bits and a saturation block (see the output of adder $A1$, Fig. 1). The MSB of signals b_{out}, y_{dry} and y_{wet} can be simply inferred. Note that the output signal y is saturated to 24 bits to comply with the format of the audio samples.

Underflow Error. The power of the quantization noise at the output of an Linear Time-Invariant (LTI) system can be computed analytically [6,4,5]. Fig. 2 displays the Signal-to-Quantization Noise-Ration (SQNR) for different scenarios. A digitized guitar signal composed of different arpeggios (I-IV-II-V) is used as a reference signal. The SQNR is computed by expressing in dB the ratio between the power of the signal and the power of the output quantization noise. Different values for the dynamic range of $x[n]$ and the feedback factor were tested.

The SQNR ranges from 60 dB to 120 dB, which proves that the quantization noise can be neglected. The graph shows how the SQNR decreases when the dynamic range of $x[n]$ decreases, and also when the feedback increases.

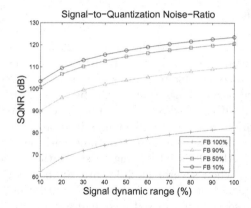

Fig. 2. SQNR for combinations of FB and the dynamic range of the guitar signal

4   Results

The effect box was implemented using the Terasic DE2-115. The components used for the prototyping of the effect modules were an Altera Cyclone-IV EP4CE115F29C7 device, 24-bit Audio CODEC (Wolfson WM8731), a 2-MB SRAM, and the set of buttons, switches, LEDs and 7-segment displays for interfacing. A guitar was directly connected to the MIC input of the board and the LINE-OUT output was connected to an amplifier. The prototype was coded using VHDL and synthesized with Quartus 12.1 from Altera.

The prototype was conformed by three blocks: i) a CODEC interface (Altera University Program); ii) a *User Interface* to set up the effects; and, iii) a *DSP* block implementing the effects. The effects can be chained as follows: A) no effect; B) Delay; C) Flanger; D) Chorus; E) Flanger+Delay; and, F) Chorus+Delay.

Four implementations were made: I) only the CODEC interface; II) whole prototype; III) only the delay; IV) only flanger; and, V) only chorus. Table 2 shows that the CODEC interface (I) requires scarce resources (less than 1%). The whole system (II) uses 8% of the resources, so there is ample room to introduce more effects. The implementation of the effects in isolation (III, IV and V) requires around 5% of the FPGA.

Delays were introduced at the inputs and outputs of each module to improve routing and to enable pipelining. Thus, each effect introduces a delay of 2 samples (0.022 msecs),so many effects can be chained together.

Table 2. Implementation results

Implementation	Total Logic Elements	Total memory bits
I	523 (< 1%)	2288 (< 1%)
II	8.727 (8%)	95.232 (< 1%)
III	5.638 (5%)	9.261 (< 1%)
IV	4.813 (4%)	37.888 ((< 1%)
V	4.749 (4%)	66.560 (2%)

5   Conclusions

We have presented the design and the implementation results of delay-based effects for electric guitar. The results yield that FPGA are suitable for real-time, high-quality audio processing (sample rates of 88 ksps and precision of 24 bits). The FPGA resource usage shows that it will be possible to implement more complex delay-based effects (stereo delays, reverb, etc.). We can safely state that these effects can be implemented leaving still room for extra effects.

As a main future line, we gather to continue with the implementation of other digital effects. Also, it is interesting to study the effect of quantization noise and saturation when several modules are chained together. The use of dual fixed-point [7] could provide some advantages in terms of dynamic range and quantization noise. The use of self-reconfigurable multipliers could reduce cost, enabling more parallelism or increase the mathematical precision [8].

Acknowledgments. We thank Altera University Program for the support given to the Laboratory of Bioengineering, University CEU-San Pablo.

References

1. Byun, K., Kwon, Y.S., Park, S., Eum, N.W.: Digital audio effect system-on-a-chip based on embedded dsp core. ETRI Journal 31(6), 732–740 (2009)
2. Pfaff, M., Malzner, D., Seifert, J., Traxler, J., Weber, H., Wiendl, G.: Implementing digital audio effects using a hardware/software co-design approach. In: 10th International Conference on Digital Audio Effects, pp. 125–132 (2007)
3. Pirkle, W.: Designing Audio Effect Plug-Ins in C++, 1st edn. Taylor and Francis (2013)
4. Constantinides, G., Cheung, P., Luk, W.: Optimal Datapath Allocation for Multiple-Wordlength Systems. IEE Electronics Letters 36(17), 1508–1509 (2000)
5. Caffarena, G., Carreras, C., López, J., Fernández, A.: SQNR Estimation of Fixed-Point DSP Algorithms. Int. J. on Advances in Signal Processing 2010, 1–11 (2010)
6. Oppenheim, A.V., Schafer, R.W.: Discrete-Time Signal Processing. Prentice-Hall, Englewood Cliffs (1987)
7. Tee, C., Cheung, P., Constantinides, G.: Dual Fixed-Point: An Efficient Alternative to Floating-Point Computation. In: Field Programmable Logic and Applications, pp. 200–208 (2004)
8. Hormigo, J., Caffarena, G., Oliver, J.P., Boemo, E.: Self-reconfigurable constant multiplier for fpga. ACM Trans. Reconfigurable Technol. Syst. 6(3), 14:1–14:17 (2013)

Design Space Exploration of a Particle Filter Using Higher-Order Functions

Rinse Wester and Jan Kuper

University of Twente, Drienerlolaan 5, Enschede, The Netherlands
{r.wester,j.kuper}@utwente.nl

Abstract. This paper presents a design space exploration methodology based on higher-order functions to facilitate the tradeoff between execution time and area usage on FPGAs. Higher-order function are transformed, resulting in parameterized nodes where the amount of parallelism and thereby performance, can be controlled. For composition and scheduling of operations, dataflow principles are used. To show the validity of the approach, a particle filter has been transformed and synthesized for FPGA. The resulting architecture is parameterizable and achieves good performance.

Keywords: Higher-order functions, Tradeoff, Particle filter, FPGA.

1 Introduction

Particle filtering is a popular Monte Carlo based technique, to perform state space estimation e.g. tracking [1]. Since particle filtering is computationally intensive, a proper tradeoff between time and space is necessary for FPGA implementation. In this paper, we propose a novel design space exploration methodology that exploits the mathematical structure in particle filters, resulting in a tradeoff between execution-time and FPGA area usage i.e. between time and space. Higher-order functions, a key abstraction technique used in functional programming, are translated into dataflow nodes using transformation rules that perform a tradeoff between time and space.

The tradeoff is explored in a particle filter written in plain Haskell [2] consisting only of normal and higher-order functions (functions that take a function as argument). Using a set of transformation rules, these higher-order functions are transformed into parameterizable CλaSH [3] hardware components. The CλaSH language is a subset of Haskell that is translated to hardware (VHDL) by the CλaSH compiler. To simplify simulation, the particle filter is implemented in both Haskell and CλaSH. For composition of the resulting CλaSH hardware, dataflow principles are used by adding logic that performs synchronization and scheduling.

The rest of this paper is structured as follows. First, related work is presented in Section 2. In Section 3.1, some background information is given on hardware design using the functional language Haskell. Particle filtering is introduced in Section 3.2. The design methodology is presented in Section 4 while simulation

D. Goehringer et al. (Eds.): ARC 2014, LNCS 8405, pp. 219–226, 2014.
© Springer International Publishing Switzerland 2014

and hardware results are given in Section 5. Finally, in Section 6, conclusions are drawn and possible directions for future work are discussed.

2   Related Work

Particle filters have become a subject of intensive research since the publication of [1]. Hardware implementations of particle filters using FPGAs for acceleration is extensively covered in [4] and [5] while hardware design methodologies can be found in [6] and [7]. In [6] a generic method is presented to implement different particle filters using a single model. [7] incorporates dataflow principles (data triggered execution) into a particle filtering architecture.

The main difference between the aforementioned papers and the methodology presented in this paper is that the tradeoff is directly applied to the mathematical definition (in Haskell) of a particle filter instead of C source code. As was shown in [8], there exists a one-to-one relation between higher-order functions and the resulting structure of components on the FPGA. It is therefore interesting to explore the transformations of higher-order functions involving a tradeoff between time and space.

A lot of research exists on using functional languages for hardware design [9], [10] including hardware design using higher-order functions [11]. However, compared to a direct register transfer level (RTL) approach, the transformations presented in this paper are applied on a higher abstraction level by exploiting the regularity of higher-order functions i.e. the transformations produce RTL style hardware.

3   Background

3.1   Hardware Design Using Haskell

All designs presented in this paper are written in Haskell or CλaSH. Haskell [2] is a functional language supporting abstraction techniques like type derivation, partial application and higher-order functions. Especially higher-order functions (functions accepting a function as argument or returning a function as result) is a very useful abstraction because it allows the designer to express the mathematical regularity of the application very concisely and semantically clear [8].

To design real hardware we use the functional hardware description language CλaSH [3], a subset of Haskell that is translated to VHDL by the CλaSH compiler. The language features that make Haskell very attractive for hardware design, like higher-order functions, are also available in CλaSH. Among others, the higher-order functions *map*, *zipWith* and *foldl* are supported by CλaSH, allowing a direct implementation of the components resulting from the design methodology. In CλaSH, all components are expressed in the form of a Mealy machine (the output and new state are a function of the current state and input). Listing 1.1 shows a small CλaSH code example of a circuit adding all elements in a vector (a list with constant length).

Listing 1.1. CλaSH code example

```
sum (State s) xs = (State s', out)
  where
    s'  = vfoldl (+) 0 xs
    out = s
```

As shown Listing 1.1, the function describing the Mealy machine of *sum* accepts two arguments (the current state *s* and vector of values *xs*) and returns a new state *s'* and output *out*. Using the higher-order function *vfoldl*, the sum of the vector *xs* is determined and assigned to *s'*. *vfoldl* accepts the binary addition function (+), an initial value 0 and the vector of numbers *xs* to be summed. *vfoldl* determines the sum incrementally adding elements from *xs* starting with the initial value 0, thereby forming a chain of adders. In the last line, the value of the internal state register *s* is assigned to the output *out*.

3.2 Particle Filtering

Particle filtering is a Bayesian filtering technique to estimate the state of a system recursively using noisy measurements [1]. The state of the system is a set of properties that should be tracked, examples are speed, position and angular momentum. For each measurement (a radar image for example), the current estimate of the real state vector is updated resulting in a more and more precise estimate. Since measurements contain noise, the resulting state will be in the form of a Probability Density Function (PDF). Analytically finding this PDF is often mathematically intractable (the integrals can not be solved) which is why approximation methods are used. Particle filters approximate this PDF by a set of N particles $x_k^{(i)}$ where $i = 1 \ldots N$ is the index of a particle and k the iteration of the filter. A higher density of particles represents a higher probability in the continuous state space (Figure 1). We focus on a commonly used type of particle filter, the Sequential Importance Resampling Filter (SIRF) which consists of four steps: *prediction*, *update*, *normalization* and *resampling* [1].

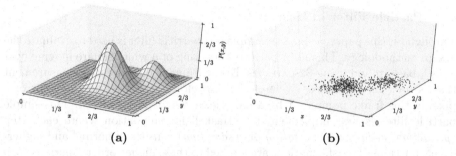

(a)   **(b)**

Fig. 1. Continuous PDF and particle representation

During *prediction*, the next state is derived from the current state using the known dynamics of the system that is being observed. This is implemented by evaluating the system dynamics function f for all N particles, $x_k^{(i)} = f(x_{k-1}^{(i)}, u_k)$. f consist of a deterministic and non-deterministic part. For each particle, the deterministic part depends only on the previous state $x_{k-1}^{(i)}$ while the non-deterministic part u_k requires a sample from a known distribution. For example, a ship moves in a straight line (deterministic) while the position might fluctuate a bit due to waves (non-deterministic).

In the *update* step, every particle $x_k^{(i)}$ is assigned a weight $\omega_k^{(i)}$, using the a likelihood function g, representing the importance of a particle given a *measurement* z_k. The function g returns a weight $\omega_k^{(i)}$ given a particle $x_k^{(i)}$, a measurement z_k and optionally noise vector v_k.

$$\omega_k^{(i)} = g(x_k^{(i)}, z_k, v_k), \quad \text{for} \quad i = 1 \ldots N \tag{1}$$

The remaining two steps in particle filtering are normalization and resampling. During normalization the weights are scaled such that the sum is equal to one, preparing them for resampling. To prevent degeneracy of weights the resampling step replicates particles zero, one or more times depending on their normalized weight $\tilde{\omega}^{(i)}$, while keeping the total number of particles constant i.e. particles with a high weight are replicated while particles with a low weight are discarded. More information on resampling techniques can be found in [4].

4   Design Methodology

As already elaborated in [8], the whole Haskell description of the particle filter can be divided into two groups, higher-order functions and normal functions. Higher-order functions are used to express structure and repetition with other functions as argument. Normal functions (base type contains no function-arguments) on the other hand are used as discrete components and correspond to combinatorial circuits like an adder for example. The design space exploration methodology consists of three phases: it starts out with 1. a definition of the particle filter in Haskell 2. applying transformation rules to higher-order functions, and 3. composition using dataflow principles.

4.1   Particle Filter in Haskell

Throughout this paper, a simple example of a particle filter is used to evaluate the design methodology. This filter performs tracking of a white square moving over a dark background using 32 particles. Every frame is considered a measurement that is used in a complete cycle of the particle filter. Based on the color of a pixel in this frame pointed at by a particle, a weight is calculated. This simple particle filter is first implemented in Haskell for simulation where each step (*prediction, update, normalization* or *resampling*) consists of normal and higher-order functions. Transformations are applied to these higher-order functions such that a tradeoff between time and space is made.

4.2 Space/Time Tradeoff Rules

Figure 2 and 3 show the transformation of *foldl*. The list to be processed (xs) is split into P sublists of size M such that $M \times P = N$. Each sublist is processed in a single cycle using $foldl_s$ (space) while the whole list is processed sequentially using $foldl_t$ (time). The amount of replication on hardware can now be controlled by the parallelization factor M, a parameter introduced by the transformation rule. A larger M results in larger sublists and therefore a higher throughput in a single clock cycle at the cost of more hardware. Similarly, smaller M requires more clock cycles but less hardware.

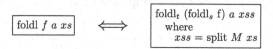

Fig. 2. Transformation of *foldl*

Figure 3 shows the transformation of *foldl* visually. As shown in Figure 3c, the final architecture requires an additional register to store intermediate results from a previous cycle. Again, the size of the sublists and the amount of parallelism in controlled by M. Similar rules are applied to the other higher-order functions (*map*, *zipWith*, *foldl* and *scanl*).

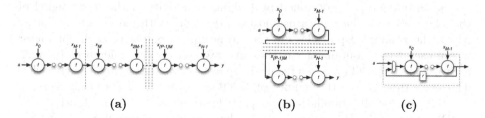

(a)   (b)   (c)

Fig. 3. Transformation of higher-order function *foldl*

4.3 Composition Using Dataflow

When all higher-order functions are transformed, the resulting components are wrapped into a dataflow node [12] for synchronization and scheduling. All these nodes are then connected together using FIFO buffers for storage of intermediate results. The data triggered behavior is implemented using a firing rule (start execution when all required data is available). When a node fires, arguments are removed from the input FIFOs while the result are written into an other FIFO.

5   Results

Before the VHDL generated by CλaSH is synthesized, the design is thoroughly simulated to verify its correctness. Since the CλaSH description of the dataflow particle filter is a valid Haskell program, simulation can be performed by just executing the code. A small framework has been built where a reference particle filter in plain Haskell is compared with the implementation in CλaSH. This framework produces a stream of grayscale images (256 × 256 pixels) for both particle filters to track. The resulting tracks are displayed in Figure 4. Both filters are able to track the square on the Lissajous path within a few pixels. However, the CλaSH particle filter deviates sometimes a few pixels more from the path due to the 18 bit fixed point implementation of arithmetic operations.

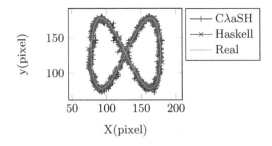

Fig. 4. Tracking of a Lissajous curve

The throughput is determined by looking at activity of the *write* signal of the FIFO between the replicator and the predictor. With parallelization factor M=4, the resampled particles are sent in groups of 8 tokens to the predictor where each token contains 4 particles. Averaging over the differences between arrival times of each first token results in an average cycle time of 69 clock cycles. This cycle time gives a throughput of $32/69 \approx 0.46$ particles per clock cycle.

After successfully simulating the particle filter, it has been translated to VHDL by the CλaSH compiler and synthesized for a Virtex 6 XC6VLX240T FPGA with parallelization factor M=2, 4 and 8 respectively. All instantiations are able run at a clock frequency of approximately 25MHz (currently limited reciprocal operation in the normalization step). Table 1 and Figure 5 show the number of LUTs used for the dataflow based particle filter. The number of LUTs required scales more or less linear with M. Similarly, M DSP48E1 multipliers are required for each instantiation.

Compared to the architectures presented in [5] and [6], the performance of the architecture presented in this paper is in the same order of magnitude. The throughput is also very similar to performance of the fully parallel particle filter in [8] but requires approximately a factor 6 fewer LUTs. Therefore, this design space exploration methodology is adequate for particle filtering.

Table 1. Resource usage of dataflow based

Component	$M = 2$ LUTs	FFs	$M = 4$ LUTs	FFs	$M = 8$ LUTs	FFs
Noisegen	70	64	138	128	274	256
Predict	37	-	69	-	133	-
Update	44	28	44	50	61	94
Sum	81	22	116	21	187	20
Recipr	923	-	923	-	923	-
Norm	20	4	29	3	48	2
Ws2Rs	204	30	333	29	592	28
Replicate	70	42	126	76	214	142
FIFOs	5210	4021	4650	3707	4435	3538
Total:	**6659**	**4211**	**6428**	**4014**	**6867**	**4080**

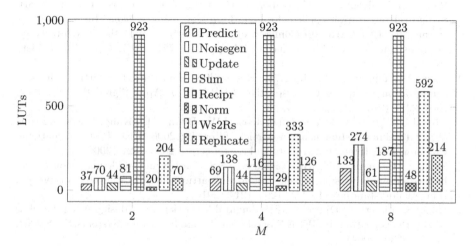

Fig. 5. LUTs used by components of particle filter

6   Conclusions and Future Work

A design methodology based on transformation of higher-order functions has been presented and applied to a particle filter application. The transformation rules produce dataflow nodes with a parallelization parameter M. By choosing a proper value for M, a tradeoff between execution time and FPGA area is made. For composition of the resulting components, dataflow principles are used. When applied to the particle filter example, the methodology produces scalable hardware in terms of throughput and FPGA area consumption. Higher-order functions are therefore an adequate abstraction to express dependencies.

All transformations and implementations of dataflow nodes have currently been done by hand, the next step is to automate this. The idea is to develop an embedded language to easily express designs using higher-order functions. A transformation algorithm then applies the transformation rules presented in this paper after which the hardware can be generated using CλaSH.

Acknowledgements. This research is conducted as part of the Sensor Technology Applied in Reconfigurable systems for sustainable Security (STARS) project www.starsproject.nl.

References

1. Arulampalam, M., Maskell, S., Gordon, N., Clapp, T.: A tutorial on particle filters for online nonlinear/non-gaussian bayesian tracking. IEEE Transactions on Signal Processing 50(2), 174–188 (2002)
2. Jones, S.P. (ed.): Haskell 98 Language and Libraries. Journal of Functional Programming, vol. 13 (2003)
3. Baaij, C.P.R., Kooijman, M., Kuper, J., Boeijink, W.A., Gerards, M.E.T.: CλaSH: Structural descriptions of synchronous hardware using Haskell. In: Proceedings of the 13th EUROMICRO Conference on Digital System Design: Architectures, Methods and Tools, Lille, France, USA, pp. 714–721. IEEE Computer Society (September 2010)
4. Bolić, M., Djurić, P.M., Hong, S.: Resampling algorithms for particle filters: a computational complexity perspective. EURASIP J. Appl. Signal Process. 2004, 2267–2277 (2004)
5. Cho, J.U., Jin, S.H., Pham, X.D., Jeon, J.W., Byun, J.E., Kang, H.: A real-time object tracking system using a particle filter. In: 2006 IEEE/RSJ International Conference on Intelligent Robots and Systems, pp. 2822–2827 (2006)
6. Saha, S., Bambha, N.K., Bhattacharyya, S.S.: Design and implementation of embedded computer vision systems based on particle filters. Computer Vision and Image Understanding 114(11), 1203–1214 (2010)
7. Hong, S., Liang, X., Djuric, P.: Reconfigurable particle filter design using dataflow structure translation. In: IEEE Workshop on Signal Processing Systems, SIPS 2004, pp. 325–330 (2004)
8. Wester, R., Baaij, C.P.R., Kuper, J.: A two step hardware design method using CλaSH. In: 22nd International Conference on Field Programmable Logic and Applications, FPL 2012, Oslo, Norway, USA, pp. 181–188. IEEE Computer Society (August 2012)
9. Sheeran, M.: mufp, a language for vlsi design. In: Proceedings of the 1984 ACM Symposium on LISP and Functional Programming, LFP 1984, pp. 104–112. ACM, New York (1984)
10. Bjesse, P., Claessen, K., Sheeran, M., Singh, S.: Lava: hardware design in Haskell. In: Proceedings of the Third ACM SIGPLAN International Conference on Functional Programming, ICFP 1998, pp. 174–184. ACM, New York (1998)
11. Sheeran, M.: Designing regular array architectures using higher order functions. In: Jouannaud, J.-P. (ed.) FPCA 1985. LNCS, vol. 201, pp. 220–237. Springer, Heidelberg (1985)
12. Lee, E., Messerschmitt, D.: Synchronous data flow. Proceedings of the IEEE 75(9), 1235–1245 (1987)

Simulation of Complex Biochemical Pathways in 3D Process Space via Heterogeneous Computing Platform: Preliminary Results

Jie Li, Amin Salighehdar, and Narayan Ganesan

Department of Electrical and Computer Engineering
Stevens Institute of Technology, Hoboken NJ 07030, USA
{jli8,asalighe,nganesan}@stevens.edu

Abstract. Biological pathways typically consist of upto hundreds of reacting chemical species and reactions within a biological system. Modeling and simulation of biological pathways in explicit process space is a computationally intensive, both due to the number of interactions and time-scale of processes. Traditional stochastic or ODE based simulation of chemical processes ignore spatial and biological information. Hence there is a need for new underlying simulation algorithms as well as need for newer computing systems, platforms and techniques. Such pathways describe exhibit considerable behavioral complexity in multiple fundamental cellular processes. In this work we present a new heterogeneous computing platform to accelerate the simulation study of such complex biochemical pathways in 3D reaction process space. Several tasks involved in the simulation study has been carefully partitioned to run on a combination of reconfigurable hardware and massively parallel processor such as the GPU. This paper also presents an implementation to accelerate one of the most compute intensive tasks - sifting through the reaction space to determine reacting particles. Finally, we present the new heterogeneous computing framework integrating a FPGA and GPU to accelerate the computation over the use of a any single platform. This framework can achieve 10-times speedup over a single GPU-only platform. Besides, the extensible architecture is general enough to be used to study a variety of biological pathways in order to gain deeper insights into biomolecular systems.

Keywords: GPU+FPGA, Process Simulation in 3D space, Heterogeneous Computing, Complex Biochemical Pathways, Stochastic Simulation.

1 Introduction

Simulation and study of such biochemical pathways will lead to deeper insights and understanding of functions of proteins, kinases and phosphotases that activate and de-activate reagents, sensitivity of various chemical species etc. There are several modeling and simulation tools that are used to study biological pathways, including but not limited to Ordinary Differential Equations(ODEs), graph

D. Goehringer et al. (Eds.): ARC 2014, LNCS 8405, pp. 227–232, 2014.
© Springer International Publishing Switzerland 2014

theoretical analysis of reaction networks, boolean networks and explicit modeling in reactive process space, with each having its own scientific, computational and implementation merits and disadvantages. Although, ODEs are a popular modeling framework and computationally very efficient, they only represent aggregate concentration of the species, and fail to capture many intricacies and local behavior mechanisms within the cell. On the other hand, reaction modeling in 3D process space is the most computationally intensive and serves as a virtual computational microscope into biological systems. Typically, modeling such biological pathways in reaction space requires millions of reagents and beyond and it is imperative to consider all-particle interactions simultaneously within the system. In this paper, we present a new heterogeneous computational framework to study the interactions enabled by the massively parallel processing capability of the GPUs and FPGAs. The computational framework will take the simulation and study of large biological systems to the next level, where in macro-biological systems such as cells, and interaction between multiple cells can be studied to gain valuable insights into real biological processes.

2   Algorithm and Implementation

Sequential Algorithm. Algorithms such as the Kinetic-Monte Carlo[1,2] and Gillespi Algorithm[3] have been used for stochastic simulation of chemical systems, on a sequential execution platform. The algorithm proceeds by listing all possible reactions and choosing to execute one of them based on the stoichiometric rate and the population of reagents. The time counter is then incremented appropriately. However, the procedure (a) doesn't capture spatial and local information and (b) is inherently sequential to be suitable for studying behavior of large number of reagents due to rapid growth of possible interactions between reagents. The number of feasible reactions grows with growing number of species as well as the the number of individual reagents. In general, the growth in the set of all possible interactions grows proportional to $O(N^2)$, for a set of N reagents and $O(M^2)$ for M different chemical species. In the above algorithm, the sequential nature of the enumeration of all possible reactions as required by the algorithm, which overwhelms the computation required to accurately simulate the process behavior. Hence the traditional algorithm above faces fundamental bottlenecks from a computational standpoint and is not scalable to simulation study of large biochemical systems within a reactive 3D space.

Scalable Concurrent Algorithm. In our previous work, we have designed and applied the following algorithm to study the growth of biofilms[4] which was implemented on on massively parallel processors such as GPUs. We have also used GPUs for simulation study of spatial molecular dynamics and their conformation[5]. However, in contrast to purely physical interactions, general chemical interactions will result in creation of new particles and consumption of others in a consistent pattern and in predefined quantities, as described by the chemical equations. Furthermore, in contrast to molecular dynamics problem, where fixed persistent agents interact with all the neighboring agents, chemical reagents interact only with select neighbors while producing new products. In order to leverage the parallel and concurrent framework, each interacting entity or particle is treated as a "autonomous agent" that interacts with other such agents of different type in an independent and autonomous fashion. This helps overcome the sequential limitations imposed by traditional algorithms. The concurrent reactions at each time step is updated to reflect the consumption of old reagent particles and production of newer agents. One of the crucial tasks in transitioning from traditional algorithms to an explicitly defined 3D process space populated by individual particles is conversion of reaction rates to equivalent interaction radii. A pair of particles within the specified interaction radius on a collision course, will react together always or with a probability that is set by their velocities in order to produce the product of the specified reaction. It is very-well possible that each particle is within the interaction radius of several other particles capable of reacting with each other, in such case, efficient parallel techniques to select a set of mutually consistent reactions to carry out, must be formulated. The concurrent algorithm can be stated as follows,

(1) Initialize: The particles positions, drift velocities. **(2) Initialize Reaction Radii:** Enumerate the set of reactions between different types along with the interaction radius of the reaction. For first order reactions of type $A \to \phi$ or $A \to B + C$, each particle of type A is assigned a life-span by sampling from an exponential distribution parametrized by its decay rate. For reactions of type $A + B \to C + D$, the reaction radius is set based on the rate-constant and drift rate of particles[6].**(3) Build Neighbor List:** Divide the simulation volume into disjoint cubic cells of dimensions equal to the largest radius of interaction. In order to identify the neighbors of each particle only the current cell and the 26 adjacent cells in 3D need to be examined. For each particle, build a list of particles of compatible types that could react. This is done efficiently with the help of a stoichiometric bit-vector. In the stoichiometric bit-vector the jth element of ith bit-vector is set to 1 if type i can react with j. A separate lookup table stores the product each corresponding reaction between types i and j. **(4) Start the Simulation:** Sift through the 3D process space of each particle in parallel, scanning for reacting particles and carefully selecting the pairs of particles in a mutually consistent manner for reaction. Increment global time and repeat steps (1) - (4) until simulation time.

2.1 Heterogeneous Computing Framework

The high-throughput and similar nature computation required to process each agent makes any massively parallel processor such as the GPU a good initial choice. However, as we outline below, the reconfigurable hardware co-processor is extremely beneficial in handling tasks that would otherwise strain the memory bandwidth and instruction throughput of the GPU. In this work we demonstrate the power of heterogeneous computational framework in accelerating an application that is not amenable to massively parallel processor alone. In the original GPU implementation of the `NeighborList` build kernel, each thread-block is responsible for building the neighbor list of all the particles within a specific cell

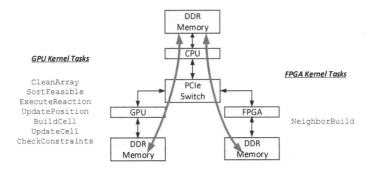

Fig. 1. Heterogeneous system framework

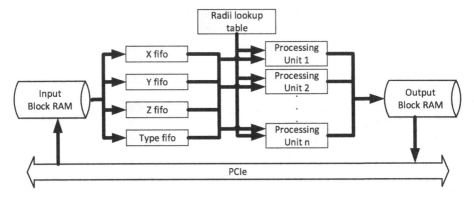

Fig. 2. processing unit architecture

with in the reaction space. To this effect each thread block sifts through the particles in 26-adjacent cells in addition to its own cell to determine the neighbors of each particle within the cell. Among all kernel functions in the table, NeighborBuild function consumes 97% of the total execution time. This is due to fact that any parallel implementation that sifts through adjacent cells will require 27x bandwidth to the off-chip global memory, as each cell performs the same task to its neighboring cells. The problem is further amplified by the fact that the NeighborBuild kernel is called far more often here than in an application such as molecular dynamics. The faster the movement of particles more often the NeighborBuild kernel needs to be called. This places undue strain on the global memory bandwidth even on a high-throughput device and throws off the instruction-to-memory ratio far from the optimal value. In order to overcome this bottleneck, we implement the NeighborBuild task on the FPGA and leverage the capability of the heterogeneous computational platform.

Hardware Design. Although the presented application is unique and the application domains are different, previous work on accelerating molecular dynamics on reconfigurable platform[7,8], is most related to the current implementation. We present the hardware design for the task to compute NeighborList and a

Device	XC6VLX240T	Resource	quantities
Logic Cells	241,152	*SliceRegisters*	54
Conf.Logic Blocks	37,680	*Memory*	40
DSP48E1	3,650	*DSP48Es*	8
Block RAM Blocks	768	*Maximumspeed*	300M

(a) Device Capability	(b) Device utilization

unified heterogeneous computing framework for large scale process simulations in 3D space. Target hardware: a generic PC and GPU GTX 580 and a PCIe plug-in board ML605 with Xilinx XC6VLX240T. It is possible to leverage the capabilities of each device via a task-level partition of the kernels as shown in Figure (1). The FPGA processes one central cell at a time. Each processing unit (figure 2)needs to compute the distance between all pairs of particles i and j, where i must be in the central cell but j can be in any of the 26 neighborhood cells or in the central cell. In order to fully parallelize each cell, the system needs as many processing units as the particles in the central cell. One particle in the neighboring cell is processed per time cycle. So, the total execution time of one central cell is 27 x the maximum number of particles in any cell.

In order to preserve the accuracy of distance calculation, floating point precision is necessary. Fortunately, modern FPGAs are equipped with ample DSP units that make floating point distance calculation within each processing element possible. With the available resources, it is usually advantageous to use the existing floating point units instead of synthesizing custom fixed precision units. In our implementation particles coordinates and reagent types are copied from GPU to FPGA. We also maintain a reaction radius lookup table on FPGA, as each reaction may have different effective reaction radius. In order to process a million particles, the total amount of data transferred to the FPGA for **coordinates** array is 1Million x 3 channel x 32 bits $\approx$ 12MB and for particle **types** array is 1Million x 32 bit $\approx$ 4MB. However, the

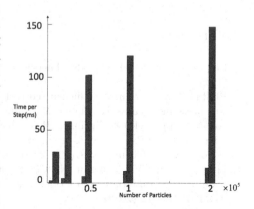

Fig. 3. Performance of the kernel with respect to the total number of particles (independent agents). The FPGA performance is shown in blue bars while the GPU performance is shown in red.

copy-back of the **FeasibleList** can be overlapped with computation. The tasks partitioned among the FPGA and GPU such that the **NeighborList** build is performed on the FPGA and the other remaining functions on the GPU. Once the computation is initiated, data transfer between GPU and FPGA would take place once per iteration. The critical resources on the FPGA are the hard multipliers, the registers and the block RAMs as shown in table (2).

2.2 Experiments and Performance

The computational framework presented here especially suitable to simulate large and complex biological pathways serving as a macro-molecular visual scope and helps observe key biochemical reactions, as the events unfold in space and time. For performance comparisons, the JAK-STAT signaling pathways was initialized with 1.23 million particles or independent reacting agents, within a simulation space of $200 \times 200 \times 200$ distance units. For performance comparisons, we set different initial number of particles for this system from 10k to 2,000K in order to measure the average time-per-step. In figure (3), we compare the performance of GPU and FPGA implementation of the compute intensive task of calculating the `FeasibleList`. The FPGA achieves approximately 10 x speedup over GPU-only implementation for all system sizes while using the 32 bit floating point to maintain simulation quality.

Acknowledgements. The authors would like to thank the Xilinx University Program(XUP) and the NVIDIA-Professor partnership for their generous support and donation helpful in carrying out the research.

References

1. Cox, D.R., Miller, H.D.: The Theory of Stochastic Processes. Methuen, London (1965)
2. Phillips, A., Cardelli, L.: Efficient, correct simulation of biological processes in the stochastic pi-calculus. In: Calder, M., Gilmore, S. (eds.) CMSB 2007. LNCS (LNBI), vol. 4695, pp. 184–199. Springer, Heidelberg (2007)
3. Gillespie, D.T.: Exact stochastic simulation of coupled chemical reactions. The Journal of Physical Chemistry 81(25), 2340–2361 (1977)
4. Li, J., Sharma, V., Ganesan, N., Compagnoni, A.: Simulation and study of large-scale bacteria-materials interactions via bioscape enabled GPUs. In: Proceedings of ACM-BCB 2012 (2012)
5. Taufer, M., Ganesan, N., Patel, S.: GPU enabled macromolecular simulations: Challenges and opportunities. IEEE Computing in Science and Engineering 15(1) (January 2012)
6. Erban, R., Chapman, S.J.: Stochastic modelling of reaction-diffusion processes: algorithms for bimolecular reactions. Physical Biology 6(046001) (2009)
7. Chiu, M., Herbordt, M.C.: Molecular dynamics simulations on high-performance reconfigurable computing systems. ACM Trans. Reconfigurable Technol. Syst. 3(4), 23:1–23:37 (2010)
8. Gu, Y., VanCourt, T., Herbordt, M.C.: Explicit design of fpga-based coprocessors for short-range force computations in molecular dynamics simulations. Parallel Computing 34(4-5), 261–277 (2008)

Efficient Buffer Design and Implementation for Wormhole Routers on FPGAs

Taimour Wehbe and Xiaofang Wang

Department of Electrical and Computer Engineering
Villanova University
800 E Lancaster Avenue
Villanova, PA 19085, USA
{twehbe,xwang}@villanova.edu

Abstract. Several studies show that the overall network performance in wormhole routers is degraded due to congestion at a specific part in the network while other parts have little or no flow of data. Our design improves the performance of the wormhole router by adding a central channel that is shared among the physical channels. Experimental results using the uniform random traffic and the hotspot traffic show that enabling the central buffer increases the performance of the network by as much as 13%. On the implementation side, buffers consume more than half of the router's area and power, and the coarse-grain nature of embedded BRAMs in most FPGAs has led to very inefficient utilization of such memory resources. We propose two different types of buffer sharing: 1. Sharing between the processors of a system on chip and router buffers; 2. Sharing BRAMs among different virtual and physical channels inside the wormhole router. Our designs target the Xilinx Virtex-6 FPGAs and the results show a decrease of 87.5% in BRAM usage on the expense of a slight register increase. Our techniques can be easily applied to any other FPGA-based buffer implementation.

1 Introduction

The growing design complexity and the ever-increasing requirements in embedded systems have been constantly driving system designers to explore more efficient interconnection networks for systems-on-chip. Packet switching networks-on-chip (NoCs) are expected to replace shared buses and point-to-point networks to provide scalable and high-performance communication for multi/many-core processing platforms [1]. Extensive research efforts have been devoted in the last decade to investigating high-performance and energy-efficient designs.

NoCs rely on routers to make data transfer decisions using various routing algorithms. Buffers are used to house arriving packet flits that cannot be forwarded immediately onto output links when contention arises. In the conventional wormhole router, each channel has a set of dedicated buffers. Their size and design have a large impact on the overall performance of an NoC, especially when the network is congested. It has been shown that buffers can consume up to almost 75% of the total area [2] leading to significant power consumption [3]. Nonetheless, several studies show that the typical utilization of these expensive buffers

D. Goehringer et al. (Eds.): ARC 2014, LNCS 8405, pp. 233–239, 2014.
© Springer International Publishing Switzerland 2014

is very low, mostly less than 30% [4]. We have proposed a network topology, called X-network, to reduce resource requirements and improve performance at the same time [5]. In the X-Network, each router is shared by four nodes and each node has direct connection with four neighboring routers in addition to the north, south, east, and west connections with neighboring nodes. This reduces the total number of routers for a given number of nodes.

With rapidly growing processing capabilities, FPGAs have been increasingly employed to implement complex SoCs. M. Papamichael et al. propose to take advantage of the routing wires in FPGAs to reduce other resource usage like the use of configurable logic blocks and on-chip memory resources based on the assumption that they are usually underutilized [6]. When it comes to implementing buffers on FPGAs, the dedicated BRAM, which is commonly found in FPGAs, is the main choice. However, such BRAM tend to have tens of Kbits, which are mostly wasted when implementing a FIFO buffer. On the other hand, a large number of such memory blocks are needed to implement all the buffers in a router. For this reason, some research proposals prefer to use distributed RAM in Xilinx FPGAs instead of dedicated BRAMs [6]. This approach, however, reduces the total logic resources available to other purposes. To make more efficient use of dedicated memory blocks, several central buffering solutions have been proposed [4,7,8]. The centralized scheme, however, improves buffer utilization at the cost of complicated control circuitry. In addition, congested output ports may consume a significant portion or all of the shared buffers, preventing smooth transportation on other ports. Other research groups, such as Kwa et al. [9], use buffer sharing between virtual channels (VCs) of a router. Kwa et al. were able to reduce the BRAM usage for Altera FPGAs by as much as 50%; however, their work imposes degradation in performance and early network saturation. Moreover, their design requires access to as many as four different memory locations during the same cycle, which is not supported by BRAMs in Xilinx FPGAs.

2   Hybrid Buffer Design and Implementation

2.1   Hybrid Buffer Design

This work is based on a 2-D 4×4 Torus in-house developed X-Network [5] which uses only 9 routers to connect our 16 PEs. Our wormhole router uses the Round-Robin algorithm in its arbiters and utilizes an XY adaptive routing algorithm to handle traffic. The development done in our design is the introduction of a shared central channel (Fig. 1). Most traffic patterns usually create congestion at specific channels inside a router [10]. The central channel here allocates specific buffers for the channels in need, reducing the latency of the network. A central arbiter controls different multiplexers and decides whether incoming flits can progress to the desired channel or to the central channel by monitoring the status of the buffers in these channels. It also modifies the credits sent between routers to include the central's channels status. In addition, a signal named central mux hold is used to prevent the apportionment of the flits of one packet in case the central arbiter switches control while a packet is being stored.

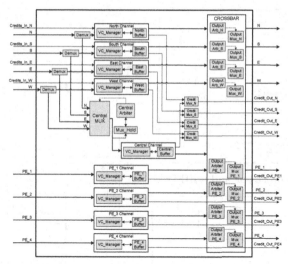

Fig. 1. The proposed router architecture

2.2   Buffer Implementation Tailored to FPGAs

Our router has eight physical channels and one central channel, each composed of eight virtual channels. Therefore, each router needs 72 BRAMs to implement its buffers. In addition, each buffer consumes only 640 bits out of each BRAM (16 flits deep x 40 bits/flit). In our design, we target the Xilinx Virtex-6 FPGA which is composed of 36 Kbits of BRAM blocks. This motivates NoC researchers to find better solutions for managing and sharing BRAM resources. We approach this sharing process in the following two different ways.

Sharing BRAMs between Processing Elements and Router Buffers. Sharing processor BRAMs with resources outside the processor system helps reduce the resources wasted for building buffers for wormhole routers. Fig. 2(a) shows how a processor's BRAM ports and BRAM controller's ports are made external to share it with a FIFO. The processor system is instantiated as a submodule in the top level design and connected to one input of a multiplexer which is used to switch between the controllers of port A of the shared BRAM. The second input of the mux comes from one port of a FIFO controller to enable the sharing process. The decision in sharing the BRAM is taken by the software (processor) to maintain its flexibility and insure that no performance degradation happens. Resource analysis of the design shows that the logic needed to implement the sharing process is minimal.

Sharing BRAMs between Virtual Channels. Sharing the memory resource in this design is based on time division multiplexing. Since BRAMs operate at a much faster speed than wormhole routers, they can be accesssed multiple times

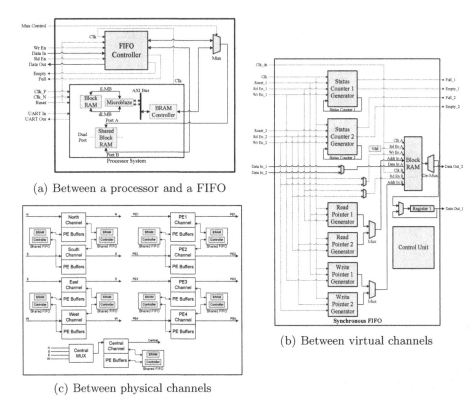

(a) Between a processor and a FIFO

(b) Between virtual channels

(c) Between physical channels

Fig. 2. Block RAM sharing

during one system clock cycle. We tried sharing a BRAM between two and four VCs yielding to the reduction of BRAM usage by 50% and 75% respectively. To do that, we used faster clock speeds to access the memory, and as a result, by the end of each system clock cycle, each of the FIFOs sharing the same BRAM will have read or written the needed data. Fig. 2(b) shows how 2 VCs share one BRAM. The control unit works at a faster clock speed and controls multiplexers to provide the sharing process and to output the needed data of each FIFO from the BRAM.

Sharing BRAMs between Physical Channels. We imported the idea of sharing BRAMs between virtual channels to physical channels. A faster clock is now used in the controller and the BRAM is shared among 8 FIFOs. Fig. 2(c) shows the new interconnection of the different physical channels of the wormhole router. The two sections of each two physical channels now share two BRAMs. The North and South physical channels share the same set of BRAMs while the East and West share another set. Similarly PE channels and the central channel share their own BRAMs.

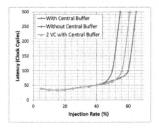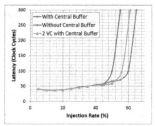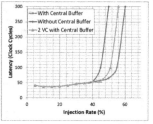

(a) Hotspot Pct: 10%   (b) Hotspot Pct: 20%

Fig. 3. Random Traffic   **Fig. 4.** Hotspot Traffic (PE2,2)

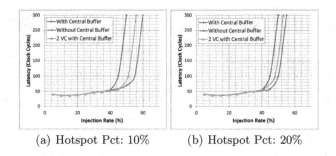

(a) Hotspot Pct: 10%   (b) Hotspot Pct: 20%

Fig. 5. Hotspot Traffic (PE4,4)

3   Experimental Results

We have implemented our designs in VHDL targeting Xilinx Virtex 6 FPGAs. Three cases are studied and compared: without central buffer, with central buffer and all channels have 2 VCs, and with central buffer and all channels have 4 VCs. Fig. 3 shows the network latency under the uniform random traffic. The plot shows that at high injection rates, the design that has the central buffer shows a performance improvement of about 13% in injection rate.

Fig. 4, 5, and 6 show the plots of the hotspot traffic pattern taking different hotspot percentages and locations into consideration. Several studies show that real-life traffic possesses a higher congestion at the center, diagonal, and corner positions of the network. Therefore, we choose PEs (2,2), (4,4) and (2,4) in our simulations for hotspot traffic. The central buffer increases the performance by 10% when the hotspot is chosen as PE(2,2) whether the hotspot percentage is 10% (Fig. 4a) or 20% (Fig. 4b) and when it is chosen as PE(4,4) with a hotspot percentage of 10% (Fig. 5a). When it is 20%, the improvement in performance is decreased to about 5% (Fig. 5b). When PE(2,4), an edge PE, is chosen as the hotspot PE, the graphs show similar results for 10% hotspot percentage (Fig. 6a) and an increase of about 8% for a hotspot percentage of 20% (Fig. 5b).

We finally evaluate the resource utilization of all the BRAM sharing designs. Table 1 shows that all the BRAM sharing designs showed an expected slight

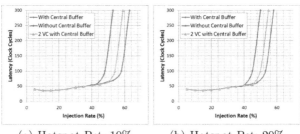

(a) Hotspot Pct: 10%   (b) Hotspot Pct: 20%

Fig. 6. Hotspot Traffic (PE2,4)

Table 1. The difference in resource utilization per wormhole router of the four designs

Resources per wormhole router	Normal Design	2 VCs share BRAM	4 VCs share BRAM	2 PCs share BRAM
Slice registers	9369	12154	13605	12998
Look-up tables	20542	20106	19407	20049
36Kb BRAMs	72	36	18	9

increase in register usage and a huge decrease in BRAM usage reaching an 87.5%. The final design makes the most efficient use of BRAMs consuming 5 Kbits out of the 36 Kbits found in each.

4   Conclusions

Our work shows that the addition of a central buffer improves the latency of the network by as much as 13%. The different proposed approaches for sharing BRAM resources shows a great resource efficiency (87.5%), which leads eventually to better power consumption. In our last design, we shared a BRAM between two physical channels leading to a more efficient use of each BRAM (14%).

References

1. Mohapatra, P.: Wormhole routing techniques for directly connected multicomputer systems. ACM Computing Surveys 30(3), 374–410 (1998)
2. Dally, W., Towles, B.: Route packets, not wires: on-chip interconnection networks. In: Proc. ACM/EDAC/IEEE Design Automation Conference (DAC), pp. 684–689 (2001)
3. Wang, H., Peh, L.-S., Malik, S.: Power-driven design of router microarchitectures in on-chip networks. In: Proc. Annual IEEE/ACM Int'l Symp. Microarchitecture (MICRO), pp. 105–116 (2003)
4. Tran, A., Baas, B.: DLABS: A dual-lane buffer-sharing router architecture for networks on chip. In: Proc. IEEE Workshop on Signal Processing Systems (SIPS), pp. 327–332 (2010)

5. Wang, X., Bandi, L.: X-Network: An area-efficient and high-performance on-chip wormhole-switching network. In: Proc. IEEE Int'l Conf. High Performance Computing and Communications (HPCC), pp. 362–368 (2010)
6. Papamichael, M.K., Hoe, J.C.: Connect: Re-examining conventional wisdom for designing NoCs in the context of FPGAs. In: Proc. ACM/SIGDA Int'l Symp. Field Programmable Gate Arrays (FPGA), pp. 37–46 (2012)
7. Nicopoulos, C.A., Park, D., Kim, J., Vijaykrishnan, N., Yousif, M.S., Das, C.R.: Vichar: A dynamic virtual channel regulator for network-on-chip routers. In: Proc. IEEE/ACM Int. Symp. Microarchitecture (MICRO), pp. 333–346 (2006)
8. Wang, L., Zhang, J., Yang, X., Wen, D.: Router with centralized buffer for network-on-chip. In: Proc. ACM Great Lakes Symp. VLSI, pp. 469–474 (2009)
9. Kwa, J., Aamodt, T.: Small virtual channel routers on FPGAs through Block RAM sharing. In: Proc. Int'l Conf. Field-Programmable Technology (FPT), pp. 71–79 (2012)
10. Mishra, A., Vijaykrishnan, N., Das, C.: A case for heterogeneous on-chip interconnects for cmps. In: Proc. Annual Int'l Symp. Computer Architecture (ISCA), pp. 389–399 (2011)

MicroACP - A Fast and Secure Reconfigurable Asymmetric Crypto-Processor
–Overhead Evaluation of Side-Channel Countermeasures–

Christopher Pöpper[1], Oliver Mischke[2], and Tim Güneysu[2]

[1] ESCRYPT GmbH - Embedded Security
[2] Horst Görtz Institute for IT Security, Ruhr University Bochum, Germany
christoph.poepper@escrypt.com, {mischke,gueneysu}@crypto.rub.de

Abstract. In this work we present a lightweight co-processor for asymmetric cryptography. While focusing on standardized elliptic curve cryptography over prime fields, the architecture has been chosen generic enough to also allow to perform RSA operations on the same hardware. Compared to previous work our processor distinguishes itself by not only having on par performance with recent work in this field, but also by being able to additionally apply state of the art side-channel analysis countermeasures to protect the implementation against timing and power analysis attacks. Different countermeasures can be dynamically selected at runtime, allowing a flexible trade-off between security and performance. Utilizing a specialized 32-bit ALU and a microcode-based control unit, it is possible to easily reprogram the controller after deployment allowing to make changes to the implemented algorithm or countermeasures by updating the microcode. This allows to keep some of the reconfigurability of FPGA-based designs even when fabricating the proposed core as an ASIC.

1 Introduction

Computing is no longer restricted to powerful mainframes or personal computers. Nowadays almost everyone carries a smartphone which is more powerful then most computers a few years back. But not only users actively interact, the Internet of Things becomes more and more a reality, where different devices autonomously communicate which each other. With the increased communication rises also the need for reliable asymmetric cryptographic primitives to provide the necessary security. This is especially true in the vehicle-2-vehicle communication where based on messages by other cars automatic actions might be performed, for example emergency brakes to prevent collisions.

Rivest-Shamir-Adleman (RSA) [9] was for a long time the algorithm of choice for asymmetric cryptography and still provides some advantages like fast verification times by using small public exponents. In case both the signing and verification of messages is needed, Elliptic Curve Cryptography (ECC) [5,7] is a better solution since it provides equal security using shorter operands which reduces not only computation time but also signature size.

D. Goehringer et al. (Eds.): ARC 2014, LNCS 8405, pp. 240–247, 2014.
© Springer International Publishing Switzerland 2014

While these algorithms remain secure from a mathematical point of view, they can easily be attacked by so called side-channel attacks if no precautions are taken. In the late 90s and early 2000s several ways have been discovered to extract secret information from a circuit by observing e.g., timing behaviour, power consumption, or electromagnetic emanation. Most notably is the work of Kocher *et al.* introducing differential power analysis [6]. Since then there exists an arms race between designers of countermeasures and attackers where the outcome is still open. Fan *et al.* [3] gives a good overview of the current state of the art in ECC countermeasures.

Implementations of pure ECC or combined ECC-RSA processors have been an ongoing research topic for some time. Many implementation techniques have been evaluated and fill different niches. As example, Batina *et al.* [1] proposed the design of an ECC and RSA processor based on systolic arrays. While this method is inherently protected against some attacks because of the static operation flow, it requires a high amount of logic resources and is not protected against e.g., differential power analysis. In [4] the authors focus on achieving a very high throughput by utilizing a large number of FPGA hard macros like DSPs and BRAMs, which makes the design less scalable and leads to high area requirements. [12] and later [11] on the other hand proposed designs based on a so called microcode architecture where a small ALU is controlled by a flexible state machine which can be easily reprogrammed by changing the microcode.

This work also uses the microcode approach aiming for a small implementation footprint and high reconfigurability. In addition our implementation is significantly stronger protected against side-channel attacks. We have implemented several countermeasures and evaluate the performance overhead. Furthermore, the designed ALU is more flexible being able to not only perform ECC but also RSA operations while maintaining a similar performance as in [11].

The remaining article is organized as follows: Section 2 describes our design architecture and the implemented countermeasures. Performance results together with a comparison to recent work is given in Section 3. This section also states the performance overhead of the chosen countermeasures and combinations. Finally, Section 4 concludes our research.

2 Our Design

In this work we are aiming to implement a design which is capable of performing both ECC and RSA operations using the same logic. We have chosen to build our design on the ideas of [12] and [11] utilizing the microcode approach. This means that a small but powerful ALU is controlled by a dedicated tiny processor which controls the program flow and the memory management based on stored opcodes in the program memory. By updating the program memory it is possible to easily update algorithms or implemented countermeasure even after deployment in the field. This gives us the highest flexibility for a very efficient ALU on a small footprint. Beside choosing an efficient architecture to perform both ECC and RSA operations, our focus is mainly on secure implementations of those by implementing several countermeasures against side-channel attacks.

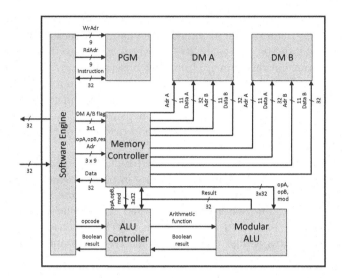

Fig. 1. Architecture overview

Our solution, the **MicroACP** is a cryptographic co-processor which imple-ments ECC over prime fields and generic RSA exponentiations with a maximum operand size of 2048 bits. For the ECC part, the core is primarily designed to work with the NIST prime curves, especially *NIST-P256*. If lower security is suf-ficient, *NIST-P224*, or even *NIST-P192* can be chosen using exactly the same hardware. It is possible to switch between different curves at runtime by up-dating the internal program code, but for the remainder of this paper we are focusing on *NIST-P256* for high security applications.

2.1 Architecture

Figure 1 depicts the architecture of the **MicroACP**. The program memory (PGM) stores the necessary algorithms for the execution of the secure ECC and RSA operations. It can either be preloaded by the bitstream or loaded via the software interface during runtime. This also allows a flexible update of the code to either support different ECC curves or countermeasures. The ALU itself utilizes a 32-bit datapath for all operations. Four hardware multipliers are used and the ALU is also able to perform addition, subtraction, compare and reduction operations. The operands and the results of ALU operations are stored in two true dual port block rams (BRAM). The interaction between the memories and the ALU is handled by the memory and the ALU controller.

2.2 Implemented Algorithms

For the fast and unprotected version of the ECC we implemented the Double-And-Add (DAA) algorithm, which is also called *Left-to-right binary method for point multiplication.* Furthermore, for an efficient computation we chose the Jacobian projective coordinates for the required point additions and doublings which results in an better overall-performance than standard affine coordinates.

Since all of the computations are made in prime fields, a reduction algorithm is required. Due to our choice of the *NIST-P256* curve, which standardized a so called pseudo-Mersenne prime number as modulus, the required reduction can be efficiently computed with simple additions and subtractions.

Similar to the ECC we choose the Square-and-Multiply (SAM) algorithm for the implementation of the modular exponentiation, used in the RSA crypto system. In contrast to ECC operations, we have to deal with random moduli for the RSA, which requires a generic reduction algorithm. For our design we implemented the Montgomery Reduction [8] which is a well-known and efficient technique.

2.3   Implementation of Countermeasures

To defeat side-channel attacks a set of countermeasures against SPA and DPA attacks on ECC were chosen. According to the work from Fan *et al.* [3] due to the usage of the following presented countermeasures the implementation is secure against all known SPA attacks and against the traditional DPA as well as against the RPA (Refined Power Analysis) and the ZPA (Zero-Value Point Analysis) attack.

All these countermeasures are not exclusive but can be combined in order to fulfill high security requirements or to choose a trade-off between security and performance.

Double-and-Add-Always. To defeat SPA attacks, J. Coron proposed in 1999 an alternative version of the DAA algorithm [2]. The principle is that an addition takes place in every loop iteration, either with the real output registers or with an unrelated dummy register. Consequently, a dependency of the scalar k and the runtime of the algorithm is prevented.

Scalar Randomization. In [2], beside the DAAA, also some DPA countermeasure are presented. The first is the *Scalar Randomization*, or also known as *Coron's first Countermeasure*. The idea is that the secret scalar k is randomized or masked. This is done by adding a random multiple of the order $\#E$ to the scalar: $r \cdot \#E + k \cdot P$. Due to this tampering of k at each ECC execution, the dependency between the secret key and the operations on the chip, and consequently the leakage of information about k is prevented.

Point Blinding. *Coron's second Countermeasure* [2] blinds or masks the input point instead of the scalar. Since in every scalar multiplication the point is blinded by adding a secret random point, the leakage of information about the scalar, and therefore the attack target, is prevented.

Randomized Projective Coordinates. The third countermeasure that was proposed by Coron in [2] is working on the projective, in our implementation on the Jacobian, coordinate representation. The principle is again a randomization of the point P. For this task the affine point P is converted to Jacobian representation. But instead of setting $Z = 1$, we use $Z = r$, where r is a random number. It is obvious, that we have to compute X and Y according to r. Due to this translation the coordinates do not have a dependency to the hypothetical values which are computed by the attacker. Since this is an appropriate representation of the input point, the inverse conversion to the affine coordinates after the multiplication returns the correct result.

Square-and-Multiply-Always. To defeat SPA attacks on the RSA computation, a dependency between the runtime and the exponent k must be prevented. Similar to the used DAAA for the ECC, we implemented the Square-And-Multiply-Always (SAMA) which was presented 1999 by Kocher *et al.* [6] and uses dummy registers to avoid runtime varieties.

3   Results

For the evaluation of the implementation, we chose the SASEBO GII platform which is equipped with a Xilinx Virtex-5 LX50 FPGA. All results have been obtained post Place&Route using Xilinx ISE 14.3.

For the ECC performance measurements, we used 256 bit random numbers as the scalar and averaged the results of the multiplication with the base point of the

Table 1. Comparison between different approaches

Design	This work	[11]	[12]	[10]	
Device	Xilinx Virtex-5	Xilinx Virtex-II Pro		Xilinx Spartan-3	
Curve	P256	P256	any	P256	not supported
RSA size	2048 bit	not supported		not supported	2048 bit
Max. Clk. (MHz)	210	210	68.17	40	95
Logic	1914	1158	2085	27597	
RAM Blocks	6	3	9	0	
HW Mults	4	4	7	0	
ECPM [cycles]	830000	949951	1074625	708000	not supported
ECPM [ms]	3.95	4.52	15.75	17.7	not supported
MEXP [cycles]	372000	not supported		not supported	74100
MEXP [ms]	1.77	not supported		not supported	0.78

NIST-P256 curve. On embedded devices such as Engine Control Units (ECUs) usually only the signature verification is required. Therefore, for efficiency reasons, in nearly all of the currently deployed real-world RSA implementations the public exponent $2^{16} + 1$ is used. As a result, this exponent was also used for the performance measurement. Usually, the signature verification with the RSA crypto system is done with a public key, which means that countermeasures against side-channel attacks are not necessary. Nevertheless, the execution of the SAMA algorithm is tested in order to show the time difference and the feasibility of countermeasure implementations for RSA using our core.

Table 1 shows the efficiency of the core compared to other recent work. The term *ECPM* denotes Elliptic Curve Point Multiplications while MEXP means Modular Exponentiations. While we have chosen a Virtex-5 FPGA for our real performance measurements, numbers obtained for the older Virtex-2 Architecture are only slightly worse then in the Virtex-5 case. Also note that our ALU is slightly more complex then in the given comparisons since we are also able to perform RSA operations.

Table 2 depicts the performance overhead required if different side-channel countermeasures are chosen. Focusing on the ECC case which requires most security for the private signing operation, overhead numbers for each of Coron's countermeasures and their possible combinations are given. The overheads are surprisingly low showing the efficiency of the countermeasures. The minimum protection against timing attacks (as well as simple power analysis attacks) can

Table 2. Comparison of unprotected and protected variants of an *ECPM* and a MEXP in terms of Runtime, Cycles and Operations per second of our approach on a FPGA with 210 MHz

ECC Countermeasures	Runtime	Cycles in 1000	Operations per second	Runtime in percent
Without countermeasures	3.95 ms	830	252	100 %
DAAA	5.22 ms	1097	191	132 %
Random projective coordinates	4.54 ms	953	220	115 %
DAAA and random projective coordinates	5.79 ms	1217	172	147 %
Point blinding	4.85 ms	1018	206	123 %
Point blinding and DAAA	6.09 ms	1279	164	154 %
Point blinding and random projective coordinates	5.46 ms	1147	28	138 %
Point blinding, random projective coordinates, DAAA	6.67 ms	1401	149	169 %
RSA Countermeasures	Runtime	Cycles in 1000	Operations per second	Runtime in percent
Without countermeasures	1.77 ms	372	564	100 %
Square-And-Multiply-Always	3.23 ms	679	309	182 %

be gained by using the DAAA countermeasure at the cost of 32% more computation time. Unifying the computation time is especially important since timing attacks can even be performed by remote attackers over, e.g., ethernet/WiFi in the vehicle-2-vehicle case. If a local adversary is assumed, additional protection against differential power analysis can be gained by applying point blinding and or randomized projective coordinates. Using all countermeasures at the same time to maximize the desired security only leads to a 69% increase in computation time which is very reasonable considering the risks caused by unprotected implementations.

4   Conclusion

In this work we have presented the design of an low-area highly reconfigurable co-processor for asymmetric cryptography. The design is focused on side-channel resistant executions of elliptic curve operations but can also be used to additionally compute RSA exponentiations. Using less than 2000 slices on a Virtex-5 FPGA and only four hardware multipliers, the proposed core is able to compute approximately 250 scalar point multiplications or double point multiplications. Because of the low area utilization, the core is inherently highly scalable since additional cores can just be instantiated in parallel to achieve the desired throughput.

We have also implemented a set of countermeasures achieving resistance against various side-channel attacks. The constant execution time and fixed program flow of the Double-and-Add-Always countermeasure thwarts not only timing attacks but also SPA or SEMA attacks. Point blinding and the use of randomized projective coordinates are state-of-the-art countermeasures to protect against DPA and DEMA attacks. We also analyzed the performance overhead of these countermeasures and found that even when using all countermeasures the core still delivers a respectable throughput of 150 scalar point or double-point multiplications per second. This overhead is quite low when compared to symmetric cryptography where masking schemes to protect against differential power analysis attacks usually lead to a performance drop of factor 3x-10x.

Using both standardized NIST curves over elliptic curve prime fields and protecting the implementation against side-channel attacks makes this work highly relevant from an industry point of view. The reason behind this is that the upcoming Federal Information Processing Standard (FIPS) 140-3 (to accredited cryptographic modules) will require mandatory side-channel testing for certain security levels. The possibility to update the core by new microcode even when deployed as ASIC allows to react to new attacks by e.g., updating countermeasures as well.

Acknowledgment. This project has been partially funded by the European Union, Investing in your future, European Regional Development Fund.

References

1. Batina, L., Bruin-Muurling, G., Örs, S.B.: Flexible Hardware Design for RSA and Elliptic Curve Cryptosystems. In: Okamoto, T. (ed.) CT-RSA 2004. LNCS, vol. 2964, pp. 250–263. Springer, Heidelberg (2004)
2. Coron, J.-S.: Resistance against Differential Power Analysis for Elliptic Curve Cryptosystems. In: Koç, Ç.K., Paar, C. (eds.) CHES 1999. LNCS, vol. 1717, pp. 292–302. Springer, Heidelberg (1999)
3. Fan, J., Verbauwhede, I.: An Updated Survey on Secure ECC Implementations: Attacks, Countermeasures and Cost. In: Naccache, D. (ed.) Cryphtography and Security: From Theory to Applications. LNCS, vol. 6805, pp. 265–282. Springer, Heidelberg (2012)
4. Güneysu, T., Paar, C.: Ultra High Performance ECC over NIST Primes on Commercial FPGAs. In: Oswald, E., Rohatgi, P. (eds.) CHES 2008. LNCS, vol. 5154, pp. 62–78. Springer, Heidelberg (2008)
5. Koblitz, N.: Elliptic curve cryptosystems. Mathematics of Computation 48, 203–209 (1987)
6. Kocher, P., Jaffe, J., Jun, B.: Differential power analysis. In: Wiener, M. (ed.) CRYPTO 1999. LNCS, vol. 1666, pp. 388–397. Springer, Heidelberg (1999)
7. Miller, V.S.: Use of Elliptic Curves in Cryptography. In: Williams, H.C. (ed.) CRYPTO 1985. LNCS, vol. 218, pp. 417–426. Springer, Heidelberg (1986)
8. Montgomery, P.L.: Modular Multiplication without Trial Division. Mathematics of Computation 44(170), 519–521 (1985)
9. Rivest, R.L., Shamir, A., Adleman, L.M.: A Method for Obtaining Digital Signatures and Public-Key Cryptosystems. Commun. ACM 21(2), 120–126 (1978)
10. Sakiyama, K., Mentens, N., Batina, L., Preneel, B., Verbauwhede, I.: Reconfigurable modular arithmetic logic unit supporting high-performance RSA and ECC over GF(p). International Journal of Electronics, 501–514 (2007)
11. Varchola, M., Güneysu, T., Mischke, O.: MicroECC: A Lightweight Reconfigurable Elliptic Curve Crypto-processor. In: Athanas, P.M., Becker, J., Cumplido, R. (eds.) ReConFig, pp. 204–210. IEEE Computer Society (2011)
12. Vliegen, J., Mentens, N., Genoe, J., Braeken, A., Kubera, S., Touhafi, A., Verbauwhede, I.: A compact fpga-based architecture for elliptic curve cryptography over prime fields. In: 2010 21st IEEE International Conference on Application-specific Systems Architectures and Processors (ASAP), pp. 313–316 (2010)

ARABICA: A Reconfigurable Arithmetic Block for ISA Customization

Ihsen Alouani[1], Mazen A.R. Saghir[2], and Smail Niar[1]

[1] LAMIH, Université de Valenciennes et du Hainaut Cambrésis
{ihsen.alouani,smail.niar}@univ-valenciennes.fr
[2] Electrical and Computer Engineering Program, Texas A&M University at Qatar
mazen.saghir@qatar.tamu.edu

Abstract. We propose a dynamically reconfigurable arithmetic block architecture for customizing embedded application processor instruction sets. Our architecture uses medium-grained arithmetic blocks and a dedicated but reconfigurable interconnection network to support a wide range of instruction-set extensions. Our experimental results demonstrate the performance of our arithmetic block compared to a general-purpose processor, and its area- and energy-efficiency compared to dedicated arithmetic circuits.

1 Introduction

Mobile computing is increasing demands for powerful *application processors* that can deliver high levels of performance and energy efficiency. To match the widest range of applications domains, application processors include several dedicated processing units to execute domain-specific machine instructions. We believe such heterogeneity can be more efficiently supported using a dynamically reconfigurable, datapath-oriented architecture and interconnection network to implement common computational structures (e.g. SIMD, VLIW, and dataflow) using simple computational building blocks.

In this paper we present ARABICA (A Reconfigurable Arithmetic Block for ISA CustomizAtion), a dynamically reconfigurable computational block that we use to extend the instruction-set architecture of the Xilinx MicroBlaze soft processor core [1]. The ARABICA block consists of a programmable network of multiplexers and four, programmable, 18×25-bit DSP48E1 slices [2]. Reprogramming the multiplexers and DSP48E1 slices at run-time enables us to modify the structural organization and functionality of the ARABICA block to support a small but versatile set of instruction-set extensions.

Our paper is organized into four sections. In Section 2 we describe the ARABICA architecture and show how it can be used to extend the instruction set of the MicroBlaze processor. In Section 3 we present our experimental methodology and results, and in Section 4 we present our conclusions.

D. Goehringer et al. (Eds.): ARC 2014, LNCS 8405, pp. 248–253, 2014.
© Springer International Publishing Switzerland 2014

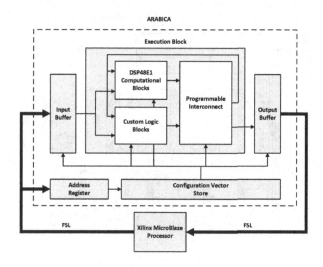

Fig. 1. ARABICA System Architecture

2   The ARABICA Architecture

Figure 1 shows our system architecture. It consists of the ARABICA block connected to a Xilinx MicroBlaze processor using a pair of fast simplex links (FSLs) [3]. The ARABICA block extends the instruction set architecture of the MicroBlaze processor using custom instructions exhibiting different formats such as SIMD, VLIW, custom data-flow, and single-precision, floating-point.

The FSL channels connect the MicroBlaze processor to the ARABICA block. While one channel transfers configuration commands and data operands to the block, a second channel transfers results back to the processor. This coupling is imposed by current Xilinx technology, which supports extensions to the MicroBlaze microarchitecture through FSL-connected co-processors only [4].

The ARABICA block is configured by a single control word sent from the MicroBlaze processor. The control word is stored in an address register and used to index into a 78-bit-wide *configuration vector store* that functions like the horizontal microcode stores of early computer systems [5]. The bit fields of a *configuration vector* determine the block's structural organization by enabling the interconnection paths that organize slices into specific computational structures. They also determine its functionality by specifying the operations that different DSP48E1 slices perform.

The ARABICA block currently supports four instruction-set extensions: four-way SIMD exclusive-or (XOR4); signed integer multiply-accumulate (MACC); a data-flow instruction that implements the integer multiply-add (MADD) function: $f = g \cdot h + i$; and two-way, single-precision, floating-point addition (SPFADD2), which demonstrates the block's support for both floating-point arithmetic and VLIW-style ILP. These extensions are by no means exhaustive and are only used

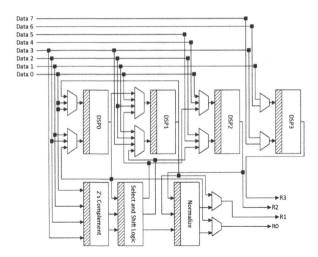

Fig. 2. ARABICA Execution Block

to demonstrate the versatility of the ARABICA architecture, which can be easily extended to support a wider set of instruction extensions. The block is fully pipelined and operates at 150 MHz.

Because a FSL channel can only transfer one, 32-bit, data word at a time, an input buffer is used to *synchronize* data operands. The number of operands used by different instruction-set extensions varies depending on the nature of the corresponding computation. For example, a XOR4 instruction uses eight, 32-bit operands, while a MACC instruction uses only two. The input buffer uses a bank of shift registers to delay different operands by different amounts until all operands become available. The operands can then be applied to the inputs of the execution block simultaneously.

The execution block consists of four DSP48E1 slices [2], three dedicated hardware blocks, and a programmable interconnection network of multiplexers overlayed on the FPGA fabric. The functionality of a DSP48E1 slice can be modified at run time by setting its control inputs appropriately. The dedicated hardware blocks implement a set of operations currently not supported by the DSP48E1 slices, but that are necessary for floating-point arithmetic. These include unsigned-to-signed number conversion, select and shift logic, and result normalization. However, from a functional perspective, we assume each of these blocks is a DSP48E1 slice configured to implement the corresponding operation.

The latency of a custom instruction depends on the structural organization and delay paths along its computational blocks. To minimize the impact of variable-latency instructions on the block's clock cycle time, we pipelined the inputs of its DSP48E1 slices and dedicated hardware blocks, which appear as shaded rectangles in Figure 2. The block's instructions vary in latency from 1 clock cycle for XOR4 to 4 clock cycles for SPFADD2. Additional cycles are also used to transfer operands and results between the MicroBlaze processor and the ARABICA block.

Once an instruction completes execution, its results are transferred back to the MicroBlaze processor over the output FSL channel. Different ARABICA instructions generate a different number of results with possibly different bit widths. For example, the XOR4 instruction generates four, 32-bit results while the SPFADD2 instruction generates two, 32-bit results. An output buffer is therefore needed to temporarily store these results before they can be transferred to the MicroBlaze processor over the FSL channel one, 32-bit, word at a time.

3   Experimental Methodology and Results

We developed three prototypes and compared them in terms of FPGA resource utilization, execution performance, and power and energy consumption. Our first prototype was a standalone MicroBlaze system configured with a single-precision floating-point unit to implement the functionalities of the ARABICA block's instructions in software. Our second prototype was an ARABICA block connected to a MicroBlaze processor, and our third prototype was a dedicated circuit block (DCB) containing hardwired circuits for each of the custom instructions supported by the ARABICA block. The circuits could only be used one at a time, and the DCB was connected to a MicroBlaze processor using the same FSL interface as the ARABICA block.

We implemented the three prototypes in the Virtex-6 XC6VLX240T FPGA found on the ML605 development board using the Xilinx Platform Studio (XPS) 13.4 tools. To measure FPGA resource utilization, we used the data reported in the XPS post-place-and-route synthesis reports. We also used a Xilinx XPS Timer/Counter IP core [6] to count the number of clock cycles consumed by different implementations of four, simple, benchmark programs that we executed on the different prototypes. We also measured the average dynamic power consumed by each prototype directly from the ML605 board [7,8]. We also estimated static power consumption using the Xilinx XPower Analyzer tool [9]. Finally, we computed energy consumption by multiplying the total power consumed by each prototype by the corresponding execution time for each benchmark.

3.1   FPGA Resource Utilization

Figure 3 shows the FPGA resources used by the three prototypes. Using the *geometric mean* of the resources used by each prototype, and normalizing the results with respect to the MicroBlaze processor, our results show that, as standalone units, the ARABICA block and DCB use 61% and 23% fewer resources than the MicroBlaze processor, respectively. Our results also show that the block uses 49% fewer resources than the DCB.

3.2   Execution Performance

Figure 4 shows the number of clock cycles consumed by the MicroBlaze processor and the ARABICA block for each of the benchmarks. These show that the block

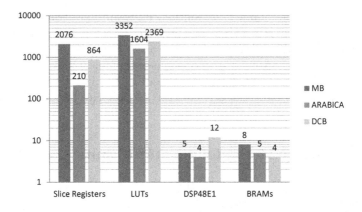

Fig. 3. FPGA Resource Utilization

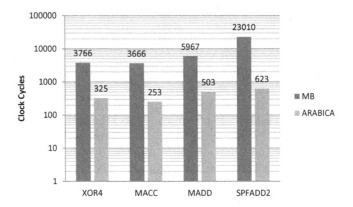

Fig. 4. Execution Performance

runs 12–37× faster than the MicroBlaze processor. The block achieves the same performance as the DCB because the latter uses the same MicroBlaze interface and hardware implementation for each instruction.

3.3   Power and Energy Consumption

Figure 5 shows the static, dynamic, and total power consumed by the three prototypes. The standalone ARABICA block consumes an average of 23% less static power, 30% more dynamic power, and 7% less total power than the MicroBlaze processor. It also consumes an average of 25% less static power, 4% less dynamic power, and 17% less total power than the standalone DCB. These results are mainly due to the block's efficient use of arithmetic and logic resources. The blocks' lower total power translates directly to lower energy consumption; on average it consumes 95% less energy than the MicroBlaze processor and 17% less energy than the DCB.

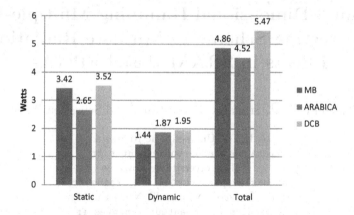

Fig. 5. Static, Dynamic, and Total Power Consumption

4   Conclusions

In this paper we proposed an architecture for a dynamically reconfigurable arithmetic block that can be used to customize an ISA at run-time. Our experimental results show that the ARABICA block achieves the same level of execution performance as dedicated hardware circuits using 49% fewer resources and 17% less power and energy. We believe these results can be further improved by eliminating the area, latency, and power overhead of the current, FSL-based, host processor interface. We are therefore working on integrating the block with the datapath of a RISC processor. We are also expanding the architecture to support a larger set of ISA extensions, and we are porting a compiler to generate ISA extensions and switch between block configurations automatically.

References

1. Xilinx, MicroBlaze Processor Reference Guide, UG081 (v12.0) (March 1, 2011)
2. Xilinx, Virtex-6 FPGA DSP48E1 Slice User Guide, UG369 (v1.3) (February 14, 2011)
3. Xilinx, LogiCORE IP Fast Simplex Link (FSL) V20 Bus (v2.11c), DS449 (April 19, 2010)
4. Xilinx, Connecting Customized IP to the MicroBlaze Soft Processor Using the Fast Simplex Link (FSL) Channel, XAPP529 (v1.3) (May 12, 2004)
5. Landskov, D., et al.: Local Microcode Compaction Techniques. ACM Computing Surveys 12(3), 261–294 (1980)
6. Xilinx, LogiCORE IP XPS Timer/Counter (v1.02a), DS573 (April 19, 2010)
7. Texas Instruments, USB Interface Adapter Evaluation Module User's Guide, Literature Number: SLLU093 (August 2006)
8. Texas Instruments, Fusion Digital Power Software
9. Xilinx, Xilinx Power Estimator User Guide, UG440 (v2012.4/14.4) (December 18, 2012)

Built-in 3-Dimensional Hamming Multiple-Error Correcting Scheme to Mitigate Radiation Effects in SRAM-Based FPGAs

B. Chagun Basha[1], Stanisław J. Piestrak[2], and Sébastien Pillement[3]

[1] IETR, Université de Rennes 1
`chagun.basheer@univ-nantes.fr`
[2] IJL, Université de Lorraine
`stanislaw.piestrak@univ-lorraine.fr`
[3] IETR, Polytech'Nantes, LUNAM Université
`sebastien.pillement@univ-nantes.fr`

Abstract. SRAM-based FPGAs have been employed extensively in many applications to implement adaptable systems whose functionalities can be changed at runtime. Unfortunately, even in terrestrial applications the SRAM configuration memory of FPGA devices is highly susceptible to radiation which may cause not only single but also multiple errors in physically adjacent memory cells, called Multiple Bit Upsets (MBUs). This paper proposes a new built-in 3-Dimensional Hamming (3DH) error correcting scheme to mitigate MBUs. The estimations of the probability of occurrence of undetected multiple errors indicate significant improvement of the error correction capabilities of the 3DH scheme proposed here, compared to known 2DH and 1DH schemes. The other important advantage of the new scheme is that it can provide faster reconfiguration of configuration frames affected by multiple errors, because error correction can be done using an internal bus alone.

1 Introduction

SRAM-based FPGAs are widely used in various application domains, due to their great advantages such as high density, fast time-to-market, flexible programmability, and cost effectiveness. However, their more widespread use in safely and mission critical applications is limited due to their high sensitivity to radiation causing so called Single Event Effects (SEEs). Amongst various types of SEEs, Single Event Upsets (SEUs) affecting SRAM-based memory cells are the most common. If an SEU alters the content of a single memory bit, it is called a Single Bit Upset (SBU). Unfortunately, besides SBUs a single particle strike can also alter the content of several memory cells (usually physically adjacent), called Multiple Bit Upsets (MBUs), which are significantly more difficult to handle than SBUs [7]. The results presented in [8] indicate that the percentage of MBUs continues to increase with each generation of FPGA devices. Recent experimental results on Xilinx Kintex7 FPGAs indicate that 9.9% of events cause multiple upsets within a frame (7.5% are double upsets); i.e., the estimated SRAM MBU rate is $1.02 \cdot 10^{-11}$, which corresponds to one MBU every

D. Goehringer et al. (Eds.): ARC 2014, LNCS 8405, pp. 254–261, 2014.
© Springer International Publishing Switzerland 2014

1515 s (about 25 min) [9]. Undoubtedly, the necessity of handling MBUs is of growing importance. On one hand, fault mitigation can be achieved by modifying the manufacturing process technology to produce radiation hardened FPGAs, but such solutions are very expensive [6]. On the other hand, fault mitigation techniques relying on using some fault-tolerance approaches are of growing interest, because they can be applied at various levels of an FPGA-based system without the need to change the standard manufacturing technology.

In this paper, we propose a new built-in 3-Dimensional Hamming (3DH) error correcting scheme, whose goal is to deal with the effects of MBUs. Section 2 addresses the need for an alternative mitigation scheme based on the study of existing soft error mitigation schemes and their limitations in recent SRAM-based FPGA devices. Section 3 explains the proposed 3-Dimensional Hamming code. Section 4 discusses how to choose the optimal size of the 3D-buffer to reduce parity memory overhead, whereas Section 5 shows the reliability improvement of the proposed scheme. Finally, Section 6 summaries achieved results and discusses further extensions of the present work.

2   Related Work

Redundancy based techniques are effective against errors affecting a single module, but they could be prone to MBUs and accumulated SEU-induced multiple errors producing erroneous outputs when more than one copy of any redundant module is affected by SEUs at the same time [6]. To avoid accumulation of SEU-induced multiple errors, fault-tolerance techniques supported by some form of configuration scrubbing can be the simplest way [3]. An alternative to scrubbing is configuration readback which enables verification of the bitstream frame data by performing a bit-by-bit comparison. However, the latter requires a mask and a readback files, a size of each is equal to the size of the original bitstream used to configure the FPGA, which is time-consuming and triplicates the memory required to perform the readback and reconfiguration process [13].

Another way of verifying configuration frames and SEU detection relies on using readback along with the Cyclic Redundancy Check (CRC). In this method, the N-bit CRC value is recorded for each frame of the configuration data. During readback of each frame, the CRC value is re-calculated and compared with the expected CRC value, any disagreement activating an error detection signal, so that the FPGA has to be reprogrammed. Because a data frame is the smallest unit of configuration memory, it suffices to re-program only the erroneous data frame, thanks to the possibility of the dynamic partial reconfiguration, [1, 3]. Nowadays, some of the high-end commercial FPGAs such as Virtex 5 and 6 series from Xilinx [5] and Stratix V Devices from Altera [1] have this kind of dedicated built-in readback and CRC logic to support faster detection and correction of configuration bit upsets. However, almost all of known reconfiguration (partial) based techniques require continuous access to an external storage device. Those external memories also need to be protected against SEUs and reconfiguration process involves an excessive delay in accessing the external storage device.

The scheme proposed here relies on using Hamming single-error-correcting/-double-error-detecting (SEC/DED) codes, because of relatively low complexity of supporting hardware compared to Low Density Parity Check (LDPC), turbo, Viterbi, and Reed-Solomon (RS) codes [10]. Some of the recent works [2, 12] propose built-in ECC-based methods of correcting configuration data which do not rely on the external golden copy. The error detecting and correcting matrix codes proposed in [2] combine the Hamming code and the parity code check bits in a matrix format. Their limitation is that if there are more than two errors in each code word, the matrix codes can correct them if and only if there are only two errors in each row of the matrix and one in each column. To deal with multiple upsets, the Hamming based 2D product code which performs Hamming SEC/DED in two different axes (directions): row-wise and column-wise was introduced in [12]. However, the latter scheme fails to correct multiple bit errors if they occur in both directions. Compared to existing 1D and 2D schemes mentioned before, the number of non-correctable multiple errors will be significantly reduced in the 3DH error correcting scheme proposed here.

3   New 3-Dimensional Hamming (3DH) Code

In this section, we will present the construction of the new 3DH code which can be implemented provided that an FPGA architecture contains a 3D memory whose buffer provides bitwise access to memory bits in all three directions (X, Y, and Z) (in contrast to conventional 2D memory where only one dimensional access is allowed). The latter allows to avoid excessive delay in multiple swapping of the configuration data in Y and Z direction. Because our work focuses on modelling a built-in configuration fault mitigation scheme, the design aspects of the 3D SRAM memory are omitted, as they can be found e.g. in recent works [4, 11] which discuss both the design of 3D SRAMs and their performance improvements.

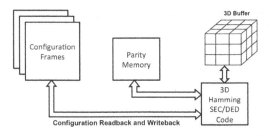

Fig. 1. General architecture that implements the 3DH error correcting scheme, proposed for SRAM-based FPGAs configuration memory protection

The basic idea of the proposed scheme is to apply a separate single bit error correcting scheme to each of three axes of the 3D data, so that the maximal number of erroneous bits could be corrected. The analysis of the hardware complexity (logic gate count) and error correction performance (bit error rate (BER)) of various ECCs, presented in [12], clearly shows that Hamming codes require the minimal hardware complexity compared to other ECCs. The general architecture that implements the proposed 3DH error correcting scheme to protect the configuration memory of SRAM-based FPGA is shown in Fig. 1.

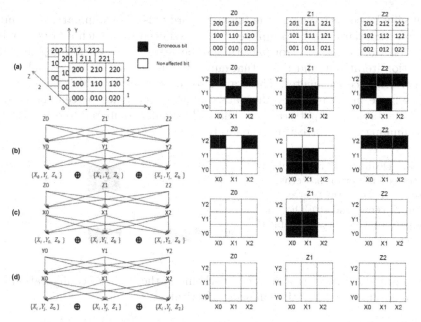

Fig. 2. Illustration of the 3D Hamming error correcting scheme: (a) Bit positions in terms of 3D co-ordinates (X, Y, and Z) and random errors introduced in data frames; (b) Error correction results after X-axis computation; (c) Error correction results after Y-axis computation; (d) Error correction results after Z-axis computation

The principles of error correction of the proposed scheme will be illustrated on a simple example of the $3 \times 3 \times 3 = 27$ bit array, shown in Fig. 2. Fig. 2a shows the arrangements of configuration bits in the 3D buffer, how bit positions are enumerated in terms of coordinate values (X, Y, and Z), and some randomly introduced multiple errors. In 27 data bits, we have introduced 13 errors which, despite they constitute almost 50% of all bits, still all will be shown correctable. Fig. 2b shows the results of the Hamming check bits generation along the X-axis, which allows to correct all single bit errors along the X-axis. Once all these errors are corrected, all errors present in the positions 110 and 020 of the frame Z0 as well as those in the positions 102 and 012 of the frame Z2 are all corrected. The same operation is performed along the Y and Z axes and its results are shown in Figs 2c and 2d, respectively. Next, once all errors are corrected along the Y-axis, the errors which were present in the positions 200 and 220 of the frame Z0 as well as those in the positions 202, 212, and 222 of the frame Z2 are all corrected. However, note that the errors in the frame Z1 are left uncorrected, because they correspond to a so far non-correctable error pattern: multiple errors in adjacent bit positions in adjacent rows and columns. Nevertheless, even this seemingly non-correctable 4-tuple error pattern can be handled, as explained in Fig. 3. Indeed, the same erroneous bits can be arranged in a correctable format, should this error pattern be viewed along the Y-axis (the latter can be seen as nothing else but a virtual breaking of the group of non-correctable errors and dispersing them in Y-frames, so they could become correctable). Then, these errors can eventually be corrected along the remaining 3rd axis Z. In summary, the sample configuration data can be completely recovered even from such a large number of errors. More complex error patterns can be corrected by performing the 3DH correction iteratively and the actual number of iterations can be considered as the performance parameter. There are also some cases for which the proposed 3DH scheme fails to recover the data, but the occurrence percentage of such non-correctable error patterns is significantly smaller compared to other 1D and 2D Hamming error correcting schemes (detailed in Section 5).

Fig. 3. Dealing with seemingly non-correctable error patterns: (a) Non-correctable 4-tuple error pattern in Z-frame; and (b) The same error pattern which is correctable in Y-frames

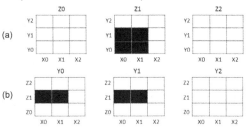

The proposed 3DH error correcting scheme of the FPGA's configuration bitstream is summarised as the following algorithm.

Algorithm 1

Step 1)   Read the N-bit configuration data frame through the serial readback bus along with corresponding parity bits stored in a separate parity memory array.

Step 2)   Perform the Hamming SEC/DED coding on the N-bit data and store the resulting data in the 3D N-bit buffer.

Step 3)   Repeat Steps 1) and 2) until the buffer is full (for the 3D buffer formatted with suitable coordinate values see Fig. 2a).

Step 4)   Read one by one the words of the 3D buffer along the Y axis and perform Hamming SEC/DED coding on them (all single bit errors are corrected during this operation).

Step 5)   If no multiple bit error is detected, perform Step 4) until the 3D buffer is fully scanned along the Y axis.

Step 6)   If multiple bit error is detected, record the current Y coordinate value and continue the same till the buffer is fully scanned along the Y axis.

Step 7)   Take the recorded Y coordinate value and perform the Hamming SEC/DED coding along the Z axis for that particular Y value.

Step 8)   Repeat Step 7) for all previously recorded Y values.

Step 9)   Once a full cycle of scanning of the 3D buffer along all three axes is completed, proceed to Step 10) if additional iteration is required.

Step 10)   Read the words one by one along the X axis and perform the Hamming SEC/DED coding on them.

Step 11)   Continue performing Hamming SEC/DED coding along the X axis until the buffer is fully scanned in the X-direction, then proceed to Step 4).

Step 12)   If any bit has been corrected, write back the corrected configuration data through the programming bus (thanks to partial reconfiguration).

Step 13)   Restart Step 1), for the next frame.

4 Determining the Optimal Size of the 3D Buffer and the Parity Memory Overhead

The size of the configuration data frame varies depending on the family of FPGA devices. Consequently, the number of check bits depends directly on the size of the configuration data frame and the error protection scheme used, like CRC and Frame ECC; for instance, in all Virtex 7 series FPGA devices: (i) all frames have a fixed, identical length of 3,232 bits and (ii) a 13-bit Hamming code and a 32-bit CRC with readback are used for error detection and correction [5, 14].

In the 3D buffer scheme proposed here, the overall parity memory overhead is given by

$$P_{3D} = (n_1 \cdot k_2 + n_2 \cdot k_1)n_3 + n_1 \cdot n_2 \cdot k_3, \tag{1}$$

where n_1, n_2 and n_3 are the corresponding sizes of X, Y, and Z co-ordinates, respectively, of the 3D buffer and k_i is the number of parity bits of the SEC/DED Hamming code for n_i data bits, $i = 1, 2, 3$. The total parity memory overhead of the proposed scheme for a particular FPGA device is

$$Total_{POH} = P_{3D} \cdot \frac{\text{Total number of configuration frames in FPGA}}{\text{Number of frames per 3D buffer}} \tag{2}$$

Because this overhead depends on the choice of the co-ordinate values of the 3D buffer, of particular interest is the so called *perfect SEC/DED Hamming code* for which the condition $n = 2^{k-1} - k$ holds, which protects the maximal number of the data bits n for a given number of parity bits k. For instance, the minimum of $k = 6$ parity bits suffice to protect $n = 12$ (minimum) as well as $n = 26$ (maximum) data bits. Fig. 4 shows the parity memory overhead of 3DH scheme for perfect Hamming codes (PH) and standard Hamming codes (SH) for k ranging from 5 to 10. Clearly, choosing the sizes of the 3D buffer which meet the perfect Hamming code condition can lead to significant overhead reduction.

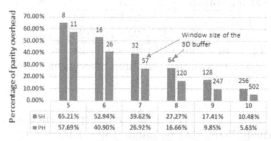

Fig. 4. Comparison of the parity memory overhead between 3D encodings using perfect Hamming codes (PH) and standard Hamming codes (SH) applied to $n = 2^j$ data bits

Unfortunately, the possibility of meeting the latter condition is hardly feasible for existing devices, because it greatly depends on the frame size of the FPGA's configuration plan. Nevertheless, it is desirable to choose the co-ordinates (n_1, n_2, and n_3) of the 3D buffer as closely as possible to the perfect Hamming code condition. As an example, we have estimated the best sizes (n_1, n_2, n_3) of the 3D buffer for Virtex 7 series FPGAs by providing 'Number of frames/buffer' and 'frame size (bits/frame)' of the FPGA as the input parameters. Two best

arrangements of 64 configuration frames of 3232 bits in the 3D format found were
(32, 64, 101) and (16, 101, 128), where all permutations of (n_1, n_2, n_3) would
obviously result in the same overheads equal respectively to 87488 and 108496
check bits. The first triple involves the minimum parity overhead equal to 42.2%,
which is significantly larger than to implement error handling mechanisms used
in the Virtex 7 series devices (the Frame ECC and CRC). Nevertheless, the
latter error correcting scheme cannot handle multiple bit errors as effectively as
the proposed scheme, because CRC must be supported by readback requiring
external circuitry to perform error correction.

5   Reliability Improvement

The reliability improvement of the proposed scheme is evaluated by comparing
the percentages of non-correctable error patterns in 1D, 2D, and 3D Hamming
code error correcting schemes. Some figures are listed in Table 1 for 3D data
cubes with $n = 3$, 4, and 5, where the occurrence percentage N_{ep} is the ratio
of the total number of non-correctable error patterns to the entire sum of correctable and non-correctable error patterns for the given bit/word/window size
of the data. All possible error patterns were generated and the N_{ep} values were
obtained using MATLAB®. Unfortunately, estimating non-correctable patterns
for $n \geq 6$ turned out computationally too complex.

Table 1 reveals decreasing nature of the percentage of non-
correctable error patterns with
the increase of the 3D buffer
size. Recall that the simple
Hamming SEC/DED scheme
is capable of correcting only
single-bit errors in a word and
that the percentage of non-
correctable error patterns in it
is very high. As for the 2D
Hamming code, any multiple
bit error in more than one
adjacent row/column is uncor-

Table 1. Comparison of non-correctable error
patterns of various Hamming schemes

	1DH scheme		2DH scheme		3DH Scheme	
n	T_b	$N_{ep}[\%]$	T_b	$N_{ep}[\%]$	T_b	$N_{ep}[\%]$
3	3	50.00	9	17.18	27	0.86
4	4	68.75	16	23.68	64	0.60
5	5	81.25	25	23.84	125	0.53

T_b: total number of protected bits;
N_{ep}: percentage of non-correctable error
patterns

rectable [12]. The data listed in Table 1 show that the percentage of such un-
correctable error patterns is relatively high. On one hand, Table 1 reveals that
the ratio of non-correctable error patterns in 1D and 2D schemes grows with the
increase of word and window size, respectively. On the other hand, it shows that
the ratio of non-correctable error patterns in the proposed 3D Hamming code
is not only very small (less than 1%) but also, unlike the other two schemes,
it tends to decrease with the increase of the window size. It suggests that the
multiple bit error correction efficiency of the proposed scheme is significantly
higher than of the other schemes.

6   Conclusion

A new built-in 3-Dimensional Hamming (3DH) multiple bit error-correcting scheme proposed to mitigate Multi Bit Upsets (MBUs) in configuration memory of SRAM-based FPGAs is presented. The major advantage of the new scheme is that it can provide faster reconfiguration of frames affected by multiple errors. This would contribute to improving performance of FPGA-based systems, because error removal (correction) can be done using internal bus alone, unlike most known methods that rely on the external configuration back-up. Since the configuration readback is a background process, the proposed 3DH error-correcting scheme operates without stalling the whole system. Only the short reconfiguration of erroneous frames results in interruption of the system operation. Quantitative estimations show that the percentage of non-correctable error patterns in the proposed 3DH scheme is significantly smaller when compared to the other schemes, thus considerably improving the reliability of the protected system. It seems that the error-correcting scheme proposed here can be also extended to other SRAM-based memory devices as well. In the future, we will evaluate the computation and hardware overhead involved in the implementation of the proposed 3DH error-correcting scheme.

References

1. Altera Corp.: Stratix V Device Handbook. Device Interfaces and Integration. SEU Mitigation for Stratix V Devices, vol. 1, ch. 9. Altera Corp., San Jose (June 2013)
2. Argyrides, C., et al.: Matrix codes for reliable and cost efficient memory chips. IEEE Trans. Very Large Scale Integr. (VLSI) Syst. 19(3), 420–428 (2011)
3. Carmichael, C., et al.: Correcting single-event upsets through Virtex partial configuration. Appl. Note XAPP216 (v1.0) (June 1, 2000)
4. Hsu, C.-L., et al.: High-performance 3D-SRAM architecture design. In: Proc. IEEE Asia Pacific Conf. Circuits and Systems, pp. 907–910 (2010)
5. Chapman, K.: SEU strategies for Virtex-5 devices. Appl. Note XAPP864 (v2.0) (April 1, 2010)
6. Kastensmidt, F.L., et al.: Fault-Tolerance Techniques for SRAM-Based FPGAs. Springer, Dordrecht (2006)
7. Quinn, H., et al.: Radiation-induced multi-bit upsets in SRAM-based FPGAs. IEEE Trans. Nucl. Sci. 52(6), 2455–2461 (2005)
8. Quinn, H., et al.: Static proton and heavy ion testing of the Xilinx Virtex-5 device. In: Proc. IEEE Workshop on Radiation Effects Data, Honolulu, HI, USA, July 23-27, pp. 177–184 (2007)
9. Takai, H., et al.: Soft error rate estimations of the Kintex-7 FPGA within the ATLAS Liquid Argon (LAr) Calorimeter. In: TWEPP 2013, Perugia, Italy, September 23-27 (2013)
10. Lin, S., Costello Jr., D.J.: Error Control Coding: Fundamentals and Applications, 2nd edn. Prentice-Hall, Englewood Cliffs (2004)
11. Pathak, M., et al.: Reliability and performance-aware 3D SRAM design. In: Proc. IEEE 54th Int. Midwest Symp. Circuits and Systems, pp. 1–4 (2011)
12. Park, S.P., et al.: Soft-error-resilient FPGAs using built-in 2-D Hamming product code. IEEE Trans. Very Large Scale Integr. (VLSI) Syst. 20(2), 248–256 (2012)
13. Xilinx, Inc.: Virtex FPGA series configuration and readback. Appl. Note XAPP138 (March 2006)
14. Xilinx, Inc.: 7 Series FPGAs Configuration: User Guide (October 22, 2013)

Adapting Processor Grain via Reconfiguration

Jecel Mattos de Assumpção Jr.[1], Merik Voswinkel[2], and Eduardo Marques[1]

[1] Universidade de São Paulo
Departamento de Sistemas de Computação
São Carlos, Brasil
{jecel,emarques}@icmc.usp.br
[2] HH Research Institute
Wehe-Den Hoorn,The Netherlands
merik@morphle.org

Abstract. Squeak is an open source Smalltalk-80 implementation created to implement high level code that is used as glue between optimized, low level "plug-ins" written in C or a restricted subset of Smalltalk and translated to C. SiliconSqueak is a hardware implementation with coarse grained processors for the high level code and fine grained "ALU Matrix" co-processors for the plug-ins. When implemented in an FPGA, a given area can either be used for a co-processor or for two more high level cores. The ideal mix varies at runtime as applications go through different phases, so the solution presented in this paper is to reconfigure the system as needed.

Keywords: Reconfiguration, Heterogeneous cores, Smalltalk.

1 Introduction

One of the defining features of a programming language is its type system. In a strongly typed language, like Haskell, there is a strict control of which kinds of objects can be used with a given operation while languages like Forth or assembly are untyped and this control is up to the programmer. Many popular languages, such as those derived from C or Pascal have a relatively strong type system with features like type casts and untagged unions to weaken the system under programmer control. While some programmers use the terms "strong typing" and "weak typing" for languages that associate type information with source text variables and runtime objects respectively, we will use the more traditional terms "static typing" and "dynamic typing" in order not to mix what are independent concepts.

Statically typed languages can get good results from relatively simple compilers while dynamically typed languages have traditionally been interpreted, which resulted in a significant performance gap. Since type declarations can be an obstacle to exploring different design options, a traditional software development method has been to write the application initially in a dynamic language (Lisp, for example) and when it is stable to completely rewrite it in a static language (like Fortran). This is even the case for embedded applications where

D. Goehringer et al. (Eds.): ARC 2014, LNCS 8405, pp. 262–267, 2014.
© Springer International Publishing Switzerland 2014

the initial algorithms might be developed in something like Matlab running on a desktop machine and the final application is a rewrite in C to run on the target machine.

This popular separation of dynamic languages for prototyping and static languages for production is being challenged by two trends: faster hardware via "Moore's Law" can make the performance of even interpreters acceptable for many applications and sophisticated compilation technologies developed for dynamic languages in the 1990s[3] are being increasingly adopted. Section 2 explains how Squeak Smalltalk[4] deals with performance issues and how this reflects on the design of the SiliconSqueak hardware. Section 3 is about the use of runtime reconfiguration of a FPGA implementation of this hardware to match the processing granularity as the application requirements change. Projects that have some features in common with the one described here are mentioned in section 4 and finally section 5 describe the next steps for this project and the results that have been obtained so far.

2   Squeak and SiliconSqueak

One problem with advanced compilation systems is that it takes significant effort to port them to different platforms and running on as many machines as possible was a major goal of the Squeak project created at Apple in 1996 [4]. It was decided that a good interpreter would meet the needs of the project given modern hardware and the fact that in multimedia applications more time is spent in library functions like codecs than inside the language itself. Java was considered as an option for the base language so that the small team could focus on the application while external groups took care of the platform but the development tools were considered too primitive compared with what Smalltalk-80 had nearly 20 years earlier back at Xerox PARC. Since Apple had a very liberal license for those tools from Xerox, they were selected as the starting point for an open source project with the idea that if development were easy enough, external groups could take care of the porting to machines besides the Mac.

Smalltalk-80 is implemented as a virtual machine which has to be simulated on different computers either with dynamic compilation or with an interpreter. Traditional interpreters were implemented in languages such as C, but the original book explaining the language[2] included a complete reference design written in a restricted form of Smalltalk without any object creation other than Integers and with no polymorphism. This made it easy for a programmer to rewrite in Pascal, C or even assembly language but it also made it possible to create a simple tool to translate it (the Squeak group called this Smalltalk subset "Slang" although there are a few actual programming languages with that name) automatically to C. Though Slang doesn't use all of Smalltalk-80's features, it can run on a normal Smalltalk implementation and make use of all the advanced development tools. Once the functionality has been fully verified, the code can be translated to C and then compiled for higher performance. This can be done not only for the main interpreter, but also for "plug-ins" like the codecs mentioned

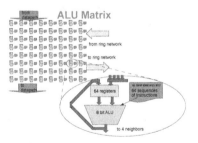

Fig. 1. 64 ALU Matrix

earlier. Or existing libraries written in other languages can be used, whichever is more convenient.

As planned, Squeak was ported by independent individuals to all the major desktop platforms within weeks of the initial release and to dozens of less known machines over the next couple of years. It is easy to make Squeak run on any soft core with a C compiler, such as the Nios II or the Leon3, to have it available in a FPGA-based reconfigurable system, but a dedicated SiliconSqueak core can be a more efficient option. The goal is to eliminate as much overhead as possible from the interpreter while at the same time including features that make it attractive as a target for adaptive compilation (a part of the project which is outside the scope of this paper, but note that other dynamic compilers have been developed for Squeak in the past and there is currently a very active project called Cog).

Most modern FPGAs are large enough that two or more SiliconSqueak cores can be used at the same time to implement course grained parallelism. This can speed up many kinds of applications, but the plug-ins written in Slang and in C don't benefit from this. So an optional co-processor, called the "ALU Matrix" and shown in figure 1, was developed specifically for that part of the code. The example shows an 8 by 8 matrix of 8 bit ALUs, each with 64 8 bit registers, but each of these parameters can be changed with no impact on the main SiliconSqueak core (though code for the co-processor would have to be recompiled). Besides its local registers, each ALU has its own program memory so that when the main core asks the ALU Matrix to execute sequence 5, for example, the exact operation can be different for each ALU making this fine grained architecture a mix of SIMD and MIMD features. It also combines computation and communication in that the instruction names two destination registers: one for the output of this ALU and one for the output of a selected neighbor.

3   Scheduling and Reconfiguration

Blue blocks in figure 2 represent generic SiliconSqueak cores, green depicts a 64 ALU matrix including the adjacent SiliconSqueak core to control it, the orange block is a 4 x 8 Gb/s networking unit to interconnect with neighboring input/output unit or FPGAs and ASIC processors in a mesh with point to point

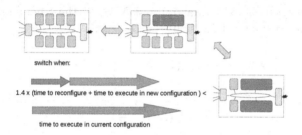

switch when:

1.4 x (time to reconfigure + time to execute in new configuration) <

time to execute in current configuration

Fig. 2. FPGA reconfiguration at work

links, yellow is the memory controller properly balanced with the optimal number of cores to avoid bottlenecks to dynamic random access memory (DRAM).
Interconnecting of cores, matrices and units is accomplished by a ring network.

With an initial configuration as in the left of figure 2, switching to the option
in the middle would replace some of the existing cores both in terms of FPGA
area and as an element in the ring networks. If that particular processor was
exclusively executing code that will now be done by hardware, there will be a
gain in performance. If, on the other hand, it was also executing unrelated code
that must now be moved to the other cores then there will be a performance
loss no matter how much faster the hardware is than the optimized code. The
scheduler should group related code under heavy loads to make it simpler to
detect the situation where a software block has one or more cores dedicated to
it and so is a candidate for a hardware replacement.

Given that an FPGA that is being reconfigured does not execute anything,
the scheduler should deal with time frames N times longer than this inactive
period. Besides the reconfiguration time itself, there is the time needed to save
all current state to external memory and then the time to restore it (adapting
to the new configuration). Since a single core with an ALU Matrix takes up the
same FPGA resources as three simple cores, any code which doesn't make use
of the co-processor will run roughly three times slower. Any code that does take
advantage of the ALU Matrix (code generated by the new compiler), on the
other hand, will run X times faster.

$$N > 1.4 \times (1 + (1 - \alpha) \times 3N + \alpha \times \frac{N}{X}) \qquad (1)$$

$$\alpha > \frac{(\frac{N}{1.4} - 3N - 1)}{(\frac{N}{X} - 3N)} \qquad (2)$$

Where α is the percent of time that code that could use the co-processor takes
on the configuration with three simple cores. To avoid needlessly switching back
and forth between configurations, a factor of 1.4 adds some hysteresis to the
system. Equation 1 shows under what conditions it is profitable to replace three
simple cores with a single one having a co-processor. Equation 2 solves for α
given X (notice that $\frac{N}{X} - 3N < 0$ given that $X > 1$). So if $X = 6$ (code becomes

six times faster with the ALU Matrix) and $N = 10$ (the scheduling time frame is ten times the reconfiguration time) then $\alpha > 84\%$.

$$N > 1.4 \times (1 + (1 - \beta) \times \frac{N}{3} + \beta \times NX) \tag{3}$$

$$\beta < \frac{(\frac{N}{1.4} - \frac{N}{3} - 1)}{(NX - \frac{N}{3})} \tag{4}$$

In equation 3 we have the condition where it is a good idea to replace a SiliconSqueak core including an ALU Matrix with three simple cores. Here β is the percent of the time in which code that uses the ALU Matrix executes in the original configuration (this is different, but related to, α). Given the same $X = 6$ and $N = 10$, then $\beta < 5\%$.

4   Related Works

Designing processors optimized for Java, such as JOP[6], are becoming more popular, as are extensions to conventional processors like the two Jazelle options for the ARM. The Lisp Machines of the 1970s to 1990s are the best known language specific architectures, but there were many designs optimized for Smalltalk including the first machine based on FPGAs, the Manchester Mushroom[8].

Among the many systems that use runtime reconfiguration to reallocate FPGA resources, the BORPH operating system[7] is interesting in its analogy to memory allocation in Unix systems. The Virtex 4 FPGAs used in the initial experiments in this project allow partial reconfiguration which has the advantage of not disrupting the part of the design that stays the same from one configuration to the next. This isn't being used yet in part because of the complexity of the tools required and in part because the plan is to build machines with multiple FPGAs which allows partial configuration at the system level.

Reconfigurable co-processors were used in projects like ADRES[1] or in NEC's IMAPCAR2 chip[5], where groups of four can be used as either a VLIW MIMD node or a SIMD machine.

5   Initial Results and Future Works

The ML401 development board from Xilinx is based on the Virtex 4 LX 25 FPGA and offers several configuration options. One of them is the SystemACE chip, also from Xilinx, which can load a configuration file from a Compact Flash memory card into the FPGA through its JTAG port. The SystemACE understands the FAT file system and can select one of eight different configuration files from subdirectories as indicated by a configuration file at the root of the memory card. Normally switches at three pins of the SystemACE device will select which file to load, but it is possible to override this choice by placing a value in a configuration register using the microcontroller port. In the ML401 board this port is connected to the Virtex 4 so a design in the FPGA can replace itself with a different one on demand.

The files to be loaded into the FPGA are all the same size (1MB) regardless of the specific design, so the time to reconfigure the Virtex 4 chip has been measured at 1.4 seconds (a transfer rate of 732KB per second, which is limited by the JTAG port but is not too far from what the memory card can achieve).

A simple benchmark was developed to draw fractal images with a computational load that varies in a 40 second cycles (so that it is worth using a configuration for at least 14 seconds, which is 10 times longer than the configuration time and there is no need to save and restore state for this simple program). This shows a limitation of the scheduler described in this paper: the model includes a constant speedup factor which can be very different from the actual speedup. In the phase of the project focused on adaptive compilation this constant should be replaced by runtime measurements.

A more realistic set of benchmarks will be implemented once the port of the Squeak interpreter is finished.

In conclusion: though all systems contain a mix of computational tasks with different levels of parallelism, the design of Squeak makes this explicit and the hardware design of SiliconSqueak reflects this by separating the course grained parallelism of the main cores from the fine grained parallelism of the ALU Matrix co-processors. On a reconfigurable platform it is possible to change the ratio of these resources at runtime to adapt to varying computing needs.

References

1. Bouwens, F.J., Berekovic, M., Kanstein, A., Gaydadjiev, G.N.: Architectural Exploration of the ADRES Coarse-Grained Reconfigurable Array. In: Proceedings of International Workshop on Applied Reconfigurable Computing, pp. 1–13 (2007)
2. Goldberg, A., Robson, D.: Smalltalk-80: the language and its implementation. Addison-Wesley Longman Publishing Co., Inc., Boston (1983)
3. Hölzle, U.: Adaptive optimization for Self: reconciling high performance with exploratory programming. Ph.D. thesis, Stanford University (1994)
4. Ingalls, D., Kaehler, T., Maloney, J., Wallace, S., Kay, A.: Back to the future: The story of Squeak, A practical Smalltalk written in itself. In: Proceedings OOPSLA 1997, ACM SIGPLAN Notices, pp. 318–326. ACM Press (1997)
5. Kyo, S., Koga, T., Hanno, L., Nomoto, S., Okazaki, S.: A low-cost mixed-mode parallel processor architecture for embedded systems. In: Proceedings of the 21st Annual International Conference on Supercomputing - ICS 2007, p. 253. ACM Press, New York (2007), http://portal.acm.org/citation.cfm?doid=1274971.1275006
6. Schoeberl, M.: A Java Processor Architecture for Embedded Real-Time Systems. Journal of Systems Architecture (2007), doi:10.101
7. So, H.K.H.: BORPH: An Operating System for FPGA-Based Reconfigurable Computers. Ph.D. thesis, Engineering – Electrical and Computer Sciences, University of California, Berkeley (2007)
8. Williams, I.W.: Using FPGAs to Prototype New Computer Architectures. In: Moore, W.R., Luk, W. (eds.) FPGAs, ch. 6.8, pp. 373–382. Abingdon EE & CS Books (1991)

Instruction Set Optimization
for Application Specific Processors

Max Ferger and Michael Hübner

Embedded Systems of the Information Technology (ESIT)
Ruhr-University Bochum (RUB), Germany
{max.ferger,michael.huebner}@ruhr-uni-bochum.de
www.esit.ruhr-uni-bochum.de

Abstract. Tools and services are available that modify the hardware
description, compilers, and tools to build application specific instruction-
set architectures (ASIPs).

This work introduces an automatic approach in identifying "hot"
code idioms: find and count recurring tuples of assembly instructions
(N-grams) in a simulator trace. Our analysis gives a short list of frequent combinations of instructions, even across control-flow boundaries.
These candidates are most promising to optimize.

On the example of an implementation of the Smith-Waterman-
Algorithm for String-Alignment in C, running on a PD_RISC by Synopsys Processor Designer, the hot part of the assembly code is identified
and manually replaced by an intrinsic function of the same behavior.
Results include the growth in logic of the processor, speed-up of the program, and reduction in energy consumption, due to the first round of
applying the proposed technique.

Keywords: Adaptive Processors, ASIP, ASIP Optimization, Instruction Set, Instruction Sequences, Instruction N-Grams, Control Flow, Intrinsic Functions.

1 Introduction

The analysis of compiled application code in order to achieve a reduction of the
code size and a speedup of the application is well known and documented in many
publications like [12]. Dutt et al.[6] specifically target the reduction of the energy
consumption of RISC processors by optimizing the instruction set architecture.
This topic is of high importance in embedded systems, especially when energy
is very limited in ultra low power and mobile applications. In these domains,
not only the well-known methods of energy saving (clock scaling, clock gating,
voltage scaling, et cetera) are possible ways to extend the time of operation
of an embedded system. Many more options, especially within the processors
data- and control path offer a variety of possibilities to optimize the hardware/
software architecture. However, these methods are often not easy to apply, since
a deep knowledge about the processor internal mechanisms and the compiler

D. Goehringer et al. (Eds.): ARC 2014, LNCS 8405, pp. 268–274, 2014.
© Springer International Publishing Switzerland 2014

is required to explore a large design space for an optimization. Furthermore, if the chosen optimization methods involve graph theory, problems of exponential complexity have to be addressed. Galuzzi and Bertels[7] give a survey on that topic.

This work includes the application's control flow graph in the analysis, as opposed to staying between basic block boundaries while analyzing the trace of a compiled application. The result of this analysis is the realization of a special instruction which leads to a reduction of cycles required for the entire program. If automated, these could be used in conjunction with reconfigurable technology, perhaps complementing works by others[1][14][4][5], if the amortization of just-in-time reconfiguration is achievable, as discussed by Grad and Plessl[8]. The introduction of a special instruction offers the advantage of no communication overhead as opposed to building an external accelerator, helping predictability in this early work.

In the paper, the analysis of the program code and integration into a real processor presents first results about cycle count, power consumption and speedup.

The remaining paper is organized as follows: Section 2 gives a short overview of techniques that influence this work. Section 3 brings the concept and realization. The evaluation of this first, manual experiment can be found in section 4. The paper is closed in section 5 with a conclusion, and an outlook to future work in section 6.

2   State of the Art

Peephole Optimization was introduced by Mc Keeman[11] and is performed on object code, as well as on intermediate code[13]. It was defined by Tanenbaum as follows: "A peephole optimization is one that replaces a sequence of consecutive instructions by a semantically equivalent but more efficient sequence."[13] The goal is to apply optimizations on the instruction level that are beneficial per sé, which can be determined at compile time. When put together with peephole-based optimizations, "Profiling information can result in small, but notable improvements in performance."[2]

The *Language for Instruction Set Architectures (LISA)*[9] allows to quickly describe a processor architecture based on its resources and available commands. A compiler can be re-targeted accordingly with the *Synopsys Processor Designer (PD)*.[1] Tools exist to generate the necessary libraries, binary tools, debugger, and instruction set simulator. It is possible to generate a Register-Transfer Level (RTL) implementation of the processor in VHDL or Verilog.

3   Concept and Realization

The current state of a processor architecture is taken as a reference point for the optimization. As the development is driven by a specific program[2], this program

---

[1] Formerly known as "CoSy Express" by CoWare.

[2] We speak of only one application, but consider a merge of several programs.

is compiled into assembly and executed on the simulator, which logs all executed instructions in a simulator trace. If necessary, exemplary input is fed into the program.

The trace either contains or is annotated with the mnemonics of the assembly instructions, which defines the order of the executed commands and their behavioral functionality. This trace is then seen as a phrase of words in the assembly language, for example ... ; ADD; CMPLE; BCC24[3]; NOP[4] ; ...

As the string of executed statements streams in, every sub-string up to a certain length is registered and counted in a prefix-tree. At depth N, this tree contains all sequences of length N, also called N-grams.

In a second phase, redundant information is removed. Due to the fact that every N-gram contains two (N−1)-grams, three (N−2)-grams and so on, overlapping sub-sequences need not be counted towards good optimization candidates, iff they don't occur on their own.

The result is a list of candidate N-grams, sorted by their execution frequency, which is inspected by the system architect. Suppose some of these high-rated N-grams are transformed into special instructions, and suppose every occurrence in the re-compiled program gets replaced, the performance gain is highly predictable by multiplying the reduction in cycles with the respective frequency. This fact might be mitigated by a poor choice of input data while tracing the program.

This analysis can be mapped back onto a control flow graph of basic blocks of assembly instructions. In the presence of a-cyclic control flow (consisting only of If-Then, If-Then-Else and short-circuit-evaluation schemes), the combination of "parallel" sequences that cross basic block boundaries is important.

So far, data-flow dependencies have been disregarded, because we search for optimization *candidates*. Obeying dependencies is work for the compiler and puts in many constraints that should not narrow down our search in the first place.

The Synopsys Processor Designer (PD) framework used for the tests comes with a "starter kit" processor, the PD_RISC which has a 5-stage pipeline, but no other instruction-level parallelism. The produced assembly is therefore very linear and orderly, when compared to the C source code.

We used an example implementation of the Smith-Waterman Algorithm for the alignment of sequences[5], which is based on dynamic programming. In its innermost loop, the maximum of three values and zero is calculated, as highlighted in the middle of Fig. 1.Determining this maximum involves three If-Then-Else-constructs: one within each branch of an outer If-Then-Else.

A special 32-bit instruction PMAX was built, that supports three non-zero operands via registers. The forth operand, zero, is implicit.

All tools, libraries and Register-Transfer Level (RTL) description are re-generated with the tools by Synopsys.

---

[3] Branch/Jump on Compare/Carry Condition.

[4] The PD_RISC can operate with one cycle delay-slot-filling[10].

[5] This algorithm might be seen as classic in Bio-Informatics.

Because of the easily and far abstracted nature of this instruction, all its potential parallelism can influence hardware generation. Unfortunately, we were unable to identify the corresponding parts of the RTL logic.

To use the special instruction, an intrinsic function was necessary as it was not possible (yet) to write a matcher pattern for the elaborated control flow scenario.[6] The C code is thus modified in two places within the inner loop: once at the place of discovery, plus another occurrence of a maximum of two values and zero. The new Control Flow Graph (CFG) is depicted in Fig. 2.

Both programs are run on their special architectures and compared as illustrated in Fig. 3, Fig. 4 and Fig. 5.

4 Evaluation

The gain in execution time of the inner loop is as expected: where the original program uses 44.25 cycles in average, the optimized version with the PMAX instruction iterates every 33 cycles, saving −25.4%. Or, otherwise said, the optimized loop runs up to $1.33x$ faster by comparison of its statically scheduled assembly.[7]

Under the assumption that an estimation is feasibly, how many cycles any new instruction might be pipelined into[8] to not hurt the processor's maximum frequency, the gain in performance can be calculated without feedback from logic synthesis.

The original PD_RISC occupies 53′625 cells as reported by Synopsys Design Compiler with the power-saving defaults given by PD, on a Default 90nm process by UMC. The added PMAX instruction costs +12.25% more chip area (60′195 cells).

Both variants of the core could be synthesised for 25MHz with a slack of 21.11ns without, respective 22.08ns with PMAX. Apparently, the newly introduced instruction had no negative impact on the length of the processor's critical path.

So far, clock-gating is not used to switch off the special instruction and the average amount of power consumed by the processor growths by +4.85%, from 0.1876mW to 0.1967mW. Every iteration of the inner loop thus uses 332nWs in the original, and only 257nWs when using PMAX at 25MHz. This potentially saves −22.6% energy, when the program processes very large inputs, even without lowering the voltage, or adjusting the clock.

As our method involves manually identifying and coding a new instruction, the explored design space is still very small and justifies no deeper analysis of trade-offs. On the other hand an intelligent system architect can skip the gap between a small example input to very big ones by justified extrapolation.

---

[6] This ought to be feasible through a specialized module within the underlying "CoSy" compiler framework by ACE Associated Compiler Experts b.v., Amsterdam.

[7] The overall speedup was found to be $1.088x$ (from 9′389 downto 8′628 cycles), on a small input size that leads to 72 iterations of the inner loop.

[8] This is only 1 cycle in case of PMAX.

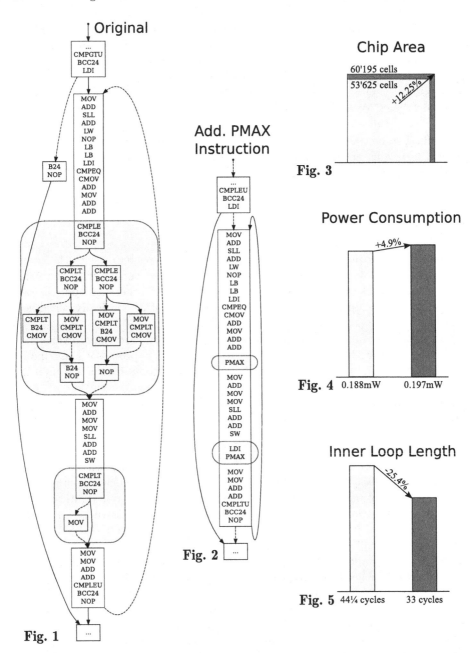

Fig. 1. Control Flow Graph of Original Assembly

Fig. 2. Control Flow Graph of Optimized Assembly

Fig. 3. Growth in Chip Area

Fig. 4. Power Consumption

Fig. 5. Gain in Execution Time

5   Conclusion

Widening trace information up to N-grams that occur frequently and filtering these by combinatorial and statistical means gives a system architect a lever on a very huge design space exploration by looking a little further than one instruction at a time. If any program code has more than one hot spot, their similarities have combined weight onto the optimization process.

By disregarding basic block boundaries in this statistical approach, it is possible to identify code idioms that span control flow patterns and quickly come up with larger blocks to optimize. Although the amount of produced logic might be arguably high, the gain in performance results in lower energy consumption.

6   Outlook

So far, we applied our technique on the level of assembly instructions. As Tanenbaum believes[13], optimizations on the Intermediate Representation (IR) within a compiler are more beneficial in most cases: the semantics of the program are still clear and side-effects of instructions are known by construction. Also, more powerful analysis techniques are available. Thus it would make sense to map our combined profiling information back onto the IR and deduce new instruction candidates for the architecture on a basis of expression (sub-)trees.

Another problem to solve will be the generation of suitable entry and exit boundaries to regions of code. We are working on an approach of combined control and data flow analysis on the IR level.

Depending on the style of the IR, efficient automatic synthesis of the required additional logic might be feasible.

On the road to achieve these semi-automatic and automatic optimizations, a much larger variety of programs and architectures should be investigated. Such automation could also be used to define a Reconfigurable Functional Unit (RFU) by terms of Barat and Lauwereins survey[3]. Energy measurements should be precised with techniques like clock-gating, clock-adjustment and voltage lowering.

References

1. Bala, V., Duesterwald, E., Banerjia, S.: Dynamo: A Transparent Dynamic Optimization System. ACM SIGPLAN Notices 35(5), 1–12 (2000),
   http://portal.acm.org/citation.cfm?doid=358438.349303,
   http://dl.acm.org/citation.cfm?id=358438.349303
2. Bansal, S.: Peephole Superoptimization. ProQuest (2008),
   http://books.google.com/books?id=DITv8TZSBbEC&pgis=1
3. Barat, F., Lauwereins, R.: Reconfigurable Instruction Set Processors: A Survey, p. 168 (June 2000), http://dl.acm.org/citation.cfm?id=827261.828228
4. Bispo, J., Paulino, N., Cardoso, J.M.P., Ferreira, J.C.: Transparent Trace-Based Binary Acceleration for Reconfigurable HW/SW Systems. IEEE Transactions on Industrial Informatics 9(3), 1625–1634 (2013),
   http://ieeexplore.ieee.org/lpdocs/epic03/wrapper.htm?arnumber=6392266

5. Clark, N., Blome, J., Chu, M., Mahlke, S., Biles, S., Flautner, K.: An Architecture Framework for Transparent Instruction Set Customization in Embedded Processors. ACM SIGARCH Computer Architecture News 33(2), 272–283 (2005), http://ieeexplore.ieee.org/articleDetails.jsp?arnumber=1431563, http://dl.acm.org/citation.cfm?id=1080695.1069993, http://portal.acm.org/citation.cfm?doid=1080695.1069993, http://dx.doi.org/10.1109/ISCA.2005.9

6. Dutt, N.D., Lee, J.E., Choi, K.: Energy-efficient instruction set synthesis for application-specific processors. In: Proceedings of the 2003 International Symposium on Low Power Electronics and Design, ISLPED 2003, pp. 330–333. ACM (2003), http://ieeexplore.ieee.org/lpdocs/epic03/wrapper.htm?arnumber=1231889, http://home.unist.ac.kr/professor/jlee/public/papers/03islped-isa-energy.pdf

7. Galuzzi, C., Bertels, K.: The instruction-set extension problem: A survey. In: Woods, R., Compton, K., Bouganis, C., Diniz, P.C. (eds.) ARC 2008. LNCS, vol. 4943, pp. 209–220. Springer, Heidelberg (2008), http://link.springer.com/chapter/10.1007/978-3-540-78610-8_21

8. Grad, M., Plessl, C.: On the Feasibility and Limitations of Just-in-Time Instruction Set Extension for FPGA-Based Reconfigurable Processors. International Journal of Reconfigurable Computing 2012, 1–21 (2012), http://dl.acm.org/citation.cfm?id=2213807.2213808

9. Hoffmann, A., Meyr, H., Leupers, R.: Architecture Exploration for Embedded Processors with LISA. Springer US, Boston (2002), http://link.springer.com/10.1007/978-1-4757-4538-2

10. McFarling, S., Hennesey, J.: Reducing the cost of branches. ACM SIGARCH Computer Architecture News 14(2), 396–403 (1986), http://dl.acm.org/citation.cfm?id=17407.17402

11. McKeeman, W.M.: Peephole optimization. Communications of the ACM 8(7), 443–444 (1965), http://dl.acm.org/citation.cfm?id=364995.365000

12. Med, M., Krall, A.: Instruction Set Encoding Optimization for Code Size Reduction. In: 2007 International Conference on Embedded Computer Systems: Architectures, Modeling and Simulation, pp. 9–17. IEEE (July 2007), http://ieeexplore.ieee.org/xpl/articleDetails.jsp?arnumber=4285728, http://www.cse.unt.edu/~sweany/CSCE6650/HANDOUTS/29.pdf

13. Tanenbaum, A.S., van Staveren, H., Stevenson, J.W.: Using Peephole Optimization on Intermediate Code. ACM Transactions on Programming Languages and Systems 4(1), 21–36 (1982), http://dl.acm.org/citation.cfm?id=357153.357155

14. Vahid, F., Stitt, G., Lysecky, R.: Warp Processing: Dynamic Translation of Binaries to FPGA Circuits. Computer 41(7), 40–46 (2008), http://ieeexplore.ieee.org/articleDetails.jsp?arnumber=4563878, http://www.inf.pucrs.br/~moraes/prototip/artigos/warp_processing.pdf

A Dataflow Inspired Programming Paradigm for Coarse-Grained Reconfigurable Arrays*

A. Niedermeier, Jan Kuper, and Gerard J.M. Smit

Computer Architecture for Embedded Systems Group
Department of Electrical Engineering, Mathematics and Computer Science
University of Twente, The Netherlands

Abstract. In this paper, we present a new approach towards programming coarse-grained reconfigurable arrays (CGRAs) in an intuitive, dataflow inspired way. Based on the observation that available CGRAs are usually programmed using C, which lacks proper support for instruction-level parallelism, we instead started from a dataflow perspective combined with a language that inherently supports parallel structures. Our programming paradigm decouples the local functionality of a core from the global flow of data, i.e. the kernels from the routing. We will describe the ideas of our programming paradigm and also the language and compiler itself. Our complete system, including the CGRA, the programming language and the compiler, was developed using Haskell, which leads to a complete, sound system. We finish the paper with the implementation of a number of algorithms using our system.

1 Motivation and Related Work

Many algorithms common in digital signal processing (DSP), like for example audio filtering, contain a high degree of instruction-level parallelism. To accelerate those algorithms, coarse-grained reconfigurable arrays (CGRAs) are often used due to their capability of large-scale parallelism. A CGRA is an array of small, configurable cores, often in combination with a general purpose processor for control operations. The cores in the CGRA usually contain an ALU and a small local memory.

Popular examples of CGRAs are MorphoSys (2000) [1], XPP (2003) [2], ADRES (2003) [3] and SmartCell (2010) [4]. Since the details of the mentioned CGRAs is out of scope of this paper, the reader is referred to the respective papers and to the surveys [5] and [6], where a good overview on CGRAs is given.

The above mentioned architectures (and also other CGRAs) have in common that they are programmed in a C-based approach. In our opinion, the choice of C for programming CGRAs is not an obvious one. Since C has been designed as a sequential language, it lacks intuitive support to express fine-grained parallelism.

Motivated by that, we developed a dataflow-inspired programming paradigm. In dataflow programming, an algorithm is represented as a directed graph [7].

---

* This research is conducted as part of the Sensor Technology Applied in Reconfigurable systems for sustainable Security (STARS) project (www.starsproject.nl)

D. Goehringer et al. (Eds.): ARC 2014, LNCS 8405, pp. 275–282, 2014.
© Springer International Publishing Switzerland 2014

The graph consists of *nodes* and *arcs*. The nodes represent the operators and are interconnected by *arcs*, which represent the dependencies between the nodes. The general idea of dataflow programming is to describe dependencies between operations instead of a sequence of instructions. Hereby, the structure of an algorithm is directly represented.

In an earlier paper [8], we presented a CGRA which is based on dataflow principles, both in the execution mechanism of the cores as well as in the configuration principle. In this paper, we present a programming language and compilation framework for this architecture.

The programming language itself is implemented as an embedded domain specific language (EDSL) in the functional programming language Haskell. This enables a designer to implement DSP applications in a concise and straightforward manner by using Haskell's higher order functions. As these functions have a notion of structure, all information on parallelism and flow of data is automatically contained in the resulting expressions.

2   Architecture

The architecture [8] for which we present our programming language and compilation belongs to the class of coarse-grained reconfigurable arrays (CGRA). It is an array of small, independent, reconfigurable cores, shown in Figure 1, the size of the array can be configured during design time.

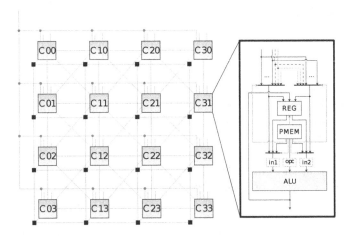

Fig. 1. Architecture

Each core in the architecture follows the rules of dataflow, i.e. as soon as all operands for a certain core are available, the configured operation is performed. Inside each core, an ALU is available, which can execute binary operations, i.e. addition, multiplication and the like. Furthermore, a local register file to store intermediate results and a storage for constants are available.

3 Programming Paradigm

For our programming paradigm, we adopt ideas from dataflow, such as the *firing rule* and the representation of an algorithm as a graph. Furthermore, we use finite state machines to extend the possibilities of pure dataflow notation.

On the conceptual level, we consider the configuration of our architecture on two different views: The *local view*, i.e. everything that is executed locally on one core, and the *global view*, which is the global flow of data through the array.

3.1 The Local View

Since it is difficult to describe iterations in pure dataflow notation [9], we decided to use a combination of state machines and dataflow notation. Iterations (or initial stages) are configured using state machines, the states itself are described using a dataflow graph. The transition conditions are determined by the number of iterations per state.

Figure 2 shows a high-level illustration of the local view. In Figure 2a, the dataflow graph is shown, in Figure 2b, the state machine.

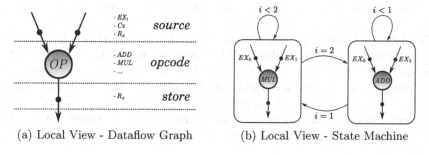

(a) Local View - Dataflow Graph   (b) Local View - State Machine

Fig. 2. Local View

The dataflow graph is defined in terms of

- **source** of each input (**EX**ternal input i, a **C**onstant value x, **R**egister x)
- **opcode** defining the current operation (**$ADD, MUL, ...$**)
- whether to **store** the result at **R**egister x

On the input arcs, a token indicates that a token is required on that arc to trigger the execution. On the output arc, a token indicates whether a token is produced or if the result is only stored locally inside the core (then, no token would be produced on the output arc).

The example state machine in Figure 2b shows a configuration of a core consisting of two states. The condition to transit between the states is defined by the number of iterations per state, indicated by the variable i on the arcs of the state machine. One iteration is defined as one firing of the dataflow graph of the current state. A core with this configuration would first perform a multiplication on two incoming token pairs, and then an addition on the next incoming token pair. In each state, it would produce an output token, but would not store the result in the internal register file.

3.2   The Global View

While the local view defines everything that happens inside a core, the global flow of data is out of the core's scope. A core only has the notion that an input can come from an external source, e.g. another core or an external input, but precisely from where is irrelevant. Consequently, for the flow of data a global dataflow scheme is required, i.e. the *global view*. The routing of the tokens is handled by the interconnection logic in the array.

4   Programming Language

In this section we present the specification of the programming language targeted at the architecture introduced in Section 2. We implemented our programming language as an Embedded Domain Specific Language (EDSL) as a recursive datatype in Haskell. Therefore, algorithms can be implemented directly using Haskell. As a consequence of implementing the EDSL as recursive datatype, the resulting expression *is* the abstract syntax tree (AST) of the expression that was specified. This means that the parser is "for free".

In Listing 1.1, the definition for the EDSL datatype is given. The names of the constructors hereby resemble their functionality. In line 1, the definition how to specify a constant number is given, line 2 specifies how a delay is defined, the definition in line 3 shows how the result from the previous clock cycle can be used (i.e. a feedback loop), line 4 represents an input where the string denotes and input stream and finally in line 5 the operation itself is defined. *Op* is a data constructor of the type *Expr* and indicates an operation, and *OpCode* defines the opcode.

```
data  Expr  =  Const  Number                        1
            |  DELAYED  Expr                         2
            |  PREV_RES                              3
            |  Input  String                         4
            |  Op  OpCode  Expr  Expr                5
                                                     6
data  OpCode  =  ADD  |  MUL  |  SUB  |  AND  ...    7
```

Listing 1.1. Recursive EDSL definition for an expression

To implement the graph defining the right state of the state machine in Figure 2b, a designer would write *Op ADD* (*Input "x"*) (*Input " y"*). To implement a multiplication with a constant value 5, one would write *Op MUL* (*Input "x"*) (*Const* 5). In the following section, we will illustrate in more detail how the proposed language can be used to construct more complex algorithms.

5   Workflow

In this section, we will describe the workflow of our system, i.e. all the required steps to implement an algorithm on our architecture using the herein presented framework.

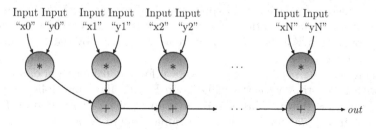

Fig. 3. Structure of the dot product

As illustrating example, we will use the *dot product*, i.e. the multiplication of two vectors, throughout this section. The dot product of two vectors x and y of length $N + 1$ is defined as $\sum_{i=0}^{N} x_i y_i$. The structure for the dot product of two vectors x and y is shown in Figure 3.

5.1   Implementing the Algorithm

The computation of the dot product contains two steps: 1. The two vectors have to be multiplied pair-wise, and 2. the results have to be accumulated. A straight-forward implementation of these two steps can be achieved by using the two higher-order functions *zipWith* and *foldl1* as shown in Listing 1.2.

```
vxvEDSL  x  y  =  out                              1
    where                                          2
        ms  =  zipWith  (Op MUL)  x  y             3
        out =  foldl1   (Op ADD)  ms               4
```

Listing 1.2. Implementation of the dot product in the EDSL

In line 1 of the code, the function name *vxv* and its arguments x and y, which are the two vectors to be multiplied, are defined, *out* is the resulting output. In line 3, the vectors are pair-wise multiplied which leads to the row of multipliers in Figure 3. Finally, in line 4, the results of the multiplications are accumulated, which leads to the row of adders in Figure 3. Please note that instead of the mathematical operators + and *, the constructors of the proposed embedded language are used, namely *Op ADD* and *Op MUL*, respectively. Also, at this point the expression *vxvEDSL* directly represents the abstract syntax tree (AST), since the EDSL was implemented as recursive datatype in Haskell as explained in Section 4.

5.2   Code Generation

In order to generate code for the hardware architecture, the compiler traverses through all nodes in the AST and generates the corresponding configuration code.

Each node in the AST is one of the five different possible cases given in Listing 1.1: 1. A constant, 2. a delayed expression, 3. a pointer to the previous result, 4. an input, or 5. an operation. Code is only directly generated for nodes that define an operation. All the other cases are used as inputs by the operation nodes and are handled there.

In Figure 4a, the resulting graph is shown for a multiplication of an external input with a constant with the value 2. In Figure 4b, a multiplication of two external inputs is shown. This is also the graph which is generated for the multiplications in the *dot product* of our example. Figure 4c shows the addition of two external inputs, as required for the additions in the *dot product*.

Figures 4d and 4e show two slightly more complex examples where either one input is delayed (*Op ADD (DELAYED x)y*) or where one of the operands is the previous result, thus forming a feedback loop (*Op ADD PREV_RES y*).

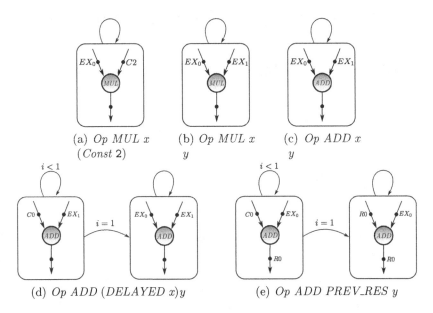

(a) *Op MUL x*
  (*Const* 2)

(b) *Op MUL x*
  y

(c) *Op ADD x*
  y

(d) *Op ADD (DELAYED x)y*

(e) *Op ADD PREV_RES y*

Fig. 4. Code generation

5.3   Mapping to the CGRA

To execute the expression on the CGRA, each node in the AST is mapped to one core using simulated annealing. The cost function is the distance between communicating nodes, i.e. the communication costs. After a mapping has been determined, the routing information is added to the configuration of each node which completes the configuration of the array.

The resulting mapping for the *dot product* maps one operator node on one core each, for the communication only p2p links are used, i.e. the network-on-chip is not required. This is an optimum mapping for our case, since we define the communication costs to be the cost function during the mapping step.

5.4   Evaluation

The previously presented usecase of the *dot product* was targeted towards a CGRA with 4x4 cores. Since our array is scalable, we implemented a number of test cases on a 4x4 array and on a 8x8 array to evaluate the usability of our compiler. The results are shown in Table 1.

For each of the implemented algorithm, the number of used nodes (and hence required cores in the architecture) and connections are shown. On the 4x4 array, we implemented an 8-tap FIR filter, the 8x8 dot product which we used in Section 5, and a 4 point FFT kernel. On the 8x8 array, we implemented a 32-tap FIR filter, a 32x32 dot product, an 8 point FFT kernel and an 8 point DCT kernel. For every test case, an optimum mapping was achieved, i.e. only p2p connections were used which ensures the highest throughput.

Table 1. Test cases for the different array sizes

array size	Algorithm	nodes	connections
	FIR8	15	14
4x4	*8x8 Dot Product*	15	14
	FFT4	16	16
	FIR32	63	62
8x8	*32x32 Dot Product*	63	62
	FFT8	60	80
	DCT8	40	50

6   Conclusions

We developed a complete framework for implementing, mapping and verifying DSP algorithms on a (previously presented) CGRA architecture. The framework consists of the CGRA itself, a programming paradigm and language, a compiler and a verification environment. All the parts of the framework were implemented using the functional programming Haskell.

The programming paradigm was developed in order to express instruction-level parallelism. Furthermore, we considered a DSP application to be composed of two views: The local view, which represents everything that happens within one core, and the global view, which represents the flow of data through the array. For our programming paradigm we adopted principles from dataflow and finite state machine (FSM) notations, which made it possible to express algorithms in the form of dataflow graphs with extended control.

For the implementation of the compiler, we used Haskell as a base, since it inherently has a notion of structure and, thus, can easily express parallelism and data dependencies. We implemented an embedded domain specific language (EDSL) as recursive datatype. In combination with higher order functions, this EDSL can be used to construct expressions that directly resemble the structure of a given algorithm. Consequently, the abstract syntax tree does not explicitly have to be extracted. We believe that by using a programming paradigm that closely resembles the structure of DSP algorithms, expressions can be implemented in a very intuitive and straight-forward manner.

References

1. Singh, H., Lee, M.-H., Lu, G., Kurdahi, F.J., Bagherzadeh, N., Chaves Filho, E.M.: MorphoSys: an integrated reconfigurable system for data-parallel and computation-intensive applications. IEEE Transactions on Computers 49(5), 465–481 (2000)
2. Baumgarte, V., Ehlers, G., May, F., Nückel, A., Vorbach, M., Weinhardt, M.: Pact xpp - a self-reconfigurable data processing architecture. The Journal of Supercomputing 26(2), 167–184 (2003)
3. Mei, B., Vernalde, S., Verkest, D., Man, H.D., Lauwereins, R.: ADRES: an architecture with tightly coupled VLIW processor and coarse-grained reconfigurable matrix. In: Cheung, P.Y.K., Constantinides, G.A. (eds.) FPL 2003. LNCS, vol. 2778, pp. 61–70. Springer, Heidelberg (2003)
4. Liang, C., Huang, X.: SmartCell: an energy efficient coarse-grained reconfigurable architecture for stream-based applications. EURASIP Journal on Embedded Systems 2009(1), 518–659 (2009) 00012
5. Hartenstein, R.: A decade of reconfigurable computing: a visionary retrospective. In: Proceedings of the Conference on Design, Automation and Test in Europe, DATE 2001, pp. 642–649. IEEE Press, Piscataway (2001)
6. Tehre, V., Kshirsagar, R.: Survey on coarse grained reconfigurable architectures. International Journal of Computer Applications 48(16), 1–7 (2012)
7. Davis, A., Keller, R.: Data flow program graphs. Computer 15(2), 26–41 (1982) 00374
8. Niedermeier, A., Kuper, J., Smit, G.: Dataflow-based reconfigurable architecture for streaming applications. In: 2012 International Symposium on System on Chip (SoC), pp. 1–4. IEEE (2012)
9. Gajski, D., Padua, D., Kuck, D., Kuhn, R.H.: A second opinion on data flow machines and languages. Computer 15(2), 58–69 (1982) 00232

Thread Shadowing: Using Dynamic Redundancy on Hybrid Multi-cores for Error Detection

Sebastian Meisner and Marco Platzner

Computer Engineering Research Group, University of Paderborn, Germany
{sebastian.meisner,platzner}@upb.de

Abstract. Dynamic thread duplication is a known redundancy technique for multi-cores. The approach duplicates a thread under observation for some time period and compares the signatures of the two threads to detect errors. Hybrid multi-cores, typically implemented on platform FPGAs, enable the unique option of running the thread under observation and its copy in different modalities, i.e., software and hardware. We denote our dynamic redundancy technique on hybrid multi-cores as *thread shadowing*. In this paper we present the concept of thread shadowing and an implementation on a multi-threaded hybrid multi-core architecture. We report on experiments with a block-processing application and demonstrate the overheads, detection latencies and coverage for a range of thread shadowing modes. The results show that trans-modal thread shadowing, although bearing long detection latencies, offers attractive coverage at a low overhead.

1 Introduction

Hybrid multi-cores combine instruction set based cores that are software-programmable with cores that are implemented in reconfigurable logic. Much like heterogeneous multi-cores, which typically combine different CPU cores, hybrid multi-cores are of interest for applications that exhibit parallelism at the thread-level and can benefit from mapping the threads to different core types in order to improve performance or energy efficiency. A main challenge for hybrid multi-cores is to create a software architecture that allows for a convenient integration of reconfigurable logic cores with software-programmable cores. In our work we leverage ReconOS [1], a programming model and runtime environment that extends multithreading to reconfigurable logic cores. In ReconOS, cores mapped to reconfigurable logic are turned into so-called hardware threads that can call an operating system running on the system's main CPU much like a software thread. In general, a ReconOS system can comprise several CPUs and reconfigurable hardware cores and run dynamically created software and hardware threads on their respective cores.

This work focuses on detecting errors at the thread level in single-chip hybrid multi-cores. Such errors arise when faults at the physical level are not masked and thus propagate up to the level of application threads. There are several causes for faults. Continuously shrinking microelectronic device structures lead to an

D. Goehringer et al. (Eds.): ARC 2014, LNCS 8405, pp. 283–290, 2014.
© Springer International Publishing Switzerland 2014

increase in components per chip area. This increase in functional density comes at the cost of reduced reliability due to increasing variations in device behavior and device degradation, as described by Borkar [2]. One particularly important source of unreliability is heat. Thermal hot spots and extensive temperature swings should be avoided since these effects accelerate aging which in turn leads to degradation [3] and, eventually, to total chip failure. Another and external cause for faults are single-event upsets [4]. Especially FPGAs, which are currently the main implementation platform for hybrid multi-cores, are vulnerable to single-event upsets since they store their configuration data in SRAM cells.

One traditional approach to detect faults is dual modular redundancy (DMR). DMR duplicates elements of a system and compares their results. This approach can be applied at hardware and software levels. At hardware level, the simplest form is lockstep execution [5]. A number of improvements over simple DMR have been presented to balance the trade-off between area/energy consumption and error detection rate [6,7,8]. At software level, DMR can be applied to threads or processes. Compared to hardware, DMR at the software level offers higher flexibility, but comes with the challenge of encapsulation, as all interactions of the thread or process with the environment have to be observed and compared. Works like [9] and [10] present prototypes for thread and process level DMR under Linux and POSIX, respectively.

The main contribution of this paper is the presentation and evaluation of *thread shadowing*, a thread-level error detection technique for hybrid multi-cores. Thread shadowing is a dynamic redundancy technique that duplicates (shadows) a running software or hardware thread for some time period. During shadowing, we compare the signatures of the two threads and detect an error if they deviate. The novel option unique to hybrid multi-cores is *trans-modal error detection*, i.e., hardware threads can shadow software threads and vice versa.

Allowing for dynamic redundancy across the hardware-software boundary opens up new potential for optimizing efficiency and overheads, as well as new ways of designing reliable systems. Thread shadowing eliminates the need for dedicated redundant cores and it can use idle cores of any modality. Additionally, error detection can be activated per thread either permanently or on a spot sample basis, which supports applications with mixed reliability requirements.

2   Shadowing Prototype Implementation

2.1   ReconOS and Shadowing Extensions

Our work leverages ReconOS [1], a programming model and runtime environment that extends multithreading to reconfigurable logic cores. ReconOS builds on a host operating system such as Linux or eCos and distinguishes between hardware threads and software threads. Both thread types, denoted as thread modalities, can call operating system functions to interact with other threads and the operating system kernel using well known programming objects such as semaphores, message boxes and shared memory. Figure 1 depicts an exemplary ReconOS system architecture comprising a main CPU, three reconfigurable

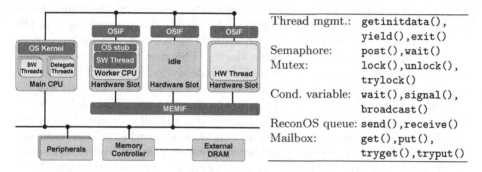

Thread mgmt.:	`getinitdata()`, `yield()`,`exit()`
Semaphore:	`post()`,`wait()`
Mutex:	`lock()`,`unlock()`, `trylock()`
Cond. variable:	`wait()`,`signal()`, `broadcast()`
ReconOS queue:	`send()`,`receive()`
Mailbox:	`get()`,`put()`, `tryget()`,`tryput()`

Fig. 1. Exemplary ReconOS architecture   **Fig. 2.** List of shadowed function calls

hardware slots, a memory controller and peripherals. Every hardware slot has two interfaces, an operating system interface (OSIF) for calling operating system functions and a memory interface (MEMIF) enabling direct access to the shared system memory. ReconOS uses a main CPU which runs an operating system kernel and user software threads. Hardware slots either accommodate hardware threads or worker CPUs that run additional software threads. Worker CPUs implement an operating system stub to embed their software thread into the multithreading environment. Hardware threads and software threads running on worker CPUs communicate with the operating system kernel by means of delegate threads. These delegates call operating system functions on behalf of their corresponding hardware threads or software threads on worker CPUs. Since ReconOS supports run-time reconfiguration, both thread types can be instantiated, loaded and started at run-time.

We have extended the ReconOS architecture and runtime system to monitor the calls listed in Figure 2 for thread synchronization, communication and management. We denote the original thread as *thread under observation* (TUO) and its duplicate as *shadow thread* (ST). The shadowing system is implemented in form of a user space library. The library substitutes each of the monitored functions with a version that wraps the original function and, in case shadowing is activated, implements function call tracing and comparison. At start-up, the runtime system creates all required STs and puts them to sleep state for later activation by the shadowing scheduler. While in our prototype this consumes some memory and, for hardware STs, a hardware slot, the ST activation time is greatly reduced. At runtime, the shadowing scheduler chooses a thread from the thread list to shadow.

2.2   Thread Signatures and Shadowing Schemes

As thread signature we use the sequence of OS calls and their parameters. Since in ReconOS, all OS calls issued by hardware threads and software threads on worker CPUs are relayed by delegate threads, it is sufficient to monitor delegate threads and software threads on the main CPU. The data structure for one OS call includes a pointer to the function name, the parameters, the return value and some meta data such as the lengths of data fields and a timestamp. For OS calls that involve a pointer to a block of writable memory, the shadowing system creates a copy of the memory block for the ST. This way, the ST gets a pristine copy of the input data that can be modified independently of the TUO.

In this paper, we report on two different shadowing schemes. The first scheme shadows n TUOs by another n STs, with the characteristics that all TUOs are of the same modality, i.e., software or hardware, and all STs are of the same modality, i.e., software or hardware, as well. This shadowing scheme basically doubles the number of required cores but runs for each thread a permanent copy and thus fault detection covers the complete runtime, which makes it suitable for SEU detection. The second shadowing scheme shadows n TUOs of one modality with only one S in a round-robin fashion. This scheme performs error detection on a spot-sample basis, but requires only one additional core, which makes it preferable for permanent fault detection, when single errors are acceptable. We have selected these two schemes for presentation in this paper since they represent interesting corner cases. Obviously, there a many more schemes with arbitrary modalities for the single TUOs and STs.

3   Experimental Evaluation

We have conducted experiments on a ReconOS implementation extended for thread shadowing running under Linux kernel version 2.6.37 on the Xilinx ML605 Evaluation Kit, which is equipped with a Virtex-6 LX240T FPGA. We have set up a static architecture with a MicroBlaze soft core as the main CPU, seven MicroBlaze worker CPUs for additional software threads and seven hardware slots for hardware threads. In the experiments shown in this section we use at most three worker cores and three hardware slots. The main CPU, the worker CPUs and all hardware slots have been clocked at 100 MHz. For testing, we have implemented a sorting application that sorts integers in 8 KiB blocks. The main application thread distributes the workload over several software and hardware sorting threads. A software sorting thread is able to sort data at a rate of 0.537 blocks/s; a hardware sorting thread sorts at a rate of 8.333 blocks/s. Therefore, using a hardware thread results in a speedup of 15.518. The number of software and hardware sorting threads used, as well as the number of blocks to be sorted are parameterized, but for the reported experiments we have fixed the number of blocks to 64. The sorting application communicates the data/results to/from the threads via ReconOS message queues which utilize only the OSIF (cmp. Figure 1). Since the shadowing system checks the OS call names *and* parameters, all input and output, including the sorted data, is checked for consistency.

Figure 3 shows the simplified main loop of a sorting thread with its operating system interactions. The first `receive()` call returns the number of integers to be sorted, while the second `receive()` call provides the actual data to be sorted. The sorted data is written back to the main thread via a `send()` call. Since the sorting application operates on blocks of data, there is actually no state

```
while (true)
{
  yield();
  receive(&recv_queue,
          &len, 4);
  if (len == UINT_MAX)
    { exit(); }
  receive(&recv_queue,
          buffer, len);
  /* sort buffer ... */
  send(&send_queue,
       buffer, len);
}
```

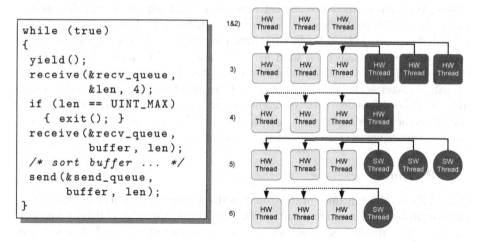

Fig. 3. Simplified main loop of the sorting thread

Fig. 4. Visualization of thread shadowing modes. Dark shapes are STs, light shapes are TUOs, and arrows indicate shadowing.

between the processing of consecutive blocks. Such application models are widespread, especially in the signal processing domain. The shadowing scheduler can deactivate/activate a thread at the yield() call issued at the beginning of the thread's main loop. Based on the two shadowing schemes described in Section 2.2 we have experimented with the following six different shadowing modes:

1. *Original:* Reference sorting application on ReconOS without shadowing support for baseline comparison.
2. *Shadowing Off:* The shadowing system is in place, but no ST is activated. This mode measures the overhead of the shadowing system, i.e., the tracing of operating system calls.
3. *Shadowing On:* Intra-modal shadowing for all threads, i.e., n hardware STs shadow n hardware TUOs or n software STs shadow n software TUOs, respectively, with $n = 1 \ldots 3$.
4. *Shadowing Round-robin:* Intra-modal shadowing for all threads with one ST switched on every yield() call in a round-robin fashion, i.e., one hardware ST shadows n hardware TUOs or one software ST shadows n software TUOs, respectively, with $n = 1 \ldots 3$.
5. *Shadowing On Trans-modal:* Trans-modal shadowing for all threads, i.e., n hardware STs shadow n software TUOs or n software STs shadow n hardware TUOs, respectively, with $n = 1 \ldots 3$.
6. *Shadowing Round-robin Trans-modal:* Trans-modal shadowing for all threads with one ST switched on every yield() call in a round-robin fashion, i.e., one software ST shadows n hardware TUOs or one hardware ST shadows n software TUOs, respectively, with $n = 1 \ldots 3$.

Figure 4 visualizes these modes of operation for the case that the TUOs are hardware threads and $n = 3$. All modes are symmetrical for software threads as

TUOs. We have verified the correct functionality of our shadowing implementation by modifying the source code of one hardware and one software thread to include an error that leads to a different thread OS call signature. These erroneous threads have been used as TUOs and STs in varying configurations to successfully test the shadowing system. In the following, we report on three measured metrics: the slowdown of the TUOs inflicted by using thread shadowing, the time difference between identical OS calls of TUO and ST, which we call the error detection latency, and the shadowing coverage. All data presented has been averaged over 10 runs of the application.

3.1   Runtimes

Table 1 shows the runtimes of the different shadowing modes for different system configurations, i.e., number of software and hardware threads. The data has been normalized to mode "Original" for the given number of TUOs. Using software TUOs, the absolute runtimes for sorting 64 data blocks in the "Original" mode decrease from $119.1\,s$, over $59.94\,s$ to $41.46\,s$ when going from one to three cores. Similarly, using hardware TUOs the absolute runtimes in the "Original" mode decrease from $7.73\,s$, over $4.24\,s$ to $3.19\,s$.

Table 1. Normalized runtimes of the sorting application under all shadowing modes over different numbers of software and hardware TUOs

Thread Count	Software TUOs			Hardware TUOs		
	1	2	3	1	2	3
Original	1.00	1.00	1.00	1.00	1.00	1.00
Shadowing Off	1.00	1.00	1.00	1.02	1.02	1.01
Shadowing On	1.00	1.01	1.01	1.06	1.09	1.13
Shadowing Round-robin	1.00	1.00	1.00	1.07	1.03	1.02
Shadowing On Trans-modal	1.00	1.01	1.01	15.22	13.81	12.50
Shadowing RR Trans-modal	1.00	1.01	1.01	15.07	1.72	1.82

The data for software TUOs in Table 1 shows that the overhead posed by the shadowing scheme and the slowdowns for different shadowing modes are negligible with at most 1%. The data for hardware TUOs shows that the overhead posed by the shadowing system alone (Shadowing Off) is at most 2% and thus negligible. For intra-modal shadowing, i.e., hardware STs shadow hardware TUOs, the sort application is slowed down by 13% at maximum for three TUOs for mode "Shadowing On". In mode "Shadowing Round-robin" the slowdown reduces to 2% for three TUOs. As expected for the given application, trans-modal shadowing where software STs shadow hardware TUOs severely affects runtimes due to the speed difference between software and hardware threads, e.g., 1422% for shadowing one hardware thread by one software thread. In the trans-modal round-robin shadowing mode, the hardware TUOs are shadowed by one software thread only for a fraction of the overall runtime. Hence, the slowdown decreases with the number of hardware threads down to 82% for three TUOs.

3.2 Latencies and Coverage

To determine the error detection latency, we measure the time difference between two identical operating system calls of the TUO and the ST. Since our shadowing scheme is symmetrical with respect to TUO and ST roles, we report on positive values for the detection latency, where an ST lags behind the TUO, as well as negative values, where an ST actually called the operating system function earlier than its TUO. As our measurements show, the results differ significantly between intra-modal and trans-modal shadowing modes. While for intra-modal shadowing the latencies lie between $-0.35\,ms$ and $2.92\,ms$, trans-modal shadowing results in latencies increased by orders of magnitude, lying between $-578.24\,ms$ and $580\,ms$. These increased latencies are easily explained by the differences in execution speed of hardware and software implementations.

Table 2. Average percentage of shadowed application cycles per thread in round-robin modes 4 and 6

Thread Count	Software TUOs			Hardware TUOs		
	1	2	3	1	2	3
Shadowing Round-robin	100%	31.09%	17.81%	100%	31.09%	17.97%
Shadowing RR Trans-modal	100%	31.25%	17.66%	100%	4.69%	6.25%

In the round-robin shadowing modes, the TUOs are not shadowed for the complete runtime. In order to quantify the coverage of shadowing, we measure the number of application cycles a TUO is actually shadowed and relate it to the overall number of the application cycles a TUO executes. In our sorting application, one application cycle consists of one iteration of the while-loop in Figure 3. Table 2 shows the percentage of shadowed application cycles. Obviously, if only one TUO is to be shadowed by one ST in a round-robin fashion the coverage is 100%. With an increasing number of TUOs shadowed by one ST in a round-robin fashion the coverage decreases. While one would expect that with n TUOs the coverage decreases to $\frac{1}{n}$, the measured coverage is lower since de-attaching and attaching STs to TUOs is always synchronized to the TUOs `yield()` operating system calls, thus adding a synchronization delay when changing the TUO. Another result is that hardware TUOs in trans-modal round-robin shadowing mode have a rather low coverage of around 5%. Since hardware TUOs are slowed down by their software STs, every other non-shadowed TUO is able to complete a lot of application cycles in this time period, thereby decreasing the number of potential application cycles for shadowing.

4 Conclusion and Future Work

In this paper we have presented thread shadowing, our thread-level dynamic redundancy technique for hybrid multi-cores that allows not only for intra-modal but also for the novel technique of trans-modal error detection. We have discussed its implementation on a ReconOS system. Our multi-core setup allows us to systematically experiment with different shadowing schemes and determine their overhead, application slowdown, detection latency, and achieved coverage. In this paper we have studied several shadowing schemes for a sorting application and we have identified two interesting configurations: First, if one can accept the high cost for doubling the number of cores intra-modal shadowing for all threads results in with full coverage, minimal slow down and low error detection latency. A reasonable alternative that requires only one additional core is intra-modal round-robin shadowing at a somewhat reduced coverage. Second, the novel technique of trans-modal shadowing is an attractive option when hardware threads shadow software threads. Here, especially the trans-modal round-robin shadowing mode is very appealing since often a hardware thread implementation will be fast enough to shadow a number of software threads.

Future work will include experimenting with more applications, studying alternative thread signatures and setting up fault injection experiments to quantitatively characterize the effectivity of the different thread shadowing modes.

References

1. Lübbers, E., Platzner, M.: ReconOS: Multithreaded Programming for Reconfigurable Computers. ACM Transactions on Embedded Computing Systems (TECS) 9(1) (October 2009)
2. Borkar, S.: Designing Reliable Systems from Unreliable Components: The Challenges of Transistor Variability and Degradation. IEEE MICRO, 10–16 (November/December 2005)
3. Stott, E.A., Wong, J.S., Sedcole, P., Cheung, P.Y.: Degradation in FPGAs: Measurement and Modelling. In: Proceedings of the 18th Annual ACM/SIGDA International Symposium on Field Programmable Gate Arrays. FPGA 2010, pp. 229–238. ACM, New York (2010)
4. Lesea, A., Drimer, S., Fabula, J., Carmichael, C., Alfke, P.: The Rosetta Experiment: Atmospheric Soft Error Rate Testing in Differing Technology FPGAs. IEEE Transactions on Device and Materials Reliability 5(3), 317–328 (2005)
5. IBM: PowerPC 750GX Lockstep Facility. Application Note (March 2008)
6. Austin, T.: DIVA: A Reliable Substrate for Deep Submicron Microarchitecture Design. In: Proceedings. 32nd Annual International Symposium on Microarchitecture, MICRO-32, pp. 196–207 (1999)
7. Vadlamani, R., Zhao, J., Burleson, W., Tessier, R.: Multicore Soft Error Rate Stabilization using Adaptive Dual Modular Redundancy. In: Design, Automation Test in Europe Conference Exhibition (DATE), pp. 27–32 (March 2010)
8. Rodrigues, R., Koren, I., Kundu, S.: An Architecture to Enable Life Cycle Testing in CMPs. In: 2011 IEEE International Symposium on Defect and Fault Tolerance in VLSI and Nanotechnology Systems (DFT), pp. 341–348 (October 2011)
9. Mushtaq, H., Al-Ars, Z., Bertels, K.: A User-level Library for Fault Tolerance on Shared Memory Multicore Systems. In: 2012 IEEE 15th International Symposium on Design and Diagnostics of Electronic Circuits Systems (DDECS), pp. 266–269 (April 2012)
10. Shye, A., Blomstedt, J., Moseley, T., Reddi, V., Connors, D.: PLR: A Software Approach to Transient Fault Tolerance for Multicore Architectures. IEEE Transactions on Dependable and Secure Computing 6(2), 135–148 (2009)

Diffusion-Based Placement Algorithm for Reducing High Interconnect Demand in Congested Regions of FPGAs

Ali Asghar and Husain Parvez

Karachi Institute of Economics and Technology
Korangi Creek, 75190, Karachi, Pakistan
{ali.asghar,husain.parvez}@pafkiet.edu.pk

Abstract. An FPGA has a finite routing capacity due to which a fair number of highly dense circuits fail to map on a slightly under-resourced architecture. The high-interconnect demand in the congested regions is not met by the available resources as a result of which the circuit becomes un-routable for that particular architecture. In this paper we present a new placement approach which is based on a natural process called Diffusion. Our placer attempts to minimize the routing congestion by evenly disseminating the interconnect demand across an FPGA chip. For the 20 MCNC benchmark circuits, our algorithm reduced the channel width for 6 circuits. The results showed on average 11% reduction in standard deviation of interconnect usage at an expense of an average 5% penalty on wire length. Maximum channel width gain of 17% was also observed.

1 Introduction

With every passing year the logic density inside a chip increases approximately following Moore's Law, which makes more and more complex problems solvable and applications realizable. But with these advancements, the efficiency of CAD tools to map and optimize these new applications is decreasing. These highly dense circuits introduce new kind of challenges for CAD tool designers; especially longer run-time of algorithms, higher power dissipation and inhomogeneous heat distribution are of primary concern.

In this paper we present a new congestion driven placement approach that attempts to reduce the variations in interconnect usage via diffusion. The major contribution of this work is a new placement cost function which pays attention to both wirelength and congestion.

Diffusion is a natural transport mechanism under the influence of which particles from a region of higher concentration move towards a region of lower concentration. The diffusion of a dye in water, the distribution of heat in a metal plate and the spreading of gas molecules in a room are all examples of diffusion.

In our case, the regions with high-interconnect demand act as high concentration regions while the surrounding regions with relatively low-interconnect

D. Goehringer et al. (Eds.): ARC 2014, LNCS 8405, pp. 291–297, 2014.
© Springer International Publishing Switzerland 2014

usage act as low concentration regions. Hence a concentration gradient exists between the two regions due to which diffusion takes place. During the diffusion process, logic blocks with high-interconnect demand are moved towards regions of relatively low-interconnect demand. Consequently, the variations in interconnect demand are reduced and a solution with better routability is produced.

The remainder of this paper is organized as follows: In Sect. 2, we review some prior research work in the domain of congestion driven placers along with some other techniques which have been used to reduce high interconnect variations. In Sect. 3, we propose our diffusion based placement algorithm and introduce the cost function used in this placer along with some techniques used to improve the run-time of our placer. In Sect. 4, we present the experimental results, while Sect. 5 cover the conclusion and future work.

2   Background and Previous Work

In the standard CAD flow for FPGA, synthesis and technology mapping are followed by clustering. In clustering, LEs are grouped together on the basis of connectivity of the mapped netlist to form configurable logic blocks (CLBs).

The clustering stage is followed by placement in which the clusters are placed onto the fixed array of CLBs. The cost function used by the VPR's placement algorithm [1] is wirelength driven i.e. it attempts to optimize the total wirelength of the current placement. The total wirelength is estimated on the basis of a semi-perimeter bounding box metric using the following equation:

$$Wiring\_Cost = \sum_{i=1}^{N} q(i) \cdot (bb_x(i) + bb_y(i)) \tag{1}$$

where N is the total number of nets, $bb_x(i)$ and $bb_y(i)$ are the horizontal and vertical span of the net i. $q(i)$ is a compensation factor for nets with more than three terminals [2].

To reduce high interconnect variation or congestion; a placement algorithm must pay attention to the routability of the final design. The semi-perimeter bounding box metric used by VPR's placement algorithm does not address this issue because a semi-perimeter based cost function brings the CLBs as close as possible unaware of the routing resources available in the target architecture. Such a placement could result in a large number of nets getting restricted to a relatively small area of the chip generating regions with high interconnect demand which in some cases exceeds the resources available in the architecture. To address these issues the authors of [10] have presented a congestion driven placer which considers the effect of overlapping bounding boxes. A congestion coefficient is generated from a congestion map which indicates the number of bounding boxes or nets which overlap each CLB. This coefficient is then multiplied with the cost function in (1) which penalizes the moves resulting in congestion.

Another congestion driven placement approach was presented in [8] which uses the well-known Rent's rule to estimate the routing requirements of the design. A novel approach for the reduction of high interconnect demand [9] is to iteratively perform re-clustering until a target channel width constraint is met.

The approach used in this paper for reducing congestion i.e. diffusion based placement has been applied in placement algorithms for ASICs. The authors of [7] used diffusion to overcome a very critical post-placement design closure issue called Legalization.

Jaffari and Anis [3] applied the concept of diffusion to address the uneven heat distribution problem in an FPGA by targeting thermal uniformity as the main objective function. The proposed placer tool uses a simulated annealing engine with a weighted common driver cost function to account for the issues of wirelength and performance requirements. The CLBs with high temperature are moved away from each other in such a way that the overall thermal profile of the FPGA smooth out. The cost function used in this placer is similar to the wirelength cost function of simulated annealing in which a negative cost is desirable for the move to get accepted. This work shows a significant improvement in standard deviation (up to 51%) and average reduction (up to 73%) in temperature with a 4% penalty in wirelength and delay.

3   Implementation

Our proposed idea focuses on improving (i.e. reducing) the standard deviation of interconnect usage, which attempts to reduce the peak channel occupancy of a congested region, this may later reduce the overall channel width of the architecture. Our congestion driven placer strives to reduce the interconnect variations by evenly spreading the routing demand across the entire chip. We have adopted the same diffusion based placement technique as proposed in [3]. However, instead of using the technique for reducing high temperature spots, as done in [3], we have used the technique for reducing high-interconnect usage. Moreover, unlike the work done in [9], size of FPGA is not increased.

Our placer uses a weighted common driver cost function similar to the one used in [3] except for the fact that the common driver weight in [3] corresponds to thermal cost extracted from the temperature profile of an FPGA while in our case it corresponds to the occupancy (defined in section 3.1) of each CLB which we call the congestion cost.

3.1   The Cost Function

The equation for calculating the congestion cost is:

$$Congestion\_Cost = \sum_{i=0}^{n}(\sum_{j=1}^{n} \frac{c_i \cdot c_j}{r_{ij}}) \qquad (2)$$

where n is the number of CLBs used in the FPGA, c_i and c_j are the occupancy of the ith and j^{th} CLB while r_{ij} is the distance between the ith and j^{th} CLB, c_i and c_j are obtained from a pre-placed and routed file which we call *Congestion File*, this file contains the occupancy of all the used CLBs. The term *occupancy* refers to the number of connections a CLB has with the adjacent routing channels.

The cost function of our placer incorporates both the wirelength cost obtained from (1) and the congestion cost.

$$\Delta Cost = \alpha \left(\frac{\Delta Wiring\_Cost}{Wiring\_Cost} \right) + (\beta) \left(\frac{\Delta Congestion\_Cost}{Congestion\_Cost} \right) \tag{3}$$

where α is the weight assigned to wiring cost and

$$\beta = 1 - \alpha$$

is the common driver weight assigned to congestion cost. The formula for calculating $\Delta Wiring\_Cost$ is same as the one implemented in VPR framework [1]. The calculation details for $\Delta Congestion\_Cost$ are discussed in 3.3.

3.2   Flow Overview

Our placement flow has three stages as described below.

1. First a routine placement is performed using the conventional wirelength driven cost function (1). Routing is performed using PathFinder routing algorithm [5].
2. After the completion of placement and routing, a congestion file is generated that contains the occupancy of all used CLBs.
3. Now the placement is performed again using the weighted common driver cost function (3), the values for c_i and c_j are obtained from the generated congestion file. Routing is again performed.

3.3   Improvements in Run-Time

The complexity of the congestion cost function is quadratic in nature which makes the run-time of our placer un-scalable for large designs. To improve the run-time of our placer we have made following attempts:

3.3.1   Calculating the Incremental Change in Congestion Cost

Instead of calculating the overall (global) congestion cost we calculate the change in congestion cost. Change in congestion cost which results when a block is moved or swapped is added to the global congestion cost which should produce the same result as computing the overall congestion cost.

The equation for calculating the $\Delta Congestion\_Cost$ is:

$$\Delta Congestion\_Cost = \sum_{i=0}^{n}(c_i \cdot c_j)(\frac{1}{r_{ij(new)}} - \frac{1}{r_{ij(old)}}) \qquad (4)$$

where n is the number of used CLBs in the FPGA, c_i is the occupancy of the logic block which is moved, c_j represents the occupancy of all the other logic blocks, $r_{ij(old)}$ and $r_{ij(new)}$ represent the distance between the ith and j^{th} CLBs before and after the move. For $\Delta Congestion\_Cost$ to be negative in (3) the distance between the congested logic blocks should increase.

3.3.2 Creating a Priority Queue

The incremental $\Delta Congestion\_Cost$ improves the run-time considerably but still suffers from long run-time penalty when the number of used logic elements is very high. To counter this problem we have made a priority queue in which CLBs are arranged in ascending order according to their occupancies. Now instead of computing the $\Delta Congestion\_Cost$ for all used CLBs at each move, only the CLBs present in the priority queue are considered because in (4) there is a greater probability of acceptance for the moves which involve logic elements having high values of occupancy. Hence, the idea of considering only a percentage of highly congested elements is justifiable.

4 Results

To fully check the functionality and performance of our proposed placer we have performed rigorous testing on all the 20 MCNC benchmarks circuits [6] by varying different key parameters which include:

1. Common driver weight.
2. Top percentage of CLBs inserted in the priority queue (discussed in 3.3.1).
3. Varying the cluster size (for $N=1$ and $N=4$).

Note: The FPGA architecture used for experiments consists of clusters with size $N=1$ and 4, LUT size k=4. For all the benchmark circuits [6] the FPGA logic utilization is close to 100%. The architecture is based on directional wires which are prevalent in the modern commercial architectures due to their better area and delay performance [4].

During experimentation we empirically tested different combinations of driver weight and percentage of CLBs. From our experiments we observed that setting the driver weight between 0.1–0.2 while inserting top 15–20% CLBs in the priority queue generates optimum results.

We compare our results with the VPR's placement algorithm. The results from VPR are obtained by running it in the wirelength driven mode for placement and routing.

Figure 1 shows the values of standard deviation in interconnect demand, wirelength and channel width required for the 20 MCNC benchmark circuits normalized to the values obtained from VPR's placement algorithm. For all the

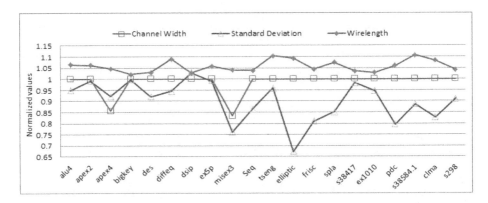

Fig. 1. Comparative results of Channel width, Standard deviation and Wirelength for diffusion based placement algorithm normalized to the respective results from VPR's placement algorithm for cluster size $N=1$

20 benchmark circuits common driver weight was set equal to 0.1 while top 20 percent CLBs were considered (i.e. inserted in the priority queue).

The results show on average ~11% reduction in standard deviation of interconnect demand at an expense of an average ~5% penalty on wirelength. The highest gain (reduction) in standard deviation was observed for elliptic (~32%) and misex3 (~24%). For misex3 a gain of (~17%) was also achieved in channel width, which further justifies the idea that significant gains can be achieved in channel width by reducing standard deviation.

Figure 2 shows the results obtained when the cluster size is increased to N=4, the same parameters (shown in Fig. 1) are normalized to the results from VPR. The common driver weight was again set to 0.1 while top 15 percent CLBs were inserted in the priority queue.

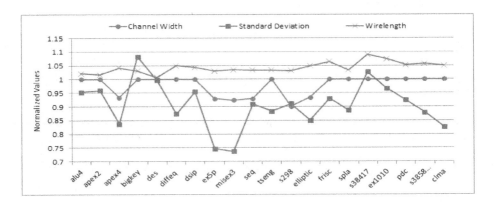

Fig. 2. Comparative results of Channel width, Standard deviation and Wirelength for diffusion based placement algorithm normalized to the respective results from VPR's placement algorithm for cluster size $N=4$

The results on average show ~10% decrease in standard deviation of interconnect demand at an expense of ~4% penalty on wirelength. The channel width was reduced for 6 benchmark circuits with the highest gain in channel width achieved for s298 (~10%) at an expense of ~3% wiring penalty. One important thing to note is that the routing channel width required by our placement approach never exceeds VPR which proves its stability.

5 Conclusion and Future Work

In this paper we have proposed a new diffusion based placement algorithm which attempts to minimize variations in interconnect demand to achieve gains in channel width. The average results for the 20 MCNC benchmark circuits show ~11% decrease in standard deviation with ~5% penalty in wiring cost. The highest gain in channel width was observed to be ~17% with only ~4% penalty in wiring cost. The average results can be further improved once this technique is applied to the circuits with inherent congestion as used in [9]. Our router lacks a delay estimator. We plan to implement it and measure the delay penalties caused by the increase in wiring cost. A proper scaling of the run-time is also needed, which becomes a critical parameter when the circuit to be mapped is fairly dense.

References

1. Betz, V., Rose, J.: VPR: A New Packing Placement and Routing Tool for FPGA research. In: International Workshop on FPGA, pp. 213–222 (1997)
2. Cheng, C.: RISA: Accurate and Efficient Placement Routability Modeling. In: ICCAD, pp. 690–695 (1994)
3. Jaffari, J., Anis, M.: Thermal Driven Placement for Island-style MTCMOS FPGAs. Journal of Computers, 24–30 (April 2008)
4. Lemieux, G., Lee, E., Tom, M., Yu, A.: Directional and Single-Driver Wires in FPGA Interconnect. In: ICFPT (2004)
5. McMurchie, L., Ebeling, C.: Pathfinder: A Negotiation-Based Performance-Driven Router for FPGAs. In: Proc. FPGA (1995)
6. MCNC. LGSynth93 benchmark suite. Microelectronics Centre of North Carolina, Tech. Report (1993)
7. Pan, D.Z., Alpert, C.J.: Diffusion based placement migration with application on Legalization. In: ICCAD (December 2007)
8. Parthasarathy, G., Marek-Sadowska, M., Mukherjee, A., Singh, A.: Interconnect Complexity-Aware FPGA Placement Using Rent's Rule. In: International Workshop on System-Level Interconnect, pp. 115–121 (2001)
9. Tom, M., Leong, D., Lemieux, G.: Un/Do Pack: Re-clustering of large system-on-chip designs with interconnect variation for low-cost FPGAs. In: ICCAD, pp. 680–687 (2009)
10. Zhuo, Y., Li, H., Mohanty, S.P.: A congestion driven placement algorithm for FPGA synthesis. In: FPL (2006)

GPU vs FPGA: A Comparative Analysis for Non-standard Precision

Umar Ibrahim Minhas, Samuel Bayliss, and George A. Constantinides

Department of Electrical and Electronic Engineering
Imperial College London
South Kensington Campus, London SW7 2AZ
umar.minhas12@imperial.ac.uk

Abstract. FPGAs and GPUs are increasingly used in a range of high performance computing applications. When implementing numerical algorithms on either platform, we can choose to represent operands with different levels of accuracy. A trade-off exists between the numerical accuracy of arithmetic operators and the resources needed to implement them. Where algorithmic requirements for numerical stability are captured in a design description, this trade-off can be exploited to optimize performance by using high-accuracy operators only where they are most required. Support for half and double-double floating point representations allows additional flexibility to achieve this. The aim of this work is to study the language and hardware support, and the achievable peak performance for non-standard precisions on a GPU and an FPGA. A compute intensive program, matrix-matrix multiply, is selected as a benchmark and implemented for various different matrix sizes. The results show that for large-enough matrices, GPUs out-perform FPGA-based implementations but for some smaller matrix sizes, specialized FPGA floating-point operators for half and double-double precision can deliver higher throughput than implementation on a GPU.

Keywords: GPU, FPGA, High Performance Computing (HPC), Non-standard Precision, Half Precision, Double-double Precision.

1 Introduction

Over the past three decades, improvements in semiconductor process technology have delivered an exponential increase, over time, in the number of transistors that can be economically manufactured on a single silicon die. Until recently, each shrink in process technology was accompanied by a reduction of supply voltage in line with scaling rules established by Dennard et al.[1]. In recent process technologies, where leakage power dominates, higher transistor density has been accompanied by reductions in energy-efficiency. The industry response to this has been a shift to multi-core parallel processing.

In the world of High Performance Computing (HPC), this has meant an increase in the use of specialised parallel architectures such as Graphic Processing

D. Goehringer et al. (Eds.): ARC 2014, LNCS 8405, pp. 298–305, 2014.
© Springer International Publishing Switzerland 2014

Units (GPUs) and Field Programmable Gate Arrays (FPGAs) in heterogeneous supercomputers to achieve energy-efficient computation.

Numerical Analysts continually seek to improve the accuracy of numerical approximation under the constraint of finite arithmetic precision. For floating point computation on both GPUs and FPGAs, there is a trade-off between the resource utilization and precision of arithmetic primitives. GPUs commonly contain specialized units for computation on single and double precision floating-point operands and FPGAs contain hardened DSP primitives which may be composed into floating point units supporting a variety of different precisions. Existing studies show that the area, power and delay of floating point operations is increased when double precision operators are used in place of single precision operators. However very little existing work seeks to answer the question of how to efficiently implement a wider range of different precisions on both FPGAs and GPUs. The unique contributions of this paper are :

- An investigation into how half (16-bit) and double-double (128-bit) precision floating point operations can be efficiently implemented on both GPUs and FPGAs.
- A comparison of the performance achievable by GPUs and FPGAs for half and double-double precision computations.

Our hope is that this can be used to guide future work on 'heterogeneous' computing. This will allow numerical analysts to efficiently implement high-precision at the points where it is needed in a computation, and optimize for power and throughput in areas where it can be safely reduced.

2   Methodology

In this section we provide an overview of the equipment and benchmark used for our experiments. We follow this in Section 3 with a deeper look at the GPU and FPGA implementations and report comparative performance in Section 4.

2.1   Equipment

For these experiments, the NVidia Tesla C1060 [2] has been selected as an exemplary GPU architecture. The Tesla range of products is purposely designed for parallel high performance computing and GPGPU programming. The C1060 is implemented in a 55nm process and has hardware support for IEEE-754 compliant single and double precision data-types. It has 240 streaming processor cores running at 1.3GHz. These cores are clustered together in groups of 8 as SIMD processors, with those 8 cores sharing a 16KByte local memory. Either OpenCL or CUDA APIs can be used for programming, expressing computation as explicitly parallel kernels for offload to SIMD processors within the GPU.

We have selected a Xilinx Virtex-6 [3] FPGA (XC6VLX195T) for this comparison study. This device is implemented in a 40nm process and our synthesis scripts targeted a 250MHz clock rate for each implementation. It was programmed using RTL design-entry incorporating floating-point cores from Xilinx Coregen[4] and FloPoCo[5].

2.2 Benchmark and Metrics

Matrix-Matrix multiplication has been chosen as a benchmark algorithm for this work. It forms a core component of many numerical algorithms and the cornerstone of the LINPACK benchmarks. For input matrices of size $n \times n$, the computational complexity of a naïve matrix-matrix multiplication algorithm varies as $O(n^3)$, exceeding the communications requirement which scales as $O(n^2)$. This means that for large-enough matrices, we can be sure that the algorithm performance is bounded by the computational capabilities of our two platforms. We measure the performance of our applications by counting the throughput in FLOPs (floating-point operations per second). Both peak power and total energy consumption are also useful metrics in large HPC environments, but a comparison of these lies outside the scope of this work.

3   Implementation

In this section, we consider how to design an efficient implementation of a matrix-matrix multiplication on GPUs and FPGAs using half and double-double precision arithmetic operands. Section 3.1 and Section 3.2 demonstrate how this can be achieved on a GPU and FPGA platform respectively. We then follow this in Section 4 with a performance comparison.

3.1   GPU Implementation

Many optimized GPU implementations exist. We have selected the SGEMM implementation from [6] which was distributed in early versions of the CUBLAS [7] library. The Tesla C1060 GPU does not have dedicated support for *computation* using half-precision data types. We instead implement these using native single-precision floating-point units. However, we can still exploit reduced-precision operands to improve performance by improving the storage density of operands in global and local memories. Where the asymptotic compute bounds are not reached, we would expect this to deliver an improvement in performance. In global-memory, CUDA stores half-precision operands as `unsigned short` and provides interfaces via `__half2float()` and `__float2half()` intrinsics [8]. These conversions are hardware-accelerated single-cycle GPU operations.

Neither CUDA nor the GPU architecture provide hardware support for double-double precision operations. Researchers have built libraries for use of double-double precision [9][10] based on underlying double precision primitives. We chose a library based on [9] for our experiments. The library stores double-double precision numbers in an abstract data type and provides functions for arithmetic operations using double-double precision based on the IEEE-754 standard. A high accuracy double-double addition requires 16 basic double-precision operations and a multiplication requires 3 basic and 4 fused multiply-add double-precision operations.

The library only supports double-double precision operations on the GPU (not on the host processor), therefore numbers are transferred to the device using double-precision and then transformed to double-double precision using a library function. Since a double-double number was represented as a struct of two double precision numbers and additional temporary numbers were used for mathematical operations, the additional register pressure means computation must spill into local memory within each GPU multiprocessor. This has an impact on performance that is explored in Section 4.

3.2   FPGA Implementation

Current FPGAs do not include hardened floating-point units. Instead floating points units are constructed using a combination of hardened DSP-block primitives and LUT logic. We have used floating-point cores from two vendors to implement our experiments. Xilinx LogiCORE IP [4] (Version 5.0) exploits the low-level architectural details of Xilinx FPGA fabric to provide high quality floating-point operators. For precision beyond 80 bits, arithmetic operators generated by FloPoCo [5] were used. FloPoCo does not offer as wide a range of options as Xilinx IP cores for trading-off latency and resource usage but allows us to generate cores with a wider range of precisions. All the operators selected were fully pipelined.

In our experiments, we have aimed to maximize the design throughput by targeting full utilization of the FPGA. To ensure this, we ran preliminary experiments to calculate how many adders and multipliers would fit on the selected FPGA. For matrix-matrix multiplication of square matrices of order $n \times n$ (where n is a power of 2), a naïve algorithm requires n multipliers and $n - 1$ adders. After having an estimate of resources used by each precision's arithmetic operators, the next step in the design process was to divide up the total available resources on the FPGA and find the approximate number of arithmetic units that can be implemented.

For matrix-matrix multiplication of large matrices, blocking was used to divide up the matrix. The block size should be small enough to be stored on the on-chip RAM but large enough to hide external memory latency. A moderate size of 64×64 was chosen that suits both conditions. However, for this section it is assumed that all the data is already stored in on-chip Block RAM for multiplying 64x64 matrix and the results are to be stored in the same memory as well. A discussion of more realistic memory architecture can be found in [11] but for large enough matrices, the throughput of calculations on individual 64×64 blocks should limit performance.

The FPGA logic utilization supports an implementation of 2^n multipliers and $2^n - 1$ adders for a particular precision. This means, a block of 2^n row elements and 2^n column elements can all be multiplied in parallel. A binary reduction tree is then used to produce each element of the output matrix.

4   Results

In this section, we first consider the performance of different numerical precisions on each separate platform. We follow this with a comparison of the relative performance achievable on an FPGA or GPU when deploying different numerical precisions.

For the GPU platform, Figure 1 shows the relative performance using each different precision. For each precision, the vertical-axis shows the number of floating point operations which can be completed each second (in GFLOPs). In all precisions, where large enough matrices are multiplied, the problem is compute-bound by the throughput of the individual floating-point operators. This throughput varies for each precision with double-precision calculations achieving approximately 2.3× lower throughput than single-precision operators (200GFLOPs vs 85GFLOPs).

The double-double precision computation implemented on the GPU platform achieves fewer than 8GFLOPs, approximately 11× slower than the double precision computation. This is in line with predictions since each double-double operation requires 7 double-precision operators and each addition requires 16 basic double precision operations. The half-precision floating point results deliver on our expectation that when compute-bound, they mirror the single-precision results.

Each different precision becomes compute-bound at a different matrix size. This reflects the different memory-system overheads for each implementation. Curiously, the half-precision does not deviate from the single-precision results. This indicates that reduced-precision data storage has not delivered significant benefits in improving memory-throughput. An interesting comparison would be to compare these results with those generated using different matrix-blocking

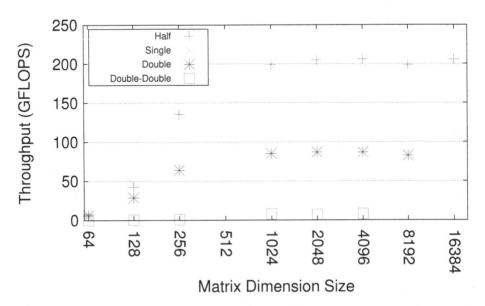

Fig. 1. Comparison of GPU performance using different matrix sizes and operand precisions

Table 1. Logic utilization for FPGA implementations with varying precisions

Logic Utilization	Half	Single	Double	Dbl-dbl
Number of Slice Registers	35%	61%	43%	32%
Number of Slice LUTs	56%	92%	66%	82%
Number of Block RAM/FIFO	83%	83%	55%	27%
Number of DSP48E1s	80%	60%	100%	87%

sizes and thread-group allocations. This might be achieved using an auto-tuned GPU library such as Atlas [12].

For the FPGA platform, Table 1 shows how logic utilization varies for various target precisions. Each precision must match the ratio of addition operators to multiplication operators necessary for the algorithm to the ratio which can be delivered by the FPGA fabric. For single and double precision implementations, the designs utilize greater than 90% of LUT and DSP48 resources respectively. This high-utilization is not achieved for the half precision implementation, where Block RAM availability, specifically port availability, limits the number of operators which may be implemented on the FPGA.

Table 2 shows the performance that can be achieved using the FPGA implementations. All implementations target 64×64 matrix block sizes. The table indicates that single precision FPGA implementations achieve approximately $3\times$ the compute throughput of double-precision implementations ($\sim$68GFLOPS vs $\sim$23GFLOPS). Where double-double precision is used, the FPGA implementation achieves 5GFLOPS, a $16\times$ reduction over the performance of single precision. The specialized compute operators for half-precision operators mean a half-precision implementation can reach 83GFLOPS, a $1.2\times$ improvement over single precision.

To compare the performance of the two platforms, Table 2 shows the achievable performance (in GFLOPs) for different matrix sizes and precisions. Where results are presented in grey, they indicate the FPGA implementation has achieved greater computational throughput than the equivalent GPU implementation. These cases occur when smaller matrices are multiplied and is a direct result of the large overhead of executing a GPU kernel and higher memory latency in our GPU implementation.

These results are represented graphically in Figure 2. This graph makes clear the very significant performance penalty that GPUs face when moving from hardware-supported single and double precision operation to using non-native double-double precision operations. By comparison, the FPGA implementations see a much more gradual degradation of performance as the numerical accuracy of operators is increased. This can be attributed to the specialized circuits produced by the Coregen [4] and FloPoCo[5] tools.

Overall, the results suggest that for large dense matrices and for sufficiently large matrices, GPU platforms deliver greater throughput than competing FPGA platforms, but for smaller matrices, the combination of specialized operator structures and the absence of large kernel setup times makes FPGA implementation competitive.

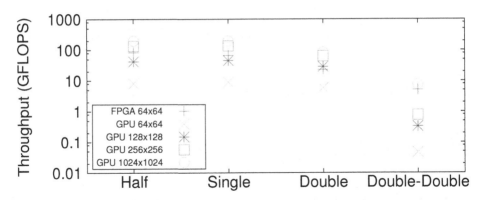

Fig. 2. Comparison of FPGA and GPU performance for various precisions and matrix sizes

Table 2. Performance (in GFLOPS) for varying precisions and matrix sizes in FPGA and GPU implementations

Precision	Performance (GFLOPS)				
	FPGA 64x64 (on-chip)	GPU 64x64	GPU 128x128	GPU 256x256	GPU 1024x1024
Half	83.12	8.09	42.45	135.3	199.17
Single	67.68	9.039	45.59	137.5	198.98
Double	22.9	5.825	28.72	63.79	85.06
Double-Double	4.93	0.047	0.33	0.771	7.60

5   Conclusion and Future Work

This work focused on analyzing the performance of non-standard precision on GPU and FPGA. An arithmetically dense program, matrix-matrix multiply, was implemented for various data sizes. The results showed that GPU implementations outperforms FPGA for larger data sizes but underperform for smaller sizes where the memory latency and kernel start overhead become significant. FPGAs have good vendor support for custom floating-point formats and we would expect this gap to increase further, in favour of FPGA implementation if even more exotic number representation were selected.

While this work has delivered a comparison of the *throughput* of the two platforms, other performance metrics warrant further investigation. Firstly, the accuracy of computations; in this work the non-standard precision results were converted to single or double precision on the same platform and compared for correctness with a verified matrix-matrix multiplication running on the same platform. Because of the error induced while converting between formats, this error criteria may be unduly lenient. However for future work, the results can be compared with a verified library to precisely estimate the correctness of non-standard computations.

Comparison of power and energy usage will also be an interesting study. With massively parallel supercomputing systems comprising of hundreds of GPUs and FPGAs a specific value of watts/GFLOPS for non-standard precision can be a key specification in system design.

Finally, the comparison can be extended to different benchmarks. GPUs are tuned to deliver very high performance for matrix-matrix multiply calculations. We would expect the gap in performance between the two platforms to narrow in other algorithms where the flexible memory systems and efficient synchronization allow FPGAs to achieve a higher proportion of peak performance than GPUs.

References

1. Dennard, R., Gaensslen, F., Rideout, V., Bassous, E., LeBlanc, A.: Design of Ion-Implanted MOSFET's with Very Small Physical Dimensions. IEEE Journal of Solid-State Circuits 9(5), 256–268 (1974)
2. NVIDIA Corporation, Santa Clara, U.: Tesla C1060 Computing Processor Board (January 2010)
3. Xilinx Corporation: Virtex-6 Family Overview. Technical Report DS150 (January 2012)
4. Xilinx Corporation: LogiCORE Floating-Point Operator v5.0. (2011)
5. De Dinechin, F., Pasca, B.: Designing Custom Arithmetic Data Paths with FloPoCo. IEEE Design & Test of Computers 28(4), 18–27 (2011)
6. Volkov, V., Demmel, J.W.: Benchmarking GPUs to tune Dense Linear Algebra. In: Proceedings of the 2008 ACM/IEEE conference on Supercomputing, p. 31. IEEE Press (2008)
7. NVIDIA Corporation: CUBLAS library v5.5. Technical report (2013)
8. NVIDIA Corporation: CUDA library documentation 4.1,
   http://developer.download.nvidia.com/compute/cuda/4_1/rel/toolkit/docs/online
9. Thall, A.: Extended-Precision Floating-Point Numbers for GPU Computation. In: ACM SIGGRAPH 2006 Research posters, p. 52. ACM (2006)
10. Lu, M., He, B., Luo, Q.: Supporting Extended Precision on Graphics Processors. In: Proceedings of the Sixth International Workshop on Data Management on New Hardware, pp. 19–26. ACM (2010)
11. Minhas, U.: GPU vs FPGA: A Comparative Performance Analysis for Non-Standard Precision. Master's thesis, Imperial College London (2013)
12. Whaley, R.C., Petitet, A., Dongarra, J.J.: Automated Empirical Optimizations of Software and the ATLAS project. Parallel Computing 27(12), 3–35 (2001)

Instruction Extension and Generation
for Adaptive Processors

Chao Wang[1], Xi Li[1], Huizhen Zhang[2], Liang Shi[3], and Xuehai Zhou[1]

[1] School of Computer Science, University of Science and Technology of China
[2] School of Computer Science, Huaqiao University
[3] School of Computer Science, Chongqing University
saintwc@mail.ustc.edu.cn, zhanghz@hqu.ustc.edu.cn
shiliang@cqu.edu.cn, {llxx,xhzhou}@ustc.edu.cn

Abstract. Adaptive reconfigurable instruction-set processors (RISP) is an emerging research field for state-of-the-art VLIW processors. However, it still poses significant challenges to generate and map the original codes to the custom instructions. In this paper we propose an architecture framework to extend new instructions for adaptive RISP. The selected hotspot is considered as a custom instruction and implemented in reconfigurable hardware units. An instruction generator is used to provide a mapping mechanism from hot blocks to hardware implementations, using data flow analysis, instruction clustering, subgraph enumerating and subgraph merging techniques. To demonstrate the effectiveness and performance of the framework and to verify the correctness of the mapping mechanism, a prototype instruction generator has been implemented.

Keywords: Instructions Extension, Adaptive Multicore Processors.

1 Introduction and Background

Reconfigurable instruction-set processor (RISP) is one of the most important domains to which reconfigurable computing technologies have been applied. RISP combines a general purpose processor and a reconfigurable logic unit into a sound framework, which enables RISP to adapt instruction-set architectures to a specific application. Compared to other state-of-the-art reconfigurable systems, RISP is also taking benefits from traditional application specific instruction processor (ASIP) design methodologies with the additional implementation of reconfigurable instruction-set.

However, RISP design still poses significant challenges on several key issues. The ISA of RISP can be adaptively reconfigured after fabrication, which makes comprehensive differences with traditional processors [1]. Due to the hardware resources limitation of a single FPGA device, it is essential to carefully choose the hotspots of applications for hardware implementation. During the instruction extension process, the identification, definition and implementation of those selected operations providing the largest performance improvement should be hardwired.

In this paper, we propose a custom instruction generation and mapping method for RISP. The main contributions of this article are extensions to our previous research in

D. Goehringer et al. (Eds.): ARC 2014, LNCS 8405, pp. 306–311, 2014.
© Springer International Publishing Switzerland 2014

[2] and can be summarized as follows: we present instruction-set extensions and candidates selection algorithms; we propose a custom instruction-set extension algorithm for RISP, including data flow analysis, instruction clustering, subgraph enumerating and subgraph merging. Experiments show that the algorithm could handle all the non-trivial custom instruction candidates efficiently.

2   Instruction Extension and Generation

Given the target functions as hotspots, custom instructions should be selected and considered to be implemented via hardware logic blocks. Traditionally custom instructions are usually generated from data flow chart in front-end analyzing tools. In this paper, the custom instructions are generated statically after hotspot information is obtained. In our algorithm there are two parts: data flow analysis and instruction-set extension. Moreover, the instruction-set extension process includes both the instruction selection and generation.

2.1   Data Flow Analysis

Data flow analysis is employed to analyze the generated instruction sequence and choose the custom instructions. Since all the instructions are regarded as the nodes in a data flow graph (DFG), we first designed an algorithm named BuildDFG to generate the target custom instructions. The instruction extension process is shown in Fig.1.

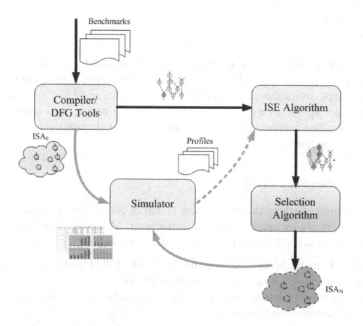

Fig. 1. InstructionSet Extension Process

In this paper, the codes between two branch instructions are regarded as a basic block. BuildDFG maintains a register table to keep the record of the producers of data flow. Once a new instruction arrives, the register table is looked up to check whether data already exists in the table. If not, then the associated registers are marked as LiveIn registers; once the basic block is finished, all the non-empty registers are marked as LiveOut registers. The BuidDFG algorithm is shown in Algorithm 1.

Algorithm 1. BuildDFG algorithm
Input: Basic Block, SrcReg, DestReg
Output: LiveIn Registers and LiveOut Registers
1:    **for** $i = 0$ to num of insts in basic block **do**
2:        $dreg = getdestreg(bb [i])$;
3:        $sreg1 = getsrcreg1(bb [i])$;
4:        $sreg2 = getsrcreg1(bb [i])$;
5:        $sindex1 = getproducer(sreg1)$;
6:        **if** $sindex1 == -1$ **then**
7:                $marklivein(sreg)$;
8:        **end**
9:        $sindex2 = getproducer(sreg2)$;
10:      **if** $sindex2 == -1$ **then**
11:              $marklivein(sreg2)$;
12:      **end**
13:      $setproducer (dreg,i)$;
14:      $setrefindex (sreg1,i)$;
15:      $setrefindex (sreg2,i)$;
16:      **end**

This algorithm outlines how the data flow is analyzed by building a data flow graph. The input parameters of BuildDFG consist of the basic block, source and destination registers, while the output parameters are LiveIn and LiveOut registers. The algorithm looks up for every basic block to mark the registers to source registers (Sreg) or destination registers (Dreg). The Sreg and Dreg identify the input and output parameters for custom instructions.

2.2   Instruction-Set Extension

Some instructions, such as memory access (Load & Store) instructions, are not cost effective and are not included in custom instructions. Moreover, there are limitations that should be considered during instruction-set extension:

— Number of Operands. Considering the limitation of the register ports, the operand number must not overpass the number of registers.
— Number of custom instructions. The size of instruction code limits the number of generated custom instructions.

— Area constraints. All the custom instructions are implemented in hardware (e.g., FPGA, CPLD), thus their hardware implementations area must not exceed the area limitations.

Generally, the instruction-set extension problem can be defined as a graph problem which is described as follows:

Definition 1: Construct a directed acyclic graph G (V, E) which represents the data dependencies between different instructions, in which V represents instructions, while E represents data relations. In the graph, each vertex v represents nodes included in custom instructions. Assume P is the node set under processing. All nodes which require external data are in $IN(P)$, and those producing external data are in $OUT(P)$. The limitations of the number of inputs and outputs are M_{in} and M_{out}, respectively. $PATH$ (u, v) is the path from node u to node v. The custom instruction problem is to find a suitable node set P to meet the following constraints: first the node number in $IN(P)$ and $OUT(P)$ should not exceed the limitation of M_{in} and M_{out}. Then for each pair of nodes v_i and v_j in P and v_k not in P, the path between v_i and v_k and v_j and v_k should not share any common nodes.

Since in the instruction sequences not all the instructions have data hazards, the sequences can be divided into several clusters. All the clusters have no data dependence between each other, so we only need to check the constraints inside each cluster and then combine the clusters.

The number assigned to each node indicates the execution order. In one cluster, each instruction has data paths to every other instructions. Different clusters need to be marked with different colors corresponding to different categories. The algorithm is described in Algorithm 2.

Algorithm 2. Cluster marking algorithm
Input: G (V, E)
Output: Mark for G (V, E)

```
1:    for i = 0 to num_nodes do
2:        n = g.vGraph [i];
3:        if isValidNode(n) != OK then
4:                continue;
5:        end
6:        regmark=(mark[i]==-1)?regionnum + 1 : mark [i];
7:        regmark = getminregmark();
8:        if regmark = =regionnum + 1 then
9:                regmark = regionnum++;
10:       else
11:               collectremarknodes(remarklist);
12:               mark [i] = regmark;
13:               for j = 0 to succ_index do
14:                       mark [successors [j]] = regmark;
15:               end
16:               regmark(remarklist,regmark);
17:       end
18:   end
```

The marking algorithm checks each node in the graph. First it checks whether the current node is valid. The term *regmark* refers to the number of successor nodes already marked. The function ***getminregmark()*** in line 7 returns the minimum ID from the current node and all its successor nodes. If all the successor nodes and the current node have not been marked, then a new cluster is created including all these nodes. Otherwise, the marks of the successor nodes should be updated (lines 12-17).

3   Mapping Instructions to Reconfigurable Logic

In this section, we illustrate an example of mapping instructions to reconfigurable logic. The hardware architecture is based on our previous starnet architecture [3], while the scheduling method [4] and programming models [5] are from the state-of-the-art. Custom instructions are mapped to our reconfigurable logic array architecture. In this paper, we introduce an automatic mapping method using producer-consumer techniques. The logic array is deployed when the program is executed for the first time. The producer of a parameter refers to the hardware module where the instruction is mapped to.

The automatic mapping procedure first looks up the producers of sources registers. If a certain register has no producers, then it is marked as LiveIn Registers, and the instruction is mapped to current level; otherwise, which means the register is produced by other instructions, the instruction can be only mapped to the next level. All the subsequent instructions cannot be mapped higher level than current instruction.

In order to support the mapping method, three tables are integrated, one is used to store all the producers, and other two tables keep the records of LiveIn and LiveOut registers. The numbers of LiveIn and LiveOut registers refer to the input and output operands of custom instructions, respectively. Fig. 2 shows an example of the automatic mapping scheme.

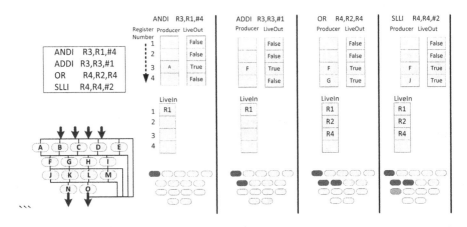

Fig. 2. An Example of Instruction Mapping

Assume we have four custom instructions: ANDI, ADDI, OR and SLLI. The mapping process is described as follows: (1) **ANDI R3,R1,#4**. After checking the producers of the instruction, R1 is marked to LiveIn registers since it does not have any producer. Meanwhile R3 is marked to LiveOut registers. The ANDI instruction is mapped to module A, which is also the producer of R3. (2) **ADDI R3,R3,#1**. The process is similar to (1). Since the R3 has a producer A, it should be mapped to the F block in level 2. The producer of R3 is updated to F as well. (3) **OR R4,R2,R4**. There are no producers for both R2 and R4, hence the OR instruction is mapped to G. R2 and R4 are LiveIn registers, R4 is also the LiveOut register and G is the producer. (4) **SLLI R4,R4,#2**. The SLLI instruction can only be mapped to next level since the R4 has a producer J.

After the mapping procedure is finished, the reconfiguration controller needs to examine for the constraints, including whether the number of LiveIn and LiveOut registers exceed the table size, or if they could not be deployed simultaneously due to device limitations. Anyway, if a certain custom instruction fails the checking examination, the instruction is removed from the table.

4   Conclusion and Future Work

In this paper, we have presented an instruction-set extension method with dynamic compiler support for reconfigurable VLIW processors. The first step is to generate the custom instruction with a data flow analysis method. Due to area constraints, only part of the candidate instructions can be extended. Here we use a clustering algorithm to generate and select the instructions paths. Then the custom instructions are mapped to reconfigurable array units. We demonstrated the effectiveness of the mapping scheme and the instruction generation algorithm. Preliminary experiments on the Altera Nios II based FPGA board with NetBench and MiBench revealed speedups from 1.7x to 5.1x of our approach over the traditional sequential execution.

Acknowledgments. This work was supported by the National Science Foundation of China under grants No. 61379040, No. 61272131 and No. 61202053, Jiangsu Provincial Natural Science Foundation grant No. SBK201240198.

References

1. Galuzzi, C., Bertels, K.: The Instruction-Set Extension Problem: A Survey. TRETS 4(2), 18 (2011)
2. Wang, C., Zhang, H., Zhou, X., Ji, J., Wang, A.: Tool Chain Support with Dynamic Profiling for RISP. In: 9th IEEE International Symposium on Parallel and Distributed Processing with Applications (ISPA 2011), Busan, Korea, May 26-28, pp. 155–160 (2011)
3. Wang, C., Li, X., Zhang, J., Zhou, X., Wang, A.: A Star Network Approach in Heterogeneous Multi Processors System on Chip. The Journal of Supercomputing 62(3), 1404–1424
4. Wang, C., Li, X., Zhang, J., Zhou, X., Nie, X.: MP-Tomasulo, A Dependency-Aware Automatic Parallel Execution Engine for Sequential Programs. ACM Transactions on Architecture and Code Optimization (TACO) 10(2), 9
5. Wang, C., Chen, P., Li, X., Feng, X., Zhou, X.: FPM, A Flexible Programming Model for MPSoCs. In: 19th Reconfigurable Architecture Workshop (RAW 2012), pp. 477–484 (2012)

DeSyRe: On-Demand Adaptive
and Reconfigurable Fault-Tolerant SoCs*

I. Sourdis[1], C. Strydis[6], A. Armato[7], C.-S. Bouganis[5], B. Falsafi[3],
G.N. Gaydadjiev[1], S. Isaza[6], A. Malek[1], R. Mariani[7], S. Pagliarini[2],
D.N. Pnevmatikatos[4], D.K. Pradhan[2], G. Rauwerda[8], R.M. Seepers[6],
R.A. Shafik[2], G. Smaragdos[6], D. Theodoropoulos[4], S. Tzilis[1],
and M. Vavouras[5]

[1] Computer Science and Engineering, Chalmers University of Technology, Sweden
[2] Computer Science Dept., University of Bristol, UK
[3] Computer and Communication Sciences, EPFL, Switzerland
[4] ICS, Foundation for Research and Technology Hellas (FORTH), Greece
[5] Electrical and Electronic Engineering Dept., Imperial College London, UK
[6] Neurasmus B.V., The Netherlands
[7] Yogitech SpA, Italy
[8] Recore Systems B.V., The Netherlands
sourdis@chalmers.se

Abstract. The DeSyRe project builds on-demand adaptive, reliable
Systems-on-Chips. In response to the current semiconductor technology
trends that make chips becoming less reliable, DeSyRe describes a new generation of by design reliable systems, at a reduced power and performance
cost. This is achieved through the following main contributions. DeSyRe
defines a fault-tolerant system architecture built out of unreliable components, rather than aiming at totally fault-free and hence more costly chips.
In addition, DeSyRe systems are on-demand adaptive to various types and
densities of faults, as well as to other system constraints and application
requirements. For leveraging on-demand adaptation/customization and
reliability at reduced cost, a new dynamically reconfigurable substrate is
designed and combined with runtime system software support. The above
define a generic and repeatable design framework, which is applied to two
medical SoCs with high reliability constraints and diverse performance
and power requirements. One of the main goals of the DeSyRe project is
to increase the availability of SoC components in the presence of perma-
nents faults, caused at manufacturing time or due to device aging. A mix
of coarse- and fine-grain reconfigurable hardware substrate is designed to
isolate and bypass faulty component parts. The flexibility provided by the
DeSyRe reconfigurable substrate is exploited at runtime by system optimization heuristics, which decide to modify component configuration when
a permanent fault is detected, providing graceful degradation.

1   Introduction

In the coming nanoscale era, chips are becoming less reliable, while manufacturing fault-free chips is becoming increasingly more difficult and costly [2].

---

* The DeSyRe Project is supported by the European Commission Seventh Framework
Programme, grant agreement no 287611. www.desyre.eu

D. Goehringer et al. (Eds.): ARC 2014, LNCS 8405, pp. 312–317, 2014.
© Springer International Publishing Switzerland 2014

Prominent causes for this are the shrinking device features, the sheer number of components on a given area of silicon, as well as the increasing complexity of current and future chips. It is expected that a significant number of devices will be defective already at manufacture time and many more will degrade and fail within their expected lifetime. Furthermore, process variations as well as the increasing number of soft errors introduce more errors in future chips.

As feature size continues to shrink and chips become less reliable, the cost for delivering reliable chips is expected to grow for future technology nodes. Providing reliable systems incurs substantial overheads in power and energy consumption, performance and silicon area. However, it is a well-known fact that power consumption is becoming a severe problem, while performance no longer scales very well (mostly due to power-density limitations). To reduce some of the above overheads, the DeSyRe project aims at reliable systems containing and tolerating unreliable components rather than targeting totally fault-free systems [1]. Our goal is to describe a new, more efficient design framework for SoCs, which provides reliability at lower power and performance cost.

Although technology trends make the design of future SoCs harder, one of them can be turned to our advantage. The increasing power density limits gate density. In a few years, significant parts of a chip will be forced to remain powered-down in order to keep within the available power budget [4]. In DeSyRe, we capitalize on this observation and propose to exploit the aforementioned unused resources to offer flexibility and reconfigurability on a chip. Until recently, reconfigurable hardware had a significant resource overhead; however, as explained above, this limitation no longer exists as on-chip resources are becoming cheaper. A dynamically reconfigurable hardware-substrate can provide an excellent solution for defect tolerance; it can be used to adapt to faults on demand, isolate and correct defects, as well as to provide spare resources to substitute defective blocks. In the DeSyRe project, we intend to use such a reconfigurable substrate and combine it with system-level techniques to provide adaptive and on-demand reliable systems.

The remainder of the paper is organized as follows: Section 2 gives an overview of the DeSyRe design framework. Section 3 describes the DeSyRe reconfigurability that offers the flexibility to tolerate permanent faults on a SoC. In Section 4, we present the DeSyRe runtime system adaptation techniques, which exploit the above hardware flexibility and provide graceful degradation. Finally, we draw our conclusions in Section 5.

2   The DeSyRe Project: On-Demand System Reliability

The DeSyRe project describes a generic design framework for fault-tolerant heterogeneous SoCs. The DeSyRe framework is partitioned across two orthogonal design dimensions: a physical and a logical abstraction. The physical partitioning considers that different parts of the chip are manufactured to have different vulnerability to faults, considering for instance different technological substrates (with different fault densities) or having different design approaches. The logical

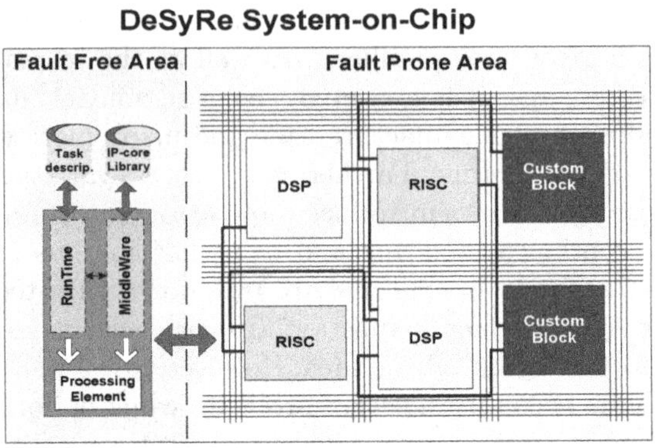

DeSyRe System-on-Chip

Fig. 1. DeSyRe SoC physical partitioning with a fault-free section for SoC management and a fault-prone section for SoC functionality

partitioning considers the same framework from the viewpoint of functionality (i.e. which part of the system does what).

Figure 1 illustrates the physical partitioning of the DeSyRe SoC. The design area is physically divided into a fault-free (FF) section providing overall system management and a fault-prone (FP) section providing the actual system functionality. The motivation for this partitioning is to reduce the chip cost: Designing a totally fault-free system is expensive, thus having a small and lightweight FF SoC part is expected to incur lower overheads. The FF section is required to provide centralized, system-wide control of the SoC, aiming to provide Quality of Service (QoS) attributes such as performance, low power consumption, resource utilization and fault tolerance. The various techniques through which this will be achieved involve an efficient combination of: online fault tolerance, runtime task scheduling and resource allocation, reconfiguration schemes to achieve flexible and defect-tolerant operation. The FP section is under the direct control of the FF section. It contains various components realized in the DeSyRe reconfigurable substrate. The components implement the main system functionality based on the target application (domain). They are required to exhibit, among others, self-checking and self-correcting properties, working in tight synergy with those of the FF section.

The logical partitioning organizes the DeSyRe SoC in three main layers. Figure 2 depicts the layers from bottom to top: components, middleware and runtime system. This subdivision is based on the abstraction level involved and the tasks handled by each layer. The bottom layer deals with fault-tolerance issues of each **Component** (i.e. unit which delivers a specific functionality) in the FP section, individually. Each component is enhanced with local fault detection and possibly correction mechanisms, hardware reconfigurability options, and a wrapper to interface with the FF part of the SoC. The second (software) layer, called **Middleware**, is located in the FF part of the SoC and is responsible for the dynamic reconfiguration of hardware resources implemented in the (fine- and/or coarse-grain) reconfigurable substrate of FP section. The third (software) layer is the **Runtime System**, also located in the FF part of the SoC. The basic functionality of the

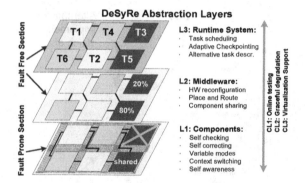

Fig. 2. Logical partitioning of a DeSyRe SoC: Components layer (SoC functionality), Middleware layer and Runtime-System layer (SoC management)

Runtime System is to schedule tasks to components, to ensure the best quality of service for the soft real-time portion of the applications, and to adapt the system in the presence of faults. Finally, DeSyRe has three distributed tasks that span across the three logical layers, since all three of them need to deal with and support them: (i) **online testing**, for permanent fault detection and diagnosis, (ii) **graceful degradation** of performance and/or functionality when the availability of SoC resources is reduced, (iii) **virtualization** support to allow tasks to be executed on different, heterogeneous components.

3   The DeSyRe Reconfigurable Substrate

The DeSyRe framework relies significantly on a flexible and dynamically reconfigurable hardware substrate to isolate, replace and (when possible) correct design and manufacturing defects as well as other permanent faults due to aging. In previous works, the design choice was either coarse- or fine-grain granularity of substitutable units; these are units that can be replaced when defective. In the first case, the substitutable unit can be an entire sub-component (e.g. a microprocessors pipeline stage) [3], while in the latter case an FPGA logic cell [5,6]. There are tradeoffs between these two alternatives. Coarse-grain approaches are less defect-tolerant - fewer defects can have large impact to the system - but lead to solutions that are more power and silicon efficient. Fine-grain approaches can tolerate a larger number of defects, but utilizing an FPGA-like substrate introduces performance, power, and cost overheads.

One of the primary challenges in the DeSyRe project is to investigate the architecture of the underlying hardware substrate for the DeSyRe SoC. DeSyRe explores a granularity mix of fine- and coarse-grain underlying hardware in order to provide increased defect-tolerance without giving away significant parts of the system performance and power efficiency. Figure 3 depicts such an example with two DeSyRe RISC components. In this example, each RISC processor is divided in smaller sub-components (pipeline stages implemented in fixed hardware) surrounded by reconfigurable interconnects/wires. In the absence of

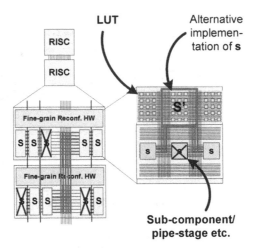

Fig. 3. The novel DeSyRe flexible/reconfigurable hardware substrate

defects, the sub-components S will form the RISC component. However, in case a sub-component is defective, it can be isolated using the reconfigurable intercon- nects, and subsequently be replaced either by an identical unused neighboring sub-component (S), or by a functionally equivalent instance (S) implemented in fine-grain reconfigurable hardware.

Our preliminary results indicate that, for a given silicon area, compared to core-level redundancy, the above mixed granularity reconfiguration increases the availability of components up to ×4 when the probability to have a permanent fault in a component is above 30%. Even when defect density increases above 1 defect per component, the DeSyRe reconfigurable substrate is able to preserve the functionality of more than 50% of components. The overhead of coarse-grain reconfigurability in the cycle time is about 15%; this overhead increases to ×3 when using fine-grain reconfigurable blocks.

Besides component reconfigurability, DeSyRe provides flexibility to tolerate permanent faults at links and routers of a Network-on-Chip, while additionally network traffic can be redirected to bypass and avoid faulty NoC resources. Finally, another (compiler-assisted) fault avoidance technique is developed to preserve the usage of partially faulty components; it offers alternative binaries of the same application task, which avoid specific functional units of a processor.

4   Runtime System Adaptation and Graceful Degradation

A DeSyRe SoC is designed to be capable of managing the accumulation of faults in the system in a graceful manner; in other words, to refrain from crashing and instead decide to sacrifice part of the system *functionality* and/or *performance*. Graceful Degradation is achieved in 3 different ways:

- Reconfiguration: The Runtime System exploits the reconfigurability capa- bilities of the components, in order to tolerate permanent faults and tailor the set of working components to the application needs. Reconfigurability is used to increase the availability of the SoC components, while partially defective components are potentially used with reduced functionality.

- Workload Adaptation: The Runtime System has the ability to adapt the workload of the system by dropping (low-priority) tasks or replacing tasks with other that have different processing requirements (possibly less computationally intensive and less efficient/accurate).
- Task (re-)mapping: Given the dynamic nature of both the available system resources and the software workload, the binding of tasks to resources may also need to be modified. This can be used to facilitate Graceful Degradation: If the number of available cores is reduced, the Runtime can either queue more tasks on the remaining cores and expect them to be carried out slower (performance degradation) or drop the least important tasks so that the rest are performed without performance loss (functional degradation).

The runtime system contains fast heuristics to modify hardware configuration, functionality (workload), and task mapping, using objective function, which reflects the system constraints (e.g. peak-power, available energy) and application requirements (e.g. performance, functionality).

5 Conclusions

The increasing need for fault tolerance imposed by the currently observed technology scaling introduces significant performance and power overheads. In our attempt to alleviate these overheads, the DeSyRe project will deliver a new generation of by design reliable systems, at a reduced power and performance cost. This is achieved through the following main contributions. Rather than aiming at totally fault-free chips, DeSyRe designs fault-tolerant systems built using unreliable components. In addition, DeSyRe systems are on-demand adaptive to various types and densities of faults, as well as to other system constraints and application requirements. A new dynamically reconfigurable substrate is designed and combined with runtime system software support in order to leverage on-demand adaptation, customization, and reliability at reduced cost.

References

1. DeSyRe Project official website, http://www.desyre.eu/
2. Borkar, S.: Designing reliable systems from unreliable components: the challenges of transistor variability and degradation. IEEE Micro 25(6), 10–16 (2005)
3. Gupta, S., Feng, S., Ansari, A., Blome, J., Mahlke, S.: The stagenet fabric for constructing resilient multicore systems. In: IEEE/ACM MICRO, pp. 141–151 (November 2008)
4. Hardavellas, N., Ferdman, M., Falsafi, B., Ailamaki, A.: Toward dark silicon in servers. IEEE Micro 31(4), 6–15 (2011)
5. Skaggs, B., Emmert, J., Stroud, C., Abramovici, M.: Dynamic fault tolerance in fpgas via partial reconfiguration. In: IEEE Symp. on FCCM (2000)
6. Tzilis, S., Sourdis, I., Gaydadjiev, G.: Fine-grain fault diagnosis for fpga logic blocks. In: Int. Conf. on Field-Programmable Technology (FPT 2010) (December 2010)

Effective Reconfigurable Design: The FASTER Approach*

D.N. Pnevmatikatos[1], T. Becker[2], A. Brokalakis[8], G.N. Gaydadjiev[3], W. Luk[2], K. Papadimitriou[1], I. Papaefstathiou[8], D. Pau[7], Oliver Pell[6], C. Pilato[4], M.D. Santambrogio[4], D. Sciuto[4], and Dirk Stroobandt[5]

[1] Foundation for Research & Technology - Hellas, Greece
[2] Imperial College London, UK
[3] Chalmers University of Technology, Sweden
[4] Politecnico di Milano, Italy
[5] Ghent University, Belgium
[6] Maxeler Technologies, UK
[7] STMicroelectronics, Italy
[8] Synelixis, Greece

Abstract. While fine-grain, reconfigurable devices have been available for years, they are mostly used in a fixed functionality, "asic-replacement" manner. To exploit opportunities for flexible and adaptable run-time exploitation of fine grain reconfigurable resources (as implemented currently in dynamic, partial reconfiguration), better tool support is needed. The FASTER project aims to provide a methodology and a tool-chain that will enable designers to efficiently implement a reconfigurable system on a platform combining software and reconfigurable resources. Starting from a high-level application description and a target platform, our tools analyse the application, evaluate reconfiguration options, and implement the designer choices on underlying vendor tools. In addition, FASTER addresses micro-reconfiguration, verification, and the run-time management of system resources. We use industrial applications to demonstrate the effectiveness of the proposed framework and identify new opportunities for reconfigurable technologies.

1 Introduction

Fine-grain, reconfigurable devices have been available for years in the form of FPGA chips. Many of these devices support the dynamic modification of their programming while they are operating (Dynamic Reconfiguration). However, this ability remains mostly unused as FPGA devices are mostly used in a fixed functionality, "asic-replacement" manner. This is due to the increased complexity in the design and verification of a changing system. In addition to design requirements, the process of creating (partially) reconfigurable designs is less widespread and the corresponding tools are less friendly to the designers.

* The FASTER project is supported by the European Commission Seventh Framework Programme, grant agreement #287804. http://www.fp7-faster.eu/

D. Goehringer et al. (Eds.): ARC 2014, LNCS 8405, pp. 318–323, 2014.
© Springer International Publishing Switzerland 2014

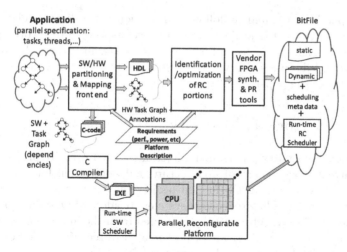

Fig. 1. The FASTER tool-chain

We believe that in order to exploit the opportunities presented by flexible and adaptable exploitation of fine grain reconfigurable resources, better analysis and implementation tool-chains are needed. For example, in a Network Intrusion Detection System, packet contents are compared against suspicious content. This can be efficiently done in FPGAs [1]. New threat identification results in new rules that must be added to the system. Reconfigurable logic allows the incorporation of new functions to the baseline hardware system, combining hardware speed with software-like flexibility.

The FASTER project (http://www.fp7-faster.eu/) aims to provide a methodology and a tool-chain that will enable designers to efficiently implement a reconfigurable system on a platform combining software and reconfigurable resources hiding as much as possible low-level technology details from the user. Figure 1 illustrates the envisioned tool-chain. Starting from a high-level application description and a target platform, our tools analyse the application, evaluate reconfiguration options, alter the application description to include reconfigurability, and implement the designer choices on the underlying vendor tools. In addition, FASTER addresses micro-reconfiguration, a technique to reprogram very small portions of the FPGA when a set of infrequently-changing parameters define the function of a block [2], verification, and the run-time management of system resources. We use industrial applications to demonstrate the effectiveness of the proposed framework and identify new opportunities for reconfigurable technologies.

Technical progress of our work has been documented in technical papers that can be found in http://www.fp7-faster.eu/. Practical achievements include the integration of partial reconfiguration functionality in the Maxeler design flow [3], and its demonstration of partial reconfiguration in a Maxeler platform using a canny edge detection code, the use of micro-reconfiguration for a NIDS application, and the application of our verification tools on a large scale application (Reverse time migration) [4].

The paper is structured as follows: In Section 2 we discuss related efforts within the context of EU projects and the novel aspects of our work. Section 3 presents the designs methods and how we combine them to form the tool-chain, while Section 4 discusses the way the system is controlled at run-time. Finally Section 5 closes the paper.

2   Related Work and Novelty

Several efforts exist towards similar directions with FASTER project such as the concurrent development of architecture and application for heterogeneous systems. hArtes [5] was an EU-funded project targeting automatic paralleliza-tion and generation of heterogeneous systems. It adopted OpenMP pragmas to specify the parallelism automatically extracted from the initial sequential speci-fication but it did not address any aspect related to reconfiguration or dynamic execution. In FASTER we use the same formalism to represent the parallel ap-plication, even if the partitioning is provided by the designer since automatic parallelization does not fall into the project's scope. Other EU-funded projects such as REFLECT [6], ACOTES [7] and ANDRES [8] conducted research on the necessary stages of a tool-chain and addressed similar issues with FASTER, but they focused more on system-level or architectural aspects of reconfiguration. Moreover, they did not explicitly emphasize on the design and runtime aspects of partial and dynamic reconfiguration, or, on choosing the best reconfiguration grain-size. Finally, the ERA project [9] adopts dynamic reconfiguration (with low-level OS support) but it targets only a specific platform developed by the consortium.

None of the existing approaches abstracts from the designer complex manip-ulations needed to control effectively hardware accelerators, in particular when these are designed as dynamically reconfigurable modules. Towards this direc-tion, we aim at providing a general formulation, capable to deal with different multiprocessor systems (targeting the embedded, desktop and high-performance computing domains), supporting different hardware implementations for the tasks and proposing a tool-chain that efficiently partitions the application, while performing considerably more exploration on the possible solutions for the prob-lem. In addition, it takes reconfiguration into account from the early stages of the design process all the way to its runtime use, hiding most of the implementation details from the user.

Other novelties of FASTER are the study of the way micro-reconfiguration is integrated into a tool-chain and interacts with the other tools, and our verifica-tion approach which applies equally to static, region-based, or micro-reconfigura-tion without modification. Finally, we envision a Run-Time System Manager (RTSM) able to support a wide range of platforms, thus we are studying the extent to which it will be developed as a generic library.

3   Methods and Tool-Chain

The starting point of our front-end is a C application, whose initial decomposition is described with OpenMP pragmas, and an XML file containing the target architecture definition (#processing elements, HW/SW tasks characterization, their different implementations and so on). The application task graph is derived and partitioned to determine which processing element (PE) will execute each of the tasks. Our tool-chain performs the following processing steps:

Application profiling and identification of reconfigurable cores: This step analyses the C-code, identifies tasks that could be moved to reconfigurable hardware, and partitions the application accordingly. Based on the initial source code of the application and the description of the target architecture, it decomposes the application into tasks and assigns them to the different components of the architecture. It can also receive information about the achieved performance of the current task assignment, and feedback after the identification of the schedule (e.g. how the partitioning affects the computed schedule) to improve the solution. It also determines (i) the best reconfiguration level (none, region- or micro reconfiguration) for each of the HW cores, and (ii) the properties of the identified tasks, such as the frequency of call functions and parameters changing, the resources required by the implementations, and the execution performance. This processing includes analysis of the call graph, estimation of data transfers, and source code profiling.

High-level Analysis: This step explores various implementation options for applications (or parts of applications) that target reconfigurable hardware and identifies automatically opportunities for run-time reconfiguration. The exploration is performed based on high-level design estimates to avoid time-consuming iterations in the design process, and produces estimates of implementation attributes such as area, computation time, and reconfiguration time; these can be looped back to the *Application profiling and identification of reconfigurable cores* step, to perform iterative design optimizations for arithmetic operations presentation, computational precision, and parallelism in the implementation. The High-level Analysis also provides an automatic way to suggest opportunities for reconfiguration, such as partitioning of the application into several reconfigurable components.

Optimizations for region- and micro-reconfiguration: This step receives the descriptions of the tasks, i.e. the corresponding source code, that could benefit from the reconfiguration and it produces new and optimized implementations for them to be considered for the task mapping. This analysis will be performed also through dynamic profiling of the application tasks to determine the parameters for the micro-reconfiguration and through the identification of isomorphic sub-graphs for supporting the data-path merging and thus reducing the number of reconfigurations.

Compile-time scheduling and mapping onto reconfigurable regions: It receives information about the application and the architecture from the two previous processing steps, focusing on the tasks assigned to the reconfigurable hardware, and it determines their scheduling along with the mapping of the cores onto the reconfigurable regions. In particular, it determines the number and the characteristics (e.g. size) of these regions, the number and the size of each input/output point, and also takes into account the interconnection infrastructure of the system (e.g. bus size). Also, it schedules the resulting implementation and annotates the characterization part with such information to further refine the specification. It annotates the tasks with information about the feasibility of the implementation where the solution is specified (i.e. if the reconfigurable region can satisfy the resource requirements) and it provides feedback to the partitioning methodology to further refine the solution.

Verification: To verify that a simple, unoptimized design (the source) implements the same behaviour as an optimized, possibly reconfiguring design (the target), we combine symbolic simulation with equivalence checking. The source and target designs are first compiled for a symbolic simulator, which then stimulates the design with symbolic inputs, rather than the numerical or Boolean inputs used in traditional approaches. Equivalence checking is used to check symbolic outputs from source and target designs that may differ but still be equivalent (for example $b + a$ instead of $a + b$). If symbolic outputs from source and target designs are equivalent for all inputs, the designs are proved equivalent, otherwise, the first input with different outputs can be used to debug the target design.

4   Run-Time System

The Run-Time System Manager (RTSM) is responsible for managing resources, scheduling SW and HW tasks, and enforcing adaptation of the system according to functional and non-functional parameters (e.g. temperature) for applications developed with the FASTER tool-chain. Its basic components and functionality were presented abstractly in [10]. The concept of its development relies on the work initially published in [11]. Here we describe briefly its first implementation, which takes into account all known restrictions imposed by the current PR technology.

Figure 2 illustrates how the RTSM is generated, its basic components and actions. RTSM basic functionality is specified by the baseline scheduler contained in the XML file. The XML contains the available runtime alternatives to reconfigure the regions, the representation of the task graph, the number of iterations for each task, and additional information about each task which will be used for the scheduling, e.g. power consumption, reconfiguration time, execution time. The necessary information retrieved from the XML file is used for feeding the RTSM structures.

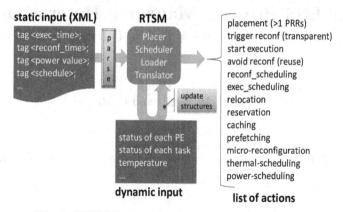

Fig. 2. RTSM inputs, characteristics and operations

5   Conclusions

The FASTER project enhances various aspects in designing modern computing systems. The main challenge is the inclusion of reconfiguration as an explicit design concept. To do this we are developing new design methods and a tool-chain for efficient and transparent use of reconfiguration.

References

1. Sourdis, I., Pnevmatikatos, D., Vassiliadis, S.: Scalable Multi-Gigabit Pattern Matching for Packet Inspection. IEEE Transactions on Very Large Scale Integration (VLSI) Systems 16(2), 156–166 (2008)
2. Bruneel, K., Stroobandt, D.: Automatic Generation of Run-Time Parameterizable Configurations. In: IEEE International Conference on Field Programmable Logic and Applications (FPL), pp. 361–366 (August 2008)
3. Cattaneo, R., Pilato, C., Mastinu, M., Kadlcek, O., Pell, O., Santambrogio, M.D.: Runtime Adaptation on Dataflow HPC Platforms. In: NASA/ESA Conference on Adaptive Hardware and Systems (AHS) (June 2013)
4. Todman, T., Luk, W.: Verification of Streaming Designs by Combining Symbolic Simulation and Equivalence Checking. In: IEEE International Conference on Field Programmable Logic and Applications (FPL) (August 2012)
5. http://www.hartes.org/ (accessed 2012)
6. http://www.reflect-project.eu/ (accessed 2012)
7. http://www.hitech-projects.com/euprojects/ACOTES/ (accessed 2014)
8. http://andres.offis.de/ (accessed 2014)
9. http://www.era-project.eu/ (accessed 2014)
10. Pnevmatikatos, D., Becker, T., Brokalakis, A., Bruneel, K., Gaydadjiev, G., Luk, W., Papadimitriou, K., Papaefstathiou, I., Pell, O., Pilato, C., Robart, M., Santambrogio, M.D., Sciuto, D., Stroobandt, D., Todman, T.: FASTER: Facilitating Analysis and Synthesis Technologies for Effective Reconfiguration. In: Euromicro Conference on Digital System Design (DSD) (September 2012)
11. Durelli, G., Pilato, C., Cazzaniga, A., Sciuto, D., Santambrogio, M.D.: Automatic Run-Time Manager Generation for Reconfigurable MPSoC Architectures. In: IEEE International Workshop on Reconfigurable Communication-centric Systems-on-Chip (ReCoSoC) (July 2012)

HARNESS Project: Managing Heterogeneous Computing Resources for a Cloud Platform*

J.G.F. Coutinho[1], Oliver Pell[2], E. O'Neill[3], P. Sanders[2], J. McGlone[3],
P. Grigoras[1], W. Luk[1], and C. Ragusa[3]

[1] Imperial College London, UK
[2] Maxeler Technologies, UK
[3] SAP HANA Cloud Computing, Systems Engineering, Belfast, UK
jgfc@doc.ic.ac.uk

Abstract. Most cloud service offerings are based on homogeneous commodity resources, such as large numbers of inexpensive machines interconnected by off-the-shelf networking equipment and disk drives, to provide low-cost application hosting. However, cloud service providers have reached a limit in satisfying performance and cost requirements for important classes of applications, such as geo-exploration and real-time business analytics. The HARNESS project aims to fill this gap by developing architectural principles that enable the next generation cloud platforms to incorporate heterogeneous technologies such as reconfigurable Dataflow Engines (DFEs), programmable routers, and SSDs, and provide as a result vastly increased performance, reduced energy consumption, and lower cost profiles. In this paper we focus on three challenges for supporting heterogeneous computing resources in the context of a cloud platform, namely: (1) cross-optimisation of heterogeneous computing resources, (2) resource virtualisation and (3) programming heterogeneous platforms.

1 Overview

The current approach for building data centres is to assemble large numbers of relatively inexpensive personal computers, interconnected by standard routers and supported by stock disk drives. This model for cloud computing leverages commodity computation, communication, and storage to provide low-cost application hosting. The efficacy of this platform depends on the providers' ability to satisfy a broad range of application needs while at the same time capitalising on infrastructure investments by making maximal use of the platform's resources. Two key concepts related to cloud data centres are managed *multitenancy* and *elasticity* [6]. To support multitenancy, the provider must accommodate and reconcile the resource needs of several applications simultaneously, while elasticity allows an application to run on a platform using a pool of resources that can

---

* The HARNESS Project is supported by the European Commission Seventh Framework Programme, grant agreement no 318521 http://www.harness-project.eu

D. Goehringer et al. (Eds.): ARC 2014, LNCS 8405, pp. 324–329, 2014.
© Springer International Publishing Switzerland 2014

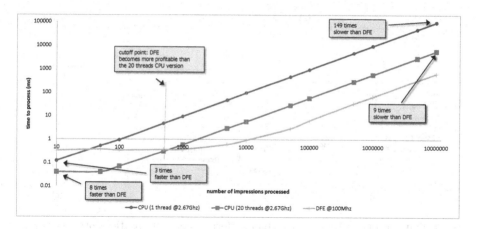

Fig. 1. Results comparing three AdPredictor implementations running on a CPU and DFE platforms. In this example, the size of the task (number of impressions to be processed) affects how each implementation fares against other implementations.

grow and shrink over time. At play here are many conflicting concerns involving application requirements, resource capacity and availability, and pricing.

The HARNESS project envisions an enhanced cloud Platform-as-a-Service (PaaS) software stack that not only supports existing commodity technologies, but also incorporates heterogeneous technologies such as Dataflow Engines (DFEs) [5], programmable routers and different types of storage devices, to provide vastly increased performance, reduced energy consumption, and lower cost profiles. To realise this goal, we are working on a platform design that abstracts the underlying infrastructure, enabled by runtime management systems, programming tools and middleware layers.

In this paper, we focus on the problem of making effective use of specialised computing resources, including DFEs and GPGPUs, in the context of a cloud platform. In particular, we have identified three key challenges in addressing this problem: performing global optimisation across a set of provisioned heterogeneous resources (Section 2), virtualising computing resources to enable sharing in a multitenant environment (Section 3), and programming heterogeneous platforms (Section 4).

2   Cross-Optimisation of Heterogeneous Resources

In current computational systems, heterogeneity is largely invisible to the operating system, and only minimal management functionality is provided. Accelerators such as GPGPUs and FPGAs are often accessed by applications as I/O devices via library-call interfaces. These accelerators must be manually managed by the application programmer, including not just execution of code but also in many cases tasks that are traditionally performed by the operating system such as allocation, de-allocation, load balancing, and context switching. If resources

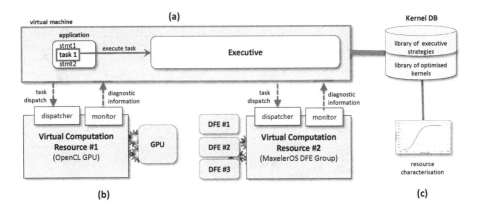

Fig. 2. Our runtime management system performs cross-optimisations over set of provisioned heterogeneous resources

are shared between several hosts, issues of contention, fairness and security become further pronounced. Since heterogeneous computing elements are generally outside the control of the operating system or other system software, global optimisation of resources for performance and energy efficiency, for instance, requires considerable programming effort and expertise.

The need for a system that automatically performs global optimisation of resources is illustrated in Fig. 1. In this example we compare the performance of the AdPredictor [2] training process (a computationally intensive machine-learning application) with three different implementations: a single-threaded CPU version (CPU-1), a 20-threaded CPU version (CPU-20) and a 100Mhz DFE version. The CPU platform is based on a dual Intel Xeon X5650 with 24 cores running each at 2.67Ghz. The DFE platform [5], on the other hand, contains a Virtex-6 FPGA as the computation fabric and external RAM for bulk storage. The AdPredictor training module processes a log of online advertisement views, called ad impressions, to update a model that predicts whether a user will click an ad when visiting a website. The size of an AdPredictor task corresponds to the number of ad impressions to be processed. It can be seen from Fig. 1 that the DFE version is not efficient for small tasks, however, at 10 million impressions, the DFE version runs an order of magnitude faster than the multithreaded version. In this example, the task size influences the relative performance of these three designs, with smaller task sizes performing better on the single and multithreaded CPU, and large tasks performing better with the DFE.

We are developing a computation management system [4] that automatically makes these allocation decisions at runtime (Fig. 2). In particular, our runtime management system processes jobs dispatched by the cloud platform using the set of provisioned computing resources to satisfy a given goal or policy, such as minimising job completion. Each job, triggered when an application is launched on a cloud platform, is processed in a virtual machine (VM). An application contains two types of code: *standard code* that is executed directly by the CPU hosting the VM, and *managed tasks*. Managed tasks are special program functions

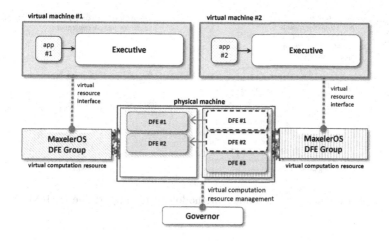

Fig. 3. Virtualisation of Maxeler DFEs to support resource sharing and elasticity

that are executed onto one or more provisioned computing resources through a queue-based mechanism. In particular, during the application execution, managed tasks are dispatched to a component called the *executive* (Fig. 2(a)), which decides how to allocate workload (Fig. 2(b)) based on the availability of optimised kernel implementations stored in a database (Fig. 2(c)) along with associated performance models, such as the one presented in Fig. 1. These performance models allow the executive to make intelligent decisions about how to optimise workload based on runtime conditions, such as task size. Other factors that can affect these decisions include accrued historical data, dependencies between tasks and availability of computing resources.

3   Virtualising Specialised Computing Resources

Specialised computing resources, such as FPGAs and GPGPUs, are designed to be single-tenant devices and typically do not provide native mechanisms that allow these resource to be shared by multiple users. In contrast, CPUs are managed by the operating system which transparently stores and restores the context of a process, so that multiple processes can share a single CPU.

We have designed a virtualisation mechanism for DFEs that in addition of supporting resource sharing, also supports elasticity where a single virtual computing resource can accumulate or shed multiple physical resources according to workload. Virtual computing resources (Fig. 2(b)) supported by our runtime management system adhere to the same interface, which allows the *executive* component to dispatch tasks and acquire diagnostic information, such as temperature and power consumption, without having to deal with proprietary interfaces.

To illustrate our virtual computing resource mechanism we present an example in Fig. 3 in which two applications are running each on a VM. In this example,

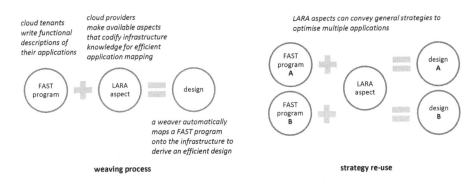

Fig. 4. Aspect-oriented programming methodology to support the HARNESS Cloud Platform

each of the applications has one virtual DFE provisioned. A virtual DFE can be instantiated to employ a fixed or variable number of physical DFEs. If the virtual DFE (also known as a *DFE group*) is configured with variable physical resources then physical DFEs are automatically re-allocated from one virtual resource to another depending on the workload. This management of shared resources is performed by a component called the *governor*. Shared resources are particularly important for online jobs: cloud tenants, rather than provisioning exclusive resources that are only used some of the time due to temporary bursts of workload, can instead share those resources with other tenants to minimise their cost, while cloud providers are able to maximise resource utilisation.

4   Application Development

Developers must acquire considerable knowledge and expertise to effectively program heterogeneous platforms. Heterogeneous platforms may include an arbitrary number of computing resources, such as DFEs, GPGPUs and multi-core CPUs. Developers of these platforms must, therefore, be aware of a number of architectural details including: the different types of processing cores which may exhibit various levels of complexity, the communication topology between processing elements, the hierarchy between different memory systems, and built-in specialised architectural features. There are two common programming approaches that address heterogeneity: (1) a uniform programming framework supporting a single programming language and semantics to target different types of computing resources; (2) a hybrid programming framework in which developers must manually partition and map their applications using the most suitable languages and tools.

We are developing the *Uniform Heterogeneous Programming* approach (see Fig. 4), which aims to combine the benefits of the above two approaches by using two complementary languages: FAST [3] and LARA [1]. With FAST, developers (cloud tenants) use a single software language (based on C99) to implement their applications with the possibility of using multiple semantics to describe alternative versions of the same algorithm. For instance, with dataflow semantics, C99 code is translated into functional units that are mapped into reconfigurable logic to realise deep pipelined architectures, in which data is computed in parallel and the output is forwarded synchronously to the next functional unit. We believe FAST simplifies not only the compilation and optimisation design-flow using a single code base, but also simplifies the programming effort when targeting specialised computing resources. With LARA, on the other hand, hardware infrastructure experts (for instance, working on behalf of cloud providers) can codify domain specific knowledge into special programs called *aspects* which analyse and manipulate (naive) FAST programs. Subsequently, a process called *weaving* automatically combines non-functional (LARA aspects) and functional concerns (FAST programs) to derive designs that are optimised for a specific cloud platform and infrastructure.

5   Conclusion

In this paper we presented HARNESS, an FP7 project which aims to develop the architectural principles that enable the next generation of cloud platforms to provide increased performance, reduced energy consumption, and lower cost profiles. In the context of this project, we are developing a runtime management system that supports cross-optimisation and virtualisation of heterogeneous resources to provide managed multitenancy and elasticity. In addition, we are developing an aspect-oriented programming approach which allows programs capturing multiple semantics to be mapped efficiently to the HARNESS cloud platform. Future work includes integrating and evaluating our heterogeneous cloud platform and development tools with industrial use cases.

References

1. Cardoso, J.M.P., Carvalho, T., Coutinho, J.G.F., Luk, W., Nobre, R., Diniz, P., Petrov, Z.: LARA: An aspect-oriented programming language for embedded systems. In: Proceedings of the Annual International Conference on Aspect-Oriented Software Development, pp. 179–190 (2012)
2. Graepel, T., et al.: Web-scale Bayesian click-through rate prediction for sponsored search advertising in Microsoft's Bing search engine. In: Proc. of the Intl. Conf. on Machine Learning, pp. 13–20 (2010)
3. Grigoras, P., Niu, X., Coutinho, J.G.F., Luk, W., Bower, J., Pell, O.: Aspect driven compilation for Dataflow designs. In: Proc. of the IEEE Conference on App-Specific Sys. Arch. and Proc. (ASAP), pp. 18–25 (2013)
4. O'Neill, E., McGlone, J., et al.: SHEPARD: Scheduling on HEterogeneous Platforms using Application Resource Demands. In: Proc. of the Intl. Conf. on Parallel, Distributed and Network-based Processing (2014) (to appear)
5. Pell, O., Averbukh, V.: Maximum performance computing with Dataflow engines. Computing in Science Engineering 14(4), 98–103 (2012)
6. Schubert, L., et al.: Advances in clouds: Research in future cloud computing. Expert Group Report, European Commission, Information Society and Media (2012)

Profile-Guided Compilation of Scilab Algorithms for Multiprocessor Systems

Jürgen Becker[2], Thomas Bruckschloegl[2], Oliver Oey[2], Timo Stripf[2],
George Goulas[1], Nick Raptis[1], Christos Valouxis[1], Panayiotis Alefragis[1],
Nikolaos S. Voros[1], and Christos Gogos[3]

[1] Karlsruhe Institute of Technology, Germany
[2] Technological Educational Institute of Western Greece, Greece
[3] Technological Educational Institute of Epirus, Greece
`{becker,bruckschloegl,oey,stripf}@kit.edu`
`{ggoulas,nraptis,cvalouxis,alefrag,voros}@teimes.gr, cgogos@teiep.gr`

Abstract. The expression of parallelism in commonly used programming languages is still a large problem when mapping high performance embedded applications to multiprocessor system on chip devices. The Architecture oriented paraLlelization for high performance embedded Multicore systems using scilAb (ALMA) European project aims to bridge these hurdles through the introduction and exploitation of a Scilab-based toolchain which enables the efficient mapping of applications on multiprocessor platforms from a high level of abstraction. To achieve maximum performance the toolchain supports iterative application parallelization using profile-guided application compilation. In this way, the toolchain will increase the quality and performance of a parallelized application from iteration to iteration. This holistic solution of the toolchain hides the complexity of both, the application and the architecture, which leads to a better acceptance, reduced development cost, and shorter time-to-market.

Keywords: MPSoC, Parallelization, Multicore, Profiling, Optimization.

1 Introduction

Chips are needed that are efficient, flexible, and performant. Many performance-critical applications (e.g. digital video processing, telecoms, and security applications) that need to process huge amounts of data in a short time would benefit from these attributes. Research projects such as MORPHEUS [8] and CRISP [3] have demonstrated the feasibility of such an approach and presented the benefit of heterogeneity and parallel processing on a real hardware prototype. Providing a set of programming tools for respective cores is however not enough. A company must be able to take such a chip and program it, based on high-level tools and automatic parallelization/mapping strategies without having to know the underlying hardware architecture. Only then, when combining the advantages of an *Application-Specific Integrated Circuit* (ASIC) in terms of processing density,

D. Goehringer et al. (Eds.): ARC 2014, LNCS 8405, pp. 330–336, 2014.
© Springer International Publishing Switzerland 2014

with the flexibility of an *Field-Programmable Gate Array* (FPGA), in addition to it being affordable since it could be manufactured in larger numbers (like general purpose processors or FPGAs), it will profit from benefits of programmability and system level programming.

The *Architecture oriented paraLlelization for high performance embedded Multicore systems using scilAb* (ALMA, Greek for "leap") European project [1] intends to provide a full design framework for designing parallel and concurrent computing systems. The design framework will rely on Scilab, an open source language for developing high-level system models. Scilab will be extended to provide explicit parallel directives, which will allow high-level optimization of Scilab system models, based on user defined cost functions and the constraints of the underlying architecture. The ALMA parallel software optimization environment will be combined with a fully functional SystemC simulation framework for multicore heterogeneous SoCs, which will be defined through generic SystemC interfaces/protocols to connect existent *Multiprocessor System-on-Chip* (MPSoC) simulation modules targeting multiple architectures.

In this paper, we present our concept of the ALMA toolchain enabling profile-guided compilation of Scilab source code to multicore architectures. The organization of the paper is as follows: Section 2 gives an overview of the ALMA toolchain. The profile-guided compilation and optimization of applications within the ALMA toolchain is described in Section 3. Section 4 presents the current status of the project evaluation and its results. A conclusion of the paper is given in Section 5.

2   ALMA Toolchain

The *Architecture oriented paraLlelization for high performance embedded Multicore systems using scilAb* (ALMA) toolchain aims to enable engineers to produce parallel programs for a variety of *Multiprocessor System-on-Chip* (MPSoC) embedded systems in a special Scilab [7] subset dialect. In order to maintain platform quasi-agnostic, the ALMA toolchain has a set of requirements for the target platforms. The target platform has to be described in a language developed within the ALMA project, an *Architecture Description Language* (ADL). The toolchain requires a platform simulator that conforms to relevant ALMA specifications in order to be able to optimize parallel code. In addition, the platform should have a C toolchain with *Message Passing Interface* (MPI) [6] support. Two different parallel multicore embedded platforms are used as initial targets, KIT's Kahrisma architecture from the academia and Recore Systems' tiled multicore SoC architecture from the industry.

The ALMA toolchain components are presented in Figure 1. At first, *Scilab Front-End* (SAFE) will consume the ALMA-specific Scilab dialect source code to produce a C representation of the original code. This C source is then loaded into *Generic Compiler Suite* (GeCoS) [2] to generate a special *Intermediate Representation* (IR) extended to meet the needs of the ALMA project. Different GeCoS modules provide parallelism extraction tools on fine-grain as well as coarse-grain levels. Fine-grain parallelism extraction aims to exploit platform SIMD features and optimize code sections known as *Static Control Parts*

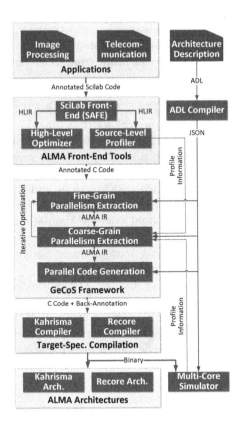

Fig. 1. ALMA Toolchain Overview

(SCoPs), while coarse-grain optimization aims to consider the whole *Control and Data Flow Graph* (CDFG) and optimize it for parallel execution. The ALMA ADL provides platform information on instruction set or core architectures, thus supporting the parallelism extraction phases. These steps will produce parallel C code for the platform compilers. The toolchain provides a full system simulator allowing application profiling and performance analysis. Simulation and profiling results are feed back to the coarse-grain parallelism extraction to increase the quality and performance of the parallel application.

3   Profile-Guided Optimization

The ALMA coarse-grain optimization process aims to minimize the parallel program running time considering the *Control and Data Flow Graph* (CDFG) *Intermediate Representation* (IR). In order to remove cycles from the CDFG, which are introduced by loop structures, the CDFG is converted to the *Hierarchical Task Graph* (HTG) IR [5]. The HTG IR transforms the CDFG by defining a new layer for each control structure and the resulting graph for every layer is a *Directed Acyclic Graph* (DAG). The vertices of each DAG layer are instruction sequences which we call *tasks*, while the edges represent data dependencies and mandate the order of execution of tasks as well as which program variables should be available before a task is executed. For each DAG two synchronization tasks are introduced: All tasks in a DAG depend on the *start* task, while the *end* task depends on all tasks in the DAG.

The result of coarse-grain optimization is to label the tasks to run on specific processing elements, as well as to define their relative order of execution. For a correct schedule, which is a schedule that does not violate the dependency constraints, if task execution times as well as data transfer times are known, task start and end execution times can be assigned. The goal of the optimization process is to minimize the running time, which is the difference in task start times between the start and end tasks of the top level task of the HTG.

In order for the coarse grain optimization to work, accurate times for each task execution as well as for the possible data communications are required. Estimating running and communication times without simulating the program at hand is not straightforward and is vulnerable to more than one order of magnitude errors. To avoid this problem, the coarse grain optimization generates a sequence of program schedules and uses the simulator to derive profiling information. As the optimizer attempts various solutions, more profiling information is available and the predictive accuracy of the running times increases.

Feedback Loop. The coarse grain optimization process generates the initial HTG IR and labels weights using inaccurate and broad estimations. The initial running time estimation for a task is the number of instructions, while the initial communication overhead is the size in bytes of the data to be transferred. The initial step for the coarse grain optimization process generates a sequential schedule that is a schedule to run on a single processing element. The sequential schedule is passed to the next steps of the tool flow, the parallel code generation and the simulator. The next coarse grain optimization step labels the tasks with the profiling information results and produces an initial parallel solution. Now, two samples are available for each task execution and one sample is available for each data dependency that has created a data communication event. This iterative process continues for several steps.

As the initial communication time estimates and the profiled ones may differ by orders of magnitude, a strong bias towards specific schedules is possible. In addition, the profiler is not able to profile all tasks dependencies in a single run, as the communicating tasks should be scheduled on different processors. In order to avoid this strong bias, a simple learning model is used to predict the communication times between tasks. For all profiled communications, the profiled time as well as the amount of data transferred in bytes is used in a linear regression model. The parameters of the model, intercept and slope, correspond to the basic communication parameters latency and bandwidth. The communication times for the non-profiled dependencies finally are predicted using the parameters above.

Profiling Information. The information used as feedback from the profiler includes a number of profiling parameters for each task and task dependency. For a task, the parameters include mean, maximum and minimum running time as well as number of executions. The number of executions is used to calculate the number of iterations for loops. For task dependencies, the information includes the amount of data transferred as well as mean, minimum and maximum communication time.

As the solution process advances, a number of samples are available for every task or dependency. In order to produce estimates for the optimization process, the samples are averaged. An idea to use a weighted average to favor latest results was not used, as there is no indication that the final solution that would be produced would be more similar to the last solutions.

Simulator Support. The ALMA Multicore Simulator supports application profiling by handling the profiling instructions added to the application, aggregating the profiling information as well as output generation. The system profiler consists of different profiling events that listen to the instrumentation function within the application. According to the generated event one or multiple information generation phases will be triggered. This allows the profiler to aggregate information about task execution and communication between different tasks.

A single task within the application is referenced as a code block between a *start_task_profiling* and an *end_task_profiling* instrumentation function. Each of these functions generates a profiling event that will be handled by the system profiler. Each task is given an id that becomes unique in combination with the id of the core executing this task. Communication is recognized by using *start_send_profiling* and *end_send_profiling* in combination with *start_recv_profiling* and *end_recv_profiling*. The system profiler can handle different combinations of instrumentation functions for information aggregation and output generation. This results in the generation of different output files that contain the necessary information for iterative parallelization and application compilation.

4   Evaluation

As the project is at integration phase, concrete end-to-end speedup results for ready programs are not yet available, although independent components present promising results, as the *Mathematical Programming Module* (MPM) [9]. Several simple and more complex C codes are used to test the integration of the Coarse Grain optimization modules with the Code Generation and Simulator, including an edge detection algorithm. The author of the edge detection application is cited as Mazen A.R. Saghir from University of Toronto, 1992, while the code comments cite the book from Embree and Kimble [4] as the source of algorithms and routines. Edge detection is used in image processing, image compression and computer vision in order to detect sharp changes in image brightness and is used to define objects boundaries, boundaries of surfaces, discontinuities in surface orientation. The particular code example detects edges in a 256 grayscale 128 × 128 pixels image and is available in four flavors, covering Arrays versus

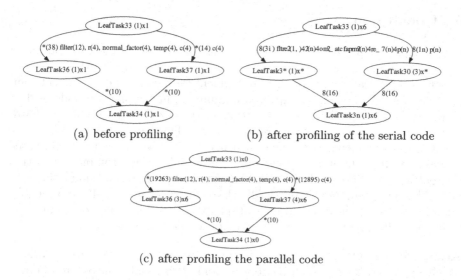

(a) before profiling   (b) after profiling of the serial code

(c) after profiling the parallel code

Fig. 2. The DAG for a specific while loop for the edge detection application

pointers and normal versus software pipelining versions. The arrays with software pipelining code are slightly modified to satisfy current limitations of the toolchain, such as implementation of standard library functions like `abs()`.

The hierarchical task graph extraction identified 25 total hierarchical layers in a structure 5 layer deep that contain 149 leaf tasks inside them. Each layer has a DAG with vertices, a set of layer tasks and leaf tasks and task dependencies between them that refer to data dependencies. In addition, each DAG has a special source node as a single entry point and a special sink node as a single exit point. All tasks in each DAG have zero weight dependencies with those nodes. The whole HTG for the edge detection application has a total of 331 edges, including the zero-weight edges between the tasks and the special nodes.

Figures 2 presents the DAG for a specific while loop of the edge detection application. The labels on the arcs represent the cost for communication and the symbols involved for every dependency. When a label is starred, the communication cost is predicted, otherwise it is the profiled communication cost. Figure 2(a) shows the DAG before the usage of the profiler. All communication costs are estimated to be the size of the data structure in bytes, while the task durations are set to be one. Figure 2(b) shows the DAG after the first usage of the profiler on the serial version of the application. Now the tasks durations have durations assigned, while the communication costs are still estimated. Figure 2(c) shows the DAG for the same loop, after profiling the parallel code for the first time. For this specific DAG, the communication costs have been updated. In this example, the labels are starred, thus the coarse-grain algorithm decided that leaf tasks 36 and 37 should not be executed on different processors and the particular costs are predicted based on the profiling information of other communications.

5 Conclusion

In this paper, we presented profile-guided compilation of parallel application for multiprocessor architectures as part of the ALMA EU project. ALMA intends to deliver a full framework for the development for parallel and concurrent computer systems. The main concept is programming in the platform-independent high-level language Scilab and still getting an optimized binary for a given hardware architecture automatically from the tools. This can be achieved by using fine-grain as well as coarse-grain parallelism extraction working on a graph-based representation of the input application. The profile-guided compilation within the toolchain provides application instrumentation, profiling and simulation support. This will generate valuable feedback to the toolchain as well as to the programmer about application parallelization, execution times and communication to increase the quality and performance of the parallel application.

Acknowledgments. This research is part of the collaborative project ALMA, which is partially funded by the European Commission under the Seventh Framework Programme (FP7/2007-2013) with Grant Agreement 287733.

References

1. Architecture oriented paraLlelization for high performance embedded Multicore systems using scilAb (ALMA), http://www.alma-project.eu
2. GeCoS, https://gforge.inria.fr/projects/gecos/
3. Ahonen, T., ter Braak, T.D., Burgess, S.T., Geißler, R., Heysters, P.M., Hurskainen, H., Kerkhoff, H.G., Kokkeler, A.B.J., Nurmi, J., Rauwerda, G.K., Smit, G.J.M., Zhang, X.: CRISP: Cutting Edge Reconfigurable ICs for Stream Processing. In: Cardoso, J.M.P., Hübner, M. (eds.) Reconfigurable Computing: From Fpgas to Hardware/Software Codesign, pp. 211–238. Springer, London (2011)
4. Embree, P., Kimble, B.: C Language Algorithms for Digital Signal Processing. Prentice Hall (1991)
5. Girkar, M., Polychronopoulos, C.D.: The hierarchical task graph as a universal intermediate representation. Int. J. Parallel Program. 22(5), 519–551 (1994)
6. Message Passing Interface Forum. MPI: A Message-Passing Interface Standard Version 2.2 (September 2009)
7. Scilab Consortium (Digiteo). Scilab, http://www.scilab.org
8. Thoma, F., Kuhnle, M., Bonnot, P., Panainte, E., Bertels, K., Goller, S., Schneider, A., Guyetant, S., Schuler, E., Muller-Glaser, K., Becker, J.: Morpheus: Heterogeneous reconfigurable computing. In: International Conference on Field Programmable Logic and Applications, FPL 2007, pp. 409–414 (August 2007)
9. Valouxis, C., Gogos, C., Alefragis, P., Goulas, G., Voros, N., Housos, E.D.: Scheduling using Integer Programming in heterogeneous parallel execution environments. In: Multidisciplinary International Scheduling Conference, MISTA, Ghent, Belgium (2013)

SAVE: Towards Efficient Resource Management in Heterogeneous System Architectures*

G. Durelli[1], M. Coppola[2], K. Djafarian[3], G. Kornaros[4],
A. Miele[1], M. Paolino[5], Oliver Pell[6], Christian Plessl[7], M.D. Santambrogio[1],
and C. Bolchini[1]

[1] Politecnico di Milano
{gianlucacarlo.durelli,antonio.miele,marco.santambogio,
cristiana.bolchini}@polimi.it
[2] STMicroelectronics
marcello.coppola@st.com
[3] ARM
karim.djafarian@arm.com
[4] Technological Educational Institute of Crete
kornaros@ie.teicrete.gr
[5] Virtual Open Systems
m.paolino@virtualopensystems.com
[6] Maxeler Technologies
oliver@maxeler.com
[7] University of Paderborn
christian.plessl@uni-paderborn.de

Abstract. The increasing availability of different kinds of processing resources in heterogeneous system architectures associated with today's fast-changing, unpredictable workloads has propelled an interest towards systems able to dynamically and autonomously adapt how computing resources are exploited to optimize a given goal. Self-adaptiveness and hardware-assisted virtualization are the two key-enabling technologies for this kind of architectures, to allow the efficient exploitation of the available resources based on the current working context. The SAVE project will develop HW/SW/OS components that allow for deciding at runtime the mapping of the computation kernels on the appropriate type of resource, based on the current system context and requirements.

1 Current Trends and Challenges in System Architecture

Since the 1960s processors have shown an exponential improvement in performance fueled by advances in semiconductor technology, allowing to increase the clock speed, and architectural innovations increasing the amount of work done per cycle, e.g., pipelining, branch prediction and out-of-order execution. Since about 2005 this exponential growth of single-core performance has significantly flattened out. While further increasing the clock frequency would be possible,

---

* This research is partially supported by the European Commission, EU Seventh Framework Program, Project 610996-SAVE.

D. Goehringer et al. (Eds.): ARC 2014, LNCS 8405, pp. 337–344, 2014.
© Springer International Publishing Switzerland 2014

the energy-efficiency of the computation would drastically decrease. The answer of the semiconductor industry to this challenge was to move away from maximizing single-core performance towards maximizing the aggregated computational power and efficiency of the complete processor. This objective is addressed using two main techniques: *on-chip parallel computing* and *customization.*

On-chip parallel computing exploits the fact that shrinking semiconductor process geometries allow for integrating several CPU cores into a single package while keeping power dissipation constant. We can witness this trend of parallelism by the rapid proliferation of multi- and many-core processors. The former provide *fine-grain* parallelism through SIMD, and *coarse-grain* parallelism by integrating different cores onto the same chip. The concept of on-chip parallel processing is carried further by *many-core processors*, which integrate several dozens of simpler CPU cores in a single processor. This concept is for example used in the Intel Xeon Phi co-processor, Kalray [3], or the STM research platform "Platform 2012" [5]. Massively parallel processor architectures even increase the number of cores to several hundreds, while reducing the complexity of each core and imposing a more restrictive execution model. The prototypical representative of this class of architectures are GPGPUs, which use a SIMD-like execution model that is targeted by dedicated programming and runtime environments, such as, CUDA, STREAM, OpenCL, C++ AMP.

The other direction for improving the performance and computation efficiency is to use programmable hardware devices, in particular field-programmable gate arrays (FPGAs). These devices can be used to implement *customized* application-specific computing engines that are perfectly tailored to the needs of a given application. One instance of this approach that is currently receiving a lot of attention in high-performance computing (HPC) are dataflow engines (DFEs), that implement custom, high-throughput processing pipelines for scientific computing or big data analytics.

In practice, neither massively parallel on-chip processors nor customized DFEs are used as the sole computational resource. Instead, these technologies are used as accelerators in combination with conventional multi-core processors. The resulting heterogeneous computing systems are integrated either as system-on-chip solutions for the embedded and mobile computing segment or by attaching the massively parallel architectures as acceleration co-processors via PCI express/Infiniband for the HPC domain.

While the performance and energy-efficiency potential of heterogeneous computing systems is widely acknowledged and many heterogeneous systems are being deployed, it is still an open research question how to program, operate, and manage these systems to reap the benefits of heterogeneous computing while keeping the complexity in bounds. For example, GPUs' and DFEs' computing resources are currently not managed by the OS but by the applications that use them, preventing a global optimization of resource usage at system-level.

2 The Objectives of the SAVE Project

According to recent technology studies the demand for computing will continue to rise rapidly and the number of computing devices will be more than triple by 2020. Given that each device contributes to our society's energy and carbon footprint, new technologies to address this challenge must be found. Indeed, we are moving towards an on-demand computing scenario, characterized by varying workloads, constituted of diverse applications with different performance requirements, and criticality. With the end of Dennard Scaling [1] in sight and a slowdown in supply voltage scaling, the entire ICT industry is currently going through an inflection point where energy efficiency, which used to be the key design concern of embedded and mobile systems, is becoming the ultimate design constraint for the entire computing spectrum ranging from embedded systems (ES) to HPC systems.

In this scenario, heterogeneous computing is currently the most promising approach to address these challenges. The flip side of heterogeneity is increased complexity. To reach an optimal solution, a system architect needs to take into account the efficiency of the computational units, the workload, the working conditions and so on. As a result, heterogeneous computing is often considered too complex or inefficient, except for very specific application environments, where the working context is delimited and the design space to be explored is suitably contained. Hence, it is key to find answers to the question how to integrate, exploit, and manage heterogeneous resources to reach the desired performance goal at minimal cost while limiting the complexity for development.

The EU FP7 project SAVE (Self-Adaptive Virtualization-aware high-performance/low-Energy heterogeneous system architectures) [2] aims at addressing the challenge of exploiting specialized computing resources of a heterogeneous system architecture (HSA) by pooling them and taking advantage of their individual characteristics to optimize the performance/energy trade-off for the resulting system, without constraining the applications or operation context. To this end, we strive for defining a more general approach for exploiting HSAs, lowering the complexity of managing the available resources, while enabling the overall system to pursue an optimization goal that can depend on the current working conditions (application requirements, workload, ...). More precisely, SAVE will address these limitations by providing *self-adaptivity* and *hardware-assisted virtualization* to allow the system to dynamically and autonomously decide how to optimally allocate the workload generated by applications to the specialized resources for achieving an effective execution of the application while optimizing a user-defined goal (e.g., performance, energy, reliability, resource utilization).

SAVE will define the necessary SW/HW technologies for implementing self-adaptive systems exploiting heterogeneous architectures that include two classes of accelerators: GPUs and DFEs that enhance heterogeneous architectures to cope with the increased variety and dynamics of workloads observed in the HPC and ES domains. Virtualization and self-adaptiveness are jointly exploited to obtain a new self-adaptive virtualization-aware Heterogeneous System Architecture, dubbed *saveHSA*, that exhibits a highly adaptive behavior to achieve the requested performance while minimizing energy consumption by allocating the tasks to the most appropriate accelerators, based on the current status of the overall system. The effectiveness of SAVE's technologies will be validated in two applications scenarios, financial risk computing and image processing algorithms, to cover the ES and HPC domain. We strive for an energy-efficiency improvement of 20% with respect to today's architecture that use DFEs or GPUs in a traditional fashion. At the same time, system manageability, ease of deployment and resilience will be greatly improved.

3   The SAVE Concept

SAVE will enable the system to decide at run-time, based on the observation of collected information that characterizes the changing scenario, how to use the available resources, to pursue a defined, but changeable, optimization goal. The overall project outcome are technologies suitable for a cross-domain adoption ranging from the data centers and HPC, where virtualization plays a relevant role, to ES, where heterogeneity and customized execution prevail. An important issue is how to move one step forward in the way operating systems view such computational resources, traditionally perceived as secondary components that hide their complexities behind pre-defined device drivers that expose high-level programming API. In this perspective hardware-assisted virtualization offers the opportunity to simplify the sharing of such heterogenous resources, without compromising performance. In SAVE, the various computing HW resources, will execute workloads constituted from multiple applications running in a virtualized environment. Since device drivers determine how accelerators are shared, this restricts scheduling policies and optimization criteria for the computational resources. If resources are shared between several guest OSes running in virtual machines (VMs), issues of contention, fairness and security become further pronounced. In addition the hypervisor has limited control on how the heterogeneous computing resources are used, and whether sharing is possible in time, space or both, because there is no direct control over the scheduler actions beyond the proprietary interfaces.

Therefore, to benefit from the opportunity that heterogeneous platforms offer SAVE exploits virtualization and integrates it in a self-adaptive perspective, to obtain a performance/energy cost-effective solution.

The final goal is to provide a set of technologies implementing a **self-adaptive virtualization-aware Heterogeneous System Architecture**, consisting of:

1. an architecture able to run any kind of applications (through *virtualization*),
2. a *scalable, cache coherent heterogeneous* platform that exposes the heterogeneity (different kinds of virtualizable computation islands, such as GPUs and DFEs) reducing power consumption and simplifying management,
3. a *dynamically adaptable* saveHSA management, driven by different environment inputs that may change at run-time, exploiting a runtime and just-in-time code generation infrastructure that allows for dynamically offloading computational hotspots to heterogeneous computing resources, and

4. an integrated hypervisor layer that promotes the specialized islands of computation as schedulable entities, that can be shared by multiple VMs.

This goal will be achieved by developing new technologies deeply integrated to obtain efficiency and optimality: (i) an *advanced run-time self-adaptiveness OS support layer*, (ii) a *hardware-assisted virtualization support for the specialized computing resources*, (iii) new *hypervisor extensions* that expose a virtual computation interface to applications, and (iv) a *just-in-time compilation and offloading infrastructure*.

3.1 Advanced Run-Time Self-adaptiveness OS Support Layer and Adaptive Hardware Layer

The first main target of the SAVE project is the development of a self-adaptive and virtualization-aware HSA, able to modify itself according to the changing scenario, thus exposing *autonomous* **adaptation** capabilities driven by the system itself, as a response to a variation in the workload, in the architecture resources, or in the user (optimization) requirements.

While reconfigurability for some classes of architectures (e.g., homogeneous multi- and many-core platforms, FPGAs) has been tackled to some extent in both the ES and HPC scenarios, each one exploiting the peculiarities of the domain, we aim at tackling the challenge by referring to a more general architectural platform, that is *across the two domains*, to serve as a means for both low-cost HPC or high-end ES. Fig. 1 shows the SAVE self-adaptiveness concept, where a *self-adaptive orchestrator* module integrated in the host operating system dispatches the submitted kernels onto the most appropriate kind of resources available in the saveHSA, where the appropriateness depends on the currently pursued goal (power consumption, performance, overall load) and the kernel nature, in terms of computational requirements. To support the runtime *self-adaptive orchestrator* module, SAVE will develop an enhanced communication infrastructure, monitors combining cache coherent on-chip interconnects with off-chip (PCI-E) with knobs to observe their behavior and configure them to act in a specific mode, along with the design of a common interface towards hardware components, called Dynamically Manageable Component (DMCs), suitable for the realization of adaptive systems. On top of this, a novel parametric versions of existing OS components (e.g., observable and controllable schedulers, device drivers with adaptive and introspective data structures) will be developed, able to orchestrate the execution of the kernels on the heterogeneous architecture, by adjusting at run-time the adopted policies, and set the ground for a novel OS with new self-aware components to support self-awareness and run-time adaptability. Furthermore, the development of a library of optimization policies allowing the system to decide, on the basis of the observed behavior (achieved performance, monitored temperature, ...), the actions (on what resource to map kernels) to be carried out to fulfill the optimization goal, has to be implemented.

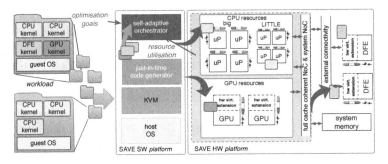

Fig. 1. SAVE self-adaptiveness concept

3.2 Hardware-Assisted Virtualization Support for the Specialized Computing Resources

The second main target of the project is the definition of an innovative hardware support for virtualization for the components constituting the heterogeneous platform, such that their *exploitation and sharing* can be facilitated. More precisely, within the perspective of a self-adaptive system that may migrate VMs running kernels from one resource (e.g., CPU) to a different one (e.g., GPU), as shown in Fig. 2, the foreseen proposed solutions will need to be flexible and sophisticated to allow virtualization not to introduce overheads and prevent the exploitation of the peculiarities of the platform.

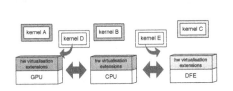

Fig. 2. SAVE virtualization concept

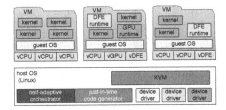

Fig. 3. SAVE hypervisor extensions

This goal will be achieved through the development of APIs to expose to the *self-adaptive orchestrator* the performance, power information of kernels running in VMs on the specific accelerator (GPU, DFE). The APIs shall provide the access to the dynamic characteristics of the kernels being executed to support the decision of the orchestrator on where to map the VM kernels to pursue the optimization goal. Moreover hardware cache coherency between the host processor and the different on-chip islands of computation resource will be introduced. This mechanism will simplify the communication cost related to data and code of executing kernel in specific accelerators. In this way, kernels can be efficiently transferred to accelerators reducing the number of copies between accelerators and host processor. Another advantage is the usage of a common virtual memory system for host processors and accelerators, to allow accelerators to access virtual memory addresses that are not yet available in the physical memory.

3.3 Hypervisor Extensions

The third target of the project is a set of elements (Fig. 3) needed to integrate the two previously discussed objectives in the realization of a self-adaptive virtualization-aware HSA. This integration will be accomplished by developing extensions to enable multiple VMs to directly access virtualized GPU/DFE, by means of the hardware-assisted virtualization. This will add the concepts of vGPU and vDFE to the already existing, in the virtualization scenario, vCPU. The hypervisor will manage these resources, enabling multiple VMs to safely interact with them concurrently. Furthermore, it will be necessary to provide extensions for allowing inner and outer migration. The former enables the "smart" orchestrator to migrate and schedule directly the tasks of different VMs among vCPUs/vGPUs/vDFEs. The latter will provide scalability in the HPC scenario (such as that of Cloud computing data centers), giving to the VMs the possibility to migrate among different saveHSA platforms. Finally, the development of an efficient communication mechanism that permits the interaction between the host and the VMs will be done. In this way, the just-in-time code generator and the orchestrator will be able to dispatch tasks to the appropriate resources and achieve the self-adaptiveness of the system.

3.4 Just-in-Time Compilation and Offloading Infrastructure

Finally, SAVE aims at exploring a novel approach of offloading computational hotspots to heterogeneous computing resources. To this end, a runtime system based on the LLVM compiler and virtual machine infrastructure [4] will be developed to autonomously analyze applications for computational hotspots that could be executed more efficiently with DFEs or GPUs. If such hotspots are identified, the smart orchestrator can initiate a just-in-time compilation for the optimal resource. Once the compilation has completed, the runtime system transparently migrates the computation to the targeted computing resource.

4 Conclusions

The heterogeneity, generated by the acceleration cores (e.g., GPUs, DFEs), consists of specialized islands of computation in architectures where different executions models can be used to exploit the peculiarities of the resources. However heterogeneity has a price too; chips have limited resources and all units on the chip compete for the shared resources, thus receiving only a limited share of load, so being under- To reach an optimal solution, it is up to the architect to distribute the resources among the different units by taking into account the efficiency of these units as well as the workload. SAVE will address this issue by developing a customizable and adaptable computing capability that manages the available resources, through virtualization, to decouple the relation between the applications and the complex underlying heterogeneous architecture.

References

1. Dennard, R., Gaensslen, F., Rideout, V., Bassous, E., LeBlanc, A.: Design of ion-implanted MOSFET's with very small physical dimensions. IEEE Journal of Solid-State Circuits 9(5), 256–268 (1974)
2. EU FP7 project SAVE, http://www.fp7-save.eu
3. KALRAY, http://www.kalray.eu
4. Lattner, C., Adve, V.: LLVM: A compilation framework for lifelong program analysis & transformation. In: Proc. Int. Symp. Code Generation and Optimization, pp. 75–86 (2004)
5. STMicroelectronics and CEA: Platform 2012: A many-core programmable accelerator for Ultra-Efficient Embedded Computing in Nanometer Technology. In: Research Workshop on STMicroelectronics Platform 2012 (2010)

Data Parallel Application Adaptivity and System-Wide Resource Management in Many-Core Architectures

Giuseppe Massari, Edoardo Paone, Michele Scandale,
Patrick Bellasi, Gianluca Palermo, Vittorio Zaccaria,
Giovanni Agosta, William Fornaciari, and Cristina Silvano

Politecnico di Milano
Dipartimento di Elettronica, Informazione e Bioingegneria (DEIB)
Piazza Leonardo da Vinci 32, I-20133 Milano, Italy
{name.surname}@polimi.it

1 Introduction

Since the silicon technology entered the many-core era, new computing platforms are exploiting higher and higher levels of parallelism. Thanks to scalable, clustered architectures, embedded systems and high-performance computing (HPC) are rapidly converging. We are also experiencing a rapid overlapping of the challenges related to efficient exploitation of processing resources. Platform-specific optimization and application boosting cannot be considered independently anymore. Thus the increased interest towards broader and versatile methodologies, which could easily scale from the embedded up to the general-purpose domain.

Scalable platforms enable also new application scenarios, where the parallelism could be exploited to support intensive computation. Augmented reality and advanced image processing are just examples of computation intensive multimedia applications which are now required also on high-end mobile devices, while exhibiting classical HPC traits. To simplify the exploitation of increasing processing capabilities, programmers are supported by specialized parallel programming models. Custom paradigms have been proposed by different industry players, targeting their own many-core platforms, but the convergence of architectures is now pushing for more generic and *portable programming models*. The OpenCL[1] industry standard [4] is considered one of the most promising solution, which supports portability while still effectively exploiting the available computational power. From the software perspective, even in the industrial embedded domain, the increased computational power has fostered more and more the opportunity to run multiple applications. This configures new *mixed-workload scenarios* where applications with different priorities and requirements compete for the usage of shared resources. While the workload set is generally known in advance, its *run-time variability* is instead unpredictable, since the workload mix as well as the application requirements are generally defined by asynchronous conditions not knwon "a priori".

---

[1] OpenCL is a trademark of Apple Inc., used by permission by Khronos.

D. Goehringer et al. (Eds.): ARC 2014, LNCS 8405, pp. 345–352, 2014.
© Springer International Publishing Switzerland 2014

Considering that the new generation of many-core systems is manufactured using advanced technology nodes, these systems are also subject to a wide spectrum of variability issues. Thus, the run-time variability could also be generated by resources, mainly due to aspects related to the fabrication process or to the run-time thermal and reliability issues. Overall, the hardware and software scenario defined above represents a classical run-time management problem, but it requires the definition of efficient yet portable solutions. Due to the problem complexity, an effective proposal could not disregard any of the different facets related to design-time profiling and run-time control possibilities as well as application-specific tuning and system-wide multi-objective optimization.

This paper proposes an innovative methodology, defined during the 2PARMA project [7], based on a properly defined run-time support to enable an effective exploitation of design-time information. The synergy between design-time and run-time provides an efficient yet portable run-time management solution which could scale from embedded to general purpose systems. The methodology proposes the integration of independent tools to provide effective compilation of OpenCL code, multi-objective design space exploration, system-wide run-time resource management and application-specific monitoring and tuning.

The rest of this paper is organized as follows. Section 2 outlines the proposed approach. Section 3 provides an experimental assessment of the tools. Finally, Section 4 draws some conclusions and highlights future research direction.

2   Proposed Approach and Toolchain

Design Space Exploration. In our approach, Design Space Exploration (DSE) is applied to the optimization of parallel streaming applications, provided that the application is designed to expose a set of parameters that impact on both performance and quality metrics. The designer is interested in a set of objectives, such as performance or CPU usage. Multi-objective optimization techniques allow to efficiently explore the space of feasible solutions (parameter configurations in the design space), thus reducing the simulation time while ensuring close-to-optimal results. To automate the DSE phase, we use the open source Multicube Explorer framework, which includes a set of optimization algorithms and Design-of-Experiment (DoE) sampling techniques [5]. The proposed approach exploits the synergy between the design time exploration framework and the *BarbequeRTRM (BBQ)* framework driving the system at runtime [9]. Such combined approach has two main advantages: a *simplified low-level profiling* and exploitation of *isolated execution context* created by *BBQ* for each application. *BBQ* has access to both software and hardware performance counters available in the platform, which can be easily exported to the DSE framework through a standardized interface[2]. This enables the designer to save effort which would be otherwise spent to write *ad-hoc* wrappers for application profiling. The output of DSE is a set of application Operating Points (OPs), which represent the Pareto-set in the

---

[2] For more details, the reader can refer to the open source MULTICUBE XML interface specification at http://www.multicube.eu

multi-objective space, to be used at runtime to support application adaptivity. Moreover, OPs are filtered with respect to platform specific metrics, to identify a set of Application Working Modes (AWMs), which represent the amount of resources required to obtain a certain application behavior. The set of AWMs represents the application *recipe* to be used at runtime by the *BBQ* for optimal resource allocation.

System-Wide Resource Management. The *System-Wide Run-Time Resource Manager* (SW-RTRM) module, *BBQ* [3], represents the central component of the proposed run-time management approach, as shown in Fig. 1. At high abstraction level, the SW-RTRM is in charge of collecting: 1. variable requirements from the running applications, when they are demanding for more resources; 2. changes in resource availability from the computing platform. This information can activate an *optimization step*, where a system-wide optimization policy is executed to identify a different assignment (*resource partitioning*) of the available computational resources. Once a new resource assignment has been identified, the SW-RTRM module provides all the control actions required to setup platform specific constraints and to notify the interested applications. The configured set of platform specific constraints will grant a predefined amount of resources to each application, while applications will be also notified about the updated resource availability.

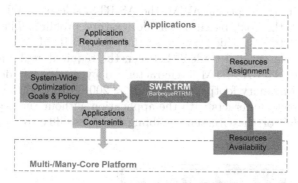

Fig. 1. Overview of *BBQ*'s role to support system-wide run-time resource management

A detailed description of the optimization policy can be found in [1]. Briefly, our resource management problem can be formulated as a *multi-choice multi-dimension multiple knapsack* problem (MMMKP) [3]. Even if such a problem is known to be NP-hard, we employ state-of-the-art heuristics [8] to find near-optimal solutions fast enough for an effective run-time exploitation. Then, an OS-specific method is employed to enforce the resource partitioning. For example, in a generic multi-core Linux machine, the standard Control Groups framework could be exploited to this purpose [2]. This allows to setup a set of isolated execution contexts, one for each scheduled application, matching the optimal resource requirements identified at design time. Finally, resource assignment is notified to each application through a dedicated interface.

---

[3] Open Source project website at http://bosp.dei.polimi.it

Application Specific Runtime Manager. The DSE output (Sec. 2) is a set of application configurations that are optimal with respect to the objectives defined at design-time. These configurations expose different tradeoffs in terms of performance and quality metrics, as well as different requirements in terms of platform resources. In our approach, they are called Operating Points (OPs) and are used for application tuning at run-time. Each application is linked to the *RTLib* library that provides an Application-Specific Run-Time Manager (the AS-RTM). The AS-RTM component itself is generic, while its behavior can be customized for each application by passing a different set of operating points and defining one or more application goals. The goal represents a soft-constraint (such as the frame-rate) that can be dynamically set by the user or selected by the application itself depending on external events. The main purpose of the AS-RTM is to manage application adaptivity, by changing parameter configurations and/or requesting resources to the *BBQ*. At this aim, the AS-RTM uses high-level monitors of the performance (such as a throughput monitor or a Quality-of-Service monitor), but even user-defined monitors can be added for application-specific metrics. Although the DSE results are averaged over a large set of workloads/datasets, the run-time behavior might not completely fit the profiled values. Thus, the AS-RTM component is also in charge of absorbing small fluctuations due to the run-time workload conditions. As shown in Fig. 2, given a constraint on a specific AWM, the AS-RTM selects an OP which is expected to satisfy the goal, based on the design-time profiling. The OPs can be sorted according to a specified metric so that the AS-RTM will select the OP which provides the optimal tradeoff between the required goal and the metric to be optimized. The AS-RTM is characterized by a very low delay ($< 20\mu s$ on average) and memory footprint (typically $< 200KB$ to load the list of OPs). Moreover, it directly interacts with the application without the need of passing through the *BBQ* or the OS, thus enabling the possibility to activate it with

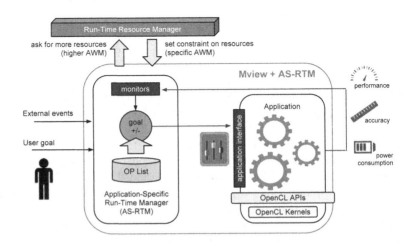

Fig. 2. Application adaptivity through the AS-RTM

higher frequency with respect to the *BBQ* reconfiguration. The AS-RTM has to interact with *BBQ* only when no OP in the current AWM allows to reach the goal. Then, the AS-RTM can request a higher AWM to the *BBQ*, by calling the *setGoalGap()* API. The goal-gap is a normalized measure of the distance from the goal, which enables *BBQ* to take into account dynamic requirements from all running applications for optimal resource allocation.

Compiler and Language Runtime. *OpenCRun* aims at providing a multitarget OpenCL infrastructure, based on the LLVM and *Clang* open source frameworks. The infrastructure is composed by four logical components: 1. the **host runtime**, which implements the OpenCL APIs; 2. a **device description**, as seen by the host; 3. a **device runtime** providing for each device the OpenCL runtime; 4. a **device runtime library**, providing the implementation of OpenCL builtin functions. Currently we target two devices: *X86* multiprocessors and *P2012*. The former uses pthread library to map a thread for each core in a X86 NUMA architectures. The latter is a clustered accelerator composed by four cluster of sixteen STxP70 cores.

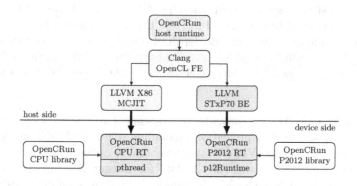

Fig. 3. OpenCRun toolchain flow

Figure 3 describes the complete toolchain overview: from the host runtime the OpenCL source code is compiled using the OpenCL frontend. After the translation in LLVM IR and the LLVM optimizer, depending on the selected device, native code is generated. For the X86 device, native code is emitted directly in memory through the MCJIT component. For P2012, a shared object must be generated to be later deployed on the device memory. The execution enviroments are specific for each device. For the X86 device, a POSIX thread is pinned to each physical core and each workgroup is scheduled on a single core. For P2012, an active runtime layer is used to coordinate the exection of OpenCL commands. The generation of OpenCL builtins implementation is fully automated using a TableGen-based tool[4]. The generation is based on an abstract

---

[4] TableGen is a component of the LLVM framework.

Table 1. Performance of Multiview Stereo Matching Kernels [s]

Kernel	LLVM xp70 back-end	P2012 SDK back-end
WinBuild	34.673	33.539
WinBuild	34.635	33.512
CostAggreg	128.344	124.193
FinalDecision	1.812	1.549
Refinement	19.312	36.929

description of each builtin variant, a basic implementation for scalar variants, and the strategy that must be used to build the vectorized variants. Target specific overrides are allowed for optimized implementation.

3   Experimental Evaluation

In this section, we provide an experimental assessment of techniques and tools. We consider a study case based on the OpenCL implementation of the Stereo-Matching (SM) algorithm described in [10]. The algorithm works on stereo images, with the aim of estimating the depth of the objects in the captured scene. The algorithm computes the *pixel disparity* between the left and the right frame of the stereo input: the higher the pixel disparity, the closer the object is to the viewpoint (e.g., a camera).

OpenCL toolchain. We first provide an assessment of the back-end compiler, using a large suite of media applications, including H264 and JPEG, implemented in C. When using a single VLIW way, our compiler outperforms on average by 4.3% the one provided in the P2012 SDK for integer benchmarks. The gain is limited to 2.56% when the VLIW bundle formation is enabled, using both ways. We then compare our OpenCL compiler toolchain with the one provided in the P2012, running the kernels that compose the Multiview Stereo-Matching Application. The comparison, shown in Table 1 is done using the P2012 SDK for the runtime components, since our language runtime is not yet optimized. Overall, the timings reflect the performance of the back-end on C benchmarks. It is worth noting that for one kernel, *Refinement*, the LLVM-based compiler performs remarkably better than the SDK compiler.

System-Wide Resource Management. Three experimental scenarios have been considered by using 1, 3 and 6 instances of the Stereo-Matching application, and comparing a non-adaptive version of this application with the runtime adaptive version. In the first case, every Stereo-Matching instance spawns a fixed number (8) of threads, while in the second case the number of threads is set dynamically, up to a maximum of 8. A first analysis has been done, by observing performance metrics listed such as workload completion time, power consumption, and number of context switches. To state the significance of the statistics, we repeated the execution of each scenario 30 times, with a mean confidence interval of 95% and 99%. The scenario stops when all the instances have completed their input stream. In the case of a single running instance, there is an increase of the completion time of about 40%, but a reduction of the system power consumption of 12%. Benefits are higher when the system is subjected to resource contention. In a 3-instances scenario, without noticeable changes in power consumption, the completion time decreases by 35%, while, in the 6-instances scenario, both completion time and power consumption decrease by approximately the 15%.

Application-Specific Tuning & RTM. The goal of this section is to assess the benefits of using the AS-RTM proposed in Sec. 2. We have seen that the behavior of the Stereo-Matching application can be tuned by changing some parameters, which affect the performance in terms of *frame-rate* and *disparity error*. This set of parameters defines a wide space of configurations but DSE allows to identify a sub-space of useful ones (Operating Points). In this experiment, a single Stereo-Matching instance is deployed on a quad-core Intel CPU and has an input stream of 100 frames to process. The optimization goal is set on the frame-rate, while we consider a Quality-of-Service (QoS) metric, computed as the inverse of the *disparity error*, to sort the list of OPs. Thus, application reconfiguration on a different OP is triggered by the AS-RTM if either the current goal is not met (the application is too slow) or the application is running faster than requested, to improve the QoS. We define 3 application working modes (AWM), with 1-2-3 processing cores available respectively. The test is repeated 12 times for each AWM, with the frame-rate goal incremented at each run from 0.5 to 6.0 frames/s with a fixed step. The three curves in Fig. 4 show the reconfiguration in each AWM. The yellow points correspond to the highest AWM (2). In this AWM, the AS-RTM has enough computational resources to meet the frame-rate goal up to 5.0 frames/s. However, for goal values higher than 2.0 frames/s, the AS-RTM starts selecting OPs with lower accuracy. In other words, there is a range of goal values, different for each AWM, where the AS-RTM can trade off between performance and QoS to meet the goal. After a certain frame-rate threshold, the AS-RTM (already on the OP with lowest QoS) cannot find any suitable OP to meet the goal, then it requests a higher AWM to *BBQ*. This technique, when combined with system-level runtime management, allows to absorb performance fluctuations due to varying workloads, reducing the interaction with *BBQ*.

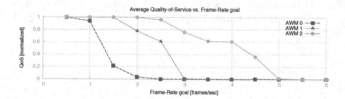

Fig. 4. Observed frame-rate and QoS by varying the frame-rate goal and the Application Working Mode

4 Conclusions

The paper proposes a design approach to support application adaptivity, exploiting a RTRM framework operating at both the application and system level. The hierarchical and modular nature of the approach makes it promising for scaling with the application performance requirements and platform computational capabilities. Future developments include a closer integration of the tools, to enable a stronger demonstration of the benefits of the approach. In particular, the OpencCL compiler and language runtime can benefit from an integration with the DSE tools, for a co-exploration of the compiler parameters [6], and with the runtime manager, to propagate decisions to the language runtime, allowing it to adjust to the new conditions.

References

1. Bellasi, P., Massari, G., Fornaciari, W.: A RTRM proposal for multi/many-core platforms and reconfigurable applications. In: ReCoSoC, pp. 1–8 (2012)
2. Bellasi, P., Massari, G., Fornaciari, W.: Exploiting Linux Control Groups for Effective Run-time Resource Management. In: PARMA 2013 Workshop HiPEAC 2013, Berlin, Germany (January 2013)
3. Kellerer, H., Pferschy, U., Pisinger, D.: Knapsack Problems. Springer (2004)
4. Khronos Group: OpenCL, http://www.khronos.org/opencl
5. Palermo, G., Silvano, C., Zaccaria, V.: ReSPIR: A Response Surface-Based Pareto Iterative Refinement for Application-Specific Design Space Exploration. IEEE Trans. on CAD of Integrated Circuits and Systems 28(12), 1816–1829 (2009)
6. Silvano, C., Agosta, G., Palermo, G.: Efficient architecture/compiler co-exploration using analytical models. DAES 11(1), 1–23 (2007)
7. Silvano, C., Fornaciari, W., Reghizzi, S.C., Agosta, G., Palermo, G., Zaccaria, V., Bellasi, P., Castro, F., Corbetta, S., Di Biagio, A., et al.: 2parma: parallel paradigms and run-time management techniques for many-core architectures. In: VLSI 2010 Annual Symposium, pp. 65–79. Springer Netherlands (2011)
8. Ykman-Couvreur, C., Nollet, V., Catthoor, F., Corporaal, H.: Fast Multi-Dimension Multi-Choice Knapsack Heuristic for MP-SoC Run-Time Management. IEEE (2006)
9. Ykman-Couvreur, C., Avasare, P., Mariani, G., Palermo, G., Silvano, C., Zaccaria, V.: Linking run-time resource management of embedded multi-core platforms with automated design-time exploration. IET Computers & Digital Techniques 5(2), 123–135 (2011)
10. Zhang, K., Lu, J., Lafruit, G.: Cross-based local stereo matching using orthogonal integral images. IEEE Trans. Circuits and Systems for Video Technol. 19(7), 1073–1079 (2009)

Author Index